AGRARIAN REVOLT IN THE
SIERRA OF CHIHUAHUA, 1959–1965

AGRARIAN REVOLT IN THE SIERRA OF CHIHUAHUA, 1959–1965

ELIZABETH HENSON

THE UNIVERSITY OF ARIZONA PRESS
TUCSON

The University of Arizona Press
www.uapress.arizona.edu

© 2019 The Arizona Board of Regents
All rights reserved. Published 2019.

ISBN-13: 978-0-8165-3873-7 (cloth)

Cover design by Nicole Hayward
Cover photograph: Demonstration at the DAAC Offices, courtesy of Comité Primeros Vientos

Publication of this book is made possible in part by the proceeds of a permanent endowment created with the assistance of a Challenge Grant from the National Endowment for the Humanities, a federal agency.

Library of Congress Cataloging-in-Publication Data
Names: Henson, Elizabeth (Elizabeth Anne), author.
Title: Agrarian revolt in the sierra of Chihuahua, 1959–1965 / Elizabeth Henson.
Description: Tucson : The University of Arizona Press, 2019. | Includes bibliographical references and index.
Identifiers: LCCN 2018026895 | ISBN 9780816538737 (cloth : alk. paper)
Subjects: LCSH: Protest movements—Mexico—Chihuahua (State)—History—20th century. | Chihuahua (Mexico : State)—Politics and government—20th century. | Insurgency—Mexico—Chihuahua (State)—History—20th century.
Classification: LCC F1261 . H397 2019 | DDC 972.08/29—dc23 LC record available at https://lccn.loc.gov/2018026895

Printed in the United States of America
♾ This paper meets the requirements of ANSI/NISO Z39.48-1992 (Permanence of Paper).

To Toni Sodersten

***and** Augusto Urteaga Pozo-Castro*

CONTENTS

List of Illustrations	*ix*
Preface	*xi*
Acknowledgments	*xvii*
List of Individuals	*xix*
List of Abbreviations	*xxiii*
Map of Chihuahua	2
Introduction	3
1. The National Context	21
2. Chihuahua, *El Estado Grande*	34
3. "The Cattle Get 30 Hectares"	57
4. 1964	100
5. "A Bomb Ready to Explode"	149
6. Aftermath	178
Conclusion	199
Appendix: El Corrido de Arturo Gámiz	*205*
Note on Methodology and Sources	*209*
Annotated Bibliography: Works About Madera	*213*
Notes	*217*
Selected Bibliography	*253*
Index	*263*

ILLUSTRATIONS

1.	Complaint filed against the FBI for harassment	xii
2.	The FBI searching our drawers	xiii
3.	Pablo Gómez	63
4.	Arturo Gámiz	64
5.	Road sign outside Madera City	76
6.	Rancheria in the sierra	91
7.	UGOCM meeting in Parral	92
8.	Normalistas accompany Pablo Gómez in a face-off with Hipólito Villa	106
9.	"Citizen Governor: The cattle get 30 hectares, and us, how many? and when?"	114
10.	Demonstration at DAAC offices	115
11.	Cover of "Participación de los estudiantes en el movimiento revolucionario"	167
12.	This photo is widely reproduced alongside stories about the assault	176
13.	Tombstone over common grave	181
14.	*Ellos sabían por qué* by Alberto Carlos	195
15.	Monument in Madera City	197

PREFACE

CHICAGO, 1977. When I went for my deposition (an evidentiary procedure in a civil lawsuit), there were four FBI agents in the room, two in front and one on each side, watching my reactions. In front of me was the lawyer representing the FBI who asked the questions, and my lawyer sat at my side. I think we drew our chairs up tight and pressed together. The questions lasted several hours. I remember being asked about people I didn't know. I answered nothing. In memory the room seemed dark but would not have been. I was twenty-seven years old.

We—the people in my household, other community leaders, the Rafael Cancel Miranda High School, the Committee to Free the Five Puerto Rican Nationalist Prisoners, and others—had sued the attorney general, the director of the Federal Bureau of Investigation (FBI), the Chicago FBI, and a number of named and unnamed agents for "harassment, intimidation, surveillance and 'counter-intelligence'" in the investigation of the Puerto Rican independence movement and the Armed Forces of National Liberation of Puerto Rico (Fuerzas Armadas de Liberación Nacional [FALN]). The FALN had claimed responsibility for a number of bombings in New York City and Chicago over the past three years. Bomb-making paraphernalia was discovered in a nearby apartment rented by Carlos Alberto Torres, who disappeared, and the FBI made regular visits to our household, searching our dresser drawers for Carlos. After my deposition, we dropped the lawsuit, realizing we could never outspend the

IN THE UNITED STATES DISTRICT COURT
FOR THE NORTHERN DISTRICT OF ILLINOIS
EASTERN DIVISION

MYRNA SALGADO LOPEZ, JOSE LOPEZ, JUAN)
ALBERTO LOPEZ, RICARDO MORALES, JOSE)
DAVID QUIÑONES, ALFONSO MORALES, EDDIE)
IRIZARRY, PETRA ALBINO, BETH HENSON,)
MOISES MORALES and PEDRO ARCHULETA,)
THE RAFAEL CANCEL MIRANDA HIGH SCHOOL,)
and THE CHICAGO COMMITTEE TO FREE THE)
FIVE PUERTO RICAN NATIONALIST PRISONERS,)
for themselves and others similarly)
situated,)
)
Plaintiffs,)
)
vs.)
)
GRIFFIN BELL, Attorney General of the)
United States; CLARENCE KELLEY, Director)
of the FBI; JOHN DOE and MICHAEL MOE and)
others, his Deputies and Assistants;)
WILLIAM BEANE, Special Agent in Charge)
of the Chicago Office of the FBI; THOMAS)
DEAN and ZACHARY ZOE, his Deputies and)
Supervisory Assistants; Agents SCOTT ,)
JENNINGS, GREG PARISH, AL JORDAN, DEFEN-)
BAUGH, MARTINEZ, RODRIGUEZ, RICHARD ROE,)
PETER POE, and other unknown FBI agents)
assigned to the Chicago Office; all such)
individual Defendants individually and in)
their official capacities as members of)
the U.S. Justice Department and Federal)
Bureau of Investigation; and the FEDERAL)
BUREAU OF INVESTIGATION, entirely,)
)
Defendants.)

FILED

JUL 25...

H. Stuart Cunningham, Clerk
United States District Court

77 C 2673

COMPLAINT AND CLASS ACTION FOR INJUNCTION,
DECLARATORY JUDGMENT, AND MONEY DAMAGES

INTRODUCTION

This is an action by a number of individuals and groups, for themselves and a class of others similarly situated, seeking declaratory, injunctive and monetary relief for Puerto Rican and other Latino people and groups who have been or will be subjected to harassment, intimidation, surveillance and "counter-intelligence" by the Federal Bureau of Investigation, through the actions of some of the Defendants and under the supervision and direction

FIGURE 1 Complaint filed against the FBI for harassment.

FIGURE 2 The FBI searching our drawers.

FBI. The government then initiated a criminal grand jury against us, and nearly a dozen people were jailed for refusing to testify.

Puerto Rico was a possession of Spain that passed to U.S. control, along with Cuba and the Philippines, at the end of the Spanish-American War in 1898. It is now a U.S. colony, "belonging to, but not part of, the U.S." Initially compelled to produce sugar for export, in the 1950s the island was partially industrialized, again for the benefit of the mainland. More than half of its population—and more since the recent crisis and hurricane—has migrated to the mainland, where they face discrimination for being both dark-skinned and Spanish speaking. Beginning in the 1930s, eugenics and family-planning experts targeted Puerto Rico, and more than one-third of the women of childbearing age have been sterilized. The island has been subjected to both a polluting pharmaceuticals industry and prolonged medical experimentation.[1] The U.S. Navy used the island of Vieques off the east coast as a bombing range for decades; massive protests finally forced the base to close in 2003 when celebrities joined the cause.[2] Today the debt crisis and the federal government's response to Hurricane Maria demonstrate the abysmal neglect—at best—of the colonial relationship.[3]

The independence movement has fought for Puerto Rican sovereignty through legal and illegal means. In 1950 the Puerto Rican flag was raised (it was illegal) over a number of towns during an armed uprising led by the Nationalist Party. When the U.S. Army retaliated, destroying the town of Jayuya and imposing martial law on the island, patriots on the mainland attacked President Truman's house. In 1954, a commando led by Lolita Lebrón fired shots into the U.S. House of Representatives in a call for independence. She and her comrades, including one from the 1950 action, were given long prison terms. The Five Puerto Rican Nationalist Prisoners were Lolita Lebrón, Oscar Collazo, Rafael Cancel Miranda, Irvin Flores, and Andrés Figueroa Cordero.

In Chicago, the Rafael Cancel Miranda High School was founded as an alternative school in 1972 by Oscar and José López. In the early 1980s, a total of fifteen community leaders, including Oscar López, were arrested and convicted of seditious conspiracy and membership in the FALN; they announced that they were prisoners of war and demanded treatment according to the Geneva Convention. They got lengthy sentences.

Lebrón and the remaining nationalists were released by President Carter in 1979; most of the FALN prisoners of war were released by President Clinton in 1999; and Oscar López, the last Puerto Rican POW, was released by President Obama in 2017. When Cancel Miranda was freed after twenty-five years, he requested the high school change its name from his to that of Pedro Albizu Campos, the legendary Nationalist Party leader, and they did. While independence remains elusive, the community in Chicago is thriving. The high school continues to provide critical education, the Puerto Rican Cultural Center offers a variety of programs, and at each end of the six blocks of Division Street known as the *Paseo Boricua* (Puerto Rican Promenade) is a huge metal Puerto Rican flag, once forbidden to fly, the largest one in the country.

Why was I so deeply moved? Why did I risk my freedom and acquire an FBI contact who came every month until I left Chicago? Who broke into my apartment and went through my files? Who interviewed someone I worked with? Who searched the boxes I left in storage? Our house on the corner of Haddon and Hoyne, near Division and Damen, was an informal and vibrant community center. My roommates were *independentistas* and students from Northeastern Illinois University, including the singer Marta Rodríguez. I worked in a nearby factory, Stewart Warner, running a keypunch machine on the shop floor alongside young Puerto Rican women. At home we sang, we assembled exhortatory pamphlets, we cooked *mofongo* (mashed plantains) and *arroz con gandules* (rice with peas), and I learned to make *tostones* (twice-fried plantains) and *pasteles* (turnovers). We received refugees from the debacle in Chile when the military came to power in 1973. We published a community newspaper, *El Coquí*, whose masthead read "Don't speak, but act. For those who struggle, victory is their reward."[4] One day sheets went up on the windows of the vacant house across the street from us, and we saw two white men in suits coming out and two others taking their place. Twelve hours later the shift changed again. This continued for months.

Around that time the solidarity movement—North Americans in support of Puerto Rican independence—split over the issue of the armed struggle being waged in New York, Chicago, and on the island while a new Puerto Rican and Mexicano-Chicano organization, the Movimiento de Liberación Nacional (National Liberation Movement), emerged in Chicago and the Southwest. I had joined a small Marxist-Leninist organization, the Sojourner Truth Organization (STO), several years before.[5] Our position was one of unconditional support for Puerto Rican self-determination, including the use of force to resist a half century of military occupation. I traveled to San Juan to meet Don Juan Antonio Corretjer—poet, militant, leader of the Liga Socialista Puertorriqueña (Puerto Rican Socialist League)—to arrange to translate their documents.[6]

In the fifth issue of STO's journal, *Urgent Tasks*, I published an appreciation of *Armed Struggle: Both a Strategy and a Tactic*, written by Massoud Ahmadzadeh, a member of an Iranian guerrilla group, which included many schoolteachers, that emerged from an attack on a rural army base in 1971.[7] Ahmadzadeh's pamphlet included a discussion of Régis Debray's *Revolution in the Revolution?*, noting the similarities between Iran and Latin America, where U.S.-backed regimes relied on military force to suppress open agitation for social change "undisguised by the concessions to democracy that are required in the metropolis," and the masses of people were contained through apathy, despair, and torture, and their resistance could only "emerge . . . within the space created by successful armed actions."[8] I ended my article, which was an extended discussion of *foquismo*, the theory that sporadic small-scale armed attacks could detonate a broader revolutionary movement, by quoting Ahmadzadeh's warning that clandestinity can create "an atomized, corrupted, alienated cadre which knows nothing but warfare, destruction, and drama and is unprepared for the painstaking work of creating a new society."[9]

Around the time I joined, STO had changed their focus from concentration on workplace organizing to one of supporting national liberation within and outside U.S. borders. We argued that anti-imperialism had to be central to any revolutionary movement and that black and brown movements had long represented the most compelling challenge. Our task was to organize the so-called white workers to renounce the privileges that make them "more white than worker" and join with black, Puerto Rican, Mexican, and other oppressed peoples. These debates were complex; I cannot do them justice here. Members of STO, especially Noel Ignatiev (then Ignatin) and our friend Theodore Allen, were pioneers in what became known as the social construction of whiteness.[10]

I left Chicago in 1979 and continued to work with STO in the Bay Area, where my activities included a campaign against sterilization abuse and translating articles on Palestine and Iran for *Newsfront International*. In 1982 I edited a report for the United Nations Human Rights Commission on violations in Iran under the Khomeini regime for the International Solidarity Front for the Defense of the Iranian People's Democratic Rights. By then I had resigned from STO, not from any disagreement but because I could no longer maintain the necessary optimism of the will. I moved to the Arizona-Sonora borderlands and spent extensive periods of time in Zacatecas, Chihuahua, and Mexico City. I think of myself as an unrepentant soldier in an army that was defeated. Nothing I have done since has convinced me we were wrong to fight for revolutionary transformation, and nothing has so fully engaged me. This book is an effort to work through what John Beverley called "the melancholia of defeat" by examining armed struggle in another context.[11] The protagonists of this book are not the revolutionaries who attacked the base but the movement itself that started in late 1959 in a long march from the sierra to the capital. For many young people—and not only young—a life dedicated to collective and not individual striving is inconceivable; the term *movement* is an empty signifier. I hope this book conveys the everyday life of the movement, both the *mística*—the dedication—and the challenge.

ACKNOWLEDGMENTS

I SPENT MANY YEARS on this book and accumulated debts too great to number, but I would like to thank the U.S. Department of Education, the Fulbright Commission, the Comisión México-Estados Unidos, and Georgia Ehlers of the University of Arizona for a Fulbright-Hays Doctoral Dissertation Research Grant supporting a year of research in Mexico City and Chihuahua. I thank the Centro de Investigaciones y Estudios Superiores en Antropología Social, Patricia Ravelo, and El Grupo Permanente sobre Violencia, Género, y Sexualidades Diversas de CIESAS for providing an academic home, a library, and ongoing discussions that illuminated my topic even when they seemed tangential.

I would like to thank the Tinker Foundation for a Summer Field Grant and the University of Arizona history department for initial funding.

My eternal gratitude goes to the University of Arizona history department for their continued support; I could not have found a more dedicated, engaged, and critical community of scholars. I thank my committee for their patience, support, good humor, and examples: William H. Beezley, John Womack Jr. (Harvard University), Kevin Gosner, and Fabio Lanza. I thank Karen Anderson and Katherine Morrissey for getting me started and members of the Sojourner Truth Organization (1969–86) and *Race Traitor* (1995–2002) for preparing me for graduate school. I thank Victor Orozco of the Universidad Autónoma de Ciudad Juárez for facilitating my research and publishing an early version. Thanks to Susan Deeds, John Mason Hart, Carmen Nava, Benjamin Smith, and Mary Kay Vaughan for encouragement and suggestions. All the errors and judgments here are mine.

Thanks also to the anonymous reviewers who pushed me to make this book better; I took nearly all their suggestions.

I thank Liliana Rascón and Bill Israel of the Archivo Histórico de Chihuahua for their generous assistance and for rescuing archives throughout the state; Maestra Concepción Franco of the State Normal School; Mitchell Alberto Garnica Flores and Arturo Santana M. of the Supremo Tribunal de Justicia del Estado and Pedro Muñoz Grado; Juan Hernández López, Colecciones Especiales de la Universidad Autónoma de Cuidad Juárez; and the archivists at the Hemeroteca Nacional at the Universidad Nacional Autónoma de México and the Archivo General de la Nación. Special thanks to Eduardo Gómez Caballero and the Comité Primeros Vientos.

Many thanks to friends who opened their homes and hearts, who fed me, who told me their stories and made introductions, who listened to years of obsessive formulations and discoveries, who kept me sane: Ramón Antonio Armendáriz, who brought me to Chihuahua; Mary Ann Capeheart; Hugo Carrillo; Lourdes Carrillo; Nithia Castorena; Adela Cedillo; Susan Deeds; Estela Fernández; Randy Gingrich; Ilse Gradwohl; Pety Guerrero; Lori Keyne; Mague, Adela, and Beatriz Lozoya; Carmen Megeath; Patricia Ochoa; Joel Olson; Patricia Ravelo; Sergio Sánchez; Lorena Talamás; Maritza Urteaga; and Robin Zenger.

Preliminary and abbreviated versions of this work, including some translated into Spanish, were published in Fernando Calderón and Adela Cedillo, *Challenging Authoritarianism in Mexico*; *Chihuahua Hoy*; *El Heraldo de Chihuahua*; *La Jornada del Campo*; and the *Oxford Research Encyclopedia*. I have presented this work at the Rocky Mountain Council on Latin American Studies, La Escuela de Antropología e Historia del Norte de México, CIESAS, El Congreso Internacional de la Historia Regional de Chihuahua, the American University of Beirut, the Oaxaca Summer Institute, and the Southwest Conference on Latin American Studies.

Special thanks to my editor, Kristen Buckles, and the staff at the University of Arizona Press, and to Adela Cedillo again for translation.

INDIVIDUALS

Alemán, Miguel. President of Mexico, 1946–1952.
Alvarez, Francisco Javier. State Director of Education.
Borunda, Teófilo. Governor of Chihuahua, 1956–1962.
Caballero, Alma. Wife of Pablo Gómez.
Caldera, Rito. Commander of detachment of judicial police in Madera.
Cárdenas, Lázaro. President of Mexico, 1934–1940.
Cárdenas Barojas, Lorenzo. Retired army captain. Gave Grupo Popular Guerrillero (GPG) military training in Mexico City, 1965.
Cardona, Hilario. Student at State Normal School. Imprisoned for six months in 1964.
Díaz Ordaz, Gustavo. President of Mexico, 1964–1970.
Echeverría, Luis. President of Mexico, 1970–1976.
Fernández, Matías (José Juan). Member of GPG. Escaped from assault on September 23, 1965.
Gámiz, Arturo. Student at State Normal School, then teacher in Mineral de Dolores. Leader of Unión General de Obreros y Campesinos de México (UGOCM), Juventud Popular (JP), and founder of GPG. Died in assault on September 23, 1965.
Gámiz, Emilio. Student at State Normal School and Arturo's brother. Member of GPG. Died in assault on September 23, 1965.
Gaytán, Rosendo. Ranchero in Mineral de Dolores.
Gaytán Aguirre, Juan Antonio. Rosendo Gaytán's son, active in UGOCM and GPG. Died in a *guerrilla* action in 1968.

Gaytán Aguirre, Salomón. Son of Rosendo Gaytán. Active in UGOCM and GPG. Died in assault on September 23, 1965.

Gaytán Aguirre, Salvador. Son of Rosendo Gaytán. Active in UGOCM and GPG.

Giner Durán, Práxedis. Governor of Chihuahua, 1962–1968.

Gómez Ramírez, Pablo. Medical doctor and teacher at rural normal school for girls in Saucillo. Leader in Partido Popular Socialista (PPS), UGOCM. Member of GPG. Died in assault on September 23, 1965.

Gómez Ramírez, Raúl. Teacher in Delicias and Ojinaga. Leader in PPS, UGOCM, and Pablo's brother.

Gómez Velazco, Antonio. Commander of the Fifth Military Zone beginning in 1963.

González Eguiarte, Oscar. Student at the preparatory school of the UACH then at the UNAM. Returned to Chihuahua and became member of UGOCM and Urban Support Network for GPG. Died in *guerrilla* action in 1968.

Gutiérrez, Clara Elena. Student at rural normal school for girls and member of Urban Support Network for GPG.

Ibarra, Florentino. José's brother. Killed in 1964.

Ibarra, José. Member of Four Friends. Landowner in Madera region. Led gangs of gunmen against communities in the sierra.

Jacott, Guadalupe (Lupe). Student at rural normal school for girls, officer in UGOCM, and member of Urban Support Network for GPG.

Juárez Santos Coy (Santoscoy), Eduardo. Director of State Department of Agrarian Affairs.

Lombardo Toledano, Vicente. National leader of PPS.

López, Jacinto. National leader of UGOCM.

López Mateos, Adolfo. President of Mexico, 1958–1964.

Lugo, Raúl Florencio. Member of GPG. Escaped from assault on September 23, 1965.

Luján, Francisco. Retired schoolteacher in Madera. Assassinated in November 1959.

Martínez Noriega, Roberto. Army officer who practiced repression on communities in the sierra.

Martínez Valdivia, Rafael. Schoolteacher in sierra. Member of GPG. Died in assault on September 23, 1965.

Mendoza, Ramón. Ranchero from Madera region and member of GPG. Escaped from assault on September 23, 1965.

Mendoza Domínguez, Manuel. Chief of the state judicial police.

Montemayor, Carlos. Wrote three novels about the assault on the base, the first published in 2003.

Ornelas, Francisco (Paco). Nephew of Pablo and Raúl Gómez. Student at State Normal School. Member of GPG. Escaped from assault on September 23, 1965.

Portillo, Francisco. Owner of the Hacienda Sírupa adjacent to Ejido Cebadillo de Dolores.

Quiñónez, Miguel. Schoolteacher in sierra. Member of GPG. Died in assault on September 23, 1965.

Reyes, Judith. Singer and songwriter. Journalist and publisher of *Acción: Voz Revolucionario del Pueblo*.

Ríos, Alvaro. Organizer of UGOCM in Madera, then UGOCM leader in Chihuahua and Durango.

Ríos, Carlos. No relation to Alvaro. Member of UGOCM and Indigenous Pima. Assassinated by Florentino Ibarra in March 1960.

Sánchez Lozoya, Dionisio. Veteran of revolution of 1910. Led struggle for land on Hacienda Santo Domingo.

Sandoval, Oscar. Student at State Normal School. Member of GPG. Died in assault on September 23, 1965.

Santos Valdés, José. School inspector for Northern Mexico. Wrote sympathetic account of assault on base, published in 1968.

Scobell (or Escóbel) Gaytán, Guadalupe. Nephew of Salomón Gaytán, ranchero in Madera region, and member of GPG. Died in a *guerrilla* action in 1968.

Scobell (or Escóbel) Gaytán, Juan Antonio. Nephew of Salomón Gaytán, ranchero in Madera region, and member of GPG. Died in assault on September 23, 1965.

Toro Rosales, Salvador del. Attorney with federal attorney general's office. Sent to Chihuahua on several occasions to mediate and report.

Uranga, Pedro. Student at the preparatory school of the UACH and member of Urban Support Network for GPG.

Vallina, Eloy. Empresario and part owner of Bosques de Chihuahua.

Vega, Tomás. Member of Four Friends and landowner in Temósachic. Harassed communities in the sierra.

Villa Rentería, Hipólito. State attorney general.

Villarreal, Lázaro. Businessman, financial supporter of various progressive movements.

ABBREVIATIONS

AGN	Archivo General de la Nación (National General Archive)
CCI	Central Campesina Independiente (Independent Campesino Central)
CDP	Comité de Defensa Popular (Popular Defense Committee)
CIDECH	Centro de Investigaciones y Documentación del Estado de Chihuahua (Center for Investigation and Documentation of the State of Chihuahua)
CIG	Certificado de Inafectabilidad Ganadera (certificate of livestock exemption)
CNC	Confederación Nacional de Campesinos (National Confederation of Campesinos)
CNED	Centro Nacional de Estudiantes Democráticos (National Center of Democratic Students)
CNOP	Confederación Nacional de Organizaciones Populares (National Confederation of Popular Organizations)
Comité Pro	Comité Pro Defensa de las Guarantías Individuales y Sociales (Committee for the Defense of Individual and Social Rights)
CROM	Confederación Regional Obrera Mexicana (Regional Confederation of Mexican Workers)
CTM	Confederación de Trabajadores Mexicanos (Confederation of Mexican Workers)

DAAC	Departamento de Asuntos Agrarios y Colonización (Department of Agrarian Affairs and Colonization)
DF	Distrito Federal (Federal District)
DFS	Dirección Federal de Seguridad (Office of Federal Security)
EMP	Ejército Mexicano Popular (Mexican Popular Army)
EZLN	Ejército Zapatista de Liberación Nacional (Zapatista Army for National Liberation)
FECH	Federación Estudiantil de Chihuahua (Federation of Chihuahua Students)
FECSM	Federación de Estudiantes Campesinos Socialistas de México (Federation of Socialist Campesino Students of Mexico)
FEP	Frente Electoral de Pueblo (People's Electoral Front)
FOCECH	Federación de Obreros y Campesinos del Estado de Chihuahua (Federation of Workers and Campesinos of the State of Chihuahua)
GPG	Grupo Popular Guerrillero (Popular Guerrilla Group)
IPN	Instituto Politécnico Nacional (National Polytechnical Institute)
IPS	Dirección General de Investigaciones Políticas y Sociales (General Office for Political and Social Investigations)
JCM	Juventud Comunista de México (Communist Youth of Mexico)
JP	Juventud Popular (Popular Youth)
LCA	Liga de Comunidades Agrarias (League of Agrarian Communities)
MAR	Movimiento Armado Revolucionario (Armed Revolutionary Movement)
MLN	Movimiento de Liberación Nacional (Movement for National Liberation)
MRM	Movimiento Revolucionario del Magisterio (Revolutionary Teachers' Movement)
NCP	New Center of Population
PAN	Partido de Acción Nacional (National Action Party)
PARM	Partido Auténtico de la Revolución Mexicana (Authentic Party of the Mexican Revolution)
PCM	Partido Comunista Mexicana (Mexican Communist Party)
PPS	Partido Popular Socialista (Popular Socialist Party)

PRD	Partido Revolucionario Democrático (Democratic Revolutionary Party)
PRI	Partido Revolucionario Institucional (Institutional Revolutionary Party)
RAN	Registro Agrario Nacional (National Agrarian Registry)
SEP	Secretaría de Educación Pública (Department of Public Education)
UACH	Universidad Autónoma de Chihuahua
UACJ	Universidad Autónoma de Ciudad Juárez (Autonomous University of Juárez)
UGOCM	Unión General de Obreros y Campesinos de México (General Union of Workers and Campesinos of Mexico)
UIEF	Unidades Industriales de Explotación Forestal (Industrialized Forestry Units)
UNAM	Universidad Nacional Autónoma de México (National Autonomous University of Mexico)

AGRARIAN REVOLT IN THE SIERRA OF CHIHUAHUA, 1959–1965

Map of Chihuahua by Hugo Carrillo Domínguez.

Introduction

MADERA CITY, SIERRA OF CHIHUAHUA. Just before dawn on September 23, 1965,[1] a squad of thirteen poorly armed young men who called themselves the Grupo Popular Guerrillero (GPG; Popular Guerrilla Group) attacked an army base on the edge of this town of twelve thousand inhabitants. They had expected to find some seventy soldiers asleep in the barracks. Instead, there were 125, who, after a brief fire fight, killed eight guerrillas while five escaped with the help of townspeople into the surrounding mountains. Four soldiers were killed and a fifth later died of wounds; one civilian was killed by soldiers. The bodies of the dead guerrilleros were paraded around town in the rain and tossed on the plaza overnight. The governor of the state, General Práxedis Giner Durán, refused efforts to remove the bodies and ordered them thrown into a common grave without shrouds. "¿Querían tierra? ¡Dénles tierra hasta que se harten!" (They wanted land? Give it to them until they choke!) he proclaimed.[2]

On September 28, the governor signed an order granting thirty-nine thousand hectares to seventy-seven campesinos of Huizopa, affecting 1,534 hectares of Los Alisos belonging to José Ibarra, four hundred hectares of El Naranjo and Arroyo Bonita belonging to the son of Tomás Vega, and five thousand hectares of Dolores along with lands belonging to Bosques de Chihuahua and the federal government.[3] Ibarra and Vega were the principal caciques of the region, and Bosques de Chihuahua (Chihuahua's Forests), a timbering company owned by a consortium of Mexican politicians and entrepreneurs, was the guerrilla's principal antagonist; the town of Dolores was central to their activities.

On October 1, 1965, *El Heraldo de Chihuahua* announced the distribution of five thousand hectares to the Ejido Cuauhtémoc, in the municipality of Ascensión, on former lands of the latifundium Palomas.[4] In 1971, President Luis Echeverría added some 252,000 hectares taken from Bosques de Chihuahua to the largest ejido in the republic, that of El Largo, whose members continue to harvest lumber.[5] The ejidatarios included previous smallholders and some of the fiercest opponents of the governor and the caciques.

Direct Action and Armed Struggle

Mid-twentieth-century industrial growth—the so-called Miracle—had long put pressure on the rural population, both landless workers whose demands for ejidos had languished for decades and *serrano* (inhabitant of the sierra or backlands) smallholders harassed by encroaching timber barons. The GPG arose from a sustained movement of campesinos and students, particularly *normalistas* (students of teaching schools), who organized direct action protests to complement petitions to the Departamento de Asuntos Agrarios y Colonización (DAAC; Department of Agrarian Affairs and Colonization). Campesinos, students, and teachers had occupied downtown plazas, invaded land, and marched throughout the state during the five years before the assault on the base. Their means of struggle were innovative and incorporated large numbers of people, urban as well as rural, whose political participation was not mediated by the usual forms of representation; while some participants were members of organizations, the organizations did not act in their stead. Prolonged coexistence and years of mobilizations strengthened bonds among participants and announced to the bureaucrats, politicians, timber barons, latifundistas, and caciques that the protesters were political subjects who continued to be present and to resist anonymity and displacement.

The armed component of the struggle developed in early 1964 in the sierra of Madera from a long-standing tradition of armed self-defense against the aggressions of local caciques, while the students and rural teachers, through their readings on Marxism and especially its Cuban variant, developed an ideological justification for sporadic episodes of vengeance that finally led to the assault on the barracks on September 23, 1965. Recent interest in these events has focused on the armed component as the first socialist *guerrilla*, the Primeros Vientos (first winds). My interest is primarily in the public, direct action aspect of the movement. This focus requires resisting the teleological collapse into a narrative focused on the *guerrilla*, whose glamor eclipses the earlier, more inclusive and heterogeneous movement that, unlike the armed component, included women as actors in their own right. One has to resist the conviction that taking up arms was more revolutionary, more radical, and that the mass public movement did not go far enough and look at what was potentially revolutionary in the land invasions, the occupations, the confrontations on the patio of the statehouse. The direct action strategy prefigured the participatory movements from below of subsequent decades, especially Chihuahua's Comité de Defensa Popular (CDP; Committee for Popular Defense), whose core members established the Colonia Francisco Villa north of the capital in 1968 following a series of urban land invasions. Direct action was a break from earlier methods of land solicitation that focused on petitioning the government for relief. Direct action relied on new methods of pressure and incorporated broader issues, such as support for Cuba and student demands. The campesinos ceased to be objects of manipulation by their representatives and became subjects acting for their own benefit. Their eruptions into public space, particularly their sit-ins and protests in the heart of downtown Chihuahua City, their highway marches, and their symbolic encampments were intended to make them visible to more than just the state authorities. They were assertions of their determination to claim their rights and announce their presence.

The popular movement responded to specific local events within a series of nested contexts that ranged from the expansion of timbering in the sierra of Chihuahua to midcentury industrialization developing against the interests of Mexican campesinos to the global contending forces of the Cold War and the Cuban Revolution. In Chihuahua, diverse social forces, from serrano smallholders besieged by timber barons to landless agriculturists in the Conchos valley, worked together under the leadership of the Unión General de Obreros y Campesinos de México (UGOCM; General Union of Workers and Campesinos of Mexico), an affiliate of the Partido Popular Socialista (PPS; Popular Socialist Party). Rural teachers and *normalistas* (students of teaching colleges) were frequently of campesino origin and remained in the countryside; they had long supported campesinos with their petitions to the DAAC. While some teachers who emerged from the normal schools became rural power brokers themselves, many were heirs to the *agrarista* tradition of the revolution of 1910 as transmitted through Lázaro Cárdenas's socialist education. Chihuahua's rural normal schools, located first in Flores Magón and then in Saucillo (girls) and Salaices (boys), were crucial centers of resistance and provided passionate foot soldiers for the campesinos' occupations and demonstrations.

From late 1959 to its denouement with the attack on the base in 1965, the movement broke with previous limits to legality and engaged in public acts of defiance: symbolic occupations, intercity caravans, and refusal to respect legally constituted authority, particularly the governor. The invasions in particular were new methods; while there were precedents, such as invasions of the Hacienda Babícora in the 1930s, they had not been widely used. In Chihuahua during the 1960s, they were pioneered by UGOCM leader Alvaro Ríos, who arrived in Chihuahua in late 1959. Before his arrival, the union had been content with petitions and delegations to Mexico City. The campesino movement was a school for protest that relied on the enthusiastic participation of vast numbers and enjoyed support throughout the state, especially from recent migrants from the countryside now living in the capital city. (By 1970, 55 percent of the state's population lived in towns with more than fifteen thousand inhabitants.[6]) The movement was strong enough to support three progressive newspapers: the daily *El Norte*, published by Luis Fuentes Saucedo; the weekly *Indice: Un Periódico sin Cadenas*, founded in 1958 and published by the attorney Guillermo Gallarda Astorga; and the monthly *Acción: Voz Revolucionaria del Pueblo*, founded in 1962 and published by the protest singer Judith Reyes, which focused on the campesino movement. Together they circulated invective, grievances, and news of confrontations, knitting the movement together.

Landholding and Violence

Since the Porfiriato, much of Chihuahua had been held by large landowners, many of them foreigners. The revolution of 1910 left many latifundistas in place while promoting new ones. In the mid-twentieth-century sierra, smallholders with unsecured property rights battled local caciques allied with Bosques de Chihuahua. Bosques had received a forestry concession in 1952 from Mexican president Miguel Alemán and responded to federal injunctions to divide the land by selling to a consortium of local cattlemen and landowners, the Four Friends, who repaid the sales by acting as thugs for the company, driving out smallholders and stealing their land and livestock, through murder, rape, and accusations of rustling. The campesino movement protested the existence of expired *certificados de inafectabilidad ganadera* (CIG; certificates of livestock exemption). First promulgated by President Lázaro Cárdenas and codified in the Agrarian Code of 1942, the twenty-five-year certificates were intended to increase the food supply by exempting grazing lands from agrarian distribution. In arid lands, permitted extensions could be as large as fifty thousand hectares. By midcentury, many were about to expire; others covered extensions of territory greater than those limited by law or lands fraudulently divided among family members. Landless agricultural workers throughout the state, particularly in the fertile agribusiness region of the Río Conchos, fought for ejidos. Yet another target of protesters was the accumulation of vast tracts of land by foreigners, some within fifty miles of the U.S. border as forbidden by the constitution of 1917. The Hacienda of Santo Domingo, near Villa Ahumada and owned by an absentee U.S. landlord, was targeted for years of land invasions and protests. Finally Mennonites, encouraged to settle on lands expropriated by Alvaro Obregón in the early 1920s, were targeted as foreigners despite being citizens.

The serranos revolted against modernity in the form of an extractive industry expanding at their expense. The sierra had been settled by mestizo pioneers recruited to form a line of resistance against indigenous raids and U.S. encroachment. They had a long tradition of municipal autonomy and resistance to imposed authority. These ranchers, described by Alonso, Katz, Knight, Nugent, and Orozco in similar terms,[7] fought to defend a way of life based on semiautonomous rural communities in isolated hinterlands with an economy of livestock, orchards, and migrant labor. No longer needed to defend the frontier and so now an obstacle to progress, the serranos were to be swept from their homeland and engaged in wage work. Chihuahua's future was urban: in 1965, the first maquiladora was established in Ciudad Juárez, one year after the bracero program ended.[8]

Battles between smallholders in the sierra and caciques allied with state agents were face-to-face confrontations between armed actors with specific grievances. The inhabitants of the region had shown a long-standing propensity for armed self-defense that adapted easily to the *foquismo*[9] being studied by radicals. Unlike later armed movements of students frustrated by their inability to bring about social change through peaceful methods during the Dirty War, the roots of the original GPG were native to the sierra. The attack on the base grew from the confluence of this endemic movement with the explicitly revolutionary and Guevarist ideology developed in the group around Arturo Gámiz, a rural teacher and leader of both public and armed movements. In late 1964 or early 1965, Gámiz took members of the group to Mexico City for military training and political networking. There they lost the support of family networks and the advantage of familiar terrain. The move followed a decision to expand the sporadic armed actions in the sierra into a larger arena. Once decided, participants were corralled into activities that could only end in total victory or defeat. They had taken up arms as a people in arms, encouraged by a series of victories in the field, and they became a vanguard separate from their supporters. Deluded by their own rhetoric, young people impatient with the popular movement and maddened by the intransigence of state authorities hurled themselves into an adventure whose spectacular failure put an end to the movement itself. We remember them for the audacity of the attack, but it was the long, preliminary, legal and illegal organizing that made the attack possible.

The story of Madera 1965 is not about the Dirty War but about its prelude. The urban guerrillas of the seventies were largely educated and middle class; they were moved by ideological convictions and were willing to act in arenas far from their homes. The majority of the GPG and its supporters were of humble origins; only a few were university students. The indiscriminant violence unleashed on both guerrillas and their innocent associates during the Dirty War was largely absent in Chihuahua, although serious abuses were common in the sierra and predated the GPG. The torture of Chihuahua's serranos confirms Gladys McCormick's argument that techniques of authoritarian repression were first practiced against dissidents in the countryside before being used in the cities. The rural areas, dispersed, far from the public gaze and the government-controlled media, provided a "laboratory—sometimes intentional and sometimes not—to test and hone coercive strategies that officials later used against urban activists."[10] The regime's strategy reflected the growing marginalization of the rural population, who were systematically sacrificed to the needs of industry and the cities. Their consent, once secured by bonds of patronage, was undermined by economic trends that made their cooperation—and they themselves—dispensable.

Although under surveillance by agents of the federal secret police, as shown in extensive files in the Archivo General de la Nación (AGN; National General Archive), no one who took part in the early protest movements in Chihuahua was disappeared or assassinated, and family members were left alone—again, with the exception of the sierra. Nor did the guerrillas, until they attacked the base, torture or kill their adversaries, with the exception of one retaliatory execution. The repressive apparatus of the state was still on the eve of its consolidation.

Chihuahua's governor Práxedis Giner Durán (1962–68) refused to honor the code of protest, negotiation, and incorporation that was the cornerstone of rule by the Partido Revolucionario Institucional (PRI; Institutional Revolutionary Party, which held presidential office until 2000). Former head of the Cattlemen's Association and a military general, Giner defied presidential resolutions and the transfer of land to ejidos, insisting that not one meter remained subject to affectation. He repeatedly called out troops against protests. Federal officials regarded Giner as incompetent and sent federal attorney general Salvador del Toro Rosales to Chihuahua on several occasions to ameliorate the damage.[11] Enraged by the students' participation, Giner closed a series of dormitories and entire schools and cast aspersions of promiscuity on the girl students. His vulgarity was legendary, and he engaged in at least one shouting match with Arturo Gámiz on the patio of the statehouse. His recalcitrance did more than Che's *Guerra de Guerrillas* to turn a mass social movement into an attack on the federal army.

Slavoj Žižek described three sorts of violence: subjective, meaning overt acts, such as using guns and bombs; objective, which is structural and inherent in the social system; and symbolic, embedded in language and the social hierarchy reproduced in speech that forms an imposed "universe of meaning."[12] The latter two are obscured by the drama of the first; the point is to resist fascination with the violence exercised by the desperate subject and see the background, the objective and symbolic violence, that continues to produce such actions. According to the logic of capitalism, wealth is generated by expansion; when Bosques de Chihuahua and the big cattlemen encroached on smallholders, their wealth generated poverty, resentment, and finally subjective violence.

Carlos Montemayor wrote extensively about the GPG and other contemporary armed groups and drew a distinction between rural and urban guerrilla movements.[13] The rural movements, rooted in specific local conditions and made up of family networks, could not extend to other areas; the origins of the urban movements were ideological, their members transcended local conditions and could take action far from home, as Che Guevara did in Africa and Bolivia.[14] In Chihuahua, serranos who fought to defend their families' land were at the heart of the rural *guerrilla*, continuing a centuries-old tradition, while the urban component consisted of students and teachers nourished on Marxist-Leninist texts who were frequently from a campesino background.[15] Because the movement was rooted in campesino demands and because it was the serranos and not the students who took up armed struggle, the ideological and the local converged for several years. As Montemayor remarked, referring in part to Chihuahua, "It is not possible . . . to point to a clear division between the armed groups properly speaking and the popular organizations, which were active, changing, and complex and took up the banner of causes that were agrarian, or related to teaching."[16]

Individuals cycled through the public and armed phases of the movement. Alvaro Ríos, who pioneered the use of direct action, organized armed self-defense in Santa Rita in 1962, where armed militants stood guard against evictions, but he broke with supporters of the GPG three years later. Campesinos Ramón Mendoza and Florencio Lugo, along with members of the Gaytán family, participated in Marxist study groups in Chihuahua and later Mexico City; they all took part in subsequent armed *guerrillas* far from their homes. Several teachers who had apparently not engaged in previous actions in the sierra took part in the assault on the base, among them Pablo Gómez, Rafael Martínez Valdivia, and Miguel Quiñónez, while several individuals whose names came up repeatedly in the armed actions of 1964 were not among the attackers.

Was armed struggle the only path to follow—had peaceful means been exhausted—as the GPG claimed?[17] The Social Democratic Christian Movement emerged in Chihuahua in the early 1960s with a focus on workplace organizing and was leading strikes while the UGOCM was at its height in 1964. Followers of Paolo Freire who raised the slogan, *La guerra moral* (the moral war), the Christian left posed an alternative to both the official Christian party, the Partido de Acción Nacional (PAN; National Action Party), and the secular left.[18] It is interesting that neither group mentions the other in their literature. A few years after the attack on the base, Chihuahua's urban poor formed the Comité de Defensa Popular (CDP; Popular Defense Committee) and led successful urban land invasions, showing that direct action still brought results. While the national labor movement had been defeated when the railroad workers' strike was lost in 1959, demands for union autonomy continued. In late 1964–1965, Mexico City doctors and medical students mobilized for independent representation and, in 1971, a reinvigorated labor insurgency initiated actions among automobile, railway, mining, and metalworkers, while the Democratic Tendency emerged among electrical workers. These workers went beyond economic concerns to demand democratic union representation and greater control of the labor process.[19] The 1970s also saw resurgent agrarian protests throughout the republic.[20]

The UGOCM, PPS, and PCM

The Unión General de Obreros y Campesinos de México was founded in 1949 as a radical alternative to the government-controlled Confederación Nacional de Campesinos (CNC; National Confederation of Campesinos) and Confederación de Trabajadores Mexicanos (CTM; Confederation of Mexican Workers). While it never acquired a base among workers, by the late 1950s it had achieved substantial influence among campesinos, particularly in the north. The events that led to the attack on the base began in Madera in late 1959, shortly after Alvaro Ríos arrived from Mexico City to lead the organization. Ríos, originally from Sonora, was a lifelong agrarian activist. He did not participate in the armed actions of 1964–1965, instead shifting his activities to the neighboring state of Durango.

The Partido Comunista Mexicano (PCM; Mexican Communist Party) was formed in 1919 and affiliated with the Third International, the Moscow-directed association of communist parties. Never hegemonic among workers and doomed to struggle against the PRI's monopoly of revolutionary rhetoric, it was arguably most influential among intellectuals, with important support among railway workers, miners, petroleum workers, and teachers and in the north-central cotton-growing region of La Laguna. Unsuccessful in its battles to create enduring autonomous organizations, its expanding influence during the popular front era of the 1930s was undermined by Cárdenas's authoritarian incorporation of organizations of workers and campesinos into the government, which thereby captured the PCM's potential base. Its stance toward the state vacillated between uncritical support and violent rejection. The PCM suffered from periodic internal purges, which weakened its connections to popular movements and made former cadres into implacable foes. With the Cold War, its members agreed to suspend the struggle for socialism in favor of an alliance with the "progressive, national bourgeoisie" who would modernize the country and rescue it from agrarian feudalism. Heavy industry would liberate the productive forces, creating a proletariat to seize power in the future. National sovereignty would come from industrialization that would be fueled—paradoxically—by foreign investment. The PCM was dissolved in 1981 and its members dispersed, many joining a series of leftwing organizations and ultimately the Partido Revoluciónario Democrático (PRD; Democratic Revolutionary Party).[21]

The Partido Popular (PP; Popular Party) was formed in 1948 by Vicente Lombardo Toledano as a broad coalition whose progressive goals were subordinated to an alliance with the ruling regime. In 1960, the PP added the term *socialist* to its name and became the Partido Popular Socialista (PPS; Popular Socialist Party) but continued to provide the regime with uncritical support. Its founders included members and former members of the PCM and a number of independent leftists, many of whom soon abandoned the party for its refusal to criticize President Miguel Alemán's rightward turn. Its influence was strongest among intellectuals and campesinos, particularly in the north and in Veracruz, and among teachers and students, especially normalistas from the rural schools with their enduring tradition of militant struggle. Lombardo, the authoritarian doyen of Mexican Marxism, regarded the party as his own fiefdom and a vehicle for his own ambitions. The UGOCM, mentioned above, was affiliated with the PP(S).[22] Engaged in struggle on the ground, regional chapters of the PPS and UGOCM were frequently more radical than their national leaders.[23]

The PCM and PPS shared an analysis of Mexico as semifeudal and needing industrialization to develop the preconditions for socialism, among them a proletarian vanguard, an analysis that subordinated them to the "revolutionary nationalism" of the state. They both saw U.S. imperialism as a greater foe than their own ruling elite. Their ideological convergence was not surprising, as each was shaped by an alliance with Moscow. They diverged in strategy, the PPS being more willing to conciliate the regime.[24] The state responded to both by alternately co-opting cadres into its ranks and throwing them into prison, as it did the leaders of the railway strike and David Siqueiros, the prominent muralist.[25]

Barry Carr emphasized the importance of statism—a high degree of state control—both in Mexico, where the state has incorporated blocs of citizens into government and where civil, or nongovernmental, organizations have been weak, and in the Soviet Union, where the state owned the means of production. In both Mexico, until the year 2000, and in the Soviet Union, the official party was synonymous with the government. The PCM and PPS inherited the preoccupation with the state from the Soviets, submerging their own emancipatory goals "to the logic of merging, incorporating, capturing, or reforming the octopuslike official party."[26] They also shared an authoritarian, patriarchal internal structure at odds with their egalitarian goals.

In Chihuahua, the PCM presence grew stronger during the election year of 1964, when the affiliated Frente Electoral de Pueblo (FEP; People's Electoral Front) fielded a number of candidates. Several protagonists were close to the PCM and its youth league, notably Judith Reyes, the protest singer and publisher of *Acción*, and many students of the State Normal School and Salaices, the rural normal school for boys. Others were members of or close to the PPS and its youth organization, including Arturo Gámiz, the Gómez Ramírez brothers, and Alvaro Ríos. I found no evidence that the movement was divided in any important way along sectarian lines or that debates over conflicting ideologies played a determining role in their activities. Supporters of both the PPS and the PCM worked together on a number of campaigns, from support for Cuba in 1961 to the campaign to free Alvaro Ríos in 1964. Reyes ran for office on the FEP ticket while her newspaper supported the UGOCM; she was rumored to be romantically involved with Ríos. As noted above, the ideologies of the PCM and PPS did not differ on important points; both were rooted in Soviet interpretive texts. In Chihuahua the movement found its own direction, disregarding recommendations from its leaders in Mexico City.

Considerations of Gender

The movement failed to raise any demands relating to women. Similarly, its surviving documents, the Resolutions, do not contain any analysis specific to women. Their existence as women was not addressed, but their participation was crucial at every step. Women were central to the family-based support networks that enabled the *guerrilla* to operate in the sierra and the five survivors to escape the assault on the base. When the men decided to join the *guerrilla*, their women and children paid a high price. As Nithia Castorena pointed out, women took part in the movement in one of two ways: either they chose to participate, assuming risks and responsibilities of their own, or they became involved through the decisions of their menfolk and suffered the consequences.[27]

The agrarian code specified male heads of household as solicitors of ejidos; a widow could inherit her family's portion only if there were no adult son. Therefore, women were considered supporters and not protagonists in the struggle for land. Not every invasion included women, and the arrested leaders were apparently all men, but when women and children did take part, the stakes increased. Mobilized in the hope that their presence would minimize violence, that was not always the case. The invasions were symbolic. None of the participants expected to stay, but they enacted an alternative, parallel reality: the invaders performed the world where they wanted to live. The women cooked in field kitchens, the normalistas set up schools, the men plowed and tended the earth.

The presence of women and children made the act of symbolic possession more comprehensive. While women performed the traditional roles of preparing food and caring for children, they also undermined those roles by leaving their homes and declaring the fields they occupied to be their homes in open defiance of the landowners and the state.

The discourse of the *guerrilla* was gendered; the battles between Giner Durán and Arturo Gámiz were described as duels, as were those between Salomón Gaytán and José Ibarra. In "The Corrido of Arturo Gámiz" (see app.), Judith Reyes described an incident in the sierra:

> Soldiers pursued them and Arturo disarmed them
> And I've heard that he left them undressed.
> They had worn out Giner's little government
> Because their cause was just and because he was more of a man.

The rhetoric reducing the campesinos' struggle for land to a battle for supremacy between these two individuals continued through the years.

The gendered dimension of the conflict between the serranos and the caciques was expressed in terms of rape. There were a number of accounts of girls and women raped and left "flung down on the ground."[28] José Ibarra and the men of his family were repeatedly described as rapists. The violation of the bodies of the womenfolk—there was no evidence of the rape of boys or men—was a means to drive the smallholders out of the sierra, quiet their demands for land and justice, and reinforce their subordination. The bodies of women and girls were tokens in a battle among men whereby the caciques affronted the honor of men who could not protect their women. Rape was an aggression that inflamed the communities, exacerbating the tension that exploded in 1964.

The Rural Normal Schools

The rural normal schools created after the revolution still retained something of a socialist character despite the nation's overall turn to private enterprise during the midcentury Miracle. In Chihuahua, *rural* could mean isolated indeed; many teachers worked in remote communities without adequate roads or bridges. Normalistas were the children of campesinos and remained connected to the countryside; the schools were "centers for the reproduction of the agrarista and nationalist ideology of the revolution."[29] Tanalís Padilla has described them as "the intersection of the logic of state-building and the social rights conquered from below."[30] The rural schools, once an instrument for the inculcation of Mexican national identity, became detonators for protest movements. "The early emphasis on socialist education, the poverty from which students originated, the state's abandonment of the countryside after 1940, and the experience of these teachers in the communities where they taught all imbued rural educators with a righteousness that fueled involvement in political struggles."[31] In mobilizing against the state, the landowners, and the industrialists, they were continuing, not reversing, the legacy of the revolution. Their demands were couched in terms of respect for the constitution.

President Lázaro Cárdenas's rural education project of the 1930s had used teachers to mobilize campesinos to fight for their interests within a capitalist structure, organizing them not into their own autonomous groups but as subordinate units of the state.[32] By incorporating workers and campesinos into blocs within the regime, Cárdenas both honored them and rendered them impotent. As national policies changed during the following decades, the schools became islands of socialism within the capitalist sea, lending legitimacy to a state that did not earn it. The radical teachers of the fifties and sixties, defending the interests of a campesinado each day less advantaged and with less space to maneuver, fought against the state itself. The constitution of 1917 had codified the most revolutionary demands of the fighters still on the ground, but the state that came to power did not rest on the revolutionaries who had been outmaneuvered. Popular forces struggled to defend achievements that the new government lacked both the means and will to enforce. The agrarian movement argued their right to land according to the constitution, but the state had undermined or abandoned certain aspects of the constitution, so the movement could only defend the revolution by defying the state while it worked actively but surreptitiously against them.

The Indigenous Inhabitants of the Sierra

The sierra of Chihuahua is home to four indigenous peoples whose languages and customs are related: the Tarahumara, or Rarámuri, renowned as long-distance runners, with a current population of approximately seventy thousand people; the Tepehuan, whose homeland lies farther south in the sierra; the

Guarijío; and the Pima, whose homeland extends west to Sonora. The relationship between the protest movements and the indigenous peoples remains to be examined. Various individuals, most notably Carlos Ríos, an UGOCM activist whose assassination in 1960 provoked a revenge killing several years later, have been described as Pima; Temósachic, a central venue of struggle, was a Pima population center. The Tarahumara, whose major population centers were to the south of Madera, were often mentioned as sawmill workers, but I have found no mention of them as activists in the early 1960s, although the Tarahumara Arturo Balboa took part in the successor *guerrilla* of 1968.

Agrarismo

The *agrarismo* enshrined in Article 27 of the constitution of 1917 and institutionalized by postrevolutionary governments contained a contradiction: the campesinos' tenacious struggle for land had been enough to enshrine collective landholding in the constitution but not enough to prevent a capitalist regime from constituting itself from elements of both new and old power. According to Armando Bartra, the state "was obligated to juridically recognize the campesino's right to land, legalizing a kind of rural class struggle that questions nothing less than the sacred principle of capitalist private property."[33] The result was two sorts of agrarismo: revolutionary, based in the struggle for autonomy, and the official agrarismo of the revolution-made government. Land distributed to ejidos still belonged to the state, not the community, and its expropriation was conducted by a cumbersome bureaucracy. The Sonoran dynasty that came to power in the 1920s favored large extensions oriented toward entrepreneurial export agriculture and, while celebrating the reform in theory, avoided it in practice. They balanced the need for agricultural efficiency and economic recovery after a decade of war, dislocation, and scarcity with the need for legitimacy. The land that went to ejidos was frequently of poor quality, insufficient to support a family, and served as a locus for the reproduction of seasonal labor destined to work in commercial agriculture, while land intended for large-scale development remained in private hands. The state was caught between the insatiable land hunger of the rural poor and the need of the rural bourgeoisie for secure tenure and social stability, a stability that could only—paradoxically—be guaranteed through periodic distributions. In the new regime, the state mediated between the campesino and the landowner.

Lázaro Cárdenas came to power during a world depression following three years of civil war in the country's breadbasket. The export sector was languishing, and the internal sector was insufficient to meet growing demand. The countryside rose up demanding land, and those ineligible for land demanded unions; strikes and land invasions swept the country.[34] Cárdenas responded with expropriations and distributions; moreover, he advocated a new, more dynamic, collective agrarian unit capable of competing in commercial markets with private landholders.[35] His support for the rural poor exacted a price: the incorporation of the campesinos in an arm of government, the Confederación Nacional de Campesinos, founded in 1938 to embody official agrarismo, threatened the existence of autonomous movements.

During the Miracle years, 1940–1970, when annual growth reached astonishing rates, this expansion took place at the expense of the countryside. Industry relied on cheap natural resources and the low wages of urban workers, subsidized by low food prices, whose ranks swelled with refugees from the countryside. The era saw a massive transfer of resources from country to town. The urban population doubled by midcentury, making Mexico a predominantly urban country.

The ejido, plagued by inefficiency, corruption, soil exhaustion, and demographic increase, proved insufficient even for subsistence; ejidatarios were forced into the labor market to enrich the profits of their entrepreneurial rivals. Others abandoned the countryside for the cities or migrated to work as peons in the United States; migration was facilitated by the bracero program from 1942 to 1964, which gave Mexican workers legal contracts under substandard conditions. Agricultural resources were funneled into the export sector, revitalized during World War II, and into domestic consumption for the elite and growing middle class. A favorable balance of payments reduced the need for food imports. What little support the state did grant to the ejidos—credit and advising agronomists—increased their dependence without improving their overall situation.[36] As Bartra pointed out, "like authentic wage workers, [the ejidatarios] lack autonomy, but unlike wage workers they must assume the risks of production."[37]

The failure of the ejido system was obvious long before the dissolution of Article 27 in 1994 and cannot be blamed solely on internal problems. The ejidos assumed an impossible burden: to provide social justice and a livelihood to their members, to feed the growing cities and their march to industrialization, and to provide the state with a mechanism for the political incorporation of campesinos.[38] As an island of socialism within a capitalist sea, they shared the larger political culture of greed and corruption. Their establishment did not take into account demographic pressure on lands that were often marginal to begin with. The ejidal plot is no guarantee of independence; it is a remnant of a bygone era that perhaps never existed. At best, it is part of a mixed strategy for family survival: illegally rented out or marginally farmed and combined with wage labor, migration, handicrafts, and small-scale retail sales, it provides an additional source of income or food.

Despite its inadequacy, the beleaguered countryfolk still demanded land. During the late 1950s, a wave of land occupations, especially in the north, coincided with the strikes of urban electrical workers, doctors, railroad workers, and teachers in Mexico City. The miseries of wage labor must have been among the incentives to embrace farming. In Chihuahua, working conditions in the expanding lumber industry were grim; accident rates were high in both the forests and the sawmills. In the outback, workers camped out for weeks, endangered by wildlife, falling trees, and equipment injuries. In town the danger came from machinery, and both jobs were poorly paid.[39] Conditions in mining were equally perilous, tightly controlled, and isolated.[40] The majority of migrant workers were caught in a cycle of seasonal migration, low wages, family separation, and periodic deportation. The struggle for land enacted by a handful of young people driven by revolutionary *mística* was the tragic result of a myth of the revolution—that land would bring freedom, dignity, fulfillment of their hopes and dreams—a myth that devoured its adherents by binding them to the state.

The 1960s

The 1960s were an era of social effervescence: the Cuban Revolution had triumphed, the Algerians had driven out the French, and the Vietnamese were holding out against the United States, where opposition to the war and the civil rights movement caused massive unrest, particularly among students and African Americans. The memory of recent defeats, such as the overthrow of Jacobo Arbenz in Guatemala, was eclipsed by the image of laughing, triumphant *barbudos* entering Havana on tanks, an image that proved irresistible to tens of thousands of young people, inspiring them to risk their lives. Since the *Gramna* landed at Playa Colorada in 1956, there has not been a time when a revolutionary armed group has not operated somewhere in Latin America.[41] Attempts to apply the Cuban model to a variety of circumstances resulted in disaster.

The *guerrilla* of Arturo Gámiz was among those failures. Gámiz believed the Cuban myth, which he studied in Che Guevara's *Guerra de Guerrillas*, first published in Havana in 1960 or 1961.[42] "We consider that the Cuban Revolution contributed three fundamental lessons to the conduct of revolutionary movements in America. They are: (1) Popular forces can win a war against the army. (2) It is not necessary to wait until all conditions for making revolution exist; the insurrection can create them. (3) In underdeveloped America, the countryside is the basic area for armed fighting."[43] The GPG, impatient after years of sustained mobilizations, took the leap from being convinced of the need for armed struggle to believing that the same people who organized for land invasions were awaiting the signal to rise up in arms.

"Ellos sabían por qué"

"Ellos sabían por qué" (They knew why) is a slogan of the movement to remember the attackers. Today's interest in the guerrilla movements of the 1960s and 1970s is animated by the need for former participants and their families to vindicate the memory of struggles for justice left unresolved, including not only the guerrillas but the protesters massacred at Tlatelolco in 1968 and Corpus Cristi in 1971 and other social movements. Tens of thousands of people took part in the mobilizations of that era along with the hundreds who joined the armed clandestine forces. A generation of largely young people perished or suffered serious damage in the 1970s. The fate of many will never be known; they "disappeared" into clandestine prisons and anonymous graves. Much of the research emerging now is guided by the desire to know finally and simply, decades later, what happened.

Contemporary supporters of past armed movements have claimed them as the prelude to today's movement for human rights and democracy. "The imprisonment of the majority of the armed groups of the 1970s and mid-1980s led to the initiation of another great movement which has endured until today: the struggle for human rights."[44] After her son Jesús disappeared in 1975, accused of belonging to the 23rd of September Communist League, Rosario Ibarra de Piedra formed the Comité Eureka (Committee in Defense of Political

Prisoners, Exiles, and the Disappeared).[45] On the eve of President José López Portillo's annual address to the nation, where he was expected to announce amnesty for political prisoners and a reform allowing the PCM to compete in elections, Ibarra and a group of women demonstrated before the national cathedral, demanding the appearance of hundreds of young people, including Jacobo Gámiz, Arturo's brother.[46] The amnesty and political reform went forward, but the regime failed to acknowledge the disappeared. The direct impetus for the movement for human rights did come from the Dirty War but has grown beyond it, responding to a regime that tortures peaceful protesters as well. Ayotzinapa, Acteal, Atenco: the opposition does not have to be armed to provoke disproportionate brutality. Surely a movement for human rights would have emerged without an armed vanguard.[47]

The assertion that the armed movements opened the door to democracy is harder to defend. Looking only at Mexico and without debating the nature of democracy itself, broader economic and political issues led to the downfall of the PRI in the elections of 2000. The peso devaluation of 1976 and the economic recession—*la crisis*—of the early 1980s spelled the end of the Miracle and reduced the PRI's capacity for co-optation, a cornerstone of its rule. Rapid growth loosed the traditional clientelist, caciqual bonds that cemented the PRI's control at the bottom, particularly in the neglected countryside. As the regime ran out of money, it became less able to dominate either the electoral machine or its own corporate institutions as it once did.

The catastrophic earthquake that struck Mexico City in 1985 revealed the PRI's inability to govern and led to broad mobilizations of citizens acting in an arena outside of and sometimes hostile to the state.[48] These events, directly experienced by thousands and widely reported on, did more to undermine the legitimacy of the PRI than the brutality it exerted on its opponents during the Dirty War, known only to a few.

1

The National Context

Estoy solicitando parcela
los años fueron pasando
Cárdenas daba la tierra
y Alemán le va quitando.

(I am soliciting land
the years go passing by
Cárdenas gave the land
and Alemán takes it away.)

—JUDITH REYES, "SOLICITANDO PARCELA"

Introduction

The post–World War II push to modernize Mexico through foreign investment in industry, infrastructure development, and mechanized agriculture resulted in far-reaching social changes that the regime was unable to contain. Protest movements proliferated and were suppressed, often with violence, while the Cold War provided rhetorical cover. Internal security agencies were created with the support of the United States. The Cuban Revolution inspired new enthusiasm, further undermining the orthodox Marxist parties. While supporting Cuba in global forums, the Mexican regime worked covertly with the United States. Marxism conquered the universities, and the New Left emerged with university students as the new protagonists.

Industrialization and National Protests

During the midcentury Miracle, economic growth exceeding 6 percent per year was fueled by industrial expansion at the expense of the countryside.

Commercial agriculture expanded, accelerating the proletarianization of the countryside and the decline of the ejidal sector. In the cities real wages fell and legislation made strikes more difficult. Industrialization was largely financed by U.S. capital in a series of binational elite partnerships. Financial, tax, and tariff policies favored business and provided incentives to capital. Low shipping rates on the railroads subsidized foreign mining companies and their mineral exports, a perennial complaint of railway workers. The government invested in infrastructure, including highways, irrigation works, and tourist destinations such as Acapulco. Impoverished campesinos flooded the cities, where they crowded into expanding belts of misery and competed for substandard wages. In 1960, the urban population outnumbered the rural population for the first time.

From 1940 to 1946, Manuel Avila Camacho followed Lázaro Cárdenas as president and reversed Cárdenas's policy of socialist development. Avila Camacho used labor laws to undermine workers' organizations, and he enacted Article 145, the law of social dissolution, to imprison the regime's opponents or deport them if they were foreigners. Miguel Alemán, president from 1946 to1952, amassed an enormous personal fortune while overseeing the turn from social reconciliation to aggressive capitalist expansion. Allied with finance capital, elite industrialists, including the Monterrey Group, and the expanding urban middle classes, Alemán built highways and airports, developed Acapulco, and moved the national university from downtown to the new five-hundred-acre Ciudad Universitaria (University City). Adolfo Ruíz Cortines, president from 1952 to 1958, extended public works and public services to the poor while continuing on the path of modernizing development. And from 1958 to 1964, Adolfo López Mateos announced that he was "of the extreme left within the constitution" and distributed more land than any other president, but he continued to contain and repress worker and campesino movements.

The Miracle years were the Golden Age of the PRI, when it projected an image of social stability known as the *pax priísta*. Recent historiography reveals the social turmoil behind the myth.[1] In 1947, Alemán created the Dirección Federal de Seguridad (DFS; Office of Federal Security) with the support and training of the U.S. FBI, which had gathered "intelligence" in Mexico throughout World War II on both the Axis powers and on dissidents through telephone and cable interceptions.[2] This prepared the ground for substantial U.S. investment by promising to contain dissent. The superpower contention known as the Cold War provided a justification and the rhetoric for a state-sanctioned offensive against the domestic opposition, who were accused of subverting the nation with foreign ideology and dismissed as common criminals and social deviants. But as Judith Reyes announced, "We did not import this idea [land invasions] from the Russians who are conquering space. It was born here, in the Chihuahuan countryside, where we see the campesinos perish before the indifference of our government."[3]

The chief characteristics of the intelligence forces (the DFS and the IPS) were paranoia and an inability to analyze the vast amount of information collected by agents in the field. Since their existence depended on powerful enemies, they exaggerated the strength of the opposition in order to increase their importance and share of the budget, and they were incapable of providing a realistic assessment of the relative strength of the regime and its opponents. Without institutional controls or civic oversight and confronting an enemy weak in resources, their intellectual poverty went unchallenged.[4] Their secrecy, lack of accountability, and impunity enabled unprecedented brutality during the Dirty War.

In 1965, the DFS had fewer than 120 agents in the field, and their reports from Chihuahua, available in the AGN, revealed a pedestrian accounting of journeys, caravans, strikes, and meetings; internal difficulties within the UGOCM and the student movement; confusion about affiliations, as when Gámiz was said to be a member of the FEP; complaints to the DAAC; and movement fliers.[5] The IPS archives contain several detailed reports on conditions in Chihuahua, such as the thirty-one-page "Estado de Chihuahua," dated August 21, 1964, with an analysis of conflicts within state government, the agrarian situation, the student movement, and other issues.[6] The actions of the GPG took place just before the national state strengthened its security apparatus. In September 1965, Miguel Nazar Haro, director of the DFS from 1978 to 1982, was in Washington, D.C., attending a training session that led to the founding in November of the Group of Special Investigations C-047, formed to combat the *guerrilla*.[7]

With the advent of the Cold War, the United States purged its own labor sector, deported leftists, and forced the Communist Party U.S.A. underground. The U.S. Embassy in Mexico City initiated a campaign to "separate Mexican labor leaders from Communism," and violent purges in labor unions and workplaces became common.[8] Militant leaders were expelled, and *charros* were imposed on the three leading industrial unions: the railway workers, the miners, and the petroleum workers.[9] Two people were killed in Mexico City when police attacked the 1952 May Day march. Government thugs destroyed the PCM printing press. The regime sent riot police and soldiers to attack demonstrators. Communist leaders were kidnapped, and many were imprisoned, including Valentín Campa, a leader of the railway workers, and the painter David Siqueiros.[10]

Despite waves of repression, the social costs associated with development, including frustration with the unfulfilled promise of advance, continued to provoke substantial protests. "The spread of capitalism in its raw version in the third world created a dramatic torsion between the anticipation of development and equality and the reality of exclusion and exploitation."[11] In 1956, students at the Instituto Politécnico Nacional (IPN; National Polytechnical Institute) went on strike, and the campus was occupied by the army, beginning the student movement that culminated in 1968.[12] In 1958, students at UNAM went out in support of striking bus drivers. Rank-and-file members of the largest union in the country, that of schoolteachers, formed the radical Movimiento Revolucionario del Magisterio (MRM; Revolutionary Teachers' Movement) in Mexico City, and one hundred thousand protesting teachers filled the Zócalo and were attacked by riot police. Primary schoolteachers then occupied the offices of the Secretaría de Educación Pública (SEP; Department of Public Education) for several months, finally receiving a pay raise. Othón Salazar Ramírez, a normalista from Guerrero and leader of the MRM, was imprisoned in September 1958 and released after massive protests. In 1958–1959, doctors, telegraph and telephone workers, schoolteachers, electricians, miners, metalworkers, students, and petroleum workers went on strike. The strikes of communications workers were especially disruptive during the elections of 1958. Initial demands reflecting narrow sectoral interests expanded to encompass a broad social vision.

In 1958, on the eve of the Easter holiday, the railroad workers initiated a series of escalating strikes. With the assistance of telegraph workers, they struck for two hours and, when their demands were not granted, four hours the next day, six hours the following day, and so on. The actions by more than sixty thousand workers were nearly unanimous and demonstrated their mastery of time, an important achievement for former countryfolk whose ancestral rhythms were task oriented, synchronized by the sun and seasons. They followed up by electing new union leaders. When subsequent negotiations broke down, they announced a new strike. That strike was crushed, and the *charro* union returned to power. Progressive leaders Demetrio Vallejo and Valentín Campa were arrested and sentenced to sixteen years in prison.[13] The importance of railways to commerce had been undermined by roadbuilding projects that diverted cargo to trucking, a less efficient means of transport but one that was out of the hands of militant workers.

Protest movements in the Distrito Federal (DF; Federal District) had important repercussions in Chihuahua, where leading actors had lived in the DF in the 1950s. Alvaro Ríos had worked at the national UGOCM office, Pablo Gómez had studied medicine at UNAM, Arturo Gámiz had been one of the scholarship students made homeless when the army occupied the IPN in 1956, and Judith Reyes had spent years there before coming north.

Militant rural movements arose throughout the country as well. The UGOCM led the movement in the northern states of Durango, Sonora, Sinaloa, and Chihuahua, later giving rise to the GPG in Chihuahua. Agraristas supported the failed presidential campaign of General Miguel Henríquez Guzmán in 1952. Henríquez Guzmán, a former revolutionary general and comrade of Lázaro Cárdenas, challenged the official PRI presidential candidate and advocated independent union organization and agrarian reform. Security forces opened fire on his supporters when they protested his loss at the polls. Agrarian struggles not always recognized as such included the movement against obligatory military service and against campaigns to exterminate foot and mouth disease.[14] In the state of Morelos, just south of Mexico City, former Zapatista officer Rubén Jaramillo had led a series of battles by campesinos for effective agrarian reform since 1943, sometimes running for office and sometimes leading armed guerrillas. He formed the Partido Agrario Obrero Morelense (Party of Agrarian Workers of Morelos) and ran for governor in 1945 and 1952. In 1954, he led armed forces against the government from hiding. In 1962, he negotiated with President Adolfo López Mateos and received amnesty. Later that year, he was kidnapped and executed along with his children and pregnant wife. His death sent shock waves throughout the republic; prominent author Carlos Fuentes journeyed to the region a few weeks later and quoted a local campesino as saying, "Our leader is dead. Now we are all Jaramillo."[15]

The Cuban Revolution

In 1956, the Soviet Union celebrated its Twentieth Party Congress. In its final session, Premier Nikita Krushchev denounced the personality cult and genocidal practices of his predecessor, Joseph Stalin, including revelations of concentration camps and of show trials, and called for "peaceful coexistence" with the West. Later that year, revolts in Soviet-dominated Poland and Hungary were crushed by tanks, and the Soviet alliance with China began to crumble. Krushchev had intended his speech to strengthen the party by acknowledging past errors; instead, communist parties around the world began the slow process of reevaluating their submission to Soviet objectives. In Chihuahua, the Declarations of the First Encounter in 1963 still bore signs of Soviet preoccupations that were absent from those of the Second Encounter in 1965.

In 1959, the Cuban Revolution reverberated throughout the world, demonstrating new forms of insurgent activity and mounting a challenge to the traditional Marxist parties. Enacting their own agrarian and educational reforms, the Cubans revealed the bankrupt promises of the Mexican Revolution. The PCM and PPS had given up on social revolution in their lifetimes and were advocating a two-stage model, uncritically adopted from their Moscow tutors, without interrogating the meaning of semifeudal, semicolonial, or "national" bourgeoisie. They were content with survival, with the small favors of sustained influence among trade unions, universities, normal schools, and disaffiliated intellectuals. As Régis Debray remarked, the communist parties' vocation was not to assault power but to resist assaults from power.

In March 1961, former president Lázaro Cárdenas organized the Latin American Conference for National Sovereignty, Economic Emancipation, and Peace in response to U.S. threats against Cuba; he also founded the domestic Movimiento de Liberación Nacional (MLN; Movement for National Liberation). The MLN united members of the UGOCM, PPS, and PCM with independent leftists and civic organizations to defend Cuba and fight against an array of changing economic and political structures. Its founders included Narciso Bassols, Heberto Castillo, Carlos Fuentes, Elí de Gortari, Víctor Rico Galán, Valentín Campa, and Hernán Laborde, former secretary general of the PCM (expelled in 1940). It was an uneasy coalition of divergent interests, and it soon dissolved.

When the United States attempted to invade Cuba in April, 1961, protests erupted throughout the republic, including a march through Mexico City led by Lázaro Cárdenas. Thousands of young people clamored to join international brigades. In response, President Adolfo López Mateos, who called himself a member of *la izquierda atinada* (the sensible left), dispersed a second pro-Cuba demonstration, this one not led by Cárdenas, with tear gas and organized anticommunist demonstrations in Puebla and Mexico City.[16]

With the Cuban Revolution, the Cold War between the United States and the Soviet Union was displaced from Europe to the periphery, where the United States found Soviet agents operating within every social justice movement. Cuba's turn to socialism, announced in 1960–1961, intensified that search, although Cuba never supported revolutionary opposition to the Mexican state. Sergio Aguayo documented the cooperation between Mexican and U.S. intelligence services during the mid-twentieth century.[17] Mexico relied on U.S. training for its agents and allowed U.S. operatives to work on Mexican soil. As far back as 1939, Lázaro Cárdenas permitted an FBI agent to remain in the country. Aguayo cited "indirect evidence" for Miguel Alemán consulting with the U.S. Central Intelligence Agency and modeling the DFS on the FBI, and he gave further examples of cooperation.[18] Following the U.S. lead while failing to question its influence, the Mexican regime adopted Cold War anticommunist rhetoric and blamed every protest movement on "internal subversion supported by Cuba."[19] Had their analysis been better, they might have realized that Cuba was indifferent to its Mexican supporters. The Mexican left was punished for a relationship from which it received little benefit beyond inspiration.

Mexico hid its relationship with the United States under a nationalist cover: the PRI's perennial claim to revolutionary nationalism; the long-term tariff barrier and restriction on investments; Mexico's hospitality to dissident exiles; and President Luis Echeverría's flamboyant support for Salvador Allende and *la nueva canción*, folk-inspired protest music. Echeverría, who was president from 1970 to 1976, attempted to recover the populist legacy of Cárdenas and overcome his role in the massacre of Tlatelolco through social spending and by presenting himself as an exponent of Latin American Revolution everywhere but at home.

Cuba provided an ideal and an example to revolutionaries but never material support. The Cubans did not take the Mexican revolutionaries seriously, even as they called for continental revolution.[20] In 1973, the Frente Revolucionario Armado del Pueblo (People's Armed Revolutionary Front) exchanged the U.S. consul in Guadalajara for several dozen imprisoned guerrilleros, including two sisters of Arturo Gámiz who were flown to exile in Cuba, where they complained of maltreatment and of not being viewed as revolutionaries but as enemies of a "democratic regime."[21] The Cubans refrained from supporting either the armed or any other leftist movement in Mexico in return for Mexico's support in the international arena and maintenance of diplomatic ties.[22] An additional factor was the friendship that Fidel Castro had formed with Fernando

Gutiérrez Barrios, director of the DFS under Gustavo Díaz Ordaz and Luis Echeverría, during his sojourn in Mexico in 1955–1956.[23] Despite the high-level understanding, agents on the ground persisted in blaming dissidence on Cuba.

The Cuban Revolution would not have happened without the handful of guerrilla fighters based in the rugged mountains of the Sierra Maestra who acted despite the initial opposition of the traditional communist party, which only reluctantly offered support in 1958 when faced with a fait accompli. It also would not have happened without the mass organization of workers and students in the cities and cane fields, whose contribution has been downplayed in the official myth espoused by Che, Fidel, and Régis Debray.[24] It was not the party leaders but the *barbudos* (the bearded ones) from the sierra who entered Havana on tanks in a triumphal procession, and their achievement opened the way for a new formulation of revolutionary strategy.

While the initial overthrow of the U.S.-backed dictator, Fulgencio Batista, and the capture of state power by the 26th of July Movement in 1959 sent waves of euphoria throughout the progressive world, it was Cuba's second revolution with Fidel's announcement in 1961 that the revolution was socialist and had always been socialist that allowed Cuba to assume the leadership of Latin America's revolutionary movements. The Soviet Union, locked in Cold War rivalry with the United States, had no choice but to back Cuba with markets, technical assistance, and military aid, and it was compelled to overlook the Cubans' insistent advocacy of theories developed in opposition to the Soviet model.

Cuba not only provided an example of successful guerrilla warfare, it demonstrated revolutionary reforms in action: mass education, land reform, and expropriations, going far beyond Mexico's earlier programs, which were circumscribed by the persistence of private property. Cuban advances threw the incomplete nature of Mexico's reforms into stark relief. After 1961, the Cubans declared themselves Marxist-Leninist and allied with the Soviet Union in defiance of the United States, becoming the only Soviet ally in the hemisphere. The Cubans had a continental vision: they proclaimed their intention to spread the revolution throughout Latin America, polarizing the left and forcing it to choose between their methods and those of the past.[25]

With *foquismo*, Latin America became a source and not an importer of ideas; other exports include Liberation Theology, *la nueva canción*, and dependency theory. *Foquismo* holds that a small band of dedicated revolutionaries can plant themselves in the mountains or jungles and through armed guerrilla actions demonstrate the vulnerability of the elite, the possibility of successful struggle, and the ability to grow into a magnetic center—a *foco*—capable of attracting campesinos, students, workers, and foreign journalists and eventually maturing into a people's army that can take state power. The initial conditions were unimportant. What mattered was the subjective element or revolutionary will; as Fidel proclaimed, the duty of every revolutionary is to make revolution. In Latin America, the struggle would evolve in the countryside, not the cities. This theory, derived from the myth of the Cuban experience, received its definitive explication in *Revolution in the Revolution? Armed Struggle and Political Struggle in Latin America*, written by the French philosopher and journalist Régis Debray, who had visited the *barbudos* in the sierra and then settled in Havana in the mid-1960s. Based on interviews with Fidel and first published in French in 1967, it was translated into Spanish, English, and many other languages and became a primer for revolutionaries around the world.[26] An earlier formulation of the *foquista* strategy had circulated among members of the GPG in Chihuahua in Che Guevara's *Guerrilla Warfare*.[27]

An essential element of the *foquista* strategy was the notion that prolonged experience within the struggle itself would create cadres capable of directing the postrevolutionary society and that the transition to socialism would begin before and not after victory. This formulation owed much to Franz Fanon and his study of the Algerian Revolution in *Les damnés de la terre* (*The Wretched of the Earth*), first published in 1961, which itself owed a debt to Mao Zedong and his notion of prolonged people's war.[28]

Foquismo implied a dramatic break with existing practices and beliefs. The Cubans located the terrain of struggle in the countryside, confining the role of urban workers, students, and intellectuals to supporting the *foco* with supplies, information, and recruits. Within the *foco*, there would be no distinction between military leaders and political leaders. By insisting that the revolutionaries could by their own actions bring about the necessary conditions for the mobilization of forces sufficient to bring U.S.-backed dictatorial regimes to their knees, the *foquistas* posed a direct challenge to the doctrine that required the revolution to wait for the maturing of objective conditions. It also posed an explicit challenge to the role of the vanguard party by insisting that the vanguard would emerge in the course of struggle.

The GPG followed the strategy they learned from *Guerra de Guerrillas*. From February, 1964 through September, 1965, they secured a base in the mountains near Madera, made sporadic attacks on caciques and army and police detachments, and maintained contact with supporters in the cities. Had they retreated as planned after a lightning attack on the base, they might have gained recruits and grown instead of being annihilated.

Mexico, Cuba, and the United States

The version of the Cuban Revolution put forth by Fidel and Debray downplayed the importance of the urban student movement and workers' strikes in bringing the 26th of July Movement to power. It also downplayed the importance of one of Debray's own insights, that the revolution revolutionized the counterrevolution, or that the United States, caught unaware by rapid developments in 1958 and not foreseeing Fidel's turn to communism in 1961, might not be so lenient or unobservant the next time. Indeed, from 1961 on, the primary objective of U.S. policy in Latin America was to prevent another Cuba.

Cuba's support for regional movements became more pronounced as the U.S. blockade tightened in the early 1960s and Cuba had less to lose. The noted exception was Mexico, the one Latin American government that defied the United States in its refusal to join the Organization of American States' boycott of Cuba. The Cuban refusal to support Mexican revolutionary movements contributed to the blanket of silence that muffled the Mexican experience for years, even among activists aware of torture and repression in Brazil and the Southern Cone (Argentina, Uruguay, and Chile). None of the theoreticians of armed struggle of the 1960s and 1970s mentioned Mexico except in passing.[29] In the early 1970s, only the North Koreans agreed to train members of Mexico's Movimiento Armado Revolucionario (MAR; Armed Revolutionary Movement).

The relationship between Mexico, Cuba, and the United States was complex. In an electronic briefing, Kate Doyle revealed Mexico's double dealing with regard to Cuba. Now declassified documents from both countries provided evidence of a secret agreement between Mexico and the United States. While publicly supporting Cuba, Mexican ambassadors provided information to U.S. officials. Doyle gave a number of examples of espionage.[30]

Old Left and New Left

The New Left that emerged in Latin America differed substantially from the one in the United States and Europe. The former faced neocolonialism and frequently naked forms of state repression and exploitation abetted by foreign (i.e., U.S.) intervention. It should not surprise us that their ideology and praxis would differ from those of the latter. The New Left of the so-called First World developed under the various influences of Herbert Marcuse, the Frankfurt School,

Louis Althusser, Antonio Gramsci, and the newly translated writings of the young Karl Marx, theoreticians who modified earlier Marxist doctrine, placing, on the one hand, a greater emphasis on culture, consciousness, and humanism while others focused on the importance of structural constraints.

By midcentury, the Mexican Old Left's long romance with the Revolutionary Family and subservience to the regime were coming to an end. The military occupation of the IPN, the violent suppression of the railway workers, and the use of riot police exposed the brutality of the regime while the Cuban Revolution posed an alternative. The PRI's system of clientelism, co-optation, and corporatism was unraveling as the economy moved ahead and rapid social movement strained face-to-face bonds. While authoritarianism still permeated many social structures, the regime's capacity for control was weakening. Modernization disrupted former relations of deference; in the cities, women found themselves beyond the reach of village surveillance, and sons and daughters defied their parents. Workers and campesinos clamored for autonomous organizations and a greater share of the wealth they produced. The new middle classes demanded political democratization and autonomous organizations of their own.

While most historiography of the era has focused on the left, the Cuban Revolution also revitalized conservative forces already concerned with creeping secularization and threats to patriarchal authority. Groups known as *porros* formed among university students, both independent of and sanctioned by the regime; they were an extralegal tool of suppression, which gave the regime deniability in case of violence but enabled the continual intimidation of *revoltosos*, as they called rebellious students. Polarization extended to customs of leisure and play. Jaime Pensado showed how rituals of *relajo*, or fun, could be used to undermine student activism.[31] Left- and right-wing students battled for control of universities, each using their own personal networks to vie for influence and exploiting connections to the elite. An examination of *porros* illustrates the way that modernization of the universities "not only failed to eliminate caciquismo but rather nationalized it in the forms of porrismo and charrismo estudiantil."[32]

New social movements emerged to supplement the traditional protagonists of worker and campesino. In the cities, housing shortages and lack of basic services led to land occupations and militant protests. Elena Poniatowska described the Colonia Rubén Jaramillo, in Morelos, where in 1973 ten thousand people invaded and lived in huts erected from cardboard, tin, plastic, and sticks, eventually legalizing their occupation.[33] Students from nearby Mexico City organized

Red Sundays to help out, bringing an alphabet soup of left-wing organizations with them. In Juchitán, Oaxaca, also in 1973, the Coalición Obrera, Campesina, Estudiantil del Istmo (COCEI; Coalition of Workers, Campesinos, and Students of the Isthmus) drew on indigenous Zapotec traditions to fight for local control against political bosses, defeating the PRI in a series of municipal elections.[34] Other communities of *paracaidistas* (parachuters) included the Colonia Tierra y Libertad in Monterrey and the Campamento 2 de Octubre in DF, along with the Colonia Francisco Villa in Chihuahua, organized by the CDP. A new generation of organizers, following the Maoist slogan "Go to the people, learn from the people," ignored parliamentary and party-building politics and emphasized the here and now, the local, and the transformation of everyday life. Instead of seeking influence within the institutions, they sought enhanced autonomy for their communities.[35] These local groups have been more welcoming to women than their predecessors.

Students emerged as the predominant sector in the New Left. Crucial to the development of a managerial middle class and beneficiaries of expanded social spending, the universities and their prep schools grew rapidly. The Autonomous University of Chihuahua was founded in 1954 in a merger of several institutions. While the normal schools had been formed with the goal of creating citizens and had always been politicized, now burgeoning numbers of university students confronted authoritarian governing structures. In 1963, the PCM founded a new organization, the Centro Nacional de Estudiantes Democráticos (CNED; National Center of Democratic Students), in Morelia. Other regional formations followed. In 1965, Mexico City medical students and young doctors organized massive protests over working conditions and wages that soon became a battle for broader democratic rights. In Chihuahua, students formed their own organization, the Federación Estudiantil de Chihuahua (FECH; Federation of Chihuahua Students). The PCM and its youth group, Juventud Comunista, had recruited a number of people in the euphoria that followed the Cuban Revolution, but many students soon struck out on their own. Maoists, Trotskyists, anarcho-syndicalists, radical Christians, and proponents of *foquismo* vied for their allegiance.[36]

Marxist intellectuals triumphed in the universities, particularly in the social sciences. The study of Marx's *Capital* became commonplace.[37] A literary movement known as the Latin American Boom—characterized by magic realism, stylistic experimentation, and stream of consciousness—focused world attention on Latin America. Among its early practitioners were Julio Cortázar of

Argentina, Gabriel García Márquez of Colombia, Mario Vargas Llosa of Peru, and Carlos Fuentes. In 1962, Fuentes published *The Death of Artemio Cruz*, which described the decline and corruption of the revolution of 1910. Another masterpiece, *Where the Air Is Clear* (*La región más transparente*), offered a broad vision of Mexico City, again focused on the corruption of former revolutionary ideals. In Mexico, the Boom was followed by a younger generation of iconoclasts known as the *Onda* (Wave), such as José Augustín, whose novel, *De perfíl* (In Profile) chronicles three days in the life of a Mexico City adolescent.

New periodicals emerged, including the newspapers *Unomásuno* and, later, *La Jornada*, and the magazines *Política*, edited by Manuel Marcué Pardiñas, *Historia y Sociedad*, and *Punto Crítico*. The cartoonist Ríus satirized the PRI with the long-running series *Los Supermachos* and *Los Agachados* (The Ones Who Kneel). José Revueltas, a writer who began and ended his career in prison for subversion, published *Los dias terrenales* (Days on Earth), a portrayal of the dogmatism and inner dilemmas of life within the PCM, and many other works. Elena Poniatowska published *La noche de Tlaltelolco* (*Massacre in Mexico*), a collection of eyewitness accounts, then *Fuerte es el silencio* (*Loud Is the Silence*), which included an account of the hunger strike by mothers of disappeared political prisoners. Carlos Monsiváis produced a series of books on national culture, the growth of civil society, and social struggle.[38] The penetration of Marxist intellectuals into mainstream culture indicated both their widespread acceptance and their irrelevance. The conquest of the universities carried the inevitable risk of corruption and cronyism.[39]

The regime that imprisoned so many dissidents created its own schools for protest within the jails. Political prisoners in Lecumberri, known as the Black Palace, were generally held in separate corridors, where they organized study groups that John Womack called "our institute of political science." The Argentine-born Trotskyist Adolfo Gilly wrote his history of the Mexican Revolution there; he is now a professor of political science at UNAM.[40]

2

Chihuahua, *El Estado Grande*

To harass a Chihuahuan serrano is much more dangerous than unjust and it is pointless to try to impose any sort of authority on him.

—JOSÉ FUENTES MARES

Summary

Chihuahua, known as the *estado grande* (the big state) because it is the largest state in the republic, consists of deserts and mountains with two fertile river valleys. Its first mestizo inhabitants clustered in mining districts. Settlers arrived in the sierra, where they fought indigenous raiders until the late nineteenth century, sustaining a tradition of armed self-defense. With the pacification of the Apaches and other raiders, the frontier became a border. Under Porfirio Díaz, the sale of public lands resulted in enormous private landholdings. The serranos rebelled against imposed political bosses and encroaching haciendas. The Guerrero District was central to the revolution of 1910. In the 1920s, most land was distributed to smallholding colonies instead of collective ejidos. Irrigation in the Conchos Valley led to cotton production. The proliferation of export agriculture favored large landholders. In the sierra, the development of forestry and railroads reduced serrano autonomy. Madera City was founded as a company town for the timber industry. An elite consortium founded Bosques de Chihuahua (Chihuahua's Forests) in 1952. The Four Friends was formed to purchase grazing lands from Bosques, empowering the assassin and bootlegger José Ibarra. Ibarra harassed smallholders to drive them off their lands, provoking the emergence of a guerrilla movement. Along with the UGOCM and GPG, several other protest movements emerged, among them a radical

Christian movement and the Committee of Popular Defense in the 1970s. In the 1980s, Chihuahua was among the first states to elect Panistas (members of the opposition Partido de Acción Nacional) to government.

In mid-twentieth-century Chihuahua, both commerce and livestock favored the central plains over the sierra, which was still a sparsely settled frontier where the indigenous Tarahumara (also known as Rarámuri, the people who run) practiced nomadic agriculture and mestizo smallholders raised a few skinny cows and clung to their independence. Popular wisdom holds that Chihuahua's terrain and climate make it suitable only for concentrations of land, where immense herds can graze its arid plains. This argument is used to justify the enormous latifundia that have engulfed the region since colonial times and fails to address the possibility that those large holdings might be worked collectively.

The Sierra Madre in the western and southern parts of the state consists of a heavily forested system of mountain ranges and canyons. While mostly foreign entrepreneurs have exploited important mineral deposits there since colonial times, the sierra remained isolated until after World War II. Much of the rest of the state consists of high desert basins, which require massive hydraulic investments to produce anything but livestock. There the first big estates formed in the eighteenth century on land grants from the Spanish crown. In the southeast, the Río Conchos and its tributaries form a fertile corridor connecting Delicias, Saucillo, Camargo, and Jiménez. To the west, in the foothills of the sierra, the Río Papigochi provides water to the Guerrero District. The northwestern plains, near Casas Grandes and San Buenaventura, were eventually irrigated by the Terrazas clan, who held the largest privately owned domain in Mexico.[1]

Indian Wars

The first mestizo population arrived during colonial times in search of gold and silver in the triangle formed by Santa Barbara, Parral, and San Francisco de Oro in the southern part of the state. Haciendas and pueblos grew up nearby to supply the mines. During the seventeenth century, the indigenous Tarahumara and Tepehuan, who had inhabited the fertile river valleys before the Spanish, revolted five times against Jesuit attempts to concentrate them in villages under Jesuit tutelage. Abandoned in 1767 when the Jesuits were expelled from New Spain, they fled to the sierra and took up transhumant herding, moving seasonally between the deep barrancas and mountain highlands. Beginning in the mid-eighteenth century, raiding Indians, pushed south and west as the U.S. population moved west, subjected the area to more than a century of warfare.[2] The Spanish responded by creating a series of fortified settlements: Janos de la Frontera, Namiquipa, Casas Grandes, Galeana, and Cruces. Military settlers were given land grants, Spanish citizenship, and exemption from taxes as inducements to settle under dangerous circumstances in inhospitable territory.[3]

Chihuahua's population was sparse well into the twentieth century; the mines and haciendas had to attract workers from central Mexico. In the Guerrero district on the Indian frontier, called the longitude of war by Fernando Jordán, the federal government continued to award small land grants to individuals in return for military duty as long as the threat continued.[4]

These mestizo smallholders exhibited a propensity for armed resistance to any encroachment on their autonomy. Remote from the battles of the War of Independence of 1810, they felt abandoned when the weak central government that formed upon independence failed to provide even the minimal aid Spain had once offered. The colonial policy of pitting indigenous peoples against each other was abandoned as new state governments pursued uncoordinated and often contradictory policies, making independent treaties and leaving the serranos to fend for themselves as best they could.[5] The system of peonage that had existed on the vast haciendas and in the mining districts was weakened as the Spanish withdrew and local strongmen replaced them. The payments in rations and liquor that the Spanish had granted the indigenous peoples to induce them to settle, bringing a shaky peace to the region at the turn of the nineteenth century, stopped as well. In 1831, indigenous incursions swept the state, devastating the haciendas and overrunning the sierra. The federal army was tied down in the center of the country, where postcolonial governments formed and were overthrown in quick succession. The serrano settlers battled the raiders as best they could.

In midcentury, as the United States threatened to invade, a cholera epidemic swept the state. The U.S. menace was particularly alarming because the border inhabitants would be first to suffer a land incursion. The federal government was both unable and unwilling to act.[6] By then the state had lost considerable population and was in danger of ceasing to exist.

In 1846, the United States invaded, crossing the border at Texas, and in February 1847, the Chihuahuan forces, devastated by simultaneous Indian raids and not receiving aid from the central government, lost the Battle of Sacramento to U.S. troops. Adding insult to injury, the federal government accused the Chihuahuans of abandoning territory to the enemy.[7] Within a year, Mexico City was occupied, the Treaty of Guadalupe Hidalgo ended the war, and Chihuahua lost its northern reaches. In 1853, President Antonio López de Santa Anna sold an additional combined eighty thousand square kilometers of Sonora and Chihuahua to the United States in the Treaty of La Mesilla, known in the north as the Gadsden Purchase.

During the nineteenth century wars of the reform and the French intervention, some of the serrano communities, particularly the military pueblos of Namiquipa and Temósachic, motivated by resistance to a modernizing and encroaching state, sided with the conservatives and the French, putting the interests of their own *patria chica* (local homeland) in the foreground. When the fighting died down, the government forgave them because it needed their weapons against the Indians.[8]

During the 1860s, the government headed by Benito Juárez consolidated its hold on power, and, fearful of another attempt by the United States to annex more territory, renewed the battle against the Indians, sending troops, handing out more land grants, and enticing hacendados to return.[9] The serranos knew the terrain and had learned guerrilla warfare from their adversaries; they regarded the federal soldiers with scorn.

A gendered sense of honor predominated among the peoples of the frontier. The communities were organized in family units, kinship determined land ownership, and the heads of households exercised patriarchal rights over their descendants.[10] The reproductive function of women made them bearers of racial honor, consistent with notions of blood purity that derived from Spain's battle for "white" Catholic supremacy over Muslims and Jews. The honor of the male warrior rested on his fighting skills and ability to defend his family, particularly the women, who might be raped, impregnated, and forced to cohabit with the "savage" enemy.

The serrano fighters had organized in irregular units whose leaders rose from the ranks and were characterized by flexibility, informality, and fierce autonomy. Within the strictures of gender, frontier society was more egalitarian than that of the center; military prowess granted prestige, and relative wealth could alleviate the stigma of mixed blood or birth in poverty.[11] As the Indian wars continued, conflicts between regular federal and irregular units increased along with conflicts between hacendados and peons as prolonged warfare interfered with production and peons fled to the sierra to escape being drafted to defend hacendado interests. During the late nineteenth century, the mountainous Guerrero district of northwestern Chihuahua, populated by sturdy pioneers and free of the latifundia that dominated the plains, continued to defend its autonomy. It was the smallholders of the sierra who finally succeeded in pushing back the frontier and achieving an uneasy peace.

The Frontier Became a Border

In 1880 soldiers led by Colonel Joaquín Terrazas defeated the Apache leader Victorio in the battle of Tres Castillos, and the Indian wars came to an end. The truce between smallholders and hacendados ended as well, as the haciendas sought to expand, now free of the threat of invasion, and the rancheros defended their independence. The class alliance that had united them against the Indians broke down, and land prices, kept low by the indigenous threat, began to soar. Population in the U.S. Southwest was growing. The completion of the railroad linking Juárez and El Paso with Mexico City led to an export cattle boom and an even greater rise in land prices to the disadvantage of smallholders and communities.[12] The railroad, built by foreign investors, facilitated the rapid growth of mining and agriculture destined for export. Freight rates favored large-scale producers.[13]

The pueblos resented the railroad, which expropriated land, cut down trees, moved resources out, and brought in troops. But the railway brought benefits as well, facilitating movement throughout remote areas. The railway workers were militant and bore the germs of unionism and socialism, bringing the backwoods rancheros and peons into contact with international labor insurgency and contributing to the social unrest that led to the revolution of 1910.[14] The railroads, compelled by topography, ran north and south, carrying the nation's resources out of the country.

During the Porfiriato (1876–1911), both land concentration and foreign investment accelerated thanks to new land laws, surveying companies, and policies welcoming foreign capital. While Luis Terrazas had the largest landholdings in the state, thirty-nine foreign proprietors owned more than one hundred thousand acres each; five land companies alone controlled more than one million acres. The American Smelting and Refining Company (ASARCO), owned by the Guggenheims, maintained a near monopoly on smelting operations, employing 15 percent of the state's mining workforce in 1909. Colonel William C. Greene, owner of the copper mine at Cananea, Sonora, mined gold and silver in the Chihuahuan sierra, where he also held important lumber and railroad interests centered in Madera. The Sierra Madre Land and Lumber Company employed two thousand workers in the early 1900s.[15] The Palominas Land and Cattle Company, on the state's northern border, had 775,000 hectares.[16] The family of newspaperman William Randolph Hearst acquired the Hacienda San José de Babícora with 370,000 hectares in the Guerrero District in 1887 and held on to a portion of it until 1957. Cargill Lumber and Company had some 170,000 hectares in the sierra.[17]

Beginning in 1884, the federal government surveyed enormous tracts of unclaimed public land to which titles had not been issued, although smallholders had long used it as a commons for grazing, hunting, and collecting firewood and other resources. Many tracts were sold to large landowners, while the surveying companies kept as much as one-third of the land they surveyed; the rest was sold to investors, many of them foreign.[18] In 1904, Governor Enrique Creel passed the Municipal Land Law, which provided for the survey and sale of municipal lands, intensifying social tensions. The elite gradually enclosed the commons, depriving smallholders of essential resources; big landowners then sought to expand into the holdings of the military colonists. A political assault joined the economic threat: in line with Porfirio Díaz's centralizing policies, the governor abolished local elections and replaced local leaders with appointed political bosses who were given expanded powers and who were backed by the armed forces of the state.[19] The appointment of these political bosses was among the causes of a number of rural rebellions, especially the one at Tomóchic.

In 1892, some three hundred villagers of Tomóchic, a remote village west of Guerrero, chafed under the rule of a local cacique imposed as political boss. The villagers, long opposed to the local Catholic clergy, allied with the elite and rose up in arms against the Two Powers, the church and the oligarchy. The Tomochitecos were not Protestant but followers of a peculiar charismatic Catholic sect whose motto was "No government but that of God and no laws but those of His Divine Majesty." They were devoted to a young woman with healing powers in the nearby sierra of Sonora, Teresa Urrea, who became known as Santa Teresa of Cabora. Her followers had formed a cult that the leader of the Tomóchic rebellion interpreted in his own fashion, assuring the villagers that God would protect them. The rebellion was sparked when the political boss rerouted the annual transport of silver from the foreign-owned mine at Pinos Altos to the capital, implying that the villagers were not to be trusted. He then requested the aid of federal troops to suppress a series of tumultuous demonstrations. The villagers succeeded in repelling the troops several times. A year after the first federal assault, some 1,200 federal troops laid siege to the town and after two weeks massacred all but a handful of women and children.[20]

Teresa Urrea fled to the United States after the uprising, innocent of any involvement. Heriberto Frías, a young army officer from Mexico City, had participated in the siege and was so appalled at its savagery that he sent a series of written reports to a journalist who published them in the Mexico City paper *El Demócrata*, bringing them to the attention of the entire nation. He was deeply sympathetic to the villagers in his reports, which he turned into the novel *Tomóchic*, first published in 1893 and widely distributed throughout the republic.[21]

Other rebellions wracked the district, such as Santo Tomás in 1893 and Temósachic a year later. During the Indian wars, the people of the serrano frontier had been viewed as the embodiment of civilization in contrast to the semihuman Indians. They assumed the bravery and brutality of those same "savages" and adopted the native practice of collecting scalps, including those of women and children, for which the Mexican government paid a bounty. Once the Indians were gone, the serranos themselves, in their recalcitrant resistance to authority, became obstacles to progress. Now the elite no longer needed their military capabilities, and an expanding economy coveted their land as prices rose. Their land was close to the border and attractive to U.S. investors. In the words of Friedrich Katz, the frontier was becoming a border.

The serranos were poor and egalitarian, and their frontier democracy depended on a weak state. The culture of armed resistance forged during centuries of warfare continued to animate them while the consolidating Porfirian state sought to impose a monopoly on violence.[22] An economic downturn in the beginning of the 1890s squeezed the rural population further; miners were laid off while drought and crop failures raised food prices.[23]

Mexican hacendados and entrepreneurs prospered thanks to general economic growth and their connections to foreigners. The elite functioned as intermediaries and not rivals with foreigners, and they were anxious to preserve a stable situation for investments.[24] The central government provided military support for the suppression of popular and workers' rebellions, many of them in the sierra. Among the most powerful elites was Luis Terrazas, who was frequent governor of the state and one of the country's largest landholders, and who had banking and commercial interests that made him the wealthiest man in Mexico. His cousin Joaquín Terrazas had been famous as an Indian fighter and was admired by the serranos. Don Luis had originally been seen as an ally by the pueblos because he used them in his power struggles with the Díaz regime, acting as the traditional patriarchal *patrón*. By the beginning of the twentieth century, he had no need of that alliance and encroached on pueblo lands.

The Revolution of 1910

Drought, population growth, economic recession, and unemployment contributed to the crisis that erupted in 1910.[25] The Mexican Revolution began in the village of Cuchillo Parado in northeast Chihuahua when villagers revolted in favor of Madero and his Anti-Reelectionist Party one week before November 20.[26] Revolutionaries occupied the district capital of Guerrero in December 1910. While Sonora offered a dynasty of presidents to the revolutionary nation, Chihuahua provided the battleground where war raged continuously: the Battle of Juárez, which forced Díaz to resign, in 1911; Pascual Orozco's rebellion in 1912; Pancho Villa's Division of the North, with its victories in 1913–1914; the Pershing Expedition sent after Villa in 1916–1917; and the long drawn out series of battles between the remnants of Villa's forces and federal troops allied with the *defensas sociales* (citizen militias) until 1920.[27]

The Guerrero District was the epicenter of the revolution. The inhabitants of the former military presidios had been hardest hit by cyclical economic recessions, periodic drought, and the loss of land to encroaching hacendados. Alan Knight listed four causes for the intensity of serrano rebellion: their forced submission to the combined political and economic domination of the Terrazas/Creel elite; the recent origins of that domination and the memory of independence; the elite's espousal of progress and modernity, which undermined the pueblos' established notions of dignity and justice; and the serranos' acute perception of both the injustice being done them and their own ability to resist.[28]

The forces who went to war varied in their social composition and demonstrated considerable class fluidity. Friedrich Katz described Pancho Villa's Division of the North in its early days as not an army but "a folk migration" composed of cowboys, smugglers, and rustlers as well as workers, hacienda peons, rancheros, and *soldaderas*, women who fed and nursed the troops.[29] The people of the countryside called themselves campesinos or rancheros but were not the peasantry of the central and southern villages, who were rooted in centuries of communal life and were resistant to encroaching modernization. The land of the northern smallholders, being marginal and far from markets, could not sustain them, and they worked as part-time wage laborers in mining, railroad, and lumber industries and as farmworkers on local haciendas and in the United States. Their class identity was fluid; they had extensive links with both rural and nonagricultural society.[30] Rebellions against imposed political bosses and the modernizing state behind them often united local notables with the poor, just as the Indian wars had united hacendados with rancheros and peons. The serrano rebels also included a number of bandits, among them the legendary Pancho Villa.[31]

While the Maderistas and middle classes fought for political liberty and freedom from foreign intervention, the masses who did the fighting demanded land. Emiliano Zapata, whose home base lay in the fertile central state of Morelos, distributed land to his followers, and they continued to wage a guerrilla war while cultivating the fields. In the arid north, Villa confiscated the property of oligarchs who fled. Haciendas were to be kept intact; only upon the conclusion of the fighting would they be distributed to the campesinos and former troops. Their cattle were consumed by his soldiers or sold in the United States; the revenue paid expenses and was managed by the Administración General de Bienes Confiscados (General Office for Confiscated Goods). Villa awarded pensions to the widows and orphans of his soldiers.[32] He refused to distribute land, fearing his army would melt away and disperse to their new properties. When the Constitutionalists came back to power, they returned land to the former oligarchs, believing that the gentry were the most likely to achieve economic recovery while providing the restored Constitutionalists with allies.[33] Among them were Luis Terrazas, who returned from exile in 1920.

The Sonoran generals faced a dilemma: they had to balance the need for economic reconstruction after a decade of war with the agrarian yearnings of those who had done the fighting and whose support they needed. Chihuahua's land reform of the 1920s obeyed political necessities, reflecting both contributions to the revolution and political expediency. Half a million hectares were distributed between 1921 and 1924. Many pueblos that had lost land during the Porfiriato and joined the revolution early were beneficiaries. Lands were distributed to veterans of Villa's División del Norte; Villa himself was awarded a hacienda in northern Durango. Distributions increased with the de la Huerta rebellion and enabled the governor to raise campesino troops, but the pace slowed after de la Huerta's defeat.[34] The reform picked up again briefly with Calles's appointment of Governor Luis L. León in 1929. León vigorously pursued land distribution in the form of private smallholdings and not collective ejidos; his successor, Francisco Almada, continued his policies. In 1926 and 1927, the original military colonies of Galeana, Casas Grandes, Namiquipa, and Las Cruces recovered 112,000 hectares each of their original lands usurped by encroaching Porfirian haciendas.[35]

Ignacio Enríquez, governor from 1920 to 1924, supported private and not collective or communal property.[36] Article 27 of the federal constitution stated that the nation is the owner of the soil, subsoil, and waters but gave the states authority to regulate its distribution, either by restitution or dotation of communal ejidos or by dividing latifundia into small private holdings. The Chihuahua land law was formulated in May 1922. Its emphasis on smallholdings over collectives was consistent both with the policies of the Sonoran dynasty and with long-standing usage in Chihuahua, which lacked the communal Indian villages of the center and south. In 1934, a new provision in federal law made ejidos available, at least in theory, to any self-constituted group of solicitants who formed a population nucleus. This resulted in periodic and persistent conflicts between smallholder colonies and the ejidos who asserted claims against their lands.[37]

Distribution frequently laid the foundation for reconstituted Porfirian wealth. Of the vast Terrazas holdings, 2.7 million hectares had been purchased by the federal government after a plan to sell five million acres to the U.S. businessman Arthur J. McQuatters fell through because of popular protests. Included in the deal with McQuatters was his investment in massive irrigation projects that did not go forward. Of that 2.7 million, half a million hectares were repurchased by the Terrazas family, half a million were transferred to smallholder colonies, and 1.6 million remained in the hands of the Caja de Préstamos para Obras de Irrigación y Fomento de la Agricultura (Fund for Loans for Irrigation and Agricultural Development), the government holding company. Former Terrazas properties purchased from the Caja by elite families, including the Almeidas, Borundas, Russeks, and the Terrazas themselves, formed the basis for the recovery of the cattle industry in the 1930s.[38]

During the debate over whether to sell the Terrazas holdings to U.S. investors, the federal government obtained ninety thousand hectares of the Hacienda

Bustillos from the Zuloaga family near what would become Ciudad Cuauhtémoc (formerly San Antonio de los Arenales) and sold it on easy terms to a colony of Mennonite farmers who began arriving from Canada in 1922.[39] This was in line with Obregón's plan to colonize the north with foreigners, itself consistent with the Porfirian dream of thwarting U.S. ambitions by implanting other foreigners. The Mennonites were exempt from the military draft and had the right to determine their own educational, religious, and economic practices. Despite initial difficulties, including conflicts with agraristas who disputed their lands, the Mennonites prospered and numbered nearly ten thousand inhabitants by 1940.[40] Smaller Mormon settlements, founded in the late nineteenth century, are located near Nuevo Casas Grandes. Despite various difficulties, by 1929 there were nearly one million hectares in ejidos, and ten years later there were just over three million hectares throughout the state.[41]

Irrigation and Agriculture

In the desert north, water was as important as land tenancy. In 1926, the Calles regime had created the National Irrigation Commission with two goals besides the long-standing one of populating the desert: to augment agricultural production and to divide latifundia and create smallholder colonies and thus fulfill the nineteenth-century dream of an agricultural middle class. In 1927–1928, the federal government began building canals in the valley of the Conchos River. The area was already served by La Boquilla, a dam constructed by Canadian and U.S. investors and finished in 1915.[42]

Enhanced irrigation brought a boom in cotton production. Anderson, Clayton and Company, U.S.-based cotton dealers, expanded their operations from Juárez to the Conchos Valley, and a new town, Delicias, was founded in 1933 as the administrative center of Irrigation Zone Five. Luis Aboites described Delicias as "the new homeland of the private beneficiaries of public investment and of the workers."[43] Cotton needed seasonal wage workers, especially for harvesting, but left laborers unemployed the rest of the year. The industry was supported by U.S. agronomists promoting new methods of pest control. Cotton brought Chihuahua into a complex international network where prices were set in New York.

The cattle industry, devastated during the revolution, had begun to recover when U.S. cattlemen were given permission to pasture their herds in Chihuahua during the drought of 1922–1923, because Chihuahua's rangeland had seen less recent pressure from grazing during the revolution.[44] Its recovery was interrupted again when the global depression of 1929 brought a halt to exports.

The depression caused falling prices in agricultural products along with a crisis in mining, much of which was in foreign hands, and the expulsion of hundreds of thousands of migrant workers from the United States, many of whom remained in the border states seeking work. Unemployed miners and urban workers migrated to work in irrigation works on the Río Conchos; others solicited ejidos. In 1933 the end of prohibition in the United States caused massive layoffs in Ciudad Juárez just as the city was flooded by repatriated farmworkers.[45]

Between 1886 and 1898, U.S. senator George Hearst, father of the newspaper magnate William Randolph Hearst, had acquired 360,000 hectares in the municipalities of Madera, Temósachic, and Gómez Farías. The Hacienda Babícora was repeatedly sacked during the revolution and threatened with expropriation. Hearst responded by publishing anti-Mexican tirades in his newspapers.[46] Between 1917 and 1942, fifteen ejidos, consisting of grazing lands, were wrestled from the Babícora, while Hearst divided the remainder into eight lots, each with a certificate of livestock exemption protecting it from expropriation.[47] In 1939, white guards in his employ killed agrarian militant Socorro Rivera and his companions in a shootout as Rivera attempted to lead an invasion. In 1954, President Adolfo Ruíz Cortines canceled the certificates and expropriated the lots. They became agricultural and livestock colonies, not ejidos.[48]

The mid-twentieth-century Miracle took the initial form of agricultural expansion in Chihuahua. From 1940 to 1960, the production of cotton, basic grains, and livestock increased dramatically while agrarian dotation diminished.[49] What was distributed tended to be pasture and not farmland, while irrigated lands remained in the hands of large entrepreneurs. Meanwhile, the federal government continued building dams, drilling wells, and draining the lands around Ciudad Juárez for the benefit of private business, though not to the same extent as in Sonora, Sinaloa, and Baja California. The 1950s saw a dramatic increase in cotton cultivation because of rising prices during World War II and declining U.S. production. While many workers migrated as braceros, the cotton boom kept some of them in Irrigation Zone Five.

According to Aboites, the extension of the agricultural frontier with the opening of former grazing lands to rain-fed agriculture by smallholders and ejidatarios augmented the production of basic grains, such as corn and beans, in the 1940s and 1950s. An example was the division of the Babícora in 1954, when 250,000 hectares were divided among thirteen colonies who sowed corn, beans, and oatmeal in the former cattle ranch.[50] Aboites proposed a regionalization distinguishing between rain-fed and irrigated agriculture and described fourteen municipalities of the northwest where corn and bean farming grew as cattle raising declined.[51] In this region, and in Irrigation Zone Five, the principal protagonists of agrarian struggles in the early sixties were found, perhaps because earlier economic expansion was frustrated as Bosques de Chihuahua appropriated land from smallholders and because extreme exploitation continued in the large commercial farms around Delicias.

In 1956, responding to U.S. dumping of its reserves, the price of cotton began to fall. In 1959 the fields were attacked by weevils and worms. The year 1963 saw torrential rains, flooding, and fungus disease. Production never achieved its previous high levels.[52] Soil exhaustion must have also played a part in diminishing returns along with the growing market for synthetic fabrics, some manufactured from wood pulp.

Midcentury economic expansion favored large landholders who were either foreigners or members of the commercial and financial elite who dominated state government. Commerce and services expanded as well, and by 1951, 51 percent of the Chihuahuenses lived in cities, and the border town once called El Paso del Norte had surpassed the capitol in population. The United States' involvement in World War II and its demand for migrant workers expanded the population in the border states as well. In 1952 the last stretch of Pan-American Highway was finished, connecting Ciudad Juárez and Chihuahua to the route traced by Juan de Oñate in 1598 and continuing south to Mexico City.[53]

Forestry

Forestry, with its ready market in the United States and existing system of rail communication, offered an obvious investment opportunity in postrevolutionary Chihuahua. Roughly one-third of Chihuahua's surface area consists of the Sierra Madre Occidental, once covered with pine and oak forests. The forests became an important source of lumber during the late nineteenth century as alarms were raised in the United States about the rate of overcutting there; original extraction went to the U.S. market. Industrialists saw the forest as a vast resource to be exploited regardless of its ability to reproduce and despite its Tarahumara inhabitants, whose way of life depends on the trees that connect heaven and earth.

The defeat of the Indians opened the sierra to Porfirian exploitation and, with the removal of the menacing savage, the military colonists lost their role as defenders of civilization. Now subject to taxes and the draft, they protested the region's exploitation by outsiders avid for gain, who saw only the vast expanse of twenty million hectares of virgin forest. The local economy was subsumed in the cyclical fluctuations of speculative extraction; the smallholders were obliged to sell their produce through junior partners of the state elite. The region was rapidly transformed, both socially and ecologically; investments arrived and profits departed alongside serranos reduced to migrant labor.[54]

Railroads moved the trees to markets. Financed by foreign capital, they facilitated the export of commodities and the integration of former backlands into a world market. Financiers bought up land near the rails as prices rose; the concentration of land further facilitated the exploitation of mining and timber resources. The entire region came under the control of unstable export markets.

The Guerrero District had been in the forefront of the Indian wars; its resources were also a principal target of Porfirian investments. In 1888, four years before the rebellion, the forested area around Tomóchic was acquired by the Limantour brothers. In 1886, the Hearst family bought the Hacienda Babícora from the Valenzuela surveying company. The Río Grande, Sierra Madre, and Pacific Railroad, based in New York, built a line from Ciudad Juárez to Casas Grandes in 1897 and continued south. The Chihuahua to Pacific Railway (Chepe), based in New Jersey and including Enrique Creel among its partners, ran a line from Chihuahua City to Temósachic in 1905. Colonel William C. Greene, owner of the copper mine in Cananea, Sonora, completed a line from Temósachic to Madera in 1907 to serve his timbering interests. Other lines soon connected the capital city to Juárez, Madera, and Sonora.

In 1904, Governor Enrique Creel sold to the U.S. entrepreneur William C. Greene the timber concession that led to the establishment of the industry headquartered in Madera, formerly named the Ciénaga de San Pedro. The concession included exemption from local and state taxes for a number of years and the right to establish a company store. The Sierra Madre Land and Lumber Company installed sawmills in both Madera and Pearson, now Mata Ortiz, near Nuevo Casas Grandes.[55] In 1906, Mexican workers at Greene's Cananea, Sonora, mine went on strike, demanding equal pay with U.S. workers and an eight-hour day. The strike turned into a riot, rebellious miners burned company installations, and several people were killed. In response, Greene called on a mob of U.S. vigilantes led by the Arizona Rangers to subdue the strikers. The scandal associated with the strike exposed the shaky underpinnings of Greene's incipient empire based on speculative expansion; he went bankrupt in the recession of 1907.[56] In Madera, two thousand workers at his mills were laid off after months without pay; operations were suspended, and the town was seized by Greene's creditors. Greene's property in the sierra passed to the state government, who sold some of it to U.S. investors. These vast holdings, together with those of the Hacienda Babícora, were fought over for decades by local campesinos, many of them former smallholders dispossessed by expanding haciendas and railroad construction in the late nineteenth century.

Madera began as a company town, with a store, hospital, primary school, bank, hotel, and casino. The company housed Mexican and U.S. workers separately in disparate conditions. In 1909, the Northwest Railroad of Mexico signed a contract with Creel, who was still governor, to exploit the forests with a twenty-year tax exemption, and the Madera Company was formed. The company built new sawmills with enormous capacity, the most modern in all Latin America, their output destined for the U.S. market.[57] In 1911, Madera City was made head of a new municipality taken from Temósachic; this allowed outside merchants to challenge the monopoly of the company store and required the company to release the land under the town center and the residential neighborhoods. In early 1913, days before Francisco Madero was assassinated, the company suspended operations because of insecurity; they then claimed millions of pesos in damages from Victoriano Huerta, incurred since the revolution began in November 1910.[58] The first cannon used by revolutionary forces was forged in Madera's workshops using the axle from a locomotive.

Vast numbers of pines were fed to the industry. Those that escaped the sawmill were consumed in the kitchens of thousands of families or in the motors of the locomotives carrying the lumber. Timber fueled the operations of the sawmills themselves. Other timber went for railroad ties. The forestry laws enacted in 1926 required logging permits and plans approved by the federal government. During the Cárdenas years, Miguel Angel de Quevedo established an independent forest service promoting conservation over production. New regulations passed in 1943 and 1948 favored entrepreneurs, who were granted concessions called Unidades Industriales de Explotación Forestal (UIEF; Industrialized

Forestry Units), which gave them exclusive access to forests regardless of ownership, in return for roadbuilding, social services, and conservation measures.[59]

The forests were clear-cut, the area around Madera first, until today less than 1 percent of Chihuahua's original old-growth forest remains.[60] Other centers of timber extraction existed farther south in the sierra, in San Juanito, Bocoyna, Urique, Guachochi, and Guadalupe y Calvo. In the early 1930s, the Madera industry belonged to three Mexicans: Gilberto Armendáriz, Rodolfo Terrazas, and Antonio Guerrero. The first union was organized in 1933, the National Union of Railroad Workers, Madera Section, and in 1935, the Union of Lumber Workers of Chihuahua. When the business went bankrupt, the union took it over, forming a cooperative, Production of Lumber and Its Derivatives. Despite the success of the workers' cooperative, the former owners burned the sawmill, offices, and store and took it back.[61]

The author of an English-language publicity pamphlet for the Mexico North-Western Railway Company described the Papigochi Valley as Mexico's granary for its production of potatoes, beans, corn, and alfalfa, and he exhorted settlers to join the Mormon colonies along the new rail line to be built from Terrazas to Madera. He promoted Madera and its nearby cliff dwellings as a tourist destination and praised the region's abundant hunting and fishing. He described the pine forests as so extensive that if they were laid out on either side of a transcontinental railway stretching from New York to San Francisco, they would extend for two miles.[62]

Eloy Santiago Vallina García, the son of a Spanish exile, married into the elite and acquired banking experience in both the United States and Chihuahua. In 1934 he founded the Banco Comercial Mexicano (today Comermex) on the site of the old Creel- and Terrazas-controlled Banco Minero. The new endeavor, consolidating capital of both Porfirian and postrevolutionary origin from around the state, created a cohesive bloc capable of competing with outside financial interests. Within it were contradictory elements due to the diverse social origins of its constituents: both dynamic economic interests imbued with entrepreneurial nationalism and bureaucratic forces linked to popular struggles prepared to enact social reforms and confront the United States. By the end of the 1950s, the group had national influence, with sixty bank branches, including twenty-eight in Mexico City, and controlling interest in several telephone companies. In Colonia Anáhuac, near Cuauhtémoc, they founded several wood-processing industries; Celulosa de Chihuahua processed 60 percent of the nation's cellulose, and Plywood de Mexico supplied the growing furniture industry. Italian and U.S. companies provided technology and capital for Viscosa, the rayon industry that developed at the expense of Chihuahua's cotton fields.[63] Some of the demand for wood pulp resulted from changes in the paper manufacturing process in response to booming literacy after World War II.

Previous timber extraction had been on a small scale, exporting raw lumber to the insatiable U.S. market by depleting the forests near the Chihuahua to Pacific Railway. In 1946, a group including Eloy Vallina and the Mexico City banker and industrialist Carlos Trouyet bought the Northwest Mexico Railroad, an initial step in creating an integrated consortium from transportation to sawmills to the fabrication of moldings, boards, and plywood. In 1952, the Grupo Vallina formed the company Bosques de Chihuahua, headquartered in Madera City. The founders of Bosques included Vallina and Trouyet; Miguel Alemán; General Antonio Guerrero, former commander of the Fifth Military Zone and an owner of the industry in the 1930s; Teófilo Borunda, governor from 1956 to 1962; Tomás Valle, empresario and state senator; and members of the powerful Terrazas and Almeida families. During the final days of the presidential term of Miguel Alemán, Bosques received a fifty-year UIEF concession covering some 560,000 hectares to supply Celulosa de Chihuahua, Industrias de Madera, and Maderas de Pino Industrializadas with raw materials.[64] At the same time, the national forestry service enacted a ban on logging in the depleted zone surrounding the Chihuahua to Pacific Railway from La Junta to San Juanito and Creel, to the detriment to the small- and medium-size entrepreneurs active there, and transferred their operations farther south and east.[65]

Bosques owned nearly 260,000 hectares outright in addition to the right to receive lumber from private and ejidal owners included in the concession, who were to be compensated for their trees at mutually agreed prices.[66] Lands not susceptible to logging were to remain dedicated to livestock; Bosques sold some of this land to cattlemen, although some of what they sold was not theirs, having been settled for generations by families who had never obtained the titles they had the right to. These sales led to a triangular conflict: Bosques asserted property rights it did not have; upon purchase, the cattlemen sought the dispossession of the land's rightful owners; and the campesinos demanded that their property rights be recognized and that Bosques be divided into new centers of population for either crops or livestock.[67] The New Center of Population (NCP), codified in the Agrarian Code of 1942, was a means for persons otherwise ineligible to form an ejido and could be created far from their place of origin.

The Four Friends

Tomás Vega Portillo, Roberto Schneider, Alejandro Prieto, and José Ibarra Ronquillo formed the livestock company Four Friends in 1956 with more than two million pesos.[68] Among their purchases was Los Guerigos, with 14,000 hectares, from Bosques. Of the four, only José Ibarra had not previously been a well-established landowner in his own right. José Ibarra and his brother Florentino became notorious as the protectors of the other partners, dedicated to "repressive actions against the small cattlemen of the region, applying systems of torture and terror, and pillaging their goods and livestock, going as far as imprisonment and murder."[69]

José Ibarra was accused of "an infinite number of arbitrarities, robberies, and murders." Sometimes said to be from Tejolócachic,[70] Chihuahua, other accounts said Temósachic, where he killed a peon and fled to Mineral de Dolores, Huizopa, Cebadilla, Agua Amarilla, Yepachi, and Tutuaca, making bootleg sotol along the way.[71] In Agua Amarilla, he came across Raúl García, who had robbed the Bank of Parral; he killed García and used the proceeds of the double robbery to establish a "tienda de raya"[72] in the Mineral de Dolores to double the profit from his sotol workers. In another version, when García arrived at his store, Ibarra shot him through the heart.[73] He bought livestock with the profits from the store and the still. In 1942, he was accused of murdering Rafael Contreras of El Carrizo. In 1948, he was accused of killing the North American Roberto Knox by sending him a poisoned turkey at Christmas. The American died alone; Ibarra stole his Rancho San Augustín and his livestock.[74]

In 1956, he joined the Four Friends. He functioned as a "socio-industrial," both junior partner and protector. The association with established hacendados assured him the backing of state and local authorities, including the DAAC, and he initiated a reign of terror in Madera and Temósachic. Despite the expressed wishes of Bosques that smallholders be protected, Ibarra burned their houses and stole their livestock, terrorizing them into abandoning their homes. In 1958, he killed the cowboy Reynaldo Solís. At this, Roberto Schneider, the principal partner, called for the dissolution of the Four Friends, and the livestock and lands were sold. The DFS remarked that Schneider and Alejandro Prieto were known as morally upright but that Tomás Vega was the brains behind the Ibarra brothers. José Ibarra, his relatives, and his supporters were permitted to carry arms as agents of the state police.[75] Although the Four Friends was dissolved in 1958, it was persistently blamed for later troubles. The DFS also mentions "an innumerable number of rapes of women of campesino families" by José Ibarra and his relatives.[76] Given that rape was the ultimate dishonor and is rarely reported, it is not surprising that the archives contain little documentation. There were persistent accusations against José and Florentino.

José Ibarra was accused of orchestrating the murder of the Madera schoolteacher, Francisco Luján, in 1959. In 1960, Florentino Ibarra killed the Pima activist Carlos Ríos in front of Ibarra's store in Mineral de Dolores. Both Ríos and Luján were campesino leaders and members of the UGOCM, and these two murders had long-lasting consequences.

Ibarra was motivated by greed and lust for power; he ascended when the sierra was in flux as industrialization put pressure on traditional patterns of land tenure, and he inserted himself into battles between local inhabitants and larger forces, as in the murders of Luján and Ríos. He frequently accompanied agents of the rural police in their harassment of serranos, positioning himself as an ally of the state and the large landholders, and became a primary target of the guerrilla struggle that erupted in 1964. He allied himself with the powerful against the powerless, but there is no reason to suppose that he acted as a conscious agent of Bosques, clearing the sierra of recalcitrant campesinos to facilitate the more efficient extraction of logging profits. The habitus of the sierra was one of small-scale, face-to-face violence, shared by Ibarra and his antagonists.[77] In his personal reign of terror, in the cycle of revenge killings between his family and the Gaytáns, in his disregard for the rule of law, in his accumulation of wealth in land and livestock, Ibarra resembled those serrano smallholders far more than he did representatives of the impersonal industrial regime now being imposed.

The traditional local cacique is a political boss who intercedes between a community and the institutions of the state, embodying hierarchies of authority, linked by bonds of reciprocity, and exercising personal and arbitrary power.[78] The traditional cacique mediates, distributing benefits in return for support. But although Ibarra became a local authority, originally through his store and sotol business, and was widely referred to as a cacique, his power was volatile and short-lived, and he did nothing to mediate between the community and outsiders. Beyond a handful of hired gunmen and servants, there was nothing to indicate he had clients. The indigenous Pima who worked his distilleries were enslaved. Ibarra and his performative violence can be seen as an instance of political, and ultimately economic, violence—the imposition of an economic system of resource extraction—pushed down to local levels.[79] Ibarra's violence was useful to the state in terrorizing its opponents. He and his associates carried credentials from the state (also known as rural) police as he rode with the army in 1964, blurring the line between official and nonofficial violence.[80]

Other Protest Movements

In 1955, a broad-based movement for social justice forced the state governor and several officials to resign. In November 1954, the taxi driver Juan Cereceres defended a waitress against the belligerent advances of a well-connected junior, Gaspar Maynez, whose father was both police inspector and chief of the rural and municipal police forces and whose uncle was Governor Oscar Soto Maynez. The next day Cereceres's taxi was found with a bullet hole and a pool of blood in the driver's seat; a month later his corpse turned up. Innocent persons were charged with his murder and tortured. Two women, one a nurse and the other, Dolores G. de Villarreal, wife of a prominent businessman who would play a role in later struggles, formed the Comité Feminino Pro Justicia y Derechos Humanos (Women's Committee for Justice and Human Rights); her husband, Lázaro Villarreal, formed a male counterpart. The progressive daily *El Norte* ran a notice on every front page, changing the date accordingly: "Who killed Juan Cereceres? [so many] days have passed without the killers being captured. Was it a perfect crime? The people of Chihuahua plead for justice." Union locals joined the campaign; donations, mostly small sums and a majority from women, arrived from every corner of the state. In late January, with the temperature below freezing, a reported seventy thousand people gathered before the cathedral to demand the governor's resignation. He stepped down in August.[81] Perhaps because the criminal bore the governor's name and because the governor was also accused of financial misdealings, this incident led to a civic awakening the regime was unable to contain.

A radical Christian movement, the Movimiento Social Demócrata Cristiano (Social Democratic Christian Movement), proponents of Liberation Theology with connections to national and international groups, also developed in the effervescence of the early 1960s, led in part by twenty young people who had been expelled from the conservative Partido de Acción Nacional (PAN; National Action Party) for renouncing the PAN's electoral strategy as legitimating the regime.[82] Calling themselves *la guerrilla moral* and dedicated pacifists, they were rivals of secular radical movements such as the UGOCM, readers of Paolo Freire instead of Régis Debray, and critical of "the abstract theorizing" of the left. Much of their work consisted of creating base communities and supporting independent unions, including strikes at El Diamante, the Súper del Real, Pepsi-Cola, and later Spicer, all in Chihuahua. A national offspring, the Frente Auténtico del Trabajo (FAT), founded in 1960, continues to defend workers' rights to this day.[83]

The attack on the base at Madera had a curious prequel in the assault on the police station and cavalry base in Delicias nine years earlier. The failed attack had been meant as part of a national uprising in support of Miguel Henríquez Guzmán, who had run as a reform candidate in the presidential elections and lost amid widespread accusations of fraud. Among local demands was the creation of an ejido in Irrigation Zone Five. While the national Henriquista leadership hesitated, local forces led by former mayor Emiliano Laing attacked with fifty-eight poorly armed men. Laing had assured them that their targets would immediately surrender. Instead the attackers were routed, and Laing and several others were killed.[84]

Finally, in the countryside, there were widespread mobilizations during the 1970s: land invasions in Jiménez led by the Union of District Ejidos and the Central Campesina Independiente (CCI; Independent Campesino Central) and urban invasions, including one of the Quinta Carolinas, once the property of Luis Terrazas, organized by the CDP. In 1973, campesinos led by the CCI invaded lands in Guerrero, Cuauhtémoc, and San Francisco de Borja. When rousted, they occupied the offices of DAAC alongside student supporters.[85]

The Committee for Popular Defense

While the attack on the Madera army base in 1965 generated a certain amount of repression in the towns, it did not prevent a new urban movement from emerging before the end of the year. As the population shifted from country to city, so did the movement's focus. As displaced campesinos swarmed into the capitol, putting pressure on available housing, they began to organize tenants' organizations and press, with the support of students and members of the PCM, for equitable rents and then for building lots. Among the early leaders of the tenants' movement was Carlos Armendáriz, who later joined the successor *guerrilla*, GPG–Arturo Gámiz, in 1968 and was killed in action. In 1967, the Frente Popular de Lucha Inquilinaria (Popular Front of Tenants' Struggles) split from the PCM, accusing them of accepting inadequate lands and of imposing leaders from above.[86]

A series of land invasions in 1968 led to the founding of the Colonia Francisco Villa to the north of the city. The colony was more than a place to live: it was an attempt to organize a new way of life, inspired by the liberation movements of 1968 in Mexico City and around the world. The women of the colony organized to prevent representatives of the purported owner from fencing them out. The colonists formed a youth club and built a school with donated materials and organized fund-raising dances where liquor was forbidden. Other land invasions followed.[87]

In 1972, the Comité de Defensa Popular (CDP; Committee for Popular Defense) was formed in Chihuahua City to protest the government's assassination of Diego Lucero and Ramiro Díaz, urban guerrillas arrested after the failed simultaneous attack on three banks. Vast numbers mobilized under the slogan "For a Proletarian Revolution" and formed a popular assembly. Initial participants included the Colonia Villa, student associations, and railroad workers, teachers, electricians, and university workers along with the Frente Auténtico del Trabajo and the Movimiento Revolucionario del Magisterio (MRM; Revolutionary Teachers' Movement). Ten thousand people marched on May Day, forcing the official contingents out of the plaza. The CDP organized a series of popular tribunals and intervened in a number of workers' struggles. Efforts in Chihuahua were connected to workers' battles across the country. Both the electrical workers and the railway workers, reanimated by Demetrio Vallejo's release from prison in 1972, battled for union democracy and an end to corrupt leadership.[88] In every CDP campaign, the Colonia Villa was central. But despite the CDP's capacity for vast mobilizations of its heterogeneous base, a number of local battles were lost to superior force. With the ebb in the national movement and a series of internal conflicts within its ranks, the CDP faded away.

In the 1980s, Chihuahua took center stage with PAN's challenge to the PRI. PAN state leader, textile manufacturer Luis Alvarez, had run as its candidate in the 1958 presidential elections won by Adolfo López Mateos. In the early 1980s, successive devaluations of the peso hit hard in the border states, which were accustomed to dealing in dollars. Backed by the local Catholic church and a business community willing to confront the PRI, in 1983 Alvarez won the mayoral election in the capital city. Six other large cities went to PAN as well. When the PRI won the 1986 elections through massive fraud, protests erupted, blocking traffic on the Córdoba bridge to El Paso for six days while Alvarez undertook a hunger strike in the Parque Lerdo near downtown Chihuahua. The archdiocese announced the suspension of mass, although the PRI persuaded the Vatican to overrule. Left-wing forces, including local PCM leader Antonio Becerra Gaytán and national leader Heberto Castillo, visited Alvarez and urged him to end the strike and launch a national democracy campaign. A painstaking comparison of official lists of registered voters with census data revealed that both the numbers of registered voters and the actual ballots purportedly cast were larger than the population, especially in remote areas of the sierra.[89] In 1992, Chihuahua elected its first PAN governor.

3

"The Cattle Get 30 Hectares"

Summary

The events that led to the 1965 attack on the army base at Madera began years before in the mountainous backlands where hundreds of families had settled on land to which they had a right to title after ten years, although only a few undertook the burdensome process. The rapid expansion of timbering in the 1950s detonated a series of conflicts as Bosques de Chihuahua sought to remove families settled within its concession. Bosques backed up legal eviction orders with extralegal violence perpetrated by local strongmen. The serranos organized to demand ejidos and eventually defended themselves with arms, invoking their forefathers who had defended the frontier from Apache incursions. Meanwhile, in the cities, students joined campesinos in agrarian campaigns and agitated for their own demands. Students and campesinos organized a prolonged occupation at DAAC offices in Chihuahua City and the First Encounter of the Sierra to debate policy.

Francisco Luján and Alvaro Ríos

In November 1959, the retired schoolteacher Francisco Luján was assassinated at his home in Madera City. He had spent years helping local campesinos petition for ejidos, including the amplification of Cebadilla de Dolores, some sixty kilometers southwest of Madera, where he had been the registered agent since 1949.[1] That community would soon become a stronghold of the opposition. The Unión General de Obreros y Campesinos de México (UGOCM; General Union of Workers and Campesinos of Mexico) attributed Luján's assassination to local thug José Ibarra and organized a caravan protesting the murder; some eight hundred people marched on foot down Highway 39 then east to Chihuahua City.[2]

When Luján was killed, Alvaro Ríos had just arrived in Madera to form a local chapter of the UGOCM. Ríos was born in the small Sonoran town of Oputo, now Villa Hidalgo, to a family of poor campesinos. Without land of his own, his father worked on the Alvaro Obregón Dam, which watered the Yaqui Valley. The older Ríos was a union organizer; their home was full of workers engaged in political discussions. The teenage Alvaro worked in California's Imperial Valley picking cotton, was deported several times, and learned firsthand of the precarious conditions facing undocumented workers in the United States. He returned to Sonora to work on the dam with his father. He also began to study history.[3]

The workers solicited the new lands that would come into cultivation with the dam they were building. They joined a group allied with Jacinto López, another Sonoran and leader of the UGOCM. The lands were promised, the wait was prolonged, and the solicitants began to disperse. Alvaro Ríos was delegated to go on their behalf to Mexico City. (The case was not resolved until 1976, when President Echeverría distributed some of the Yaqui lands.) He stayed in Mexico City working with López, learning about the agrarian reform, and studying at the PPS's Universidad Obrera (Workers' University). After five years, he decided that the UGOCM did not organize people on the ground but only filed petitions and guided them through legal procedures. He concluded that the PPS only cared about theory and did not work for fundamental social change.[4]

Ríos wanted to go someplace where he could put his ideas into practice without interference from the PPS and UGOCM's national leadership. After long conversations with the Chihuahuan David Estrada, Jacinto López's assistant and a former student of Madera schoolteacher Francisco Luján, Ríos decided to come to Madera and arrived days before Luján's death. The Estrada family had ejidal rights in Huizopa, Madera, which would become the site of some of the fiercest battles and worst repression. The municipality of Madera contained some of the biggest landholdings in the country: Bosques, the Hacienda Sírupa near Cebadilla de Dolores, and the lands of the Four Friends. Ríos came to the sierra to prepare the terrain for a revolutionary movement.[5] He organized a chapter of the UGOCM.[6] The group included Leonel Luján, son of the murdered schoolteacher, who organized the first protest caravan.[7]

In early 1960, three thousand campesinos met in Madera to petition President Adolfo López Mateos to expropriate some of Bosques's hundreds of thousands of hectares of forest. They also demanded punishment for the murder of Professor Luján Adame.[8] A few months later, national leader Jacinto López arrived and founded the Federación de Obreros y Campesinos del Estado de Chihuahua (FOCECH; Federation of Workers and Campesinos of the State of Chihuahua), the state committee of the UGOCM.[9] Regional groupings in Delicias and Casas Grandes followed.

As the serranos mobilized, the repression increased along with the impunity of its perpetrators. On March 18, José Ibarra's brother Florentino killed Carlos Ríos, an indigenous Pima and leader of the local UGOCM in the Mineral de Dolores. This murder, coupled with the assassination of Francisco Luján, became an enduring rallying cry. Ibarra was brought to trial and sentenced to eight years in prison. Freed on bail, he appealed, and his sentence was revoked in November 1963.[10]

A number of other acts of violence were reported during those years. José Ibarra's gunmen assassinated the campesino Anselmo Enríquez Quintana on June 12, 1959, outside a cantina in Matachic, a small town south of Madera City, and stole his property. Ibarra was indicted, and an arrest warrant was issued but not enforced. On September 4, 1959, Rubén Ibarra Amaya, José Ibarra's son, wounded the schoolteacher Armando Mendoza Orozco in Matachic. He was indicted in February 1960 and set free on bail. An arrest warrant was issued on February 27, 1962, against Rubén Ibarra for assaulting Abelardo López Vega. On November 17, 1963, Jesús Ibarra, nephew of José Ibarra, wounded Eleuterio Olivas, a solicitant for the NCP Huizopa.[11] Salvador Gaytán claimed that it was José Ibarra Jr. who had shot Olivas, leaving him crippled, and that Fernando Solís, the police commander in Dolores, had arrested Ibarra, earning the enmity of the clan. Ibarra was soon released and rewarded with a state police credential.[12] In August 1960, *Indice* reported the murder of "the son of María L., widow of Ortega, whose intellectual authors were the Vallinas, the Arreolas, the Almeidas, and the Vegas, represented by José Ibarra."[13] In February 1961, Fortunato Gil Valenzuela accused Rosendo and Salvador Gaytán of rustling; they were ordered to stand trial. On August 13, 1961, José Ibarra was assaulted in Río Dolores; Manuel Rascón, Manuel Torres, and Guadalupe Ortega were arrested but released for lack of evidence.[14] In September 1963, Gil again accused Salvador and Rosendo Gaytán, Ramón Mendoza, and Luis Estrada of robbery and theft of land. The warrant against the Gaytáns and their associates was revoked when it was found that the land in question was being solicited by NCP Huizopa.

Arturo Gámiz and Pablo Gómez

As conflicts in the sierra multiplied, events throughout the state took on greater urgency. Among the central protagonists of that movement were Arturo Gámiz and Pablo Gómez. Arturo Gamíz García, who became a leader of the UGOCM and later the Grupo Popular Guerrillero, arrived in Chihuahua during the late 1950s. He was born in Suchil, northern Durango, in 1940. He attended primary school in Mexico City, where he was a prizewinning student, and he entered the third year of middle school at the Instituto Politécnico Nacional (IPN; National Polytechnical Institute) in January 1956, where he lived in the dormitories on a scholarship. On September 23, 1956, federal troops evacuated the dorms at gunpoint after a prolonged strike. After the occupation of the IPN, Gámiz followed his family to Chihuahua, where his father worked for Celulosa, a wood-pulp producing plant in Anáhuac, near Madera.[15] He obtained a teaching position in La Junta, a small logging town, where he taught for two years. He then applied for admission to the State Normal School.[16] He transferred a number of credits earned from 1954 to 1956 and was enrolled in 1960 and 1961, although he did not attend classes in 1961 but took exams in some subjects.[17] He did not graduate. His absences are not surprising given the scope of his organizing activities. He was brilliant, serious, charismatic, and a fiery orator.

In December 1958, in Nuevo León, he was elected a national vice president of the Juventud Popular (JP; Popular Youth), the PPS's youth group.[18] (Other officers that year included Rafael Villa Estrada, president, and Roberto Jaramillo, secretary-general, who later assisted GPG members when they fled to Mexico City in late 1965.[19]) According to the DFS, in 1962 Gámiz was sent to Germany for six months to study Marxism-Leninism, a reward for his work with the JP.[20] Another author placed him among a delegation of students and teachers who visited Cuba in 1963.[21] Either journey might help to explain the concern with Soviet objectives in the movements he led.

Pablo Gómez Ramírez, from a family of poor campesinos, was another leader. Born in Saucillo, Chihuahua, he and his brother Raúl studied at the State Normal School. A third brother, Simón, was involved in the movement to a lesser extent. Pablo married Alma Caballero, also from Chihuahua, in Mexico City in 1950. He had gone there to study medicine and complete his studies at the Normal Superior. There he joined the PPS. On the couple's return to Chihuahua, Gómez did his obligatory social service in Buenaventura, where he worked with a surgeon and taught at the rural normal school for girls, then located at the former Hacienda Carmen in nearby Flores Magón. (Many rural normal schools were established in former haciendas, transforming sites of campesino exploitation into opportunities for their children.) While Gómez treated patients and taught, his wife established a pharmacy. Their daughter Alma remembered being harassed at school when anticommunist hysteria intensified after the Cuban Revolution, since her father's sympathies were well known. She also recalled her father going to El Paso to buy a shortwave radio and inviting the neighbors to listen to Radio Habana; that students dressed as *barbudos* (bearded revolutionaries) for the parade on Day of the Students; and that the Cuban delegation showed a film she guessed might have been *Lucía* (not released until 1968). In 1961, Pablo Gómez attended the Latin American Conference for Peace, organized by Lázaro Cárdenas, as a local delegate. The family moved to Saucillo, in the irrigated agricultural district along the Río Conchos, with the relocation of the school. Both Pablo and Raúl became leaders of the UGOCM in nearby Delicias, running for office on the PPS ticket in 1964.[22]

In November 1960, one year after the serranos began organizing, President Adolfo López Mateos visited Chihuahua. A delegation of some six hundred campesinos from Madera came on foot to request the expropriation of Bosques de Chihuahua and vengeance for the murders of Francisco Luján and Carlos Ríos. Joined by students, they followed the official November 20 parade with one of their own, marching under freezing rain and carrying banners that read "The CNC has become the worst brake on the national agrarian reform," and "The millions that the assassins of Luján have should not impede the working of justice." They presented López Mateos with a lengthy written report on conditions in Madera signed by Jesús Manuel González Raizola, Alvaro Ríos, Carlos Muñoz, Francisco Márquez, and Leonel Luján.[23] They camped on the outskirts of the capital near the Chuvíscar Dam, while women students collected food for them.[24] This was one of the first actions that brought students and campesinos together.

Two weeks later, López Mateos announced the cancellation of "all fictitious forestry concessions," including Bosques de Chihuahua. He had previously canceled the permit for the forestry company Río Septentrional for violating federal forestry law.[25] In return, Antonio Guerrero, president of the state forestry association and a founder of Bosques, accused the president of "encouraging communism and stimulating professional agitators." The association was later compelled to deny that accusation. In February, *Indice* reprinted an article from the national journal *Política*, reporting that Bosques was attempting to sell its stock to its employees; copies of *Política* were prevented from circulating in Chihuahua. Despite the presidential announcements, Río Septentrional was cutting more than ever the following summer, and the Bosques concession was not canceled until years later.[26]

When the United States invaded Cuba at the Bay of Pigs in April 1961, the PPS called for volunteers to defend Cuban sovereignty.[27] The organization Friends of Cuba and the State Normal School called a demonstration in the Plaza de Armas on April 24, and the student association of Salaices obtained a truck and driver from the school. While Alvaro Ríos and Antonio Becerra Gaytán, a PCM member and teacher at the State Normal School, stood on the speakers' platform, Catholic conservatives attacked the meeting with Molotov cocktails, and five students and one professor were arrested.[28] Several years later, Ríos was accused of homicide in the death of one of the anticommunist protesters and jailed for six months. This was the first time students from Salaices, the State Normal School, the Normal Night School, the prep school of the university, and the Technical School (La Escuela de Artes y Oficios) had demonstrated together, although they did not all take part in the planning. For many, it was their first introduction to the idea of a victorious guerrilla struggle. Finally, it was their initial experience of repression, as police moved in to subdue the protesters.[29]

Meanwhile, in the sierra, reports of agrarian battles continued. In Madera, the prosecutor arrested Alberto Durán and Carlos Yáñez to force them to relinquish their lands, although they were protected by an injunction from the secretary of agriculture and livestock. Bosques had sold the land to Juan Alvarez, Ramón Molina, and José Ibarra, giving Durán and Yáñez ten days to leave and assessing a substantial fee for the use of its pasture.[30] Yáñez later joined the GPG. *Indice* accused the director of the state office of DAAC of extortion and threats in the case of the indigenous community of Panalachic in Bocoyna, another logging area. They also reported on problems in the Ejido Carlos Pacheco in Balleza, where unidentified outsiders had taken illegal possession.[31]

The campesinos of Santa Rita in Temósachic refused to pay the rising rents demanded by Bosques. They had received a presidential resolution to form the Ejido Conoachic in March, 1960; it was not executed until ten years later.[32] Threatened by gunmen, their leaders fled to Mexico City. The rural police arrived at the home of Esteban Olivas while he was gone, evicted his wife and nursing infant, and destroyed the house.[33] In 1962 Ríos would organize armed resistance for a showdown in Santa Rita that did not take place.

In December, the UGOCM chapter in Madera demanded that Bosques de Chihuahua and the Four Friends be expropriated for charging rent and evicting people from new centers of population that they were soliciting from DAAC. While the Four Friends had been dissolved several years before, their notoriety lived on. A newspaper article listed Cebadilla de Dolores, El Serrucho, El Largo, Junta de los Ríos, and El Oso as communities that had received

FIGURE 3 Pablo Gómez, Comité Primeros Vientos.

FIGURE 4 Arturo Gámiz, Comité Primeros Vientos.

presidential resolutions that had not been executed, although according to RAN Chihuahua, both El Largo and Junta de los Ríos had been executed in 1960.[34]

Judith Reyes

Judith Reyes was another central figure in the protest movement. She was born in Tamaulipas in 1924 while her father was a migrant laborer in the United States. Her mother took in laundry and sold tortillas. Judith began singing at a young age and toured as La Tamaulipeca, often composing her own songs. After an unfortunate marriage, several children, and several years singing on the radio in Mexico City, she arrived in Chihuahua in 1959 or early 1960 and went to work as a journalist for *El Monitor de Parral*, where she wrote a column called "Ubicua y yo" (Omnipresence and I) in the *Sociales* section. She interlaced news of weddings and concerts with that of Tarahumaras dead of starvation and of the former governor of Campeche, who stole fifty million pesos and fled to the United States. She solicited donations for miners who were old, impoverished, and in bad health after decades of labor.

In her autobiography, *La otra cara de la patria* (The Other Face of the Fatherland), she described her first meeting with the agrarian movement at the march in November 1960, when the campesinos came to present their demands to President Adolfo López Mateos.[35] She described the wretched crowd, the women and children sleeping under the stars, and coffee boiling in ten-gallon pots. She returned from the encounter determined to write not only articles but songs about the agrarian situation.[36] She described the campesinos' living conditions: women and children without shoes (but with crude, homemade sandals); straw and adobe huts with dirt floors; no doctors, electricity, water, sewers, or schools after the first four grades. They worked for large landholders for miserable wages or on marginal parcels insufficient to support a family. The agrarian department treated them with disdain, while they filed petition after petition and made countless, fruitless attempts to obtain their agrarian rights.[37]

Later she joined an invasion of a landholding called El Ocote City, near Parral, where she described the rules promulgated by UGOCM leader Alvaro Ríos: No alcohol, playing cards, fights, or arguments; no damage to the hacienda or to animals and crops; respect for women, old folks, and children; no arms of any kind; no confrontations or arguments with the army and its officers; only leaders to speak to the press or the authorities. During the invasion, participants should use the time to discuss their situation and national and international problems. The invasions were intended not only as struggles against the landowners and the agrarian authorities but as steps in the construction of an alternative way of life.[38]

They invaded El Ocote at night with banners that read "The land belongs to those who work it" and "Viva Zapata." They erected a Mexican flag among their banners and slept on the ground around it. Reyes described the happiness she felt at dawn, waking among people recovering their dignity, drinking coffee around a campfire.[39] The army arrived later that morning. Reyes acted as spokesperson and the dialogue ended in a lively exchange of insults with an unnamed general. While he went for instructions, Reyes called for her guitar and entertained both the campesinos and the troops with corridos. When the general returned, the invaders were driven off, and their abandoned belongings were destroyed. Reyes was ordered to report to the Fifth Military Zone in Chihuahua City. She requested and received a ride, was dropped at the doorstep of the headquarters, and entered and left by another door, on her way to report to the newspapers. Then she departed for another invasion. She calculated fifty-four invasions, nearly simultaneous, at this time, and thirty thousand campesinos in motion.[40]

Simultaneous invasions had been pioneered by the UGOCM in the northern states of Baja California, Nayarit, Sinaloa, and Sonora, where they targeted the latifundia of the Cananea Cattle Company, among others. Invasions had also been used in the Babícora in the 1930s, where Socorro Rivera and his companions had been killed.[41]

Agrarian law initially sanctioned the invasions as a means of pressuring the state to fulfill its obligations under Article 27 of the constitution of 1917, which mandated the distribution of land, regardless of prior ownership, to any group of campesinos with demonstrated need. The invasions were made a federal crime in 1960, authorizing the army to dislodge protesters.[42] Along with interrupting business as usual, the occupations of public space, the marches by the side of highways, and the land encampments were ways of saying, "Here we are, the campesinos, and we are here to stay." They asserted their own simple existence and the rights inherent in their condition as campesinos; they became political subjects.

The strategy was aimed at building participation. Earlier agrarian movements had relied on petitions directed at the state and representatives sent to offices in capital cities. While continuing to push the necessary paperwork, the UGOCM built a grassroots base, concentrating on the long-term development of a radical challenge to the state itself. By focusing on marches and occupations, the movement relied on direct participation not mediated through its leaders. Alvaro Ríos, whose goals went beyond the provision of land and on to fundamental social change, spoke of raising the consciousness of the campesinos so that they would continue to struggle even after having been granted their own land.[43] At times the movement approached "collective bargaining through riot," particularly during several tumultuous demonstrations in 1964.[44]

While the average wait between the date of the first agrarian solicitation and the survey, indicating imminent distribution, was fourteen years and two months, in some cases only a short time elapsed between the initial solicitation and the invasion—between the legal and illegal act—indicating that

Chihuahua's petitioners refused to be bound by the humiliating ritual of prolonged engagement with the state bureaucracy. "The decision to invade or the threat to do so demonstrated their inconformity with the violence signified by the monopoly holding of land and the negligence of the authorities and bureaucrats of the DAAC . . . ; that is, it was not a response exclusively concerned with the status of the agrarian file."[45] Aleida García Aguirre discussed the relation between legal and illegal acts: the solicitants were compelled to act within the framework of existing law and discourse, but the authorities were helpless to shape the solicitants' interpretation of that law.[46] For the protesters, agrarian law meant an absolute right to land, one they would exercise within or without legal boundaries.

In October 1962, Judith Reyes founded the independent semimonthly newspaper *Acción: Voz Revolucionaria del Pueblo* (Action: The People's Revolutionary Voice), which continued until 1964.[47] *Acción* was printed at the plant owned by Guillermo Gallardo Astorga, who published *Indice*, another progressive paper, and focused on the agrarian movement. The composition of its team of collaborators varied with every issue. It frequently included the crusading agronomist Víctor Manuel Bueno, who directed López Mateos's Office of Complaints; the school inspector and PCM militant José Santos Valdés; Arturo Gámiz; and for a period of time both Carlos Montemayor Aceves, author of *Las armas del alba*, who signed his articles "Bloque revolucionario de la preparatoria" (Revolutionary bloc of the preparatory school), and his father, Carlos Montemayor Díaz.

Initial issues carried a series of articles about the Cuban revolution, generally reprints of speeches by Fidel or Che, extolling their progress and attacking the United States. None of the articles on Cuba referred to the theory of *foquismo* that soon became important in Chihuahua. There was a series of unsigned articles on the history of the Mexican Revolution, praising Pancho Villa. There were long essays, particularly from Santos Valdés, on a variety of political issues; from Bueno on agrarian concerns; and later by Pablo Gómez, Arturo Gámiz, and Alvaro Ríos on the crisis in the state. Every issue contained a column by Judith Reyes, called "Taconazos" (blows from a high-heeled shoe). These were short entries attacking politicians and landowners, written with delicious sarcasm; she referred to the state attorney general, Hipólito Villa, son of Pancho Villa, the *centauro* (centaur) of the north, as the *minitauro*, or little bull. Many articles described battles in the ongoing war between campesinos and landowners, emphasizing the collaboration of state officials with latifundistas.

The language of *Acción* was frequently sarcastic but never vulgar; the editor never used sexual insults as a form of class aggression. The focus of the rhetoric was that the class enemies, *Bosques de Chihuahua*, the cattlemen, and the politicians had subverted the constitution and its promise of agrarian reform and that they were the real usurpers, the real trespassers and land invaders. *Acción* demanded equality before the law and complained that the army was used to dislodge campesinos and demanded that instead it be sent against outsiders' cattle grazing on ejidal lands. This was a discourse focused on respect for law, not on a future revolution but on the one already fought. One example was Gómez's often reprinted article, "El paracaidismo en Chihuahua": "It is not the campesino who invades the land he received from the revolution but the latifundista who once again steals it, frustrating the application of the agrarian reform."[48]

Against the persistent Cold War rhetoric employed by the official press and politicians, *Acción* responded,

> General Olachea Aviles, National Defense Minister, was surprised at the existence of guerrillas in the sierra of Chihuahua. Where did they come from? This was the first question we asked the heavenly horoscope. From Venezuela? *Made in U.S.A.* [in English in original]? The stork of Paris? The *guerrilla* came from the people to protect the people.[49]

When the occupation of Sombreretillo was violently dislodged by the army, Reyes attacked the commanding general for failing to salute the enormous flag the protesters carried, asking whether the flag were meant only for PRI propaganda.[50]

Indice, founded in 1958 and edited by Guillermo Gallardo Astorga, was another opposition newspaper. Gallardo's focus was broader; he wrote about government ineptitude and corruption, defended the interests of the indigenous, and supported striking workers and students as well as agraristas. He was vociferous in his denunciations of Eloy Vallina, a major investor in Bosques de Chihuahua, Teléfonos de México, and Comermex, whom he referred to as the "Sephardic shark," adding a dash of antisemitism to his class antagonism.

Several left-wing periodicals with national circulation were present in Chihuahua at the time, notably *El Machete*, the organ of the PCM, and *Política*, edited by PPS member Manuel Marcué Pardiñas.

In the first edition of *Acción* in October 1962, Reyes reported that in Casa Colorado, in the municipality of Madera, campesinos complained that Emilio

Portillo had cut down three thousand pines on land they had been soliciting for many years; those trees were protected by agrarian law.[51] This was a common complaint. In the same edition, she published an article by Víctor Manuel Bueno accusing the state DAAC of allowing the latifundista Emilio Pinoncely, the French Consul in Chihuahua, of grazing his cattle on the lands of the Ejido Los Sauces in the municipality of Chihuahua during a drought year. The campesinos had petitioned, saying, "We have six thousand hectares for fifty people; Pinoncely has two hundred thousand in various places," without result. They had then taken their petition to the Federal Office of Complaints, on August 21, 1961, saying, "We know that the DAAC has used public force to get rid of campesinos; they should use it now to get rid of the latifundista's cattle, in the name of equality before the law."[52]

In December, Reyes welcomed the new director of the state DAAC, Eduardo Juárez Santos Coy (sometimes written Santoscoy), exhorting him to "be loyal to his task, to be understanding of its problems, to be just and active in his intervention, and to resist the temptations of the latifundistas and to refuse their bribes." She went on to say that over the last four years, forty presidential resolutions involving more than a quarter of a million hectares for ejidos had languished despite López Mateos having ordered their swift execution. She added that the agrarian delegation had done nothing, especially in the case of forested properties where they allowed timbering, even clear-cutting, only relinquishing the properties when the trees were gone. They said that foresters were also timbering on ejidal lands. In the case of Bosques de Chihuahua, with its quarter of a million hectares, the campesinos were prevented from soliciting lands and were sometimes driven off. Bosques fooled some with promises of small private properties, but the contracts were not formalized, and the solicitations disappeared. The campesinos did not abandon their lands willingly but were forced to migrate in search of work. She stated that the DAAC should make it clear that Bosques is not permitted to rent or sell properties. She concluded by hoping, along with López Mateos, that national lands would be distributed as ejidos.[53]

Hacienda Santo Domingo

One of the first land invasions, in 1960, was led by Dionisio Sánchez Lozoya on the Hacienda Santo Domingo, property of U.S. citizen William Stevens. It was located some thirty kilometers southwest of Villa Ahumada (itself

125 kilometers south of Juárez) and contained some 166,000 hectares with thermal springs and artesian wells. The property was rented out. In a report dated 1958 to the office that became the DAAC, an agronomist reported that none of the cattle on the property belonged to the owner, although he held a CIG based on his own livestock, and that the property contained abundant artesian water, although the owner had been plugging up the springs to make the property less attractive to colonization. The land was being solicited by two groups: the NCP Santo Domingo, associated with the Liga de Comunidades Agrarias (LCA; League of Agrarian Communities), which was associated with the CNC and the PRI; and the NCP Villa Ahumada and its affiliates, El Porvenir and Ejidos Unidos Constitución de 1857 Segundo, which were associated with the División del Norte Front, named for Pancho Villa's legendary army, and the UGOCM, who invaded in May–June 1960, in February, April, August, and October 1961, and in May 1962.[54] Sánchez, a former Villista lieutenant, now in his seventies and a resident of Ciudad Juárez, often worked with the UGOCM but maintained his independence.

Judith Reyes described her participation in the occupation of Santo Domingo as follows:

> On May 22, 1960, 184 campesino families of the División del Norte hurled themselves into the occupation of the barrio known as *El Triste* [The Sad One], which corresponded to the main house of the former hacienda of Santo Domingo. . . . I arrived with eight tons of food collected by going door-to-door in Parral. . . . I was harassed by the police and soldiers who tried to take my things. When I finally arrived, a lieutenant tried to delay the distribution of food, but knowing how hunger hurts, I insisted on doing it immediately. By the end of the day, my fingers were sore, and my hands were bleeding . . . from handling so many boxes and from putting so much grain into sacks and tying them up with fibers.[55]

This invasion was dislodged on June 10, and the campesino leaders were jailed for some twenty days.[56]

In 1961 Reyes would compose and sing the "Corrido of Santo Domingo":

> Son las armas de la Patria contra los campesinos,
> las mujeres, los ancianos, y como 300 niños.
> Linda gente de Parral, linda la Ciudad de Juárez

nos trajeron alimentos a pesar de los pesares.
Año del sesenta y uno en la prensa se leía
la repartición de tierras que López Mateos hacía.
Pero sólo eran noticias lejos de las realidades
porque la Reforma Agraria es demagogia en cantidades.

(They are the arms of the country against the campesinos,
the women, the old folk, and some three hundred children.
Lovely people of Parral, lovely people of Ciudad Juárez
brought us food despite their hardships.
It was the year of sixty-one and one read in the press
of the distribution of lands by López Mateos.
But it was just news, far from reality
because the Agrarian Reform is a matter of demagogy.)

The struggle for Santo Domingo continued for years. The invasions became semipermanent and included families who had nowhere else to go. Judith Reyes described both the hardship and community she found there. Often the suffering was acute, particularly when the families lost their access to water. On July 19, 1960, the owner Stevens died. On November 24, the federal government acquired part of the property, and presidential resolutions were signed turning over land to nine new centers of population, eight associated with the LCA/CNC and one with the División del Norte and the UGOCM. This was consistent with the government's policy of distributions to campesinos associated with the CNC. The NCP Villa Ahumada and Dionisio Sánchez condemned this resolution and continued to invade the property until 1962.[57]

On January 14, 1961, Sánchez Lozoya met with Jacinto López in Mexico City to report that the day before a platoon of cavalry had attempted to dislodge four hundred campesinos representing the one thousand heads of family in possession of the center of Santo Domingo.[58] In February, *Indice* reported that the army had repelled a fourth attempt to invade on January 31.[59] Also in February, Carlota Murrieta de Estrada, a member of the UGOCM, sent a telegram to Eva Samaniego, the wife of Adolfo López Mateos, signed by four hundred women and asking the army to permit medicines and food to enter Santo Domingo to relieve a bronchitis epidemic in which four children had already died.[60] *Indice* reported that López Mateos had ordered Roberto

Barrios, director of the national DAAC, to write to Governor Teófilo Borunda and ask him to meet with Dionisio Sánchez.[61] On May 8, campesino leaders complained that the army had cut the water supply to Santo Domingo and was not letting them approach the wells.[62]

A number of other agrarian conflicts simmered in the state. Sánchez Lozoya published a list of ejidos and communities in dispute without detailing what the conflicts were: Ejido La Cruz, Municipio La Cruz; Ejido Nombre de Dios; Ejido Nonoava; Regional Campesino Committee of Parral; Ejido Anáhuac; Ejido Carbonera; Ejido Los Angeles in Balleza; Poblado Carbajal de Arriba and de Abajo; Ejido El Aguila; Ejido Carboneras; Ejidos El Cairo and Francisco Madera; Ejido Las Fuentes; Ejido Casas Grandes; Ejidos San Isidro, Jesús Carranza, Zaragoza, and Salvador Juárez, all in Municipio Juárez; and Ejido Ascensión.[63]

Sánchez Lozoya went on to report on problems in Ejido Ignacio Zaragoza in Casas Grandes:

> For seven years there had been no accounting of funds, either for the rent of pastures or from forestry contracts. For seven years, the four sawmills of the Timber Company of the Northwest, property of Deputy Teófilo Borunda [Borunda was governor from 1956 to 1962] had produced forty thousand feet of lumber daily. Yet its workers were paid with chits for the store belonging to the president of the ejidal commission, as if it were a company store. In seven years the company has processed seventy thousand pines, or forty-eight-thousand square meters, twenty million feet with a value of twelve million pesos. The latest forestry exploitations were realized without contracts or forestry studies despite repeated orders from the federal DAAC to the agrarian delegate of the state to change the ejidal commissioner, to no avail.

He finished by remarking that another invasion of the Santo Domingo had been dislodged.[64]

Strikes at Celulosa

In early 1960, Section Sixteen of the Workers of the Paper, Cardboard, Cellulose, and Raw Materials Industry in Anáhuac, site of the pulp-processing subsidiaries of Bosques, threatened an imminent strike demanding a 75 percent pay raise, the suppression of illegal rent payments, and reforms to contract clauses favoring industry. A cartoon published in *Indice* portrayed Eloy Santiago Vallina, a major owner in both Bosques and Celulosa, as an octopus lamenting that "The Chihuahuans do not understand my sacrifices."[65] Vallina was killed in a bizarre incident later that year when a retired army major whose daughter had been romantically involved with Vallina's son came to his door and shot him for insinuating that his daughter was not good enough to marry a Vallina.[66] The Vallina mansion on the outskirts of Chihuahua was modeled on the big house on the plantation Tara in *Gone with the Wind*.

When the strike at Celulosa broke out, this halted the operations of Plywood Ponderosa and Viscosa, also in Anáhuac, for lack of raw materials. Students at the State Normal School, the Normal Night School, the Technical School (La Escuela de Artes y Oficios, where men learned various trades, including carpentry, shoemaking, binding, soldering, and radio and television repair), and the Technical School for Young Ladies (La Escuela Industrial para Señoritas) organized a support committee for the workers; they held a rally on March 6 in front of the cathedral and distributed leaflets. The students also demanded the partition of Bosques de Chihuahua and its division among the campesinos of Madera and Temósachic and justice for the murder of Francisco Luján. After nineteen days, the workers had won enough demands to call off the strike and return to work. This was the first time the students had announced their public support for workers and campesinos soliciting land.[67]

A year and a half later, workers at Ponderosa Plywood were back on strike, led by the Confederación Regional Obrera Mexicana (Regional Confederation of Mexican Workers, CROM), in a battle for recognition. Three weeks later they won most of their demands.[68]

On January 4, 1963, the workers at Celulosa organized a union in three factories associated with Bosques de Chihuahua—Celulosa, Ponderosa, and Triply—but the new union officials were fired after refusing management bribes. *Indice* accused Rafael Vallina of terrorizing the workers; Vallina retaliated by closing the plants and accusing the workers of sabotage. He cut off the lights, water, and sewers to company houses along with access to the hospital and primary school, advising the workers to move to Chihuahua City.[69] In January, 1964, *Indice* reported that workers with union connections had been fired, including the leader of the 1960 Celulosa strike, Jesús González Sánchez. *Indice* quoted Article 123 of the constitution of 1917, which guarantees the rights of workers, including the eight-hour day, the right to strike, the right to rest one day a week, protection for women and children, and the right to indemnification in cases of unjustified termination.[70]

Práxedis Giner Durán

The end of Teófilo Borunda's term as governor in 1962 was marked by financial scandal focused on his construction of the canal channeling the Río Chuvíscar through the capital city. A year before, he had declared the treasury empty and suspended public services, stopped public works, and ceased to pay teachers and office workers. He had fired five hundred state employees. Borunda was closely associated with former president Miguel Alemán, while the incoming governor General Práxedis Giner Durán, the former head of the Cattlemen's Association, was close to the big ranchers.[71]

Giner Durán was born in 1893 in Camargo, Chihuahua. He fought with Pancho Villa's Division of the North, rose in the ranks, and was commander of the Fifth Military Zone before becoming governor. The PRI chose him as a hard-liner when previous governor Teófilo Borunda was accused of being soft on communism for failing to control demonstrations in support of Cuba and the formation of a local chapter of the Movimiento de Liberación Nacional.[72] Giner explained, in a memorandum to the federal government dated spring 1966, that he was the "most anticommunist" of all the governors and that the United States, which bordered his state, knew they could count on him for the suppression of communism. Giner bragged of creating problems where they had not existed by closing schools and dormitories, by delaying finding jobs for graduating normalistas, and by firing a popular teacher.[73] The communists kept him in power, since as long as they threatened, the federal authority would not remove him, and so he grafted Cold War rhetoric onto existing conflicts. Giner also faced considerable opposition from factions within the state government, discussed below, and earned the enmity of the local daily newspaper, part of the powerful García Valseca chain, for refusing to pay for his campaign propaganda.[74]

Other governors were removed for less.[75] During the last days of President López Mateos's administration, he removed the governor of Puebla for allowing protests to get out of hand.[76] And Gustavo Díaz Ordaz removed the governor of Durango for similar protests in 1966. Yet Giner Durán served out his term, despite years of tumult culminating in the attack on the army.

El Mineral de Dolores

On December 7, 1962, Salvador Gaytán won election as sectional president of the Mineral de Dolores as a candidate of the PPS against the local boss, Leonardo Olivas, who had held that office for eighteen years. Four days later, Arturo Gámiz arrived to give classes without pay to some eighty-five children; he had not graduated from normal school, and this was not a formal appointment. Gámiz had met Salvador's brother, Salomón, in Chihuahua City at a protest meeting. Dolores had been without a teacher for some twenty-eight years. Gámiz initially gave classes in the plaza, while the community rebuilt the school, naming it for Francisco Villa.[77] Dolores was close to the Sonora border and nearly inaccessible because of the lack of adequate roads and bridges.

Salvador's father, Rosendo Gaytán, had arrived in Dolores in 1925 from Moris, also in the sierra, and had fought with Socorro Rivera for the partition of the Hacienda Babícora. Rosendo's mother was of Apache descent. Members of the family had been secretaries and carpenters at the mine, employees of the Lee companies.[78] Rosendo's sons Salomón and Juan Antonio, along with their nephews Antonio and Guadalupe Scobell Gaytán, lost their lives in armed actions; Salvador participated in both the GPG and in later guerrilla movements.

Cebadilla de Dolores is often confused with the Mineral de Dolores; the Mineral, and not Cebadilla, was the sectional head of the municipality of Madera where Salvador Gaytán was president and Arturo Gámiz taught. Cebadilla de Dolores was a small hamlet that became an ejido in 1948; it was the site of the First Encounter of the Sierra Pancho Villa in 1963 and came close to constituting a guerrilla *foco*, or center of armed resistance, in the sierra. A deep barranca separates it from the Mineral de Dolores some thirty kilometers away; a photo titled *Mina de Dolores desde Cebadilla de Dolores* has been published online.[79] No paved road has ever linked the two locations.

The nucleus of the ejido was formed in 1948 when the community sought to regain land taken by Francisco Portillo to form the Hacienda Sírupa, granted a twenty-five-year certificate of exemption in 1946.[80] In 1955, a presidential decree granted the community one thousand hectares of grazing land taken from Bosques; they continued to press their petition, claiming the land was too steep and rocky and pressing for the better land occupied by the hacienda. The community repeatedly invaded the hacienda lands and over the years won possession of parcels of various sizes. In August 1963, López Mateos formally granted them the fifty hectares under the community center; in September

FIGURE 5 Road sign outside Madera City. Photo by the author.

1964, they received another three thousand hectares from Bosques. In 1970, 34,840 hectares of the former Sírupa Hacienda were finally distributed to the community with the expiration of the certificate of exemption.[81] The populated center was abandoned in the 1970s as families moved to Madera for schools, and the ejidatarios are now engaged in small-scale logging.

Following Gaytán's election in 1962, the community of Dolores regained control of its school, reservoir, and communal orchard. They built basketball and volleyball courts and initiated vaccination campaigns against diphtheria, tetanus, and measles. They built a bridge over the Sírupa River with donated materials. They renewed their petition for amplification of the ejido, which had languished for a number of years in the hands of the agrarian bureaucracy.[82]

On August 5, 1964, Leonel Chávez Reyes, treasurer of the municipality of Madera, reported on the achievements of his administration from October 1963 to June 1964, including a report of work done from October 10, 1962, to June 30, 1964.[83] The prisoners of the town jail had cleaned the municipal cemetery, and the city had erected crosses on the graves of Socorro Rivera, Manuel Jiménez, and Crescencio Macias, "martyrs of the struggle for the partitioning of the former Hacienda Babícora."[84] Under the heading "Various Public Works in the Municipality," the report contained a section on the Ex-Mineral of Dolores. First, the sectional president was changed after eighteen years, "although it seems unbelievable," during which time no public works had been done. The school, which had not functioned for some twenty years and had fallen into ruin, was rebuilt with private donations and volunteer labor. The state department of education, after repeated requests, sent a teacher paid by them in January 1963. (In fact Gámiz arrived in December and came on his own as a volunteer.) The road from Madera was repaired, again with volunteer labor and donated materials. The report says a new hanging bridge was constructed over the Río Dolores, although it was in fact the Río Sírupa, to replace one long out of service; the materials arrived on the backs of mules. A dam was repaired. The town hall and plaza were repaired, again at no cost to the municipality.[85] In the section called "Education," the final item is "Teachers." Here the author notes that eight teachers had been sent to various locations and that five more were needed "to totally resolve the problem, avoiding thus the arrival of teachers paid by outsiders, who only come to propagate foreign ideologies, the cause of the recent events in the Mineral of Dolores."[86] Here the treasurer praised the work initiated by Salvador Gaytán and Arturo Gámiz without naming them, since they were then known to have taken up arms and, in the same report, the treasurer warned against them.

In January 1963, the UGOCM led dozens of land invasions throughout the state; they were evicted by the army. *Acción* argued that the land invasions were intended to awaken the public, public attention being the campesinos' only weapon, in the face of the marked illegalities committed by latifundistas and state agents. They showed that conditions in the countryside could not continue—neither the unemployment nor the hunger—and that if the problem were not solved peacefully, violence would soon erupt.[87] The invasions were also the campesinos' way of positing an alternate reality in which they could act and not always be acted upon, in which they were not forced to wait for a remote bureaucracy to proceed on their behalf. They asserted their own interpretation of legality and justice through direct action, choosing leaders from among themselves. During the invasions they lived communally, forging ever tighter bonds.

On January 4, an El Paso newspaper published an article with the headline "Reds Leading Invaders: Hundreds Camp On Ranches." They reported three ranches, all one hundred miles from El Paso, seized by "squatters" led by "procommunists."[88] The United States was afraid of communists on their doorstep and, with no understanding of Mexican agrarian law, saw only menace in the unarmed "squatters." This was another indication of the Cold War rhetoric from the United States that Giner exploited to stay in power.

Acción reported that in January, the army had been called out against campesinos invading latifundia in Guadalupe y Calvo, in the remote southern reaches of the sierra, where few other incidents of agrarian unrest were reported during these years. Seven protesters were killed.[89] García Aguirre reported nine properties with CIGs, among them Terrenates, Peñitas, El Madroño, Ojo Peñuelas, and La Morita, invaded in January by four new centers of population: Terrenates in Buenaventura, Profesor Francisco Luján Adame, Guadalupe Victoria, and Pancho Villa.[90]

On January 14, interim governor Saúl González Herrera had another one of countless meetings with Alvaro Ríos and sent Lieutenant Colonel Roberto Martínez Noriega and Licenciado Daniel Luna to confer with the campesinos. They reported that "the members [of the UGOCM], found in various places across the state to carry on the invasions, do not do so because of instructions from their leaders, but when they see some land empty, they invade as they see fit."[91] The protesters were acting on their own behalf. The next day, González Herrera sponsored a trip to Mexico City for UGOCM members, including Ríos, Ricardo Ruelas, Dionisio Sánchez Lozoya, and Nepomucena Vargas; there, Ríos promised to end the invasions. The delegates requested that the president send agronomists to comply with existing presidential resolutions, to take censuses, and to revise certificates of exemption.[92]

In Chihuahua, the UGOCM led a protest against the Mennonite communities around Cuauhtémoc, whom they accused of evading taxes.[93] On January 26, *Indice* published an article attacking Anderson, Clayton, the U.S.-based cotton corporation, and a major landowner in Irrigation Zone Five, claiming the company was bankrupting small- and medium-size cotton-ginning interests and forcing their owners to emigrate.[94]

Víctor Manuel Bueno, the former director of López Mateos's Office of Complaints, was jailed in Chihuahua, accused of fraud. Bueno had accused the state director of DAAC, Eduardo Juárez Santos Coy, of lying about his inspection of the Haciendas La Morita and Peñuelas, property of Hilario Gavilondo, in the municipality of Janos. They had twice received CIGs, in August 1940 and August 1949, and contained double the amount of land allowed by law.[95] Meanwhile, a number of Chihuahua banks wrote to López Mateos requesting his intervention because, given the level of agitation and the invasions throughout the state, the banks were reluctant to offer credit to cattlemen since their lands could no longer serve as guarantees.[96] In February, *Indice* accused Esteban Almeida, a partner in the Banco Comercial Mexicano and scion of a former governor, of selling the Hacienda Santa Rita to Mennonites. He had previously obtained a CIG for forty thousand hectares of that property, although it was farm and not pastureland.[97]

Indice published a letter signed by Arturo Gámiz as the secretary general of the municipal committee of the PPS, claiming that two hundred new centers of population had initiated agrarian solicitations some twenty years ago that remained unresolved; he blamed official *tortugismo* (moving like a tortoise). Gámiz summarized the agrarian situation as follows: four hundred latifundistas owned eight million hectares while sixty thousand campesinos had no land.[98] He demanded that the CIGs be revised and that land near the U.S. border be expropriated.[99] He provided a list of ejidos, some promised by López Mateos, along with others that had lost their water rights to encroaching hacendados. He demanded that the Tarahumara of Urique be given their ejido, now years in process, and finally he called for punishment for the killers of Carlos Ríos and Francisco Luján.[100]

Pablo Gómez published "El paracaidismo en Chihuahua" (*paracaidismo* means parachuting, a term applied to land invaders), which began with a clear statement of the movement's legality. "It is not the campesino who invades the land given to him by the revolution but the latifundista who once again takes possession, frustrating the application of the agrarian reform." He accused cowards who hid in the United States (e.g., the landowner Luis Terrazas, who returned in 1920) of plucking the fruits of the revolution, fought by Zapata and Villa so that the campesinos might have a bit of land once the (Porfirian) regime, "creator of great socio-economic difference," was defeated. In Chihuahua, which lacked sufficient agricultural lands because of its aridity, the problems included the theft of water from the Río Grande by its northern neighbor, destroying the agriculture of the Juárez valley all the way to Ojinaga; the monopoly accumulation of land in the hands of a few, displacing economically active families; and demographic increase. The problems were more acute where the forests and pastures were in the hands of bankers, businessmen, industrialists, and government functionaries, who worked in complicity with government officials against the wishes of the agrarian reform, with the "unbelievable" connivance of the CNC, nominally charged with representing the campesinos but put in place by the bourgeoisie in power. The most frequent frauds involved certificates of exemption for livestock that covered only one-fifth of the actual property. The forests had been clear-cut, damaging the water table.[101] Lands had been fraudulently divided, as was the case of Ori (probably Otis) Jeffers in Casas Grandes, who deeded some of his land to his wife. The Spaniard Marcario Pérez, owner of vast extensions in Chihuahua and northern Durango along with a coffee plantation in Brazil, was vulnerable to application of Article 33, which prohibited landownership by foreigners. The majority of agrarian petitions were set aside for more than ten years. Gómez accused the cattlemen of hiding springs to frustrate the campesinos' desire for land. He condemned constitutional violations, the misery of the people, economic inequality, and the campesinos' betrayal by the CNC and agrarian authorities. "These cases were not invasions? This is obeying the law? Can these gentlemen not be accused of being perennial *paracaidistas*? Can they not be accused of the crime of social dissolution?" This, he concluded, was why latifundia were invaded and why the campesinos had joined the UGOCM.[102]

In April, *Acción* rhetorically asked what the UGOCM had received thanks to recent mobilizations and replied, "Promises, insults, persecution, and jail." Natividad Pérez and Rafael and Feliciano Chacón had been in jail for three months in Guerrero City. Carlos and Alberto Durán of El Naranjo had been approached by the Mayor of Madera, who offered them one thousand hectares and five thousand pesos to betray their comrades. Meanwhile, the community of Cebadilla de Dolores was being harassed by the same *caciquillo* who said that the DAAC and the President's Office of Complaints "meant less to him than a bread roll because in this region there is no law but his."[103]

The agrarian campaigns received widespread support throughout the state. Gámiz published a series of articles in *La Voz de Chihuahua*, a small radical newspaper, in May, June, and July of 1963 that were reprinted in *Indice* a year later under the headline, "Professor Arturo Gamis [*sic*] Explained Why They Took Up Arms."[104] Gámiz described the Mineral of Dolores at the turn of the century as having two thousand miners and one hundred mules mining gold and silver. Now maybe fifty inhabitants remained. Twenty years ago, when the mine shut down, the company left behind ruins and nostalgia along with the *cacicazgo* (reign of tyranny) of José Ibarra and Tomás Vega. (Ibarra appeared some years later.) "The evils portrayed in movies of the Old West are nothing compared to them." With the support of Bosques, Ibarra and Vega burned, for example, the *ranchitos* of Timoteo Castellanos in El Salitre and of Olivas in Las

Varas. They killed inhabitants of Agua Amarilla, Carrisitos, Dolores, Temósachic, and others on the highway, and they sent others to jail. They beat and robbed women. They supported the same mayor in Dolores for eighteen years. They were friends of former governor Borunda and other important people. They were the cause of the decadence, anxiety, and injustice in the sierra, and they saw no reason to make improvements.[105]

The UGOCM had now been active in Chihuahua for three years. They had overthrown the sectional president of Dolores in December, and the Four Friends had disbanded several years before. Gámiz cited the events at Santa Rita a year previously, when Alvaro Ríos had led armed campesinos to defend the community, as evidence of a new stage. The campesinos had lost their fear; they were organized and fighting for ejidos as their primary objective. The hour had struck for the *cacicazgos* and *latifundismo*.[106]

During the first days of May, Rosario Prieto and other members of the UGOCM, along with campesinos from the ejidos Zaragoza, Buenaventura, Galeana, and Benito Juárez, invaded La Morita and Ojitos, property of Hilario Gavilondo and the heirs of Carlos Villarreal. They arrived in a group of fifty families with a large number of children. Their eviction by the authorities was expected.[107]

On May 27, campesinos invaded six ranches: San Miguel, San Ambrosio, Terrenates, Las Varas, Agua Nueva, and La Morita.[108] Andrés Gastélum, national UGOCM leader, denied any knowledge of the invasions. Two days later, Gastélum denied accusations by the Cattlemen's Association that he had known of the occupations of Agua Nueva and San Ambrosio. On May 30, the army was called in. On the same day, campesinos invaded the Rancho San Carlos, property of Carlos Muñoz Leyva in Delicias. General Efrén Sámano Hernández convinced them to leave without incident.[109] On May 31, the UGOCM executive committee blamed the invasions on the DAAC.[110]

On June 1, *Indice* published a front-page editorial from Alvaro Ríos, "leader of the men without land in the state," pointing out that Chihuahua had been the state with the largest land concentrations before 1910 and that this had precipitated the revolution; that any country whose economic basis was agriculture would be poor; and that industrialization required the internal market that Mexico lacked, since 70 percent of the population were campesinos without land of their own. DAAC had become an instrument of the latifundistas. Three hundred landowners had eight million hectares.[111] His 70 percent figure was exaggerated, since half the population was urban by midcentury.

In July, *Acción* published another article by Alvaro Ríos, probably a reworking of his article published on June 1 by *Indice*. Ríos explained that Mexico was underdeveloped, with low agricultural production not oriented to popular needs but to monoculture and with a foreign policy that followed Yankee imperialists, a judicial system that hardly existed, and no tradition of planning. He blamed the United States for Mexico's low internal development, as Mexico's role was to supply raw materials and a market to the United States. The living standards of the campesinos would have to be raised to create an internal market. Monopoly landholding caused misery and backwardness, while the principle enemy was Yankee imperialism.[112] This article reflected the PPS's emphasis on U.S. imperialism over domestic reaction.

Troops of the Twentieth Cavalry dislodged the occupation of Sombreretillo, in Matamoros, a large property owned by the Chávez family that had been divided among fictitious owners, some of them family servants. *Acción* published a photo of soldiers standing behind the campesinos, who were walking away with a huge Mexican flag. Alfredo Chávez had been governor of the state from 1940–44.[113]

Judith Reyes contrasted the attitude of General Liborio Olivera Salazar, in charge of troops at Sombreretillo, with that of Major Jorge Garzón, who had dislodged campesinos from the latifundium Agua Nueva, property of Federico Sisniego, the grandson of Luis Terrazas, with "energy, courtesy, understanding, and respect for the white flag with the slogan *Tierra y Libertad*."[114] She mentioned the arrival of General Antonio Gómez Velazco, the new commander of the Fifth Military Zone, in Chihuahua.[115] A year later, Gómez Velasco would evict the cacique José Ibarra from Madera and Temósachic. On June 22, *Indice* reported that Judith Reyes had been beaten the month before by two gunmen who had followed her for two days.[116] Reyes herself published nothing about the attack.

In June, Raúl Gómez Ramírez was removed from his post as director of School Number Eighty in Delicias following the invasion of the nearby property of Arturo Grifel. *Acción* accused Francisco Javier Alvarez, state director of education, of firing him for the "crime of sympathizing with the campesinos . . . and being a communist and dangerous source of exotic ideas," while suggesting that the leader of section fifteen of the teachers' union, Adaucto González, might have a motive for firing anyone who could compete for his position in the union. Gómez announced his intention to teach adults at the night school in Delicias as a volunteer.[117] According to the DFS, the governor ordered both

Raúl Gómez and his brother Simón fired and Pablo transferred as punishment for the wave of invasions. Arrest warrants for Raúl Gómez and Alvaro Ríos were also issued. Félix Caro, accused as leader of the invasions, was arrested in Camargo, accused of robbery and criminal association.[118]

On July 7, the secretary general of the Confederación Nacional de Campesinos, Javier Rojo Gómez, convened a forestry congress in Chihuahua to organize the Tarahumara to use "powerful ejidal organizations" to defend their forests. *Acción* remarked that "powerful interests" constituted an impassible barrier that one man was unlikely to overcome, but that until they were betrayed, the campesinos could still hope. In the next issue, *Acción* accused Rojo of using the congress as part of an electoral campaign and of appointing Refugio Rodríguez as head of the state forestry association, although "he knows nothing about trees." Rojo Gómez flew back to Mexico City on the same plane as leaders of the Cattlemen's Association.[119]

On August 18, *Acción* again reported on the case of Juan and Alberto Durán and Carlos Yáñez, who were still in jail in Guerrero even though the federal office of DAAC had asked Giner to intervene on their behalf. They had been accused by Bosques, "through their puppets, Ramón Molina and Juan Alvarez," of invading land in Los Aguajes and El Durazno in Madera and of damages in the amount of one hundred fifty thousand pesos. *Acción* pointed out that Molina and Alvarez could not legally possess land that Bosques could not have legally sold, since Bosques had only "an unconstitutional forestry permit" and that the accused had lived for more than forty years (Yáñez) and twenty-six years (the Duráns) on the land in question. *Acción* demanded that the state attorney general, Hipólito Villa Rentería, take action on their behalf.[120] The DFS report on the case added that they had been arrested by Lieutenant Colonel Roberto Martínez Noriega, "who received his salary from Bosques." They also mentioned the case of Ubaldo Olivas, "arrested some time ago, although he had lived for sixteen years within the limits of what the company claims."[121]

In Cebadilla de Dolores, Francisco Portillo destroyed the ejido's corn crop, sending goons to cut it down with machetes, so that he could build a fence on ejido land that would keep the ejidatarios from watering their livestock at the artesian waterhole and would extend the Hacienda Sírupa by some thirty-four hectares. The *Acción* article stated that the campesinos had been there since 1905, while Portillo had only appeared "eighteen years ago."[122]

Indice and *Acción* published the following anonymous letters that summer:

Here comes a supposed lieutenant or colonel, a pimp for Bosques, and his gunmen threaten us, tell us that the governor gave instructions that we have fifteen days to leave, when we have lived and worked here for more than forty years. . . . Here we have our little houses, our *ranchitos*, the lands we opened to cultivation, the schools we built with so much sacrifice. . . . We can't believe the governor gave the order. When we marched in a caravan to see him, he promised to support us and said he was one of us. Leaving Agua Prieta with Villa's defeated army, he passed through here and saw only humble campesinos. Vallina, Trouyet, and Bosques were still unknown. For years we have tried to legalize our titles, and we will only leave in coffins.[123]

They trample us, tear down our fences, burn our homes, kill our companions, and all because we do not leave our lands. And why should we leave if we were born here and have lived here all our lives? When we arrived, it was all abandoned, our fathers and some of us fought against the Apaches who came from the north and defended with our blood what they want to take. What right have Don Carlos Trouyet, Don Carlos Serrano, the Vallinas, and those who have been enriched with the sweat of the poor to take what has cost us so much effort and sacrifice?[124]

A few days ago everyone who lived inside the lands of Bosques de Chihuahua was given ten days to leave. We are not leaving. Those who should go are the *gachupín* exploiters and usurers, the Vallinas. The exploitation of the forest only benefits its owners; the workers are now living in conditions that are worse or as bad as before. We are the real owners of the forests; look how they leave them clear-cut. They say they opened industries and provided jobs for thousands; that is true, but the workers now live in misery. We were better off before they arrived; there was work, money, not so much crime and harassment, and we all lived better despite our poverty. They began by taking what we all considered ours, our lands, our water, our forests. They imposed rent on those who did not want to leave. When we refused, they forced us out with their white guards, judicial police, and army; they burn our homes, pursue us, threaten us, put us in jail, and if that doesn't work, they kill us. All this has been constant since Bosques and their gunmen took over this region. But we are organized to defend ourselves—if they could not evict many before, they will evict fewer now. We ask the authorities why they don't uphold the law instead of making us defend ourselves? We do not want to resort to violence; we have suffered enough. We want the DAAC to legalize possession of the lands we have had for fifty years.[125]

The Mexico City journalist Roberto Blanco Moheno, who visited Chihuahua in 1964, reported that the root of the conflict was corruption in the DAAC, whose officials were blackmailing the state's latifundistas with the threat of expropriation, accepting bribes to protect their properties, and distributing arid lands to comply with presidential resolutions. He cited the example of Santo Domingo, where some two hundred families had been left in intolerable conditions, finally abandoning the new centers of population. Another example he cited was that of a place called Charco de Piedra (probably Charco de Peña), where eighty colonists had received property more than twenty years ago on land that would not support them any more but where the DAAC brought more than one thousand more campesinos instead of taking land from the four haciendas in the surrounding area, haciendas that the DAAC extorted instead of expropriating. In Palomas, hundreds of campesinos received worthless land. Blanco Moheno named the latifundistas in Irrigation Zone Five: General Antonio Guerrero, with half a million hectares of good land; Esteban Almeida; Emilio Pinoncely; Roberto Schneider; the former governor Alfredo Chávez; the family of former governor Quevedo; the family of Eloy Vallina; Enrique Hernández Gómez, state treasurer; former governor Teófilo Borunda; and the widow of Muñoz with more than forty lots near Delicias. In all, eight million hectares were in the hands of three hundred families. Blanco Moheno also blamed the conflicts on Giner Durán's lack of political tact as revealed in his announcement that "All this agrarismo is bullshit [*pendejada*]. The lands should go back to the hacendados."[126]

Juan José Salas, of the NCP Pancho Villa in Casas Grandes, announced that four hundred women representing eight hundred ejidatarios would depart in a caravan for Mexico City to meet with the president. For the last four years, they had been asking DAAC to survey La Morita and Ojos de Peñuela, property of Hilario Gavilondo, who lived in the United States but held a certificate of exemption for 19,666 hectares. The women accused Gavilondo of having purchased the agronomists who came to do the survey. Salas added that the women would send a document with all the details to the president and the secretary of government, complaining that the owner was using good agricultural land for grazing. They asked the president to resolve the problems without going through DAAC, since DAAC would only visit the landowner, take his money, and return to the office without having seen the land.[127] Later that month, Salas announced that three agronomists had arrived who had been sent by the president to investigate the situation.[128]

Students

The constitution of 1917 mandated that education be secular, free, and obligatory for all Mexicans. The schools created after the revolution intended teachers to serve as conduits, linking the poor and marginal with the rest of the country and creating a national identity. The schools were sites where cultural forms of belonging were negotiated between local communities and national directives. The rural schools would make citizens of far-flung indigenous villagers, teaching them Spanish, hygiene, and science. Alongside their fierce anticlericalism, the schools were imbued with a devout sense of mission. In the 1930s, President Lázaro Cárdenas created schools that were socialist, forming teachers who were community leaders and "intellectuals of the poor."[129] The schools were an essential element in the Cardenista plan to incorporate the nation's campesinos and workers into blocs to support the state against its enemies: large landholders, the industrial elite, foreigners, and the church. Teachers became advocates both for workers seeking to enforce the right to organize and for campesinos demanding land reform. But the Cardenista project used teachers to mobilize campesinos and workers within a capitalist structure. They were organized not into their own autonomous groups but as subordinate units of the state.[130]

When Manuel Avila Camacho replaced Cárdenas as president in 1940, he imposed a series of reforms: the shift from scientific to national revolutionary socialism, the purging of communists (only partially successful), and the segregation of boys and girls into separate dormitories and schools. There were also more insidious moves to isolate the schools from the surrounding countryside by means of the elimination of agriculture from their curriculum and the attempt to reduce their influence on nearby primary schools. Finally, the Secretaría de Educación Pública (SEP; Department of Public Education) ordered that the rural and state (urban) normal schools share a uniform curriculum. This reorientation was in line with the general midcentury turn from countryside to city, but it did not break the tradition of social activism that continued to animate the rural schools where the agrarian dream lived on.[131] Initially employed as vehicles of consensus, by midcentury teachers and normalistas were just as frequently agents of social change who sought to uphold the legacy of the revolution by opposing its betrayal by contemporary politicians.

The rural normalistas were the children of campesinos; many had been raised on family histories of agrarian battles. They entered the schools as young as twelve, after graduating from primary school. Candidates were selected by their teachers and often came from families who had joined collective actions. The students lived in dormitories, in austere conditions with rigorous discipline, where they formed lifelong bonds. Their food, clothes, and medical care were provided for, which meant that many students lived better than they had at home. While salaries for rural teachers were abysmal, they were a step out of extreme poverty, and teachers were respected, particularly in the countryside. The rural normal schools provided social and economic opportunities, particularly to women, who could gain authority and independence through teaching. They also provided the state with a safety valve by giving the most ambitious children of the countryside a path to social mobility.

Both rural and urban normal schools developed their own politicized culture. Many teachers were Marxist, and some were veterans of the 1930s and the heyday of socialist education. By the early 1960s, under the leadership of Luis Urías Belderráin, the State Normal School of Chihuahua "was becoming an institution where discussions and analysis of the Cuban Revolution, the Soviet Union, Yankee imperialism, or the agrarian reform were part of everyday life."[132] Students studied the Agrarian Code and counseled solicitants. García Aguirre described the continuities of the early sixties: "political discussions and arguments occurred daily. The assemblies, the democracy of majority rule, and preparing speeches for debate were resources learned and reproduced from the 1930s."[133] The students frequently interrupted everyday routine, striking to remove teachers or to obtain better living conditions. In 1964, they undertook a prolonged strike to protest the governor's closure of dormitories in the capital.

Many of the students were members of the Juventud Comunista de México, the youth group of the PCM, or the rival Juventud Popular (JP) of the PPS, but there were numerous examples of their putting aside sectarian differences to work together.

The heritage of socialist education and the persistent politicization of the schools, their poverty, and their origins in the countryside led the students to join the campesino movement then gaining force. They were radicalized not only within the schools and political parties—taught from above—but also by their daily experience of struggle, by the energy and enthusiasm of the movement and the joy of being part of something bigger than themselves, and by the corresponding recalcitrance of the state government and the brutality of the armed forces. The students who took part in campesino actions in the early 1960s did not only come from the two rural normals. There was substantial participation from the State Normal School, the Technical School, the Technical School for

Young Ladies, and their respective night schools, all in the capital. During the strike wave of 1964–1965, secondary schools throughout the state joined in.

The national Federación de Estudiantes Campesinos Socialistas de México (FECSM; Federation of Socialist Campesino Students of Mexico) was founded in 1935 with the goal of maintaining a presence in every rural normal school. They closed their assemblies singing the "Internationale," the communist anthem.[134] Unlike other organizations of the Cárdenas years, the state was unable to co-opt and incorporate them. In May 1961, there was a split in the national FECSM, when the group led by Lucio Cabañas Barrientos, then a student at the rural normal in Ayotzinapa, Guerrero, defeated the group led by Antonio Valtierra of Salaices in Chihuahua by one vote. The organization divided into groups called "the north" and "the south" until November 1964. Several members of Cabañas's group were members of the PRI, although Cabañas himself belonged to the PCM, and the Salaicinos rejected any sort of party affiliation. In Chihuahua, the Salaicinos were notably less involved in the wave of land invasions and eventually declared their opposition to armed struggle, although Miguel Quiñónez, killed in the attack on the base, was a Salaices graduate. Students in Chihuahua formed their own organization. The Federación Estudiantil de Chihuahua (FECH; Federation of Chihuahua Students) was inaugurated in May 1962 with more than three thousand delegates from schools around the state.[135]

Members of the JP helped the campesinos with their petitions to the DAAC along with UGOCM members. They also supported the invasions, providing beans and flour and connecting the campesino nucleuses with one another. The first students, and some teachers, to join the invasions did so as members of the UGOCM or JP and not as representatives of their particular schools. As leaders, they planned invasions, set up regional organizations, and met with agrarian officials.[136] Later the schools acted through their own student associations. Led by Arturo Gámiz, Eduardo and Guillermo Rodríguez Ford, Hildebrando Gaytán (not related to the Gaytáns of Madera), and Saúl Chacón, students at the State Normal and Normal Night Schools organized study groups within the JP.[137]

Because of deteriorating conditions in the former hacienda where it was housed, in September 1962 the girls' rural normal school moved from Flores Magón to a new building in Saucillo, in Irrigation Zone Five and closer to the boys' school at Salaices. The young women began taking part in invasions and collecting food for the movement. Pablo Gómez, a teacher at Saucillo, also influenced the students' participation. Clara Elena Gutiérrez, one of the most militant students, explained that the UGOCM would invite the student association to choose students to participate in invasions and would distribute them around the state.

In early June 1963, in the Plaza Hidalgo, the FECH presided over a rally of some three hundred people supporting the campesinos and protesting the firing of the Gómez brothers.[138] Simón and Raúl Gómez were reinstated, although Raúl was threatened again shortly thereafter. On June 8, *Indice* published an advertisement signed by section fifteen (the federal, or rural, teachers) of the teachers' union praising the three Gómez Ramírez brothers alongside a front-page editorial thanking the governor for their release. They also ran full-page ads, purchased by the Cattlemen's Association, warning of subversion. In the same issue, Alvaro Ríos published an article accusing the governor of defending the latifundistas and being an enemy of the campesinos, having sent soldiers against the campesinos occupying Santo Domingo when he was commander of the Fifth Military Zone and turning it into "a concentration camp." He added that Giner, before becoming governor, had helped the campesinos living on lands within the Bosques concession. But after his election, the same campesino leaders he had previously supported were met with "rudeness and insults," while the governor stated, "The problem is not agrarian but one of agitators." Ríos further remarked on the existence of a "fantasy commission of surveyors and technicians" meant to execute presidential resolutions.[139]

In June, *Acción* asked the Cattlemen's Association when they would return the camera taken from their reporter, Arturo Gámiz, in Delicias. They accused the "gachupín" (Spaniard), Macario Pérez, of illegally holding land in the state of Durango as well as in Namiquipa in Chihuahua.[140]

Acción pointed to the existence of a power struggle between Giner and his predecessor Borunda: despite his campaign promise to sweep away elements of the former regime, Giner did not notice that Borunda had a whole gestapo of spies within the government who seemed to support the governor but were actually loyal to Borunda and worked in favor of alemanismo (Miguel Alemán was the former president of the republic) and its supporters.[141] There were serious conflicts between Giner and secretary of government Enrique Hernández Gómez, discussed below, but their effect on the protest movement was unclear, and neither faction seemed to have intervened on behalf of the campesinos.[142] The significance to repeated claims that Borunda was "alemanista" may be that he was allied with Bosques, representing the state's industrial future, while

Giner, as former head of the Cattlemen's Association, a distinction he shared with several other governors, was sympathetic to the more traditional economy of large ranching.

In the same issue, Judith Reyes reported on her encounter with General Manuel Mendoza Domínguez, chief of the state judicial police, and his attempt to give her a "lesson in journalism" in the governor's waiting room, saying what she did was "not journalism but agitation" and threatening to put her in jail.[143]

In yet another meeting in Mexico City with DAAC officials, Alvaro Ríos agreed once again to suspend the invasions provided Santos Coy brought eight agronomists to begin the execution of existing presidential resolutions. If the work were not begun by the end of June, the invasions would start up again.[144]

Acción reported that Alvaro Ríos was being followed by an FBI agent hired by the local police who wore a false beard as disguise and went door-to-door in the capital asking for Ríos and saying, "Fidel [Castro] wants him at the police station." The agent had been instructed to identify Ríos by a mole behind his left ear and carried a magnifying glass the size of a frying pan and looked behind everyone's left ears.[145]

Acción accused the Cano family of attempting to dam the Río Santa Isabel, one of the few perennial rivers in the state, to make a lake and private water park in Jacales, near the town of General Trias, formerly Santa Isabel, contravening Article 27 of the constitution that decreed that the waters belong to the nation.[146]

In August, *Indice* published an editorial complaining that Giner was sending the campesinos to live in the desert, believing it was enough to simply distribute land, but that without the means to work it, the land was good for nothing. They cited Santo Domingo as an example. The same issue carried a letter of support from the wood-processing unions of Anáhuac to the campesinos of Madera.[147]

Acción published an article about a conflict in the Ejido El Porvenir, without specifying the municipality, stating that the ejidatarios were being threatened with partition as the result of an "illegal reclamation" by the Bazúa family, who had abandoned those lands some twenty-five years earlier. The ejidatarios had been working them since 1922 with a presidential resolution in their favor, but the judge of the second district court in Juárez had ruled against them, jailed their leaders twice and authorized the claimants to put up a fence. The ejidatarios' possessions had been destroyed and their harvests trampled, but they responded "with serenity, with confidence in the federal government, and without violence."[148]

FIGURE 6 Rancheria in the sierra. Photo by the author.

In late August, Rafael Hernández of the UGOCM attempted to lead invasions of Casa Colorada, Cobriza, and San Mateo in the municipality of Santa Barbara; they were prevented by the Twentieth Cavalry Regiment, who arrested fifteen campesinos and their leader, then released the campesinos. The invaders demanded permission to plow lands meant for imminent delivery, an end to repression, and the government to stop treating them as criminals. They warned that if their demands were not met by September 15, they would sit in at the offices of the DAAC.[149] Among their cases was that of the Ejido Casa Colorada, where the campesinos had generated conflicts among themselves that could only be remedied by its amplification.[150] According to RAN Chihuahua, it was never amplified.

Raúl Gómez was again in danger of losing his job. Protests broke out against Javier Alvarez's decision to replace some fifty primary and secondary schoolteachers, in many cases removing them without warning and not giving them new assignments. Three hundred parents of students at School Number Eighty in Delicias, along with the NCP Twentieth of November, the cotton workers union Section Thirty-two, and the teachers' union Section Forty demanded his

FIGURE 7 UGOCM meeting in Parral. *Left to right*: David Estrada, Pablo Gómez, Alvaro Ríos, Judith Reyes, Jesús Orta, Salustio González, and Arturo Gámiz. Comité Primeros Vientos.

retention. *Acción* asked whether the schools were preparing Mexicans to confront the problems of the nation or just teaching them to be braceros.[151]

First Occupation of the DAAC

On the morning of September 2, not waiting for the deadline they had announced earlier, eighty campesinos, most of them from Delicias, occupied the downtown street in front of the offices of the DAAC and announced their intention to stay until their demands were met. Their banners called for the disappearance of the latifundia and the distribution of land. "The cattle get 30 hectares [the amount calculated to sustain one animal], and us, how many? and when?"[152] They were led by Raúl Gómez and Rosario Prieto, leaders of the UGOCM in Delicias and Casas Grandes, and advised by the students Saúl Chacón and Arturo Gámiz.[153] President Adolfo López Mateos was expected to visit the state at the end of the month. Protesters obtained an interview with the director of DAAC and presented him with an eleven-point petition. On September 3, Gámiz, standing in for Alvaro Ríos, who was not in Chihuahua, led a commission of campesinos to speak with the interim governor, Saúl González Herrera. The state judicial police remained on alert, requesting backup from the Fifth Military Zone.

The businessman Lázaro Villarreal offered protesters the use of the offices of the Partido Auténtico de la Revolución Mexicana (PARM; Authentic Party of the Mexican Revolution), the PRI's loyal opposition, across the street from the DAAC at Calle Ojinaga 617.[154] Villarreal, who owned a large furniture store, bankrolled a number of the movement's activities. In 1955, he and his wife had led mobilizations against Governor Oscar Soto Maynez and forced his resignation. Villarreal may have had his own political ambitions and hoped to replace him. While nominally associated with the PARM, he worked with both the PPS/UGOCM and the PCM/FEP. The committee he organized in the spring of 1964, the Comité Pro Defensa de las Garantías Individuales y Sociales (Comité Pro; Committee for the Defense of Individual and Social Rights), bore a resemblance to the Comité Central Pro Justicia y Derechos Humanos (Central Committee for Justice and Human Rights), which he had organized with his wife some nine years earlier. He also led the local chapter of the Masonic lodge. While he provided substantial logistical and financial support, there is no indication that he directed the movement in ideological terms.

On the afternoon of September 3, the campesinos left the DAAC to march to the state house, a few blocks away, then returned, led by Arturo Gámiz and Raúl and Pablo Gómez. Along the way they handed out fliers explaining that they had been demanding land for years and gotten nothing but promises. In Delicias, the teacher Dolores Armendáriz called a meeting to gather more campesinos for the sit-in before the DAAC. The sit-in would remain for nearly a month, while dormitory students donated part of their meals to feed the participants.

The State Coordinating Committee of the UGOCM published an open letter to the DAAC, the governor, and the attorney general with a list of demands. All new centers of population within Bosques de Chihuahua should immediately receive land—along with others, among them La Nueva Esperanza, Renovación, Terrenates, and Pancho Villa—affecting the latifundia of Federico Sisniega, Roberto Schneider, Edward Payton, Eugene Smith, and Hilario Gavilondo, and cancelling their CIGs. The new centers of population in the regions of Cárdenas, Meoqui, Delicias, Saucillo, Camargo, and Francisco de Conchos, in Irrigation Zone Five, should be satisfied immediately, while Colonia Cárdenas should be made an ejido. The charges against Raúl and Pablo Gómez should be dropped and they should remain in their jobs. Immediate unconditional liberty should be granted to Natividad Pérez, Rafael and Feliciano Chacón, Carlos Yáñez, and Alberto and Juan Durán, all in jail in Guerrero, some of them held against the specific orders of the DAAC for their release. The NCP Conoachic and its additions, Oquirachic and Santa Rita, should receive their land. The administration of Ejido Galeana should be put in the hands of authentic ejidarios. The amplification of Tres Ojitos should be acted on. Without repression, evictions, cancellations of agrarian rights, discrimination against those who were not members of the CNC, or any other arbitrary measures, the DAAC should resolve all outstanding petitions. Only then would the campesinos suspend their mobilizations.[155]

In the governor's first annual report, he claimed to have distributed two hundred thousand hectares, but these dotations had been executed before he took office. Ninety-five percent of the agrarian petitions had been rejected. Sixty-four thousand hectares of Cuatro Vientos de Cebadilla had been rejected as an NCP, although the state had only to act on the 1961 presidential resolution.[156] The case of Sierra Oscura, in Madera (not on the list of RAN Chihuahua), had not been resolved yet either, but Giner took credit for its distribution.[157]

Arturo Gámiz, on behalf of the organizing committee for the UGOCM, wrote to Roberto Barrios, director of the federal DAAC, complaining that in the Ejido Galeano, a Señor González and others were grazing their cattle on ejidal lands without paying rent. He complained that the Mormons of Colonia Levarone (Lebarón) were foreigners and encroaching on ejidal lands. (The Mormons were Mexican citizens.) A Señor Anchonda was selling calves that belonged to the ejido without accounting for the cash received, and the community considered that robbery. Although the ejido held 112,000 hectares, its members had no milk for their children. They demanded a new census, the autonomy to choose their own leaders, an accounting for the sale of livestock and pasture rentals, and finally credit to pay for livestock and other expenses.[158]

On September 14, campesinos, students, and teachers held a rally before the state house. Among the speakers were Cristina Hurtado, director of the Abraham González School; Antonio Becerra Gaytán; Jesús Luján Gutíerrez of the PPS; and Ramón Sánchez. Their principal target was State Director of Education Javier Alvarez. They reiterated their support for the campesino struggles.[159]

More than twenty days after the sit-in in front of the DAAC began, President López Mateos arrived in Chihuahua and granted a meeting to five leaders of the UGOCM: Alvaro Ríos, Arturo Gámiz, Jesús Orta, and Raúl and Pablo Gómez. This was the only meeting he had with popular forces during his brief visit. The UGOCM denounced the governor's refusal to negotiate. The president promised to resolve the situation, saying, "Count on all my support, sympathy, and affection."[160]

First Encounter of the Sierra

During October 7 to 15, the JP organized the First Encounter of the Sierra Francisco Villa in the municipality of Madera, where seventy-five young enthusiasts discussed world and local events and formulated strategies. The meetings took place in Cebadilla de Dolores and included delegates from Tlaxcala, Mexico City, Durango, Coahuila, Sinaloa, Nayarit, and Sonora. For many of the students, it must have been the first time they traveled to the sierra; the sixty-kilometer walk between Madera and Cebadilla, up and down the rocky trail, in cool mountain air scented by pines, would have been a fine introduction. The landscape was full of possibilities not seen on the plains; one could imagine a Sierra Maestra (where the Cuban Revolution was born) with its hiding places, solitudes, and caves. This was contested territory, the homeland of campesinos they had met only in the capital or on marches. The First Encounter created a dynamic attaching the students to a place previously only imagined and the struggle for that place.

The IPS reports on the encounter include ludicrous inventions. According to the agent, on arriving in Madera, before walking to Cebadilla, the students were told to set aside their weapons, which they refused to do. They sang corridos to Fidel Castro and then detonations—presumably firearms—were heard outside town.[161]

The encounter's "Statement of Political Context" was signed by five students: Oscar González Eguiarte, a student at the preparatory school of the university; Clara Elena Gutiérrez, a student at Saucillo; Filiberto Ontiveros; Miguel Manuel Miramontes; and Rosalba Abarca, of Saucillo.[162] The statement foreshadowed the Five Resolutions passed by the Second Encounter in 1965. Like the later Resolutions, it seems to have been influenced by formulations written in a different context. The statement of the First Encounter reflected the priorities of the Soviet Union during the Cold War and may have been influenced by Pablo Gómez's recent trip to Cuba or Arturo Gámiz's purported six months in East Germany. The JP, which Gámiz and many students belonged to, was a member of the Federation of Democratic Youth, headquartered in Budapest, as was the Communist Party USA. The statement focused on disarmament and the threat of a third world war and emphasized the centrality of workers over campesinos. It also reflected the triumphalism—the exhortation to follow a rising tide—that followed the Cuban Revolution throughout the 1970s.

Only the last paragraph addressed problems specific to Chihuahua, with a list of demands for projects in the sierra beginning with the legalization of campesino property and including credit for feedlots; schools and dormitories; added-value industries such as dairies and tanneries; provision of fowl, pigs, and so forth, and consultation with agronomists; government health clinics in Madera and the surrounding area; training centers in agriculture, livestock, and forestry; telephone and mail service; and campaigns for the prevention of disease, vaccines, first aid, and so forth. These demands revealed the isolation of Madera City, to say nothing of the surrounding area. Their fulfillment required ordinary capitalist development and not the revolutionary overthrow of the system.

Two of these demands—the most important, since an end to cacuqal and state violence was not included—seem problematic in the light of the years that followed. The first was as follows: "Considering that national forestry law gives preference to exploitation by ejidos and that now exploitation is in the hands of private *rapamontes* [mountain strippers] who, without respecting the most elemental norms, clear-cut on an enormous scale, we fight for collective exploitation of the forests by ejidatarios." Today most of the sierra *is* in the hands of ejidatarios, many of them indigenous, but because they have no alternative but to sell their trees to large consortiums, their overall situation has not improved, and they cannot be responsible environmental stewards.[163]

The second demand was to "ask the government for studies regarding the potential of mining in the sierra with the aim of interesting domestic capital in the exploitation of this resource and the creation of jobs." Today there are more than one hundred mines operating in the state, many of them Canadian. Today's mines are largely automated, providing only a handful of jobs, and they cause cyanide and other water pollution, create labor and safety issues, and displace communities with huge, open-pit mines.[164] One of those mines, in El Mineral de Dolores, provoked widespread but unsuccessful protests by the Ejido Huizopa, itself a result of the UGOCM's struggles in the 1960s. The buildings of Dolores, some dating from colonial times and including Gámiz's school, were destroyed as the mine expanded.

Included in the IPS files were the "Ballad of the Encounter of the Sierra," which described the walk to the encounter, by Jesús Manuel Sánchez and the poem "Revolutionary Suffering" by Rosalba Abarca.[165]

The authors of the *Fiscalía* document, compiled from IPS and DFS files, suggested that the participants in the encounter explored the viability of armed struggle as a path to socialism and that the event marked the beginning of a break on the part of the more radicalized sectors with their leaders, whom they began to regard as "reformist."[166] This assertion was unattributed. In Gámiz's later document, "Participación de los estudiantes en el movimiento revolucionario" (The Participation of Students in the Revolutionary Movement), presented at the Second Encounter in 1965, Gámiz described the position taken by the normalistas of Salaices during the First Encounter, in which "before becoming revolutionaries and taking power, one must teach ethics to the masses," a stance Gámiz argued against.[167] "Participación de los estudiantes" was the only existing statement of theory signed by Gámiz, and it did respond to local conditions and provide detailed arguments about actual conflicts. It is clear from "Participación" that the extent of student solidarity with campesino struggles was debated at the First Encounter; however, it is not clear that they debated whether their solidarity should extend to armed struggle and a break with the UGOCM as reformist, although the documentary evidence is incomplete. The encounter's official document, the "Statement of Political Context," focused on world peace, which appeared out of place in a gathering of people engaged in daily battles with enemies whose names they knew.

After the meetings, on October 12, the students stayed on and counseled ejidatarios of Cebadilla regarding their prolonged conflicts with Francisco Portillo, owner of the neighboring Hacienda Sírupa. Portillo had recently built fences that encroached on ejido land to enlarge his property and keep the campesinos from watering their livestock at an artesian spring. The students, along with some fifty campesinos, removed the barbed wire and tore out some three hundred fence posts. Four students (Javier Romero Zamudio, Saúl Chacón, Jesús Márquez, and Oscar García) were arrested and released the next day.[168] Alvaro Ríos was arrested and consigned to the First Criminal Court in Chihuahua. He was released when a supporter posted the one-thousand-peso bail.[169]

Late in 1963, Israel González, a serrano police officer, denounced Emilio Rascón for having stolen seven cattle from González's mother, and he arrested Rascón as he passed through Dolores with the cattle. One of José Ibarra's associates saw them and took Rascón and the livestock back to the mother, where they forced her to sign a bill of sale. Then they kidnapped González and hanged him, leaving him for dead, although he escaped. He was tortured again by troops in the summer of 1964.[170]

In November, General Manuel Mendoza Domínguez signed a report describing a meeting of the UGOCM in Delicias. Miguel Moreno and Samuel García addressed a crowd of six hundred people, complaining that campesinos were paid only six pesos a day. Clara Elena Gutiérrez assured them of victory since they now had the support of the teachers. Manuel Sánchez Ibarra followed by singing two corridos. The next speakers were Rubén García of the rural normal school of San Marcos, Zacatecas; Casimiro Villalobos; and Oscar González, who said they were ready to take down any and all fences erected against the campesinos and that the real agitators were Giner Durán and Héctor Sánchez Calderón, leader of the state PRI. Then came teachers Dolores Armendáriz and Pablo Gómez followed by Alvaro Ríos, who said that instead of building schools the government maintained an army. He invited the governor to choose the path of friendship because if not, the campesinos would be forced to resort to violence because their children were hungry.[171]

In December, *Indice* printed an homage to Judith Reyes, "journalist and indefatigable fighter," by the school inspector and PCM militant José Santos Valdés.[172]

Agrarian conflicts continued throughout the state. On December 24, *Acción* reported that Secundino López Guerrero, of Ignacio Zaragoza, had been accused of robbery for working a parcel abandoned five years before by Guadalupe M., widow of Vargas. The rural police had confiscated his entire harvest of corn and beans.[173] Reyes offered a detailed accounting of his case as an example of campesinos sent to jail at planting time, although December seems a bit early for seeds. López was sixty years old, illiterate, and an ejidatario of Zaragoza, Galeana. His wife, Belem Millán, thirty-eight years old, with five children, could read. López claimed to have had an agreement with Guadalupe M., the owner of the parcel in question. She herself was a colonist and could not join the ejido but was required to live on her parcel. She proposed that López put his house on her land. She would help pay for seeds and then they would split the harvest. He had cleared the land, built a house, and erected fencing. For two years, they split the harvests, and then she began sending people to take it all. He argued his right to the parcel, having cultivated it for three years, and moreover that she could not be both an ejidatario and colonist. Instead, his fences were cut, livestock were turned loose in his fields, the harvests were stolen, and he was arrested repeatedly. He filed the paperwork to legalize his possession; he met Reyes for the first time in the offices of the DAAC.[174] It was not clear why, if he were an ejidatario already, he was not working his own ejido parcel, or whether the land he worked belonged to a colony or in what sense the widow was attempting to be both ejidataria and colonist.

In Zaragoza, Judith Reyes met a group of women who suggested breaking him out of jail themselves, because the authorities would hesitate to fire at women. Reyes replied that they would indeed fire and, moreover, they would kill López. Threatened with yet another arrest and subject to continual harassment, López fled to the sierra, while his wife traveled to Mexico City to attempt unsuccessfully to meet with officials of the DAAC. "The presence of this campesina, with her knowledge of the countryside that counted for nothing here, facing the cement jungle of the huge city, was shocking. Belem's difficulties multiplied with her inexperience of urban life."[175]

Meanwhile, when López returned home to see his children, someone denounced him, and the authorities arrived. The house was surrounded, the officials began shooting, and he returned their fire. They threw burning tires so the smoke would force him out; he threw them back. One of his daughters panicked and ran out and was taken hostage. López surrendered to protect his children. The house was burned before their eyes. The children went to stay with neighbors and their father went back to jail. When Millán returned from the Federal District, she and her children went to live with Reyes, who offered refuge to any campesino attempting to legalize possession.[176] In February López was released, but the confiscated 192 bags of corn and 198 of alfalfa were not returned.[177] Santos Valdés included photos of the family and the remains of the family home in his book.[178]

In December 1963, police and soldiers closed the rural normal schools and arrested leaders of the UGOCM and dozens of students. When informed that the students demanded the reopening of their dormitories, Giner Durán remarked, in a meeting with the state secretary of government, "I would rather convert those schools into pigsties. But in Mexico City they don't understand."[179] In response to the petition of women students, he replied, "What do they want dormitories for if they like to sleep in the fields with the campesinos?"[180]

The mobilizations of the early 1960s set the stage for the explosive confrontations of 1964 and the emergence of an armed vanguard in the sierra of Madera.

4

1964

Summary

The year 1964 brought the emergence of an explicitly socialist armed vanguard, the Grupo Popular Guerrillero (GPG; Popular Guerrilla Group), which engaged in sporadic attacks on targets in the sierra while in the cities, students battled authorities in a series of militant confrontations. The governor shut down schools and dormitories. The presidential elections heightened the tension, and a riot broke out at candidate Gustavo Díaz Ordaz's campaign stop. Land invasions continued and were dislodged by soldiers. Alvaro Ríos and several students were jailed for six months. On his release, Ríos resumed organizing intercity marches, distancing himself from the GPG. The army and state police assaulted families in the sierra. The GPG moved to Mexico City for training, leaving a handful of members to fight in the sierra. In early 1965, the state UGOCM split.

Election Year

During the election year of 1964, competition increased between the PPS-UGOCM axis and the gathering strength of the PCM-FEP axis. Lombardo Toledano announced his support for PRI candidate Gustavo Díaz Ordaz, and the state section of the UGOCM came under pressure to contain the mass movement. A split in the local UGOCM became inevitable. Raúl and Pablo Gómez ran for local offices for the PPS. Several new organizations emerged: the Association of Revolutionary Women, based in Saucillo, and the Comité Pro Defensa de las Garantías Individuales y Sociales (Comité Pro; Committee for the Defense of Individual and Social Rights,). All the groups shared the same mimeograph machine and sat on the same rented chairs.

The Frente Electoral de Pueblo (FEP; People's Electoral Front), a national group formed in the summer of 1963 and affiliated with the PCM, used the electoral campaign to attract independent leftists. Among its national leaders were the poet and journalist Renato Leduc; Braulio Maldonado, former governor of Baja California; and Othón Salazar of the Revolutionary Teachers Movement. The FEP attempted to obtain authorization to participate in the elections and was denied, but it ran candidates anyway. Four political prisoners ran for office, including the muralist David Alfaro Siquieros and Valentín Campa of the railroad workers movement, and the Sonoran Ramón Danzós Palomino, who was chosen as a presidential candidate.[1] In Chihuahua, Judith Reyes ran for the federal senate under the FEP banner, and Becerra Gaytán ran for deputy in the first district. The Gómez Ramírez brothers ran for local offices as members of the PPS.

On January 7, General Antonio Gómez Velasco, commander of the Fifth Military Zone, intervened with DAAC on behalf of the campesinos, asking that existing resolutions be executed.[2] On January 17, fifty soldiers assaulted the two hundred campesinos of NCP Pancho Villa who had invaded Gavilondo's Ojo de Peñuelas, beating women and children. The leaders of the invasion—Rosario Prieto, Jesús and Carlos Dórame, Felipe Castillo, and Rogelio Pérez—were dumped in jail cells with their wounds untreated, and the army closed the road to Sonora. With these developments, Arturo Gámiz declared, "Who is disturbing the peace? Either change the policies or build more prisons." The land was not expropriated until 1967.[3]

In January, *Indice* accused Ernesto Rosas Ruíz, director of inspections, purchasing, and complaints at the DAAC, of counseling the cattlemen Gavilondo, Graton, and Otis Jeffers to divide their land and sell to Mennonites when their CIGs ran out, as Almeida had done earlier.[4] In late January, the campesinos Ricardo Ruelas, Francisco Sánchez Ruíz, and Diógenes Ordúñoz, of the NCP Guadalupe Victoria in Madera, were released from jail. They had been charged by the Spaniard, Amador Picazarri.[5] *Acción* accused Manuel Pereda, owner of the sawmill Ranchería del Norte in Madera, of violating federal labor law by paying his workers with chits for the company store, while he bet their salaries on horse races. He had also threatened to fire and evict them.[6]

In early February, strikes broke out among students of the Technical and State Normal Schools, demanding the governor remove the director of the Technical School's dormitory, retired Lieutenant Colonel Antonio Guerra Duque. He was accused of "bad character and behavior," of beating and insulting students, holding back food, and advising young male students "how to behave with a girl."[7]

Emergence of the Grupo Popular Guerrillero

The first action of the GPG took place in Madera in February 1964 when Salomón Gaytán and local campesino Ramón Mendoza burned a bridge belonging to the Ibarras that was used to carry timber out of the area and left the message, "To the civil and military authorities: We have destroyed this bridge to support the land invasions and so that the campesinos and leaders in jail be freed, and we will continue to take drastic measures until our goal is met. Attentively, the Popular Guerrilla Group."[8] Mendoza, originally from Tres Ojitos near Dolores, was then in his early twenties. His father had been forced to sell his ranch by the Four Friends when they had him arrested for rustling and threatened his family.

On March 5, Salomón Gaytán, accompanied by his nephew, Antonio Scobell Gaytán, shot and killed Florentino Ibarra, José's brother, in revenge for the assassination of Carlos Ríos four years earlier.[9] Ignacio Gil was also wounded in the attack. When questioned by a reporter, Gaytán said he had gone to the house and asked for Florentino, then emptied a pistol into him, shouting, "This is what I came for, son of a ———," and fled. On the road Gaytán and his nephew ran into some women and he yelled, "I've killed your boyfriend, you old sluts [*viejas resbalosas*]!" It was suggested that Ibarra had tried to force Gaytán's sweetheart.[10]

On March 22, Salomón Gaytán and Antonio Scobell sent a letter to Ernesto Castellanos, Mayor of Madera, explaining their use of violence. "The fundamental reason is that we are convinced the authorities do not wish to resolve the people's problems, especially those of the workers and campesinos, but instead they harass those who ask for work and land and repress the people's movements for justice with violence." They promised to surrender when the last latifundia was divided. They said that everyone knew the Ibarras humiliated and harassed the people of Dolores and that they killed Florentino Ibarra because the authorities failed to act. Finally, they declared that Ignacio Gil had shot himself in the leg while attacking them.[11]

On February 18, twenty men and eight to ten women invaded the property of Ezequiel Chávez Bustamante in Casa Colorada, sixteen kilometers from Madera, in support of their petition for an ejido. They brought livestock and erected tents. Arturo Gámiz and two companions had left Madera en route to a meeting in Santa Rita, Temósachic, when they arrived at Casa Colorada and decided to spend the night. The three had been taking turns riding first one then two horses. A detachment of soldiers arrived the next morning, found the group gathering firewood, and arrested Gámiz and Manuel Montes Varela of Tres Ojitos, a member of the soliciting group. As they were led away, the crowd threatened to follow, and the soldiers fixed bayonets. The invaders were dislodged after "two hours of discussion." The officer remarked that they were not "local campesinos but persons dedicated to activities that are not the care of livestock."[12]

According to court records, this was Gámiz's first arrest. He was charged with occupation of property belonging to another and sent to the state penitentiary in the capital, located on Twentieth of November Street near downtown. In his declaration, he reported that the DAAC had promised to release the property in January and that the occupation was intended to pressure the authorities. During his time in jail, Gámiz met with Salvador del Toro Rosales of the federal attorney general's office, who was sent to Chihuahua to resolve the crisis; Gámiz made a favorable impression on Toro Rosales.[13]

On March 4, the journalist Pedro Muñoz Grado paid a bond of one thousand pesos, and Gámiz was released pending trial. His companion Manuel Montes Varela was released a week later when Senaido (Rosario?) Prieto Chávez of Nuevo Casas Grandes paid his bond. In July, an order for Gámiz's arrest for failing to appear was issued and the bond was forfeited.[14] Gámiz's court file ended with a letter dated October 19, 1965, noting his death and indicating the inclusion of a certified copy of the death certificate not found in the file.[15]

Whatever else happened to Gámiz in captivity, he was confronted with his own vulnerability. On his release, he renounced his role in the public movement and joined the GPG in the sierra. He may have realized his life was in danger and that further legal action was useless, while the mountains and canyons of northwestern Chihuahua offered an ideal terrain and a population accustomed to armed self-defense.

More Protests

On February 18, General Efrén Samano arrested four campesinos for a symbolic occupation of land belonging to Evaristo Rojo. The students of Saucillo called for a mute protest, demanding liberty for the campesinos and protesting the attitude of the municipal authorities. On February 20, Luis Carlos Terrazas, the mayor of Delicias, encouraged a gang of youths, including students of the secondary school, to attack a UGOCM meeting by hurling rotten oranges, onions, potatoes, and tomatoes. They also threw a live snake at the Saucillo students, trying to scare them, and the mayor's nephew shot off a pistol.[16]

While the movement assigned tasks thought appropriate to their gender to the normalistas of Saucillo, such as gathering food and donations from supporters, it also created opportunities for participation in direct action. Women from Saucillo spoke publicly as representatives of their school. As teachers in the Freedom Schools convened during invasions, they exerted a certain authority. Aleida García Aguirre noted that by working with the UGOCM, the women gained a degree of autonomy from the Salaicinos, although in turn they were subordinated to leaders of the UGOCM, namely Arturo Gámiz and Alvaro Ríos, who expected to make decisions for them and required their obedience.[17] She did not mention Pablo Gómez in this connection, although his influence at the school was transformative.

A DFS document described a series of invasions led by the UGOCM in early 1964, including eighty campesinos of the NCP Narciso Mendoza who invaded the property of Alfonso Terrazas in Delicias; one hundred campesinos of the NCP Plutarco Elías Calles who invaded the properties of Evarista Rojo and Carlos Múñoz Leyva in Saucillo; and sixty campesinos from the NCP Ignacio Allende who invaded the properties of Paula Carbona, widow of Muñiz, in Lázaro Cárdenas and Delicias. Normalistas of Saucillo and Salaices advised and sometimes joined the invasions; some of the young women dressed as men. Other invasions around the state included Lot Number Nine, property of Ezequiel and Oscar Chávez, invaded by eighty campesinos of the NCP Casa Colorada in Madera (where Gámiz had been arrested); properties of Bosques de Chihuahua by campesinos of the NCP Independencia; the property of Jorge

Quijada, within the lands of Bosques, by the NCP Revolución; unidentified properties in Nuevo Casas Grandes invaded by the NCP Plan de Sabinas; and unidentified properties in Flores Magón, invaded by campesinos of the NCP Terranetes (Terrenates). The report went on to identify Pablo Gómez Ramírez as a leader of the UGOCM teaching at a school in Delicias (actually Saucillo), and it stated that Giner Durán had previously asked the education department to transfer Gómez, without success. The report also stated, erroneously, that Arturo Gamez (Gámiz) was out of state at the time. Gámiz had joined the invasion of Casa Colorada and been arrested there on February 19. The report ended by describing a gathering of some three hundred students of Saucillo (nearly the entire student body), ninety local campesinos, and one hundred students of Salaices in front of Saucillo's city hall demanding the release of campesinos jailed for the invasions.[18]

On February 22, a crowd of normalistas and some campesinos swarmed into the offices of the DAAC and confronted Eduardo Juárez Santos Coy in his office. In the confusion, the front door was locked. The students were accused of locking it to kidnap the delegate while they claimed the door had been locked by DAAC employees to facilitate their arrest. In any case, the combined forces of riot, state, and municipal police arrived and evicted the students, arresting some thirty. The protesters regrouped in the Plaza Hidalgo in front of the state house and were attacked with tear gas. The students responded by throwing rocks and whatever they found at hand. Photos on the front page of *Acción* showed scenes of chaos: many young women among the protesters menaced by cops in battle gear. Guillermo Rodríguez Ford was arrested for catching a tear gas canister and hurling it at the feet of police chief Mendoza Domínguez, who was said to be too old to run. *Acción* claimed that Mendoza ordered live ammunition against students but that the troops disobeyed orders. *Acción* also gave the improbable number of fifteen hundred to two thousand students crowding into the offices of the attorney general to protest the arrests.[19] This was one of the face-to-face confrontations led by students that grew increasingly heated that year.

Three photos in *Indice* showed students burning Bad Government in effigy and carrying a coffin, surrounded by soldiers in gas masks in the Plaza Hidalgo. The students burned the coffin representing Giner Durán, while David Hernández, a protestant minister and member of the FEP and Comité Pro, read the funeral service. Education director Francisco Javier Alvarez called in Professor Isaias Orozco, of Secondary School Number One, and accused him of leading

FIGURE 8 Normalistas accompany Pablo Gómez in a face-off with Hipólito Villa. Comité Primeros Vientos.

the student movements and the invasion of the DAAC.[20] Most of the protesters were released; Guillermo Rodríguez Ford and the students Jesús Hilario Cardona, Guillermo Ramírez Rodríguez (Guerrero according to Toro Rosales), and Jorge Rodas were accused of rioting. All were offered bail; Jorge Rodas was the only one able to raise it. Months later, Roberto Barrios, director of the DAAC in Mexico City, ordered his delegate in Chihuahua to drop the charges.[21] Campesinos began another prolonged sit-in before the offices of the DAAC in downtown Chihuahua.

In February the authorities kept watch over the women students of Saucillo while the men of Salaices were exempt from similar surveillance and went unmentioned in *El Heraldo*.[22] Later that spring, both rural normal schools were under continual surveillance "by the state 'secret' police, by the municipal police, and by police from Mexico City, moreover by spies from the FBI and CIA, and even worse, by soldiers of the federal army," who held the students under an ineffective but menacing state of siege.[23] Students from Saucillo were invited to take part in a shooting gallery at a country fair, and there they were photographed, and those photos were exhibited as evidence of guerrilla training.[24]

Federal officials, less beholden to the interests of local cattlemen and hoping to prevent another Cuba, tried to diffuse the climate of violence by sending Salvador del Toro Rosales and Manuel Gutiérrez Zamora from the federal attorney general's office to Chihuahua in February. In a memoir published in 1996, Toro Rosales described his visit and concluded that Chihuahua's problems were rooted in the misery of the countryside and that the only solution was to put aside political interests and to proceed with the agrarian distribution through legal channels.

On the first day of their visit, the two attorneys met with state attorney general Hipólito Villa Rentería, who told them the protests and land invasions were led by communists and outsiders. Toro Rosales described General Manuel Mendoza Domínguez, director of the state police, as an "old man, who knew nothing about the police, had no idea what caused the movement, did not know who participated in it and led it, was not interested in knowing, and said that the only thing that bothered him, in his own words, was that those rude and uncouth kids [*muchachitos léperos y mal educados*] went daily to the state house to insult General Giner, which was intolerable."[25]

Mendoza complained about the young women.

> Some of them look like women of the streets, and they are the most argumentative. I ask you, Licenciado, what are these girls doing with the campesinos on the ranches? Because these are the same ones who went to the agrarian office. And so, what are they doing away from home, at night, at dawn? I tell you that in various invasions, we found half-empty bottles of sotol and even some guitars.[26]

This was neither the first nor last time that aspersions of promiscuity were cast on the young women of Saucillo. The authorities found it inconceivable that, being women, they would act on their own convictions.

Toro Rosales paid a visit to Giner Durán in his home library, with its shelves empty of books, where Giner made a speech. "In Chihuahua there are no latifundia, their leaders are lying." He went on to explain that the wealth of Chihuahua consisted of livestock, which needed a great deal of land to thrive. "What do they want? that instead of sheep we raise rats?" Giner compared the hardworking cattlemen who rose at dawn to feed and water their animals with lazy troublemakers who spend all day in the city following their leaders from one office to another and agitating. He added that he had ordered the secretary of public education to close the rural schools of Saucillo and Delicias (Salaices) for being "nests of vipers, seedbeds of communists." He urged Toro Rosales to act energetically and complained that the prisoners should be a federal and not local responsibility, since the municipal jails were full and the mayors could not afford them.[27] Giner believed that his vociferous anticommunism justified every authoritarian act.

Toro Rosales described how "one of his [Toro Rosales's] police agents, Rudy," managed to recruit a snitch among the campesinos who were sitting in at the DAAC who reported that some of the students were saving up to buy guns and that they were overheard saying, "No one will remove us from here. Now that the authorities will not give us land, then to hell with it all." The snitch confirmed that the movement had reached a slow boil. Asked who its leaders were, he replied, "No one." The protesters gathered, without knowing what to do or what would come next, because they needed to be together. They hated but did not fear either the authorities or the caciques.[28] The assertion that the movement was leaderless reflected the degree of autonomy among the campesinos.[29]

Toro Rosales received delegations of students who insisted that he release the prisoners and arrest Giner. He described their petitions as "clear and precise, but absurd, because the prisoners were not at the disposition of the attorney general." He received Pablo Gómez, accompanied by a small entourage. Gómez delivered a speech, in a voice Toro described as shrill and disagreeable, repeating that the campesinos would remain in place, whatever the consequences, until the last of the latifundia were distributed. The agrarian delegate Santos Coy insisted he had not been kidnapped and warned that in the countryside, "the campesinos do not talk, they act," and if the situation were not resolved, they would take up arms.[30]

Toro Rosales sent for Arturo Gámiz. He was impressed by Gámiz's simplicity, modesty, and intelligence. According to Gámiz, a recent UGOCM assembly in Los Mochis had agreed to effect simultaneous nonviolent land invasions throughout the northern states, allowing themselves to be arrested and replaced until only "old folks, women, and children, the relatives of prisoners" were left, but the call to begin had not been issued. Gámiz accused Jacinto López, national leader of the UGOCM, of ignoring the agreement in exchange for potential political appointments and of not wishing the protesters to be seen, during an electoral year, as "enemies of the regime." By the end of the meeting, Toro Rosales and Gámiz agreed that the situation would be resolved with the arrival of a team of agronomists and that the agronomists would be sent from Mexico City and not from the Hermanos Escobar School in Juárez because the latter were considered "children of the rich." They also agreed that the movement would accept the agronomists' decisions, whether they were favorable or not.[31]

Immediately following this meeting, López Mateos ordered the release of all prisoners, provided funds for the campesinos to return home, and sent a team of twenty agronomists, with office personnel, equipment, and vehicles, to the state office of DAAC. Toro Rosales and Gutiérrez Zamora gave a press conference, assuring the public that they had acted "not because they were pressured by agitators but because they considered the petitions of the campesinos for land to be just." One invasion, in Las Playas, Madera, on the property of Amador Picazarri, took place because the invaders had not heard of the agreement, and it was peacefully dissolved.[32] Despite the agreement, Pablo Gómez and Saúl Chacón paid a visit to Santos Coy to inform him that the campesinos would not return home but would remain until their demands were met. They would continue to stand before the offices of the DAAC in the morning and march through downtown in the afternoon, carrying banners and signs, accompanied by students with collection boxes.

There was a rally on February 21 in Delicias, and three days later there were three more: one in Saucillo, organized by the normalistas who had been called before the assistant director of the normal schools that very day to demand they cease these interventions; one organized by the FECH in the capital, where four normalistas and one campesino addressed the crowd; and one that night when there was a "symbolic burning of the authorities, beginning with the governor."[33] On February 28, three or four hundred campesinos arrived in Chihuahua City in a caravan from the south led by Saúl Chacón and Pablo Gómez. Every day, they and their supporters gathered before the offices of the DAAC in a mute protest; in the afternoon they paraded around downtown and gathered again at the Plaza Hidalgo. At night they slept in the offices of the UGOCM. The students collected money, food, blankets, and clothing.[34] These demonstrations showed that the movement had a momentum of its own and intended to continue no matter what concessions were negotiated by its leaders.

The normalistas of Saucillo agreed to stop eating dessert and sweet rolls and proposed that the school give the money to the caravan of campesinos. When the school refused, they opened the storeroom themselves and took all the food.[35] The day the caravan arrived at the state house, the State Normal School performed a funeral: the students dressed in black and marched in silence carrying cardboard coffins symbolizing Justice and Liberty, while the band played a dirge.[36]

Judith Reyes announced her candidacy for the federal senate on the FEP ticket.[37] In March, Pablo Gómez announced his candidacy as substitute deputy in Delicias for the PPS, while his brother Raúl Gómez ran for federal deputy in Guerrero. Arturo Gámiz, by then in hiding, announced his support for the Gómez brothers.[38]

Presidential candidate Gustavo Díaz Ordaz arrived in Chihuahua in early April on a ritual campaign tour, although his election was assured. Judith Reyes described the preparations for his visit. An enormous red, green, and white banner reading "PRI: Gustavo Díaz Ordaz" was hung from the Cerro de Coronel, to the southeast of the city, with its own electrical plant for illumination and soldiers to guard it, at a cost of one hundred thousand pesos. On the flanks of the same hill were caves inhabited by the Tarahumara who came to the city to sell their handicrafts, beg, and pose for tourist photos; their children's bellies were swollen from parasites. Bureaucrats and union members were forced to attend Díaz Ordaz's speeches. The attendance of the poor and unemployed was purchased for a sandwich and forty pesos in Juárez, but only twenty pesos farther south.[39] Reyes later reported that three truckloads of campesinos had refused to leave the vehicles until they were paid, and she asked, who was more despicable, "la que peca por la paga o él que paga por pecar" (she who sins for pay or he who pays for sin [from a poem by Sor Juana de la Cruz]).[40]

Díaz Ordaz made his first speech in Juárez, where students threw rotten eggs.[41] On April 6, he paraded down the principal street of the capital and then spoke in the plaza, where a reviewing stand had been erected in front of city hall. Along with the usual crowd of PRI supporters, a number of students gathered. Some observers say the disturbances occurred toward the end of his speech, others that he was prevented from speaking. Toro Rosales remarked that the crowd along the way had been unresponsive. All accounts agree that the students Cecilio Polanco and Jesús (sometimes José) Mariñelarena climbed the reviewing stand and demanded an interview with the candidate. Mariñelarena grabbed the microphone, although the power had been cut, and there was an outbreak of shouting, much of it directed against the governor and local authorities, and a hail of sticks, rocks, fruit, and bottles was thrown at the reviewing stand. The candidate was hustled back to his tour bus (other accounts said the nearby Hotel Fermont). The crowd took over the plaza while panicking bystanders fled.[42]

Judith Reyes attended the event as a reporter for the national magazine *Política*, whose director, Manuel Marcué Pardiñas, was a member of the PPS and a political prisoner in Lecumberri in Mexico City. After the candidate was led away, she was asked to sing and declined. She then entered city hall, where the mayor, Roberto Ortiz, invited her for coffee while the crowd burned the posters behind the reviewing stand. Soon the firemen arrived and put out the flames. Again the students set fire to the stand, this time breaking windows and scorching the facade of city hall, while the mayor refused to call the authorities against them. Ortiz, Reyes, and a handful of employees escaped to the roof of a neighboring building until the fire was extinguished. That night, Díaz Ordaz attended a banquet of the Cattlemen's Association, where he expressed his gratitude for the reception he had been given while soldiers patrolled the streets. Four weeks later, Reyes was arrested.[43] *Indice* published a photo of the scorched front of city hall, remarking that normally Chihuahuenses would be ashamed of such behavior, but that in this case, "If here they killed Padre Hidalgo and here the revolution began, we must expect something from Chihuahua."[44]

The protagonists of these two events, the swarming of the DAAC and the riot on April 6, were students frustrated by the recalcitrance of the governor and other authorities and responding with a show of militancy. According to Toro Rosales, on April 6 they undid the gains of the campesinos as the newly initiated agrarian campaign ground to a halt: "the informative technical works that had only begun a few weeks before were paralyzed, the agronomists returned to their base camps, and the petitions returned to the files. Complaints and new petitions went into the garbage."[45] The repression, particularly against the rural normal schools, increased. The student movement was not, however, united behind the protests. According to DFS reports on the FECH, some students wanted the protests to be orderly and peaceful.[46]

On April 8, Jesús Hilario Cardona Rodríguez, a student at the State Normal School, was accused of rioting. He was convicted on August 12 and sentenced to thirty days' time served and a twenty-five peso fine, but he was not released. He appealed, and on October 28, the conviction was overturned. He was finally released on November 5.[47] His detention, along with that of Alvaro Ríos, inspired widespread protests.

The normal schools, the Technical School, and the Technical School for Young Ladies were singled out by Giner Durán, members of the PAN, and Catholic organizations, who demanded that parents control their children and blamed the teachers who belonged to the PPS, PCM, UGOCM, and FEP for corrupting them.[48]

In Delicias, a number of agrarian leaders, among them Raúl and Pablo Gómez, were arrested. On April 8, Díaz Ordaz secured their release and met with them briefly, promising to find a solution to the agrarian question. In his memoir, Paco Ornelas included a photo of Díaz Ordaz receiving a memorandum from the Gómez brothers. The caption referred to a twenty-minute meeting on the outskirts of Delicias.[49]

Hilario Cardona's initial declaration, given on April 8, was elicited under torture and included the following details, which he later denied. Cardona was in his third year in the Normal Night School. He had joined the FEP in November the year before, invited by Andrés de la O, who told him they were forming a new revolutionary party. Reynaldo Rosas Domínguez was in charge of press and propaganda. Cardona knew Isaias Orozco, secretary of acts and agreements. He also named a tall, bald man called Félix Guzmán, a fat one named Federico Ruíz Viescas, and Ramón Sánchez, a primary schoolteacher who tried to recruit new members. Rosas told everyone to get a red marker and write FEP slogans on walls and doors. There were forty-seven people at a meeting on the patio of a carpentry shop in Calle Aldama. They collected money for fliers announcing the arrival of presidential candidate Ramón Danzós Palomino. Andrés de la O Ayala, Reynaldo Rosas, Becerra, and the accused went to pick up chairs for the meeting in Becerra Gaytán's car; Cardona thought it must have been the first meeting for this reason. After that, he attended meetings every Sunday. In the meetings it was said that they should attack the state and federal governments, that the movement would be national, and that they would pressure the president to release political prisoners such as Vallejo, Campa, Siquieros, and Filomeno Mata. Within the state they should attack the governor, attorney general Villa Rentería, and the secretary of government Saúl González Herrera, as well as Giner because he was inept, and González Herrera and Villa for being his yes-men and following his inept and reactionary policies. Cardona testified that he gave out fliers to students of the normal schools and invited his compañeros to meetings; he invited Ruperto Soto Guajardo and Rodolfo Ramos Beltrán, who attended all sessions. He painted the walls of the sports park, near the university campus, with slogans. He collected money. Federico Ruíz Viescas gave the most, and everyone gave something, sometimes one peso or less. They held meetings to plan for the arrival of the candidate and began by naming commissions, obtaining funds, and sending representatives to the reception. Lázaro Villarreal gave money under the table but was committed to the PPS. The brains of the operation were Oscar Ayala Martínez, Antonio Becerra Gaytán, Judith Reyes, Reynaldo Rosas, and Ema Becerra Gaytán, a student at the Normal Night School. The strike at the dormitory of the Technical School was organized by Andrés de la O, who had been instructed by Becerra Gaytán.

Section Eight of the national teachers union gave moral support and the use of their mimeograph machine. Cardona named Rafael Martínez Valdivia as a leader of the Juventud Popular and a girl whose last names were Espina Carpio as Gámiz's girlfriend.[50]

Cardona had accompanied Gámiz, Chacón, Pablo Gómez, and Rodríguez Ford in their discussions of guerrilla warfare and on excursions into the woods near Aldama to make Molotov cocktails and hand grenades. Gámiz spoke of preparing the people and said that only a few campesinos from the UGOCM would be good for guerrilla war. Danzós Palomino told Alvaro Ríos not to carry out land invasions in February but to wait for April 15, when there would be a general campesino mobilization, but Cardona did not know where. Alvaro Ríos did not respond. Pablo Gómez and Clara Elena Gutiérrez were going to Cuba to connect with revolutionary organizations there. The FEP painted over propaganda for Gustavo Díaz Ordaz. José Mariñelarena Rivera had planned to take the microphone (on April 6).[51]

The declaration of José Luis Franco Alvarez was included in Cardona's file. Franco declared that ten to thirteen students met before the rally and planned to challenge Gustavo Díaz Ordaz (GDO) with questions using a battery-powered microphone. Mariñelarena got up on the platform and was pulled down. An assistant took GDO to the Hotel Fermont, and a riot broke out. The Democratic Christian Party or the PAN caused the destruction. Former governor Borunda tried to calm the students and went back to the hotel. A figure dressed in black and standing on a car, whom the students called the Prophet, directed the riot. GDO came out and told them he would solve their problems, and they met for some fifteen or twenty minutes. Franco belonged to an action group, the lowest of the three grades of the FEP. The FEP had a hierarchy: above Franco was Hilario Cardona, above him was Becerra Gaytán, and above him were Judith Reyes, Othón Salazar, and Pedro Muñoz Grado, organized in concentric circles. According to Franco, Oscar Sandoval did not belong to any of the circles.[52]

Hilario Cardona made a second, undated declaration in which he repudiated his earlier statement, saying he had been tortured. He said he did not know whether the strike committee got help from Lázaro Villarreal or Section Eight. He denied knowing anything about bombs and grenades or a trip to Cuba. He said he was taken from the Normal and invited to speak with the attorney general at 7:30 a.m. on April 8 and that he was threatened in the cells of the state judicial police. The attorney general brought Daniel Luna, a cross-eyed police

FIGURE 9 "Citizen Governor: The cattle get 30 hectares, and us, how many? and when?" Comité Primeros Vientos.

agent, who questioned and insulted Cardona. First he hit him in the face, and Cardona fell off his chair. Then Luna hit him in the stomach and on the back of the head until he could not see. Luna had made him kneel to the count of five hundred, and at two hundred Cardona fell over and was beaten again on the stomach and head. They made him hold a broom above his head and beat him some more. Luna also used *la chicharra*, electric shocks from a cattle prod, and they took him out to the cemetery at night and threatened his family. The torture ended at twelve o'clock, he was shut up in a dark room, then they got him out at 8:00 p.m. and put him in a tiny bathroom. Then they took him to José Luis Franco and told him they had his house surrounded and were recording everything. The two of them were shut up in a tiny room where they could not sleep for the pain. The next day the jailers were "Machiavellian." They brought Cardona everything he wanted, and the doctor told him nothing was wrong and gave him an injection. Marks from the beatings were still visible on his body.[53]

The file ended with a Judgment that found a clear relationship between the conception and preparation and the events of the riot. Franco and Mariñelarena

FIGURE 10 Demonstration at DAAC offices. Comité Primeros Vientos.

admitted to having climbed the stand as Díaz Ordaz finished his speech. The sentence of thirty days' time served was confirmed along with a twenty-five-peso fine. There was also a letter to the director of the penitentiary releasing Cardona after thirty days' time served, dated November 5, 1964, seven months after his arrest.[54]

Guerrillas in the Sierra

On April 13, the emerging GPG released a nine-page declaration explaining that they had taken up arms to rebuild a society that was hopelessly unjust and badly structured and that power should pass to the workers and campesinos. They were not against the elections or opposed to revolutionaries running for office as long as elections did not create illusions or become the primary form of struggle. "The transition from one social system to another by means of a violent revolution is an objective law." The hour had struck for the colonial and semicolonial countries, with the maturing of objective conditions. "Only in the course of revolutionary action will the workers' movement be rebuilt, the left united, and the popular masses achieve class consciousness. . . . Victory is guaranteed beforehand because the revolution responds to the interests of the people."[55]

Salvador Gaytán reported the rape of two girls age fifteen and seventeen by Ramón Molina on the Rancho El Durazno near Cebadilla. They were the granddaughters of the campesino Leonardo Rivera, who had been killed by Molina sometime earlier for failure to pay the rent on land he leased. The girls were left thrown on the ground.[56]

Raúl Florencio Lugo Hernández, from a poor campesino family who had settled in Nuevo Casas Grandes, joined the movement during the winter of 1963–1964. Neither a student nor a campesino himself but a young man without direction, when he first encountered the movement he was in jail. Through a window in his cell he heard a loudspeaker announcing a rally in support of campesinos soliciting land. On his release, he joined the solicitors.[57]

He later wrote a memoir of his days with the GPG while in Lecumberri Prison in Mexico City. He had been sentenced to five and a half years following a fleeting contact with the Revolutionary National Civic Organization of Guerrero, years after the events in Chihuahua. The first edition of his memoir was published anonymously and contained few names or dates but a wealth of detail concerning life in the movement.

Lugo described the preparations for an invasion: a caravan of some two hundred to two hundred and fifty persons rode in sixteen vehicles supplied by small businessmen who supported the breakup of the latifundia because their markets were hurt by competition. They traveled at night through intense cold. On arrival, they set up tents made of tarps in the form of a triangle with the leaders in the middle. He described the leaders as locals advised by the UGOCM, some of them "true revolutionaries who took advantage of legal cover . . . to develop the real work of raising consciousness among the campesinos." The campesinos received word that the army was coming to dislodge them, consulted among themselves, and left before the army arrived, being unprepared for a confrontation. The occupation was symbolic, not meant as an act of expropriation but intended to complement the pressure put on the DAAC by comrades in the capital using legal means.[58]

The group returned to Nuevo Casas Grandes to evaluate the action, decided their attitude had been overly "soft," and returned to wait for the army. This time they were dislodged by fixed bayonets, taken to Nuevo Casas Grandes, and released. Again they returned with their families. The army cut off their access to water, and they tried to dig wells. They raised both white and national flags in response to the press calling them "subversives, reds." They stayed for four days and then were surrounded by soldiers, surrendered, and returned to Nuevo Casas Grandes, where they organized a rally while their leaders were jailed. Here Lugo spoke in public for the first time, taking his cue from "a letter of Fidel Castro."[59]

A leader of the UGOCM invited Lugo and a few compañeros to private meetings and asked them to commit themselves to armed struggle. Instead of taking part in further occupations, Lugo and his companions returned home to organize clubs of working class youths "to counteract the ideological permeability to which the young workers are victim through the alienating actions of the class in power." They formed a study group of some twenty persons in Nuevo Casas Grandes and rented an office where they held weekly meetings to discuss dialectical materialism and political economy.[60] Another group had been organized in Chihuahua City.

With this, Lugo's life changed, as he was introduced to a "new world that he confronted with only one means, the urge to learn, assimilating all he could of the historical experience of class struggle." Among the books he read were *Fidel Castro*, *Listen Yankee*, *The Young Guard*, and *The Regional Clandestine Committee Acts*. Lugo recalled a conversation with a leader of the UGOCM who asked him what he thought about communism. He replied that if the bourgeoisie called them communists and subversives for demanding land, "then communism might not be so bad!"[61]

Lugo made the leap from petitioner to armed revolutionary within months. Shortly after Arturo Gámiz was released from jail and joined Gaytán and Scobell in the sierra, Lugo and six companions took the train to Madera to join the nascent GPG. Guadalupe Scobell met the group at the station and took them to meet Salomón and Antonio Gaytán. They made backpacks from their blankets to carry their belongings, which included rifles. They walked all night. The next day Scobell killed a deer, which they butchered and dressed and took with them. After several days of walking, four of the seven recruits deserted. The rest spent two days with serrano supporters, helping them plant and discussing the situation in the sierra. They walked for several more days and nights, visiting ranches along the way, and finally arrived at Arroyo Amplio, home of the Gaytán family. They then continued to a place where they met Arturo Gámiz and someone whose nom de guerre was Arnulfo. There they camped in a barranca, setting guards every four hours up above. Everyone took turns at chores, even at cooking their meager provisions of jerky. While they rested, they studied Che's *Guerra de Guerrillas*: "The guerrillero is a social reformer, who takes up arms in response to the people's angry protests against their oppressors and who struggles to change the social regime that keeps all his brothers disarmed, in disgrace or misery."[62]

The rules were typical of a guerrilla movement: they could spend no more than two days in any one place. They must eliminate all signs when breaking camp. They must pay for everything they took from the community or, if they had no money, promise to pay and keep the promise. They must respect women. Desertion and lack of discipline would be judged and punished. At every stop, someone spoke to the campesinos nearby, inviting them to join their discussions. Once while they were talking about the lack of food, a campesino suggested they kill one of "his cattle." When they said they had no money, he replied that the brand belonged to a well-known cacique and "it still belongs to us." From then on, they supplied themselves with meat that had been stolen "historically." Lugo pointed out that these and other initiatives came not from them but from their supporters in the countryside.[63] Their success can be measured by the fact that when the five survivors fled into the sierra after the attack on the base, they were hidden and fed, often by strangers, and not one was denounced despite the forces sent after them.

In a report dated April 27, Miguel Morán, acting sectional president of Dolores, reported that Salomón Gaytán, Arturo Gámiz, Juan Antonio Escóbel, Enrique Torres, and Agapo (Margarito?) González had arrived at the home of José Ibarra in Dolores moments after Ibarra left. They took three long guns and cartridges from the house, then dragged the bed where Ibarra slept out to the patio and set fire to it. They placed a stick of dynamite in the radio transmitter–receiver and blew it up. They threw gasoline on the generator and burned it as well, then the house itself. The neighbors put the fire out.[64]

Elsewhere in the Movement

On April 24, students of the Normal Night School invited local groups to join Comité Pro. Headed by Antonio Becerra Gaytán and financed by Lázaro Villarreal, this committee, which called for constitutional guarantees, was another example of the movement's insistence that it was they who obeyed the laws and the government and landowners who broke them. On April 27, three hundred students rallied and demanded liberty for Hilario Cardona. On May 1, they published a manifesto calling on all citizens, regardless of political affiliation or religion, to defend their constitutional rights.[65]

In May, the students of Saucillo and Salaices published a letter disclaiming any participation in the events of April 6. Their campuses had been occupied by the soldiers of the Fifth Military Zone.[66]

In northern Durango, six hundred campesinos set out from Canutillo, where Pancho Villa had spent his last days, to march on the state capital and demand the distribution of the haciendas belonging to Marcario Pérez, Baudelio Rodríguez, "and other foreigners." Led by the UGOCM, when offered a bribe to call off the march, they took the money and continued.[67]

Reyes described her participation in that march in detail. They began with a rally for the townspeople, then marched four abreast with banners, one hour of walking and ten minutes of rest, from six in the morning to six at night, with a break for the midday meal. Then they scattered on both sides of the highway to sleep on the ground. Reyes still put on face cream and lipstick and always covered the stone she used for a pillow with a kerchief of artificial silk.

> Curled up in my poncho, I began to dream, shifting aside the pebbles under my ribs with my body. A few minutes later, thinking I was asleep, a compañero

approached and put a blanket over me, then tiptoed away. I stopped being cold and fell into a deep sleep among the campesinos. On waking, I couldn't open my eyes because the lids were swollen and stuck together with mucus, perhaps from sunburn. They brought me a damp handkerchief to clean them and when I opened my eyes, they were red as a rabbit's.

"Happy the eyes that see you," I joked while folding the blankets; two more had arrived overnight. I felt enveloped in their affection.

A local woman who came to see what was going on asked, "Aren't you afraid of spending the night among so many men?"

"No, señora, they respect me and take care of me. In all the years I've been with campesinos, I never saw one who did not respect the compañeras."

The march began early, and then, with swollen hands, blistered feet, eyes reddened by the sun, and bathed in sweat and dirt, we halted among some houses alongside the Nazas River. Immediately the committees went into action: some called the locals to a rally, others put up posters and banners, others improvised a stage, and I tuned my guitar before the curious eyes of a group of gypsies whose carts were going in the opposite direction and who had stopped in the same place. A fat old gypsy woman, in a loud voice, said to me, "Where are you taking them, woman? In the south there is nothing, take them up north to the cotton harvests. That's where the money is now." Oscar González Eguiarte laughed and commented, "She thinks you're contracting people to work. She can see you have the face of a foreman."[68]

On April 27, the army returned to the streets to beat up the students who gathered in front of the district court to support Hilario Cardona. José Humberto Rojas Ruíz, the federal attorney general, had called out the army, although district judge José Flores Sánchez insisted soldiers would only aggravate the situation.[69]

On May 16, attorney general Villa Rentería resigned at the governor's request. Villa Rentería announced that he had been scapegoated for the events of April 6, and he went on to cite the state government for bad organization and mistaken policies and their failure to resolve the crisis in the countryside. José Melgar de la Peña, former director of the state penitentiary, was named to replace him.[70]

On May 18, gunmen surprised members of the GPG near Dolores, although the group escaped without injury. The secretary of national defense sent three sections of soldiers, each with thirty-three members, to find them; the troops failed to make contact.[71] The soldiers hired guides among the serranos who led them around on the steepest trails without finding anyone. The troops used counterinsurgency methods to break the civilians suspected of supplying the guerrillas: they beat them, hung them by the arms so their feet did not touch the ground, and dangled them from helicopters flying close to the rocks.[72]

In May, the students threatened a national strike if Hilario Cardona were not released, he being the only prisoner still in jail.[73]

On May 25, Alvaro Ríos was arrested and accused of the murder of Roberto Carranza Anchondo, who had died after a beating during the riot on April 24, 1961, at the rally organized by Friends of Cuba. Ríos had been on stage with other speakers the entire time. *Indice* blamed the riot on the Catholic right. The attorney Salustio González of Parral was also arrested, making three political prisoners counting Cardona. Ríos had been accused of tearing down Portillo's fence in Cebadilla de Dolores the previous October; he had been out on bail on that charge, and the bail was revoked. Students demonstrated against the arrests at the Plaza Hidalgo.[74]

On May 26, fifty campesinos, among them some women, arrived in the capital from Charco de la Peña, formerly Felipe Angeles, in Julimes, demanding the presidential resolution of March 1963 (December 1962 according to RAN Chihuahua) be executed. On May 27, Salustio González was released from jail, and he announced that he would request that the governor of Durango intervene on Ríos's behalf. On May 30, the FECH organized a rally protesting the arrests of Cardona and Ríos. On May 31, a caravan of two hundred people left Saucillo on foot, heading to Chihuahua. Eight hundred people joined them in Delicias, carrying a banner that read "We demand unconditional liberty for Alvaro Ríos." The highway police set off to intercept them and confiscate any trucks. The campesinos in northern Durango were preparing to join them. The marchers collected food and money from bystanders.[75]

On June 1, Judith Reyes and Lázaro Villarreal were called into the office of the attorney general, who asked Villarreal if he knew Danzós Palomino. Villarreal said that he had not given money to Danzós but that he had given a truck and food to the campesino caravan and intended to go on helping them.[76] The same day, Judith Reyes was arrested without a warrant; she was held for seventy-two hours without being charged. This was the second time she had gone to jail under Giner Durán, both times on the Day of Liberty of the Press.

Indice published photos of her in jail, in her long colorful skirts with an abundance of beads around her neck and with her guitar, singing the "Corrido of Díaz Ordaz."[77]

In jail Reyes was subjected to long interrogations. They accused her of having brought three thousand students to burn the reviewing stand on April 6, saying they had 248 photos of proof, and yet, as she pointed out, it was the PRI who had trucked people in. They presented her with a document, from the Ejército Mexicano Popular (EMP; Mexican Popular Army), signed in the Sierra of Chihuahua.[78] They showed her some cylinders that they said were bombs, which they had found under the court house in Nuevo Casas Grandes. They insisted she tell them who was responsible for the events of April 6, and she replied Gustavo Díaz Ordaz, for ignoring the tensions in the state and the military blockade around the rural normal schools that are now incommunicado because the buses no longer stop there and because of the people's exasperation with the PRI.[79]

She was placed in a cell with fourteen women and girls, including a ten-year-old and a twelve-year-old detained for robbery, while the others were in for prostitution. From the door, one of the police introduced her as *apretada* (one of the decent—or uptight—ones). Reyes entered, shouting, "Make way, I've been wounded, I don't want to bleed on you!," and buried herself in the filthiest corner. There was urine on the floor. A girl approached and offered her an overcoat against the cold, and Reyes began to doze off. Then she was awakened and taken to a solitary cell with three stone beds that looked like catafalques and a hole in the floor for a toilet, which was open to the view of the guards, was full of excrement and menstrual rags, and was buzzing with flies.[80]

The press attacked her, although she had many friends who were reporters. A commission of journalists, students, and teachers brought her food, so she did not have to eat filth served in an old sardine tin. Her visitors included the journalist Pedro Muñoz Grado, Federico Guevara, Jesús Manuel González Raizola "Gonzalitos," and Ismael Villalobos, the Tarahumara, press photographer, and poet. The police forced Antonio Becerra to taste her food, saying the PCM meant to poison her and accuse the government of her death. They had also arrested Salustio González in Parral once again.[81]

She sang to the other prisoners and talked politics all day. "Being in jail eliminates the fear of jail," she said. The women talked about the authorities who owned the brothels and told her who went looking for boys instead of women. From inside her guitar she pulled a roll of fliers supporting the candidacy of Ramón Danzós Palomino, and handed them out. She wrote slogans on the walls, such as, "Giner is afraid of me and Díaz Ordaz is afraid of the FEP," and "The government goes on reforestation campaigns so we plant trees and at the same time gives permission to the forest-strippers [*talabosques*] to cut down Mexico's forests."[82]

One day the guards tried to rape two women. She heard the screams of homeless children being beaten. On the day she was released, she went to the mayor to protest the treatment of children and he insisted that there were no children in the city jail. When she left, on June 3, the prisoners cheered. She was met by friends from the FEP who brought along her three children, Magaly, Josué, and Berenice. On the way home, they passed the state house, where the campesinos maintained a sit-in, and she got out and sang for them.[83] On June 7, as she approached her home, she was attacked by an unknown person.[84]

The marchers from Saucillo were joined by twenty-two students from the rural normal school of Saltillo, Coahuila, including twelve girls no older than fifteen, who marched at the front with banners that read "We demand unconditional liberty for Alvaro Ríos" and "Freedom for political prisoners." Antonio Gómez Velasco, chief of the military zone, had a short discussion with the student Oscar González, remarking that some of the marchers were children, to which González replied that sometimes children were more aware than grown-ups. On June 2, three hundred protesters marched into the capital and gathered in front of the state house, where they sent a commission to meet with the governor.[85]

On June 3, two hundred campesinos gathered in front of the state house, to be joined by two hundred students from the State Normal School, Secondary School Number One, and the Technical School. The newspaper *Correo de Juárez* had published a major article on agrarian problems, reporting that when the governor received the UGOCM, he told them he knew they were organizing groups of agitators in Madera to prepare for a guerrilla war and that this would be taken up by newspapers in the United States. On June 8, the U.S. vice consul of Juárez had lunch in Chihuahua City with the attorney general and asked about Alvaro Ríos, the UGOCM, and the FEP, affirming the significance of the article in *El Correo* concerning the "communist plot."[86]

On June 8, the FECH organized a general assembly at the State Normal School to plan a demonstration for Hilario Cardona. Villarreal would pay for the leaflets. A strike was called for June 10 if Cardona were not freed, to result in a general strike in all the schools organized by the FECH. If Cardona were not released, the strike would become national through representatives of the

Juventud Comunista de México (JCM; Communist Youth of Mexico), whose arrival was expected. The next day, the IPS reported that the rally had failed because Villarreal had refused his support, and so the students had not been able to contact their colleagues throughout the republic. The three students sent by the JCM had not arrived.[87]

There were several indications of sectarian conflicts in the movement. On June 13, the IPS reported that the Comité Pro was still planning a rally the next day. While Villarreal distributed leaflets attacking the Gómez brothers as communists, Antonio and Ema Becerra Gaytán of the FEP were expected to participate. Two hundred people attended the rally.[88] In June, the DFS reported that students were worried about final exams scheduled for July and were reluctant to join demonstrations in support of the campesinos. In addition, they said that "Gómez Ramírez" (either Raúl or Pablo) encouraged them to support Cardona but not to mix with the campesinos.[89] They further reported that a rally had been suspended for lack of participants and that the students responded apathetically to the FEP's calls for progressive strikes.[90]

Indice published a photo of Judith Reyes behind bars with her guitar. The IPS reported that Reyes had appeared in the office of the attorney general saying she had a good opinion of the governor and that Gallardo (the editor of *Indice*) was stirring up trouble.[91]

The entire state elections team went on strike because they had not been paid and then quit, and the state hired persons without training who were working without typewriters or maps. Many people were signed up in the wrong voting district and would not be able to vote in the July 5 election. The governor refused to support the team because his faction in the state administration was in conflict with one led by the state director of the PRI.[92]

In June, the one hundred and three students of the Generation of Abraham González at the State Normal School agreed not to invite Giner to address their graduation, as was customary. Giner threatened to block their appointments to schools and denied them the use of state buildings for the ceremony. He forced Luis Urías, director of the school, to back down and print new invitations including his name. The students added Hilario Cardona to the list of graduates, although he still languished in jail. They followed graduation with a dance on the patio of the state house.[93]

On June 28, the Comité Pro held a rally at the Plaza de Armas with two hundred people, including students from neighboring states, demanding liberty for Hilario Cardona and Alvaro Ríos.[94]

On June 29, the FECH held a meeting with the National Center of Democratic Students in the offices of the Comité Pro to plan interviews with local authorities and discuss how to feed the out-of-state students. They asked the city for a sound truck to announce the installation of the National Student Council on June 29 and 30. They met with the mayor and informed him they were expecting delegates from around the country, including representatives of the normal schools of the DF and the IPN, who would remain in Chihuahua until Cardona was freed. They sent the sound truck through the Colonia Industrial, exhorting its neighbors to join them and blaming poverty and unemployment on the governor. On July 4, the IPS reported that the state was quiet. Most of the twenty-two out-of-state students went home after less than a week; the FECH and the National Center stopped holding demonstrations; and Cardona was eating again after a hunger strike. The IPS also reported that local PRI leaders ran an apathetic electoral campaign.[95]

On July 5, Gustavo Díaz Ordaz was elected president of the republic. Opposition candidates in Chihuahua lost. *Acción* published the laconic note that "the FEP was the only party not going through mutual recriminations, because they had not expected personal benefits."[96]

Indice published the curious item "Giner now has his very own Bible," saying Giner Durán carried a newspaper clipping referring to Che's *Guerra de Guerrillas* in his wallet, next to his heart, and insisted on reading it to everyone who came to his office.[97]

Acción reported that an article had been published in the *Los Angeles Times* in California about the events of April 6, quoting, "The Campesinos Defy; An Unpopular Governor Is the Cause of the Disturbances."[98]

In July, the New Mexican activist Reyes López Tijerina, "El Tigre," arrived in Chihuahua, leading his Federal Alliance of Mercedes to gain restitution from the U.S. government for lands lost after the Mexican-American War of 1846–1848. He had prepared material to distribute in the schools, explaining how the United States had violated the Treaty of Guadalupe Hidalgo and left the heirs of Spanish land grants without their properties. The alliance was leading a car caravan to Mexico City to request the federal government's support in recovering lost land. Crossing the border at Ciudad Juárez, they paid homage to the homeland of their ancestors. On July 14, López Tijerina was arrested in the offices of the Comité Pro and sent to the state prison for having invited participants at a rally to receive the caravan "in the name of five million Mexicans, residents of the southern U.S., victims for one hundred and seventeen years of violations of the Treaty of Guadalupe Hidalgo."[99] After three days he was released and warned to keep away from Judith Reyes, at whose home he had been staying. He and Reyes continued to Mexico City, where they were warmly received until he was again arrested and deported.[100] In 1967, López Tijerina led a group of land activists in an armed raid on the Río Arriba County Courthouse in Tierra Amarilla, New Mexico.

Repression in the Sierra

IPS reports indicated that federal agents were aware of depredations visited on campesinos of the sierra by the Ibarras and Tomás Vega. Agents Antonio Rocha Civera and José Sánchez Ibarra cited José Ibarra as the principal cause of local unrest. The local campesinos had formed the NCP Huizopa, naming Luis Estrada as the ejidal commissioner, since their lands had been invaded by Ibarra and by Vega, who fenced off the waters of the Río Tutuaca for the exclusive use of his own livestock. The solicitants were not poor but middling cattlemen; the Estradas sold between five and six hundred cattle a year for five hundred pesos each. In 1960, Tomás Vega expropriated ten thousand hectares and 475 head of cattle from the brothers Dionicio, Jorge, and Guadalupe Ortega in retaliation for damage their cattle had done on his land. The Ortega family was forced to emigrate when he threatened their lives. The report ended by noting that Salomón Gaytán and Antonio Scobell Gaytán killed Florentino Ibarra and Ignacio Gil (Gil was in fact wounded), a cowboy in his employ, on March 4 (March 5) and then burned a house belonging to the Ibarras in Dolores.[101]

Roberto Martínez Noriega, assistant director of the state police and commander of the flying squad of the Fifth Military Zone, arrested Luis and Amador Estrada along with Anastasio, Casimiro, and Israel González, the latter still showing marks of hanging around his neck. Agents listed the firearms found when the homes were searched, including four pistols and two rifles, along with five rifles belonging to the mining company where Luis Estrada worked as a night guard. The prisoners were set free on June 2 in Arroyo Amplio. José Ibarra accompanied the troops, with his sons Jesús and Rubén, and showed them who to arrest; he also provided provisions. The soldiers arrived on the planes of the company Servicios Aereos de Madera. They destroyed Luis Estrada's distillery, smashing forty-eight barrels of sotol. The agents reported that Salomón Gaytán and Antonio Escóbel were now accompanied by an individual named Eduardo (Arturo) Gámiz.[102]

Needing food, Lugo and Salomón Gaytán returned to Arroyo Amplio, leaving Arnulfo at the summit as a lookout. On the way back, absorbed in conversation, they ignored the pebbles Arnulfo was sending their way while the rural police occupied the heights. Finally, Arnulfo shouted, and the guerrillas retreated in disarray. Some days later the group reunited and engaged in fierce self-criticism for allowing themselves to be ambushed. The other two compañeros from Nuevo Casas Grandes who had joined with Lugo quit at that point, leaving him the only one of seven to withstand the rigors of the sierra.[103]

On July 15, the GPG attacked the Ibarras' house in Mineral de Dolores, which was being used as a base by five judicial police commanded by Rito Caldera Zamudio, a former white guard for the family. Legend has it that the men were stripped to their underwear and set free; Judith Reyes included this detail in her "Corrido of Arturo Gámiz" (see app.) According to Caldera's version, the police had been in the area since May searching for "Arturo Gámiz, Salomón and Antonio Gaytán, Juan Antonio Escóbel, and two unknown individuals." The day before, Francisco Molina had reported seeing armed men in the nearby Arroyo Los Táscates. At 4:00 a.m., Caldera told the guard, Manuel Gómez Licón, to come in for coffee; they were planning to follow up on the report. Gómez Licón had turned to enter the house when they heard gunshots, and Gómez was hit in the elbow. They heard voices shouting, "Long live the FEP! Long Live Palomino! Death to Díaz Ordaz!" The attackers threw grenades, setting fire to the house. The battle lasted approximately two and a half hours. When the defenders ran out of ammunition and fire raged through the wooden house, they decided to surrender. First, four came out, and then Caldera; he and Gómez threw their pistols into the fire rather than giving them up. The house caved in. Caldera was carrying an M2 and "an infinity of shots" rained down, wounding him in the right heel. The guerrillas confiscated his M2, two M1s, two 7 mm Mausers, and three .38 super pistols. The police were thrown to the ground, their hands tied behind their backs, and they were marched to town hall and then to the school, where they were lined up against the wall to be executed.[104]

The group deliberated among themselves and decided not to kill them, instead locking them up in a school room and taking Gómez Licón to have his wound treated by a neighbor. Caldera further remarked that each of the guerrillas wore "a hat with a small red and black flag" on the front and that each carried two cartridge belts across the chest and another around the waist, that Antonio Escóbel carried an M1 and each of the others a .30–06, and that Gámiz, seeing a portrait of Gustavo Díaz Ordaz in the classroom alongside Benito Juárez, had cursed and torn it down and said, "What a pity to see him next to Licenciado Benito Juárez." Caldera added that each of them carried a blue and white rubber backpack and that they declared they were "defending the oppressed and all the workers exploited by all the bosses."[105]

The IPS also reported on these events, remarking that since Gámiz had the men lined up for a firing squad and then pardoned them, this meant that "his struggle was not as the state government made it to appear." Then the report quoted General Antonio Gómez Velasco saying that the conflict was "personal," that the Ibarras had stolen a great deal of land, and that this had generated discontent, culminating in the actions of Gámiz and his band. In Madera, people blamed José and Florentino Ibarra and Tomás Vega for atrocities and dispossessions and for leaving many families homeless. They said that many people hated them and that even Vicente Arreola, manager of Bosques, regretted having sold to them and was horrified by their crimes. The report warned that if Gámiz were to be killed on orders of the governor, the region would erupt.[106]

According to Florencio Lugo, the six guerrilleros had camped nearby with nothing to eat but pinole, the ground toasted corn of the Tarahumara. At dawn they surrounded Ibarra's house on the outskirts of town. This was the same two-story house that served as the company store. Local campesinos had told the group where the rurales gathered inside. Someone went to the front door and threw a Molotov cocktail in, but dogs barked and sounded an alert and someone came outside and was shot in the arm. The attackers shot into doors and windows, exhorting the rurales to surrender. After half an hour, the flames consuming the house forced them out. The last to leave was their leader, Rito Caldera, who carried an M2 in such a way that it could be fired. The guerrillas tied the prisoners' hands just as the roof collapsed. They took their captives to the center of town, explaining their goals along the way, and that they were not fighting individuals but against "bad government, the caciques, and the exploiters, but that the prisoners would be executed for their servile attitude." They lined up the prisoners against a wall and Caldera fell on his knees, begging for mercy. The streets were empty, the inhabitants watching behind closed doors. Lugo, afraid of negative publicity if the prisoners were executed, argued against it, and convinced his companions to pardon their lives.[107]

Rito Caldera's version appears false on several points. A two-and-a-half-hour fire fight in a burning house was unlikely; the wooden structure would have collapsed long before. The hats and backpacks were absurd, and even more so the slogans exalting the FEP and Danzós Palomino. The targets of the GPG, not mentioned by Caldera or the IPS, were the caciques and their allies among the authorities; the attack was not an extension of the electoral arena. Neither Gámiz, Lugo, nor the Gaytán or Escóbel brothers were associated with the FEP.

On July 15, in the Tarahumara village of Humariza in the municipality of Nonoava near Balleza, agronomist Luis Villalobos Guerrero, Benjamín Chávez, and one unnamed indigenous person were killed in a firefight. The battle resulted from a conflict between mestizo villagers soliciting parcels and indigenous Tarahumara who had received an eighteenth-century land grant that had been amplified during the nineteenth century. Villalobos had been sent by the DAAC to make surveys and died with a .22 pistol in his hand. A number of other arms were confiscated.[108] Thirty-four people were arrested, two-thirds of them indigenous.[109] The IPS reported that Villalobos had a violent temper and had been attacked in another incident in Moris.[110] In the Fifth Resolution of the Sierra, this event appeared in a list of attacks carried out by the GPG as proof that "it is possible to take up arms and inflict defeat, although partial and limited, on the enemy," although it is unlikely the GPG had anything to do with the gunfight. Laura Castellanos called it an "uprising"[111] that showed the sierra to be "the ideal terrain for beginning the revolution," but it was more likely a sign of desperation.

Elsewhere in the State

Agronomist Ramón Romero Contreras of the state DAAC published a declaration a few days later saying that the year before, at a banquet of the Chihuahua Section of the Mexican Agronomy Society, he had described some of the thousand ways that they, the agents of DAAC, extorted the campesinos, using "an exquisite variety of negligence, incompetence, and corruption." Now they were guilty of the death of one of their own. He suggested ethics training for the DAAC and admitted that he, too, had engaged in corrupt practices but that now he was tired of "scrambling in the mud."[112]

Indice compared Giner Durán to "Atilla, Goldwater, and the military gorillas of Latin America, who know nothing of civilization and culture." Instead of arresting Ríos, Cardona, and Judith Reyes, the *Indice* writer went on, the federal attorney general, still in Chihuahua, should arrest Giner. On the next page, *Indice* complained that the agents sent from Mexico City were providing misinformation and that journalists only went to the authorities to learn the official version. No one had gone to Madera or Delicias or to the jail to interview Ríos or Cardona.[113]

In July, the Federation of Revolutionary Students of the Mexican Republic held its national meeting in Chihuahua and demanded the release of Alvaro Ríos and Hilario Cardona.[114] The conflicts in Chihuahua were gaining national attention. On July 22, unknown persons in Nuevo Casas Grandes dynamited the stand where the governor was to preside over the Wheat Fair.[115] Conflict continued in Julimes between the Ejido Felipe Angeles and the smallholders who had settled on the same land previously. The sharecroppers of San Diego de Alcalá, south of Chihuahua City, had been invaded by some five hundred cattle, who devoured pasture and crops with the collusion of San Diego's purported leader.[116]

In August, *Indice* printed a list of agrarian conflicts. They included the case of Humariza, stalled since the death of the agronomists, and listed a number of estates that violated the agrarian code, including La Gallina and El Pico de la Gallina, which belonged to the heirs of Eloy Vallina; Los Organos, of José Chávez López; El Anteojo, of the Almeida family; El Becerro, belonging to the Ramos Carrasco brothers; and Tacubaya, belonging to a foreigner named Beckman. They complained about the Ejido Villa López, on land of the former Hacienda Corrales, where three thousand ejidatarios had no pasture since the land had been given to colonists despite the legal preference for ejidos over colonies. The paper also criticized Giner Durán for flying to breakfast in Mexico City twice in one week.[117]

In a report dated August 21, an anonymous agent of the IPS described the problems in the state as "political" and deriving from the governor's failure to control various conflicts, among them the agrarian situation, agitation in the rural normal schools, unemployment in mining, and the lack of economic resources, particularly in Ciudad Juárez because of its rapid growth.[118] He added that former governors—among them Rodrigo Quevedo, Alfredo Chávez, and Teófilo Borunda—senators, and deputies had formed economic groupings that contested the governor's power and frustrated the attempts of the DAAC to affect their properties or those of their protégés. He noted that Governor Práxedes Giner Durán lacked political tact and was so crude that the banking, commercial, and industrial sectors distrusted his capacity to deal on their behalf with federal officials and that Giner had also been rude in his dealings with students and campesinos. He noted the existence of two groups contending for power. One, led by the secretary of government, Enrique Hernández Gómez, allied with his own department and those of economics, labor, and education, the attorney general, the chief of the state police, and most of the mayors in the southern part of the state. The other, led by Hector Sánchez Calderón, president of the state committee of the PRI, was allied with the governor's private secretary, his chief of staff, most of the local deputies, federal senators and deputies, the CTM, the LCA, the Confederación Nacional de Organizaciones Populares (CNOP; National Confederation of Popular Organizations), the teachers' unions, and local party leaders.[119] Both groups prevented the DAAC from acting on behalf of the campesinos, and their competition was so fierce that investors were scared away. He added that there were no public works in progress and that Chihuahua and Juárez were full of the unemployed; Juárez was in chaos, and the funds proportioned by the Programa Nacional Fronterizo (PRONAF) had gone to benefit private individuals, among them the Mascareñas family.[120]

The report continued to explain that large landowners held vast amounts of territory protected by CIGs or forestry concessions and that the CIGs were running out. The campesinos had come to distrust the CNC and had turned to the UGOCM and the CCI. Ejidos were awarded presidential resolutions without sufficient study because the lands awarded were already being worked by smallholders who also attempted to regularize their possession. In Madera, where enormous extensions were exploited by Bosques de Chihuahua, lands susceptible to partition were sold to private parties and the authorities ignored the pleas of the campesinos, giving rise to a *guerrilla* led by Arturo Gámiz García.[121]

The report dealt with a number of agrarian cases in detail: Charco de Peña; Belisario Domínguez; Ojo de Peñuelas; NCP Seis de Enero de 1915, soliciting lands from the former Hacienda Palomas; NCP Huizopa in Madera; Humariza; Santo Domingo; Ejido El Raíz in Madera; Netzahualcoyotl in Ascensión; La Pinta and La Joya and its additions; and Bosques de Chihuahua—with recommendations for their resolution and a breakdown of hectares exploited, sold, donated, and affected. The author noted that it was the campesino or low-income background of the students that led them to sympathize with the campesinos and join them in the invasions regardless of the left-wing orientation of their teachers.[122]

The report continued to explain that the above-mentioned conflict between the chair of the state PRI and the secretary of government had led to the state's failure to support recent electoral campaigns. The CNOP did not exist, and the LCA was weak, supplanted by the UGOCM and the CCI.[123] Nevertheless, the PRI had won the last elections. The PAN was competing for influence with the Democratic Christian Front. The PPS, whose leaders also led the UGOCM, had dedicated itself to land invasions and petitions to the DAAC and had failed to support the presidential campaign of Gustavo Díaz Ordaz, as ordered by its national convention, because they were influenced by the radical politics of the FEP and the CCI and regarded Lombardo Toledano's support for GDO as accommodationist. (The influence seems unlikely, as the FEP and the CCI were of recent origin, and the UGOCM had taken a militant posture before.) Lombardo Toledano was opposed to the activities of Alvaro Ríos and Arturo Gámiz. The Authentic Party of the Mexican Revolution was inactive, since its leader, Lázaro Villarreal, took part in every activity, including those of the FEP and the Comité Pro. The FEP had influence among students, teachers, and campesinos, with offices in the principal cities, among them Chihuahua, Juárez, Parral, and Madera. Their goals were to incite violence in agrarian struggles; organize the unemployed, especially in Juárez and Parral; and work among the proletarian communities on the outskirts of Chihuahua and Juárez. They led the PPS and the UGOCM; their own leader was Salustio González Delgado, an attorney in Parral.[124] The National Sinarchist Union had little importance, most of it in Juárez. The Democratic Christian Front, former PANistas, had some adherents in the prep school of the Universidad Autónoma de Chihuahua; they had led campaigns against free textbooks and were considered of the extreme right.[125]

When the DAAC failed to resolve campesinos' problems, the report concluded that a certain "aversion" to the army arose when it dislodged campesino occupations. General Antonio Gómez Velasco had investigated the situation in Madera and had determined that the Ibarra family was behind the disturbances. When Ibarra was invited to leave the area, the people regained their confidence in the army. Gómez Velasco was said to have influence over the governor.[126]

Lázaro Villarreal, the businessman who supported the movement for years, died on September 6, 1964, at the age of 69. He had been paying a restaurant to send three daily meals to the prisoners Alvaro Ríos, Hilario Cardona, and Guillermo Rodríguez Ford after it was discovered that their prison food was contaminated with cockroaches and excrement and they went on a hunger strike.[127]

Nominally the head of the local PARM, Villarreal had financed a number of activities by both PPS and PCM affiliates, but there was no evidence that he provided political direction.

Indice published a letter from Guillermo Rodríguez Ford, still in prison, and Arturo Gámiz, somewhere in the sierra, headlined "Alchemy in Politics," which stated that private property leads to the existence of antagonistic classes; bourgeois liberty emerges from feudalism; and the state defends the rich, becomes reactionary, and turns against the liberties it once proclaimed. The state needs to disguise itself and becomes more complex, evolving into superstructure and base. The transformation of capitalism into true democracy would be alchemy. Revolutionaries should support the legislature, although it is of secondary importance.[128] The letter indicated the widening break between Gámiz and the PPS, which supported the national bourgeoisie as a stepping stone to socialism.

According to the DFS, in the beginning of September, Gámiz offered to surrender if his safety were guaranteed and named the agents he would give himself up to in Madera, but he did not show up.[129] Lugo related an event that occurred probably around the same time. Gámiz, subject to an arrest warrant since he skipped bail in March, was recognized by a former neighbor, now a municipal cop, as he walked through Chihuahua City one evening. Without naming Gámiz, the cop called for reinforcements. While they waited, Gámiz convinced him of the justice of his struggle. The cop told him which official to bribe at the station, and Gámiz, in perhaps a rare occurrence, was carrying sufficient cash. The next morning he walked away, unidentified. Lugo used this anecdote to illustrate the power of persuasion derived from conviction. "The strength of the words goes in proportion to the clarity and firmness of the ideas." Gámiz, having been a neighbor, might have previously made an impression that influenced the cop's actions. He was indeed well known as a persuasive speaker, having education and experience. This raises the questions, would Lugo himself have been capable of the same eloquence, and why wasn't such persuasion universally effective?[130]

At this time, Alvaro Ríos was in prison for one hundred days. He refused to leave under bond because it would have meant admitting guilt.[131]

An undated card in the IPS archives stated that "The gang is divided in two groups. Salvador Gaytán: Mauricio Torres, Carlos Yáñez, Refugio Yáñez, Ramón Mendoza, Manuel Ríos. Cebadilla, Los Otates, Punto de los Ríos. Arturo Gámiz: Salomón Gaytán, J. Antonio Gaytán, Refugio Portillo Miramontes, Margarito González. Dolores. Río Ancho. Huizopa."[132] Carlos Yáñez had been jailed in Guerrero for a considerable period of time, and Manuel Ríos was the brother of the murdered activist, Carlos Ríos, and an early associate of Alvaro Ríos (no relation).

In October, *Indice* reprinted, with abundant photos, a long article by Daniel de los Reyes, including an interview with Arturo Gámiz and Salomón Gaytán. The article had originally been published in the national *Sucesos para Todos*.[133] After days of visiting hamlets in the sierra and sleeping on floors, Reyes, his unnamed photographer, and his guide, Luis Romero, were awakened before dawn by Gámiz and Gaytán. Gámiz carried a pistol and Gaytán an M2 and a .38 pistol. Gámiz did most of the talking, explaining the long-standing enmity between the Gaytán and Ibarra families. Gaytán said that when he was a child, a small plane had gone down in the sierra. It had been abandoned for months when some people rented mules from his father to go and cut soles for sandals from its tires; José Ibarra arrived with his armed guards and threw them in jail. As a young child, Gaytán had seen Ibarra burst into their home "without respect" and had vowed to exact revenge when he was older. Fortunato Gil, owner of the Charamuscas Ranch, had sent Salomón's father to jail for rustling. After Florentino Ibarra was killed, Salvador Gaytán was forced to go to the United States and work as a bracero. Gámiz insisted, responding to a direct question, that they did not rise up in arms against the government but against the caciques José Ibarra and Tomás Vega, and he cited as evidence their having released Rito Caldera's police unharmed. The reporter brought them a letter from Ernesto Castellanos, Mayor of Madera, guaranteeing their safety should they surrender. They refused.[134]

The photos published with the article included one of Fernando Solís, former police chief in Mineral de Dolores, removed by José Ibarra for obstructing his activities; Felicitas Gaytán, Salomón's sister, with Señora Carlota, widow of González, whose ten- and twelve-year-old children were abused by soldiers and gunmen; and Daniel González, who had witnessed the torture and death of Reinaldo Solís at the hands of Francisco Vega, a relative of Tomás Vega and an officer of the rural police. There was also a photo of María Mendoza, widow of Ortega, in the mayor's office. Her nephew had been killed by Ibarra and his gunmen, who stole some eight hundred head of livestock.[135]

Another witness, Israel González Ríos, declared, "They accused me of supplying the guerrillas who went to the sierra, they came to my house and, since I bring merchandise from Madera to sell to my neighbors in competition with the company store, they robbed me of everything." They arrested González Ríos and took him to the Cerritos Ranch, where a lieutenant named Fuentes put a rope around his neck and hung him from a tree. A soldier pushed on the rope while another hit him in the stomach with a rifle butt, then they cut him down and left him for dead until some women came and revived him. Meanwhile they searched his house. They gave the corn to their horses after letting them loose to trample the crops. They divided up the merchandise, and some of them left wearing new hats. An individual named José de la Luz Domínguez carried an enormous bundle of booty on his head. They held Amador Estrada for nine days, including three mornings on foot under the sun without a hat.[136]

José, Rubén, and Manuel Ibarra as well as various other gunmen, rurales, and soldiers commanded by Lieutenant Colonel Roberto Martínez Noriego had appeared in Dolores and the surrounding areas after Salomón Gaytán shot Florentino Ibarra. They came to the Rancho Arroyo Amplio, the home of Aurelia Aguirre, Salomón's mother, and rounded up the neighbors along with everyone in the household. They beat Juan Antonio Gaytán with rifle butts until his arm was useless. Then they took him, along with Loreto Amaya, Eleuterio Solís, Jesús González, Antonio González, Venancio Ríos, and some other rancheros to El Aterrizaje, a landing field high on the mountain where the soldiers were camped.[137]

Luis Estrada, a forty-seven-year-old rancher and father of five, reported,

> It was May 24 when it all began. We were arrested at one in the morning and taken to a nearby arroyo to be questioned. They kept asking where was Gaytán and who helped him, and we said we didn't know, all night long. Then the one they called the Venado [deer], of the state police, dark, average height, maybe thirty-five years old, told them to beat me, but they preferred torture. They kept me all day in the sun without a hat. In the afternoon, while I was still suffering from sunburn, they went to my house and searched it. My wife asked to see the warrant, and they shoved her in response. Someone dressed in an army uniform shouted, "With or without an order, we will search your house!" A soldier stole a case of beer and took it to the lieutenant colonel as a gift. After taking whatever they liked from all the houses in Huizopa, where the rancheros are petitioning for an ejido, the lieutenant colonel came to me and shouted, "Get the hell away from these lands. The government does not want you here. You have to stop petitioning for land."[138]

According to Estrada, since the army, being federal, represents the president of the republic, when the rancheros were ordered off their land, they understood the order as coming from the president.[139]

After beating up Juan Antonio Gaytán, José Ibarra took him to the assistant state attorney general to put him in jail. But the assistant took his statement, conducted an investigation, and released him. Juan Antonio joined the guerrillas. Ibarra announced that he himself would exact justice. He returned to the home of Señora Gaytán (Aguirre de Gaytán) at dawn, accompanied by the rurales and Martínez Noriego. They entered cursing, wrecking the furniture, and threatening to burn the house down. They put a bridle around the neck of José de la Luz, age eleven, and announced they were going to hang him. They hanged the child from a tree, with his toes touching the ground, in front of his grandmother, shoving him as he went into convulsions and nearly strangled. Neither he nor his grandmother would talk.[140]

Repeated acts of terror in the sierra had a disproportionate impact on women. As the men disappeared into jail or clandestinity, women were left in poverty with large families to provide for and few opportunities to work outside the home. While protecting and providing for the family was a key aspect of masculine honor, disappearing into clandestinity absolved men of that responsibility without prejudicing their virility.[141] As Nithia Castorena remarked, "the women did not appear among the considerations to take into account. They were completely omitted from the priorities to be resolved."[142] The assaults also constricted the family economy by forcing women to curtail their activities outside the home. While the men of the sierra had long been compelled to migrate for work, leaving women and girls to do their chores in pastures and fields, the men now disappeared without sending money home. Without them, the women worked double shifts, often far from home, searching for firewood, herbs, and wild foods, managing herds, and visiting far-flung neighbors. In these widely scattered rancherias, even staying home offered no protection.

Women sheltered and nursed fugitives, took food to their hiding places, and served as messengers. They hid and transported weapons. In 2007, I spoke with Aurelia Gaytán Aguirre, the oldest of the Gaytán siblings, then in her eighties and living in the town of Madera. She described the day she presented herself before General Antonio Gómez Velasco, commander of the Fifth Military Zone, in summer, 1964, saying,

I hear you are looking for me. You said that on May 25, I took him [her brother Salomón] a basket with food and a bottle of wine, fresh clothes, and who knows what else. Ay, I told him, listen, my general, you know this is a small town, haven't you noticed that in this rancho there's no shops selling bottles of wine, and we're not familiar with the basket. If, by chance, I had taken him food, it would be in a feed sack.

She neither admitted nor denied the accusation. In this conversation, she consistently referred to José Ibarra not by name, but as "the enemy."[143] Later that summer, her sister Felicitas accompanied a reporter and photographer documenting caciqual atrocities and allowed herself to be photographed outside her home, dressed for the occasion.[144] These women were neither passive victims of caciqual abuse nor of their menfolk's decision to join the struggle; they were actors in their own right within the limitations imposed by gender.

The Move to Mexico City

After a period of scattered small-scale ambushes, which provoked low-intensity warfare as platoons of soldiers and state police combed the rancherias looking for a handful of young men, members of the group headed for Mexico City, hoping to broaden their contacts and undergo military training. They also hoped to defuse tension and protect the leaders, Gámiz and Salomón Gaytán. Few sources are available for these events beyond participant memoirs and interviews.

On September 15, 1964, on the eve of Mexico's most important patriotic holiday, while hitchhiking, Lugo was picked up by the army as they conducted a gun-control campaign. Lugo was carrying a pistol, but it escaped detection. A few days later, he met Gámiz in Chihuahua City, who gave him a mimeographed document to distribute, now unavailable, that contained the "political foundation of the *guerrilla*." He was instructed to make contact and inform the *guerrilla* of the immediate departure for the Federal District via Chihuahua City. A small group remained in the sierra, where they would perform a handful of actions. Wearing clerical garb as disguise, some of the guerrillas traveled to Chihuahua in a late-model car provided by the urban supporters and then on to Mexico City. Lugo traveled by bus with Oscar Sandoval, a student at the State

Normal School. Sandoval's family would report his disappearance in November. In Guanajuato, Lugo and Sandoval asked a collaborator for money to continue by train.[145] If Lugo's date was accurate, some members of the GPG spent as much as a year away from Chihuahua.

The decision to leave the sierra and strike out for the center was the turning point between the GPG as armed self-defense and an armed vanguard. It was a move to recruit among strangers and not among the population of the sierra, and it implied alliances with the professional left and their parties. This called into question the nature of the enterprise; was it an elite head guiding a more or less inert—and not to be recruited from—body of campesinos? Did Gámiz and Salomón Gaytán consider their base in the sierra consolidated and secured, so they could turn their attention elsewhere? Was there nothing left to do among the scattered rancherias? Were the mountains of Chihuahua not a better venue for training? In Mexico City, they engaged in political study that could have been done anywhere. The military training, consisting of target practice and hikes in the central mountains, could also have been done in Chihuahua, where they would have learned the terrain on which they would fight. In the sierra, the movement had deep roots; now it became increasingly abstract.

With whom did Gámiz meet in Mexico City? The split in the FECSM that left Lucio Cabañas opposed to the students of Salaices was only recently healed, and the situation in Guerrero had not coalesced into an armed movement. If he met with the PPS or the JP or both, there was no indication that those groups offered support. Would he have been too closely allied with the PPS to make contact with the PCM? Did he meet with the journalist Víctor Rico Galán, who came to the sierra within weeks of the attack and wrote for a national audience? Did he make contacts in the normal schools or in the UNAM or the IPN where he had been a student leader?

How did they attempt to raise money? Lugo described an aborted plan to rob a small shop, which Gámiz called off when he realized the shopkeeper was not alone.[146] Mendoza's recollections of their attempts at stealing cars revealed a comic ineptitude.[147] In Chihuahua, they had supporters, both in the sierra and in the city; in Mexico City they had (and were) no one.

On arrival, they lodged with a family. Then they split up because they could not afford to rent a place of their own, and their presence had become dangerous and uncomfortable. According to Lugo, Gámiz took a group to Zacatecas City while another stayed in Mexico City, and Lugo went briefly to Chihuahua where he met with Pablo Gómez, and then both returned to Mexico City.[148]

Gómez's nephew, Francisco (Paco) Ornelos, in his memoir, *Sueños de Libertad*, described training in the mountains of Zacatecas with Oscar Sandoval, Rafael Martínez Valdivia, and Antonio Scobell for "three or four weeks" in June 1965. Sandoval and Martínez Valdivia had been his companions in the State Normal School. He mentioned their having rented a house near a garbage dump. They gathered cactus fruit—*tunas* and *pitayas*—in the mountains. The training consisted of hiking and sleeping outside. They took turns reading *Memorias de Pancho Villa* by Martín Luis Guzmán; *Thus the Steel was Tempered* by Nikolai Ostrovski, an inspirational novel about the Russian Revolution; and *The Young Guard: Marcelo Usabiaga; A Life of Commitment and Struggle*, about the Spanish Civil War.[149] This account left a gap of many months, from September 1964 to June 1965.

According to Ornelas, after training in Zacatecas in June 1965, they returned to Mexico City, where they were joined in August by Pablo Gómez, Gámiz, and the "rest of the compañeros." For six or seven weeks, they trained in the mountains to the east, toward Puebla. Groups of two or three would climb separately, uniting at the summit. They hunted for food with slingshots and a .22 rifle. According to Ornelas, this summer's training was the bond that united those who assaulted the base; those who did not take part were the ones who failed to arrive on September 23. In this connection he named Pedro Uranga, Juan Fernández, and Juan Aguila, who joined the group in mid-September in Chihuahua City and got lost looking for the meeting place; Saúl Ornelas Gómez, who left the group to look for Uranga, Fernández, and Aguila; and Salvador and Antonio Gaytán, who spent only a few days in DF and failed to arrive on time with the arms. Finally, he mentioned two teachers from Salaices and an unnamed woman who stole off in the night.[150] According to *Las armas*, Mendoza and Salvador Gaytán spent three months in Mexico City, leaving Chihuahua the beginning of June.[151]

Matías Fernández, who later participated in the attack and escaped, listed Zacatecas, El Vaso de Texcoco, Ajusco, Milpa Alta, San Gregorio Tlalpan, and the Cerro del Peñon as sites for military training. He listed the people who helped them economically: Doctor Rafael Estrada Villa; Roberto Jaramillo; Alfonso Pliego, a teacher at the IPN and perhaps the UNAM; Demetrio Vallejo, hero of the railway workers' strike; Doctor Ciro Jiménez Sánchez; the wrestler Arsacio Vanegas; and Heberto Castillo.[152]

According to Lugo, the group rented a headquarters in the Colonia Morelos in Mexico City. For training, they walked to Santa Martha Acatitla, the site of a prison, where subsequent activists were held. From there they walked into the hills, where they practiced with explosives and target shooting.[153]

Pablo Gómez spent the winter of 1964–1965 in Mexico City attempting to obtain permission to move to Cuba with his wife and five children, whom he had installed in an inhospitable slum. The visa was denied. Gómez blamed Lombardo Toledano and his opposition to the radical actions of the UGOCM in Chihuahua for the denial, although Lombardo might have been glad to see the last of him. The family had no resources and lived in brutal conditions. In March 1965, they returned to their home in Chihuahua, where Pablo was then in hiding. His daughter Alma, the oldest child and a student at the rural normal, described retrieving his doctor's bag from his office and doing other errands. In August 1965, Gómez returned to Mexico City, where he met several times with the school inspector José Santos Valdés, an old friend, who tried to persuade him to take the teaching job he had been assigned in Perote, Veracruz. Instead, he joined the *guerrilla*.[154]

In Mexico City the group contacted Lorenzo Cárdenas Barojas for training. Cárdenas Barojas was a retired army captain who had known Fidel Castro during his Mexican sojourn (1955–56) and had smuggled arms to revolutionary forces in Guatemala. According to Lugo, he taught the Chihuahua guerrilleros to make topographical surveys, read maps, and plan an ambush.[155] While many of the survivors regarded him as a spy who betrayed them to military intelligence and caused the attack on September 23 to fail, that assertion has not been proven. Adela Cedillo uncovered evidence that Cárdenas Barojas was imprisoned and tortured in Military Camp Number One between 1969 and 1971 and described him as an "involuntary informant."[156]

Lugo discussed the move to the center of the country, focusing on the shortcomings of the urban support network in Chihuahua, which failed to recruit for the armed nucleus and to provide adequate logistical and financial support, such as boots and cash. But the question remains, Why recruit in the city and not among the serranos themselves? Lugo did note that "theoretically" the *guerrilla* should come from among the locals and that "it is the political work among the masses that goes on everyday forming the militant, and it is the political-military capacity of the *guerrilla* that ensures the confidence of the campesinos in the struggle and their subsequent recruitment."[157]

He suggested that Gámiz should have demanded cadres from among the urban supporters, including Oscar González Eguiarte, who led an armed action in 1968 in which he was killed. Lugo accused the urban supporters of being "subjective, romantic, and frequently without political experience."[158] In abandoning the sierra for Mexico City, Gámiz was depriving them of the very movement they supported and their opportunity for political experience.

The strength of the movement was in its attachment to Chihuahua in its specificity, its vast landholdings and landless mass of returned braceros and out-of-work sawmill operatives, and its urban dwellers whose parents were still in the backlands. In describing the limited possibilities for training in arms during the initial time in Mexico City, Lugo remarked, "We knew that our real strength lay in our political capacity to join and assimilate with the people."[159] The question is, why did they move away from the people who already supported them?

When the leadership decided to work clandestinely, the impetus that had mobilized crowds in the public square was deflected, transmuted, and finally subordinated to the armed movement to which it gave birth. 1964 had seen a series of spectacular events: the occupation of the DAAC, repeated land invasions, the mobilization against Díaz Ordaz, student strikes and protests, and rallies for the political prisoners, for the reopening of dormitories, and so forth.

In Lugo's phrasing, Gómez and González Eguiarte "showed with their deaths their love for the people and for the revolution,"[160] but while this may be what he meant by ideological preparation—the willingness to make the supreme sacrifice—work in the public sphere required a different set of skills than those of a serrano fighter, who needed marksmanship, endurance, rapport with the serranos, and the ability to become invisible. The urban supporters had to be resourceful, persuasive in fund-raising, and attentive to details, combining discretion with advocacy. Arturo Gámiz embodied both: he was a talented orator, a skilled organizer, and he had the stamina to adapt to harsh conditions in the sierra. The photo of horsemen published with Daniel de los Reyes's article evoked the sort of idyll these young men briefly shared, living outdoors in the pine forests and dominating a vast area stretching to Sonora.

Are *romantic* and *subjective* code words for feminine, for the normalistas of Saucillo, in the forefront of the melee during the occupation of the DAAC and the demonstrations before the state house? In an incident widely reported but vague on the details, two or three normalistas from Saucillo attempted to board the train to Madera to join the *guerrilla* and were prevented by Pablo Gómez, in one version only days before the assault. In Montemayor's interview with Guadalupe Jacott, she named Luisina (Alvarado) as her only companion on that occasion and said that when the two were pulled off the train, she went to stay with her uncles and aunts in Anáhuac, where she heard the news of the assault.[161] But by this time Jacott had dropped out of school and was working full-time with the UGOCM, which brings into question her assertion that the two girls started from the school. And if they did start from the school, how far did Gómez go to run them down, since the train for Madera did not pass through Saucillo? In Montemayor's interview with Laura Gaytán and Clara Elena Gutiérrez, Gutiérrez named Luisina Alvarado, Lupe Jacott, and herself. In this version, the three had decided to leave school, so they went to Delicias, where they bought clothing suitable for the sierra, and then on to Chihuahua, where they met with Arturo Gámiz, Saúl Chacón, and the Rodríguez Ford brothers, and Gámiz invited them to join the *guerrilla* in Cebadilla de Dolores. But then they apparently returned to Saucillo, where their absence was noted, and Pablo Gómez, suspecting their intentions, borrowed a car and chased them down, forcing them off the train, because, according to Clara, he feared the effect on the rural schools should they be found out, since the government already wanted to shut down the school.[162] If her version is accurate, then Gámiz supported the participation of at least these young women.

According to Florencio Lugo, discussing the problems of recruitment, when "a message arrived from the city saying that seven compañeras were ready to join the armed group and asked for authorization, our response was that at the moment it was not possible or practical for them to join us, since the beginning of a *guerrilla* imposed a strength and sacrifice in every aspect that were difficult to bear."[163] Physical conditions in the sierra were brutal, especially for townsfolk, but this judgment assumed that women were less capable than men.

Régis Debray, in *Revolution in the Revolution?*, emphasized the need for mobility and flexibility: "Only at the risk of losing initiative, speed of movement, and maneuverability, can a guerrilla unit take with it women, children, and household belongings from one village to another."[164] (The Spanish translation added "animales domésticos" to the list, which is not found in the French original.) Despite his desire to "free the present from the past," Debray assumed that women would always belong with the household goods and children. While this work by Debray was not available at the time, the ideas it expressed must have been common. (It is interesting that none of Debray's critics, collected in 1968, found his exclusion of women noteworthy.[165]) Lupe Jacott denied that the women were seen as less capable; she said the leadership only wanted to protect them. She said that the women's work, as messengers and fundraisers, complemented that of the men.[166]

By the time of the Movimiento Armado Revolucionario (MAR; Armed Revolutionary Movement), in the late 1960s, with a nucleus of students from the Universidad Michoacana de San Nicolás de Hidalgo, such judgments had been overcome. A number of women participated in the MAR, including the Chihuahuenses Alma Gómez Caballero and Herminia Gómez Carrasco (Pablo and Raúl's daughters), Minerva Armendáriz, and Laura Gaytán Saldívar, all relatives of members of earlier armed movements, and Bertha Vega Fuentes, along with her four brothers, friends of the Gaytán family.

The intense emotions generated by struggle, working day and night in close quarters, and the youth of most of the participants may have led to romantic liaisons, although little evidence remains. Judith Reyes and Alvaro Ríos were romantically linked. Arturo Gámiz was rumored to have had several girlfriends, none of them leading actors among the normalistas.[167] Judith Reyes's daughter, Magaly, bore Gámiz's child.[168] In 1967 Oscar González Eguiarte, leader of the successor *guerrilla*, Grupo Popular Guerrillero–Arturo Gámiz, made the following statement regarding marriage and romantic relationships among the *guerrilla*: "we also suppress the requirement of being and remaining single . . . because this requirement restricts, limits, the participation of valuable elements . . . and we tolerate authorized courtships and marriages."[169]

Meanwhile in Chihuahua

On September 7, Augustín Olachea Aviles, the secretary of national defense, visited Chihuahua escorted by Gómez Velasco. The stated reason for the visit had to do with narcotics production in the southern part of the state. The Eighty-Second Battalion was sent to Parral to combat drug production, and additional military forces were sent to Madera.[170] Within decades, the cultivation of opium poppies and marijuana would dominate the region as it does today.

Examples of the DFS's inability to understand the information they gathered were found in a report dated October 8, 1964: an "iluminado" (wise man) named Gámiz, who began with two men and now commanded eighty, had risen against the bad government of General Giner Durán ("Giner de los Ríos") and was being supplied by José Santos Valdés, of Lerdo, Durango. He was financed by *Indice*, and the engineer Oscar Flores (who followed Giner Durán as governor) was the true soul of this little revolution. In 1960 he had appeared in the march on the capital from Madera. In 1962 he had gone to Germany to study Marxism-Leninism. In 1963 he had organized the protest before DAAC and the Encounter of the Sierra. Gámiz was with the MLN and had campaigned for Danzós Palomino and the FEP, although earlier he had urged the campesinos not to join the CCI. The incident with Rito Caldera was related more or less according to Caldera's report, with the odd detail that, leaving the burning house, Caldera had attempted to embrace Gámiz, and that was when he was shot in the heel. Finally, the report described the meeting called by Gómez Velasco described below and ended by saying that cavalry officer Tafoya wanted to exterminate the group but that Gómez Velasco held him back.[171] The report exaggerated Gámiz's strength, with eighty men, to justify the authorities' failure to contain him. It is unlikely that the group received any help from *Indice* or Santos Valdés. The agent, linking Gámiz first to *Indice* and Santos Valdés and then to the FEP and Danzós Palomino, appropriated and made use of the political conflicts he could put names to, gathering all the enemies of the state on one team and failing to understand the complexity of their affiliations and rivalries.

Military zone commander Gómez Velasco ordered José Ibarra out of Madera. There are two versions, giving different months in 1964, for that encounter. In a DFS report written after the attack, José Ibarra had been told by Giner Durán and Gómez Velasco to leave his ranch in Dolores and his family home in Temósachic to avoid greater agitation. Four months later, in October, Ibarra returned to Temósachic with the help of federal forces and the rural police and resumed living with his wife and visiting his properties.[172]

According to Daniel de los Reyes, Ibarra left the sierra, announcing he would soon return "to go on hanging bandits," and he left Rito Caldera and the rurales in charge of his house in Mineral de Dolores. Caldera sent a challenge to Salomón Gaytán, "If you are a man, come down and show it," which Gaytán accepted, attacking Ibarra's house on July 15.[173] This version would have Ibarra leaving Dolores before July 15.

In another version, Gómez Velasco announced that the recent troubles in Madera were due to the terrorism José Ibarra had exacted on its people. He summoned Ibarra to a meeting with Giner Durán and Ernesto Castellanos, mayor of Madera, and ordered Ibarra to leave the area.[174] Ibarra agreed to depart by the first of October; he would go to Temósachic with all his belongings and family members. The Fifth Military Zone would guarantee his safety during the move.[175] Gómez Velasco admitted to having given orders to the officer in charge of Temósachic to protect Ibarra but only while he gathered his belongings and herded his cattle from Madera. The point of the vigilance was to keep them from stealing anything else.[176]

The School Closings

Just before school began in the fall, state director of education Francisco Javier Alvarez, on the governor's orders, announced the permanent closure of the normal night schools in Chihuahua, Juárez, Ojinaga, and Parral, saying they had fulfilled their function. There would be no budget for new schools or teachers. He had recently closed the dormitories of the Technical School and the Technical School for Young Ladies for being "antipedagogical." Finally, he announced that teachers considered agitators would be transferred to new schools.[177] The dormitories had been in operation for some forty years and were the only way students with scarce resources could study. *Indice* argued that Giner had announced the closing of dormitories for "immorality" (homosexuality) but that such immorality was "only a factor in England and the U.S. where dormitories exist because the students' parents divorce and want nothing to do with the children beyond providing for them financially." *Indice* further insinuated that if Giner were looking for homosexuals, they could be found in the state house. They also accused authorities of robbing scholarship money and closing the dorms as if the population were already educated.[178]

The opening of the State Normal School and the rural normals was delayed. The students went out on strike soon after they did open but continued to receive rations and other habitual services while striking.[179]

Pablo Gómez complained to Jaime Torres Bodet, director of the national education department, that he had been transferred out of state. He repeated his claim that during his two years of teaching at the normal school of Saucillo, he had also acted as the students' doctor and had requested a formal appointment as such on repeated occasions, but the appointment had not been granted.[180]

On October 23, the student society of the State Normal School, of which José Mariñelarena was secretary general, warned the governor of a general strike if Cardona were not released. The DFS remarked that it was unlikely that Mariñelarena had actually signed the document since he had good relations with the state government and therefore was distrusted by Rodolfo Ramos Beltrán, president of the FECH.[181] It was Mariñelarena who had kicked off the riot against Díaz Ordaz in April, so his "good relations" would be recent. The State Normal School went back out on strike.

On October 28, Hilario Cardona's first criminal case, regarding the occupation of the DAAC offices, was dismissed on appeal. His responsibility as a "material author" was not proven. The original judgment had been based on his participation in its conception and preparation, since it was not possible to establish the identity of any of the persons who had committed the act of rioting.[182]

In October, students from Mexico City arrived in Chihuahua seeking support for the students of Puebla.[183] The crisis in Puebla began when the state government prohibited direct sales of unpasteurized milk and the milkmen's protests were taken up by the students. Governor Antonio Nava Castillo was forced to step down on October 30 for failing to contain the demonstrations, while Giner remained in office until the end of his term.

On October 31, the students agreed to continue to strike for liberty for Cardona, also demanding higher scholarships and the reopening of night schools and dormitories.[184] On November 7, a commission of strikers from the State Normal, Secondaries Number One and Five, and the Technical School for Young Ladies met with José Melgar de la Peña, state attorney general, to complain of the governor's attitude. Melgar told them to act within legal limits, then the same commission went to complain to police chief Mendoza Domínguez.[185]

Acción reported that Javier Alvarez wore a .45 pistol in the office despite the army's ongoing gun-control campaign and that he needed a pistol more than a book or a pen because he was closing schools.[186]

In November, *Indice* printed Arturo Gámiz's essay "Participación de los estudiantes en el movimiento revolucionario" (The Participation of Students in the Revolutionary Movement), where he argued that students should act in solidarity with the campesino movement and that education was acquired through participation in struggle.[187] Student mobilizations increased. One hundred students of the Secondary School of Nuevo Casas Grandes went out on strike in support of the State Normal School. Students of the prep school of the university split over the issue. Section 128 of the Miners' Union agreed to lend moral and economic support.[188] On Sunday, November 15, students of the Secondary School Justo Sierra in Cuauhtémoc, where Arturo Gámiz's sisters attended, went out as well. At a tumultuous meeting, parents voted against the strike. Strike supporters were prevented from speaking, among them Emilia García de Gámiz, Arturo's mother. The next day, soldiers entered the school where the strike committee was meeting, roughing up Dolores Gamíz, Arturo's sister, and threatening reporters at gunpoint. Student Antonio Noyola shouted, "This school is ours, if we want we'll close it down and build another!" Another student declared, "The rich parents pay tuition for the private school, why not go back to it and leave Justo Sierra for the poor!"[189]

Someone announced a plan to organize the parents as strikebreakers. By now, sixteen rural normal schools around the country were on strike, and the State Normal School had called for progressive strikes, adding one hour daily, in every school. On November 20, Day of the Revolution, masses of students gathered in the Plaza Hidalgo protesting the closing of the night schools and the plan to reassign teachers. The Group of Progressive Teachers from Section Forty called for union autonomy, education according to the constitution, the unity of all teachers, and resources for economic and professional development.[190] Javier Alvarez resigned.[191] Giner Durán later claimed to have engineered these disturbances himself to demonstrate his control.[192]

In December, *Indice* published the following letter from Arturo Gámiz and Salomón Gaytán, emphasizing their reluctance to fire on common soldiers:

General Práxedis Giner Durán, Constitutional Governor of the State, State House, Chihuahua, Chihuahua:

As we have affirmed on various occasions, we have taken up arms and confronted the caciques, gunmen, and police who come here to commit all kinds of abuses and injustices, torturing defenseless women and children, but we have nothing against the police or soldiers who respect families and refrain from committing atrocities.

Once more we declare that we only want the fundamental problems of our people to be truly resolved and above all that the lands unjustly held be divided. Only then will we give up our arms.

Observing the movements of the hundreds of soldiers who pursue us, we have noticed that many times the officers go in the rear, without disguising their cowardice; they put the ordinary soldiers in front. We have not wanted to confront them while we wait for the dotation of lands because we really do not wish to fire on ordinary soldiers, who like us are the sons of workers and campesinos, who pursue us blindly only following orders because they do not realize that what we demand is justice for the good of all.

But our patience and our desire that things should be resolved through good means are not reciprocated; on the contrary, the behavior of the government, and above all, you, Mr. Governor, are every day more recalcitrant, aggressive, stupid, and intolerable.

In view of this, we have resolved to wait till the end of the year for the lands to be distributed, the students attended to, and the repression to stop; or, better yet, for you, Mr. Governor, to step down and leave the state; if not, we will begin to fire on army officers.

You are a general, it would be good for your own prestige and that of the national army, if you were to do something right; we would like to see you here, in the sierra, leading your soldiers, and let's see whether you are as good at arms as you are at insulting the girls you hate because you cannot corrupt or bribe or intimidate them.

Victory or death. For the Grupo Popular Guerrillero. Salomón Gaytán, Chief of Operations. Arturo Gámiz, Political Chief.[193]

The government announced it would satisfy all the demands of the student strikers and failed to do so.[194] In December, students planned actions protesting the disappearance of State Normal School student Oscar Sandoval Salinas, blaming local authorities.[195] It was later learned he had joined the GPG in Mexico City. *Indice* reported a meeting between Giner and a student commission seeking the reopening of the dormitories in which Giner pointed to a sixteen-year-old girl and said, "The girl students don't need dormitories, they sleep in the fields with the campesinos asking for lands."[196]

On the last day of 1964, the United States ended the Bracero Program, which had provided agricultural work under substandard conditions to tens of thousands of Mexican campesinos since the beginning of World War II. Thousands returned, many settling in the border states, exacerbating the demand for land and work.

5

"A Bomb Ready to Explode"

Summary

In 1965, the state UGOCM leadership split over their response to guerrilla actions. Repression in the sierra continued, and so did school closures and protests. The GPG organized the Second Encounter of the Sierra, which approved the Five Resolutions that culminated in a call to armed struggle. Sporadic insurgent strikes continued in the sierra. The GPG leaders traveled back from Mexico City and held a final meeting in Chihuahua and then went on to Madera. They attacked the army base before dawn on September 23 with thirteen people. Eight, including Arturo Gámiz and Pablo Gómez, were killed, and five escaped.

Split in the UGOCM

In January 1965, the state UGOCM leadership and their supporters met without Arturo Gámiz, and the group split. The supporters of Lombardo Toledano and the PPS, who had campaigned for Díaz Ordaz, wanted to put a brake on mass actions in favor of electoral campaigns. Gámiz's supporters proposed participation in elections while continuing the broad agrarian protests and building a parallel, clandestine organization for armed campesino self-defense. This tripartite strategy of mass protests, electoral participation, and armed self-defense seemed an absurd refusal to make a decision. A third position underlay the apparent contradiction, which aimed to unite the leaders of the mass movement into a political-military group headquartered in the sierra with its own urban support network that could form alliances with organizations throughout the country.[1] This position recognized that the limits of armed self-defense in the sierra had been reached and proposed taking the struggle to a "higher level," which required a national revolutionary strategy. In other words, the split was between those who argued that the legal activities lent legitimacy to the regime and postponed the revolution, which would start with the rural *guerrilla* in the vanguard—they were willing to sacrifice the public movement for the sake of the armed *foco*, as they did when the leaders moved to Mexico City—and those who argued that it was by supporting the mass movement that the vanguard obtained its cadres.[2] Presumably members of the PPS, such as Gámiz, split from that organization as well at that time.

Alvaro Ríos had left the group earlier and had been leading protest marches in northern Durango for some time. Decades later, he spoke of the assault on the base as a "tactical military error," unplanned and not part of a long-term strategy. He pointed to ejidal dotations in Huizopa, Cuatro Vientos de Cebadilla, and Conoachi as evidence that the mass protests had achieved concessions and that "we had legal reason, moral reason, and historical reason on our side."[3] (Of these three, only Cuatro Vientos had been distributed before September 1965, leaving the achievement of concessions still in doubt when the base was attacked.) Ríos blamed the attack on the students and teachers who led the UGOCM, although it was the campesinos who taught them and not they who brought "consciousness" to the campesinos. The campesinos focused on defense of their land and on enemies with specific names and faces, while the students followed a broader vision with the impetuousness of youth.[4]

There is evidence that Ríos did participate in armed actions, both of self-defense and of a more aggressive character. In 1962, he led the armed defense of Santa Rita, Temósachic, where the community was threatened with eviction and spent nine days prepared for battle, but the authorities did not arrive. (The resolution in favor of Conoachi was executed in 1970; other parcels were sold to community members, and other petitioners joined El Largo.[5]) In interviews with Montemayor, Ríos described events at Santa Rita as a test of the campesinos' willingness to take up arms and referred to himself as leading two movements: one aboveground and thriving, and the other clandestine and armed.[6] Pedro Uranga mentioned talk of an incident in the sierra, when Gámiz and a small group stumbled on a larger group led by Alvaro Ríos, who were engaged in guerrilla training.[7] After the assault, Ríos was vilified by some of the survivors for having split from the movement.[8]

Both Ríos and José Santos Valdés blamed the attack on Cárdenas Barojas, the former army captain who provided military training to the group in Mexico City. Cárdenas Barojas's motivations remain in dispute; many but not all witnesses assumed he was a tool of the regime who alerted the authorities to the attack. Regardless of his involvement, the group had decided on a course of armed insurrection in line with their reading of Che's *Guerra de Guerrillas* before the base was chosen as a target. This was the importance of Resolution Five of the Resolutions of the Sierra and the reason for their move to Mexico City. The attack was not spontaneous but planned, however poorly.

"A Bomb Ready to Explode"

On New Year's Eve, revelers were provoked, jailed, and shot at. The UGOCM announced, "The people will have the last word, it will not be one, or two, or ten, or twenty, it will be the whole people who rise up as a judge to punish the guilty, and then, gentlemen, nothing will stop them. Chihuahua is a bomb ready to explode."[9]

Indice accused Giner of raining bribes on reporters and contributing to inflation, and reported that Giner spent too much time in Mexico City. Once again, progressive strikes were planned throughout the state to begin on January 11. Despite Giner's earlier announcement, little or nothing had been resolved.[10]

The UGOCM published a new denunciation: José Ibarra put cattle with altered brands into the Ortega family's herds in order to claim that they were stolen. He took the police to help him and stole more than four hundred cattle along with horses, saddles, and saddlebags. Families were evicted and the men were put in jail, where they remained for more than five months. Fortunato Gil had some of the cattle; Tomás Vega had taken the ranch. The families of Santa Rita were evicted, their livestock killed, and the best pasture and water fenced off. Santa Rita had received a presidential resolution that the DAAC had not executed.[11]

Giner announced his refusal to reopen the dorms or the schools: "The male teachers are lazy and the females, with legitimate and illegitimate children, spend their time asking for more [salary]." Four thousand teachers threatened to strike.[12]

The UGOCM repeated its denunciation of the dangerous situation in Madera, adding new claims. The leaders of El Naranjo had been sent to jail on various occasions by Ramón Molina, who had received an illegitimate land title from Bosques and was evicting people who had lived there all their lives. The ejido Cebadilla de Dolores was still battling Francisco Portillo, whose son sent someone to kill the Alvarez family. In Ranchería del Norte, the gunman Manuel Pereda tried to kill a compañero. Oscar Chávez and a gang of gunmen invaded the indigenous community of Yepachi, in Temósachic, where the presidential resolution dated from 1957; many indigenous had been killed and others evicted by force. In Huizopa, soldiers helped Fernando Rascón evict rancheros who were forming an ejido. In Babícora, ejido plots were being openly bought and sold. The agrarian reform was paralyzed. Bosques abused their employees, paying them less than the legal requirement and overworking them; they were also cutting more trees than the law allowed, although the same law forbid a campesino from taking pines to build himself a house. With regard to education, thirty-five teachers were needed in Madera, and the isolated rancherias needed schools with dormitories. The denunciation was signed by Miguel Moreno, as secretary general, and Oscar González Eguiarte as secretary of organization and press.[13]

The teachers' union had long campaigned to equalize wages in the state and federal systems. Giner had offered to pay three million pesos of the thirty-four million required, bringing state teachers' wages to slightly more than six hundred pesos a month, less than the pay of an army private. The union representing the DAAC employees complained that they could not execute land resolutions without budget or staff and published their own salaries to shame the state.[14]

Six hundred people attended the UGOCM congress in Madera, where Pablo Gómez, Alvaro Ríos, Oscar González Eguiarte, and Guadalupe Jacott were named officers, none of them campesinos themselves.[15] The new director of the federal DAAC, Norberto Aguirre Palancares, announced upon taking office that "all affectable lands would be distributed immediately. Neither money, nor threats, nor flattery would stop the agrarian reform."[16] He proved unable to fulfill that promise.

On April 2, 1965, Tiburcio Garza Zamora replaced Antonio Gómez Velasco as commander of the Fifth Military Zone. Two weeks later, Garza traveled to Madera, finding it "absolutely calm."[17]

On May 5, 1965, Salvador Gaytán, the sectional president of Dolores, took up arms and left office. In a letter he penned a declaration detailing the history of the town, whose inhabitants had lived in tranquility until their land awakened the greed of caciques whose names he listed. He described his tenure as president, Arturo Gámiz's arrival as schoolteacher, the violent response of the caciques, and the community's struggle for justice. Gaytán closed his epistle with a promise to lay down arms whenever the caciques were brought to justice. He made copies of the declaration and sent one to the press after every armed action he undertook.[18]

Gaytán commanded a squad, including Ramón Mendoza, that captured and disarmed local landowner Emilio Rascón as he traveled with a twelve-year-old boy near the Río Tutuaca. The guerrillas confiscated an M1 and .38 special pistol and took Rascón to the plaza in Dolores, where they forced him to write out a check for six hundred pesos to benefit the school.[19] Salvador del Toro Rosales related the same incident as told by Rascón, beginning when Rascón invited Gaytán and his companions to help him round up cattle. After several days, Rascón was awakened by four or five of them pointing guns at his head and telling him to get up. They tied his hands and got him up on his horse and took off, explaining that they had risen against the government and caciques and that anyone who did business with them was an enemy. In this version, the check was for two hundred pesos and was never presented to the bank. Rascón told Toro he had thought them his friends and felt betrayed, because he would have paid them for helping with the round up and that he was neither a latifundista nor a cacique. He asked for a license to carry arms and go after them.[20]

Pedro Uranga was recruited to the JP by Oscar González Eguiarte, a friend from prep school. Uranga provided refuge to the *guerrilla* and its supporters in Chihuahua City in a household that included his wife, Francisca (Paquita) Urías, whose father was director of the State Normal School; her sister Margarita; Pedro's friend Juan Fernández; and Juan's two sisters. They did the group's printing on a mimeograph machine hidden in the maid's room, where they produced the Five Resolutions of the Sierra and occasional news bulletins. They joked that while the machine was hidden, the papers were covered with their own ink-stained fingerprints. They stole Uranga's father's hunting rifles for the assault and frequently supplied the *guerrilla* with small sums of cash, boots, and clothing. Weeks before the attack, several persons arrived to stay at their house; Guadalupe Jacott came every day to cook for them.[21]

The Second Encounter of the Sierra

In May 1965, the Second Encounter of the Sierra "Heraclio Bernal"[22] took place in Torreón de Cañas in northern Durango at a former hacienda that had been solicited for some twenty years by six hundred families and was now being distributed to others. Students, teachers, and campesinos from Chihuahua and other northern states attended. *Indice* published a press statement signed by Oscar González Eguiarte, Hildebrando Gaytán, and Dolores Gámiz. Among the sponsors were the UGOCM, the Association of Revolutionary Women, and the indigenous Yaqui and Mayo Federations of Sonora.[23] Only Miguel Quiñónez represented the school of Salaices, whose disagreement with the armed project dated back several years.[24] Over the course of one week, participants discussed the Five Resolutions and Arturo Gámiz's "Participación de los estudiantes en el movimiento revolucionario" (The Participation of Students in the Revolutionary Movement; hereafter "Participation") and whether to move the struggle toward an armed insurrection.[25]

The group had convened several study groups—one in Nuevo Casas Grandes and another in Chihuahua City, where they kept a small office with a library and military maps, on Calle Angel Trías, behind the Posada Tierra Blanca.[26] There may have been one in Madera, and there must have been ongoing discussions, whether formal or informal, in Parral between Judith Reyes and Salustio González and the people around them and in the Conchos Valley with Pablo and Raúl Gómez. The normal schools continued to be centers for political debate. The study groups would have focused on theory connected to varying extents with their activities. In those days, the Soviet Union translated, published, and sent abroad vast quantities of Marxist literature, much of it simplified and exhortatory. Rogelio Luna Jurado remarked on the "dogmatic assimilation of texts which were already by nature schematic" in the rural normal schools.[27] According to Victor Orozco, the GPG studied "History Will Absolve Me," Fidel's speech following the assault on the Moncado barracks, a possible model for the assault at Madera; other speeches by Che and Fidel; and the First and Second Declarations of Havana.[28] Members of the group probably listened to Radio Rebelde, Cuba's shortwave station that broadcast throughout the Americas.[29]

The groups would have debated the issues in the Resolutions, which were released several months before the Encounter. They were widely disseminated throughout the state, where the group had already mobilized a broad base without any statement of principles. They may have been meant to arm the students and teachers for arguments with other political tendencies, since the split with the UGOCM in January compelled them to delineate their positions. The Resolutions also served to differentiate the group from its parent organization, the

PPS, and the leaders hoped they would help to mobilize support throughout the republic.

In nearly fifty thousand words, the Resolutions contained a statement of basic Marxist economic theory; a brief historic overview of Mexico; a discussion of Mexico's semicolonial nature, the role of the national bourgeoisie, and the stance revolutionaries should take toward the ruling regime; and a scathing critique of "armchair revolutionaries." They described the poverty of masses of people, the cyclical crises of capitalism, and the cynical machinations employed by the regime to corrupt and co-opt the leadership of popular movements. They culminated with a ringing call to armed struggle: "the hour has come to see whether bullets will penetrate where reason cannot, the hour of relying on the 30–30 and 30–06, and not on the Agrarian Code and the Constitution."[30]

They addressed the central debate facing the communist movement: the extent to which the ruling regime and the national bourgeoisie could be called revolutionary, meaning the extent to which they served as a defense against U.S. intervention and economic penetration. If Mexico were semicolonial and had exchanged a Spanish overlord for another foreign power, then an alliance between the regime and the national elite, defined as one whose interests were not tied to foreign investments, was crucial to maintaining sovereignty and developing an economic base that would withstand pressure from the giant to the north. In that case, the duty of revolutionaries was to lay aside their differences and defend patriotic unity while continuing to struggle for the class interests of workers and campesinos on terrain governed by larger geopolitical concerns.[31]

The PPS had consistently supported the regime, even to the extent of backing Gustavo Díaz Ordaz in 1964. Lombardo Toledano argued that since the United States possessed the atomic bomb, resistance courted universal nuclear catastrophe. The authors of the Resolutions pointed instead to the recent success of Algeria, Cuba, and Nasser's Egypt in confronting great power bullying.[32] The PCM's positions were complicated by their greater care in maintaining a posture of revolutionary militance. "The difference is that VLT [Vicente Lombardo Toledano] spits out his nonsense directly while the PCM is careful to guard appearances."[33]

Even as they described Mexico as semicolonial, the authors insisted there were only two classes that matter: the exploited and the exploiters. "There are two social classes. This is something a revolutionary must never, at any time, forget—the exploiter and the exploited, and which of these is served by progress?"[34] The title of the Fourth Resolution read, "The bourgeoisie has failed and is incapable of resolving the national problems." There would be no recourse to the national bourgeoisie.

Their analysis of modes of production was telescoped. The first page of the "First Resolution: Imperialism: The World We Live In" described the transition from feudalism to capitalism as driven by the demand for cash and the movement of peasants from fields to factories and the battle between the emerging "business" class and the nobility.[35] "The mode of production in a few decades passed from simple cooperation to manufacturing and to modern factory production."[36] This explanation resembled their analysis of Mexico in which the Wars of the Reform, now seen to have introduced the changes needed for emerging capitalist relations—the privatization of landholdings, the secularization of civil authority, the establishment of legal equality through the abolition of the *fueros* (separate military and ecclesiastical courts)—were characterized as a continuation of feudalism under secular and not clerical authority. They based their argument on the survival of the hacienda, where debt peonage was employed in the production of commercial crops for export, illustrating feudalism under the sway of imperialism.[37] This analysis, in which feudalism continued until the 1910 revolution, was crucial to their argument about the mode of production in the twentieth century. At no point did they reference an understanding that the new grows up within the shell of the old, that modes of production and the forces that would overthrow them are products of the same line of development. "No social order is ever destroyed before all the productive forces for which it is sufficient have been developed, and new superior relations of production never replace older ones before the material conditions for their existence have matured within the framework of the old society."[38] Instead, they posited an abrupt break, "in a few decades," between feudalism and capitalism.

Their analysis of the Mexican Revolution was brief. The revolution was anti-imperialist, Villa its most important military leader, and Zapata its social hero. While the constitution embodied popular gains, it was the bourgeois forces led by Carranza who came to power: "people had shaken off one yoke to have another put on." This occurred "because in the epoch of the revolution, the proletariat was small and had no class consciousness, no awareness of its historic mission, because there was no party to make the masses aware of the situation and embody its perspective, that would show the bourgeoisie for what it was and indicate a superior strategy, that would reveal the class interests at play and energetically reveal the dirty politics of the Constitutional Leader [Carranza]. And finally, because Villa and Zapata had no political vision." The Resolutions barely mentioned Ricardo and Enrique Flores Magón, anarchists whose newspaper, *Regeneración* (Regeneration), published from exile in the United States, and whose party, the Mexican Liberal Party, played a crucial role in mobilizing for the 1910 revolution, particularly among workers, including those in the Mexican–U.S. borderlands.[39]

The analysis continues with the postrevolutionary period. Now Mexico had ceased to be feudal and was capitalist with two social classes: "the paradise of the bourgeoisie is in the hell of the proletariat." During World War II the proimperialists returned to power, and since then they have alternated with the national bourgeoisie. Both are afraid of the masses. Now Mexico was industrialized, but the benefits went to the rich, including certain landowners of Chihuahua. The federal government pursued a policy of conciliation with the United States, and the authors quoted the Second Declaration of Havana: "the national bourgeoisie cannot lead the antifeudal and anti-imperialist struggle. Experience has shown that in our nations that class, even when its interests contradict those of Yankee imperialism, has been incapable of confronting it, paralyzed with fear of social revolution and frightened by the clamor of the exploited masses."[40]

The analysis continues to describe how the campesinos fought for land as a movement against feudalism, although the breakup of the hacienda holdings, always partial and nowhere adequate, resulted in the ejido, a communal form of landholding, and not private property, the usual result of an antifeudal movement. Meanwhile, the workers fought for improvements to their working conditions, for popular education, and for "demands that respected private property, that had nothing to do with socialism, and for this reason, the revolution was democratic and bourgeois."[41] This was a curious formulation, limiting the fighting forces to "democratic and bourgeois" goals despite the considerable Magonista influence directed against private property, the state, and the clergy. The analysis of the Resolutions was binary and schematic and failed to recognize contradictory elements within the vast heterogeneous revolutionary forces.[42] The authors identified Emiliano Zapata and Pancho Villa as the only forces fighting for justice and equity—"for their social composition, for their leadership, for their ideology, and for their program"[43]—while Venustiano Carranza represented the forces of the national bourgeoisie once held in check by the Porfiriato and its alliance with foreign capitalists. In the Resolutions, the revolution lasted but a moment, followed by "half a century of bourgeois dictatorship." It was in this half century that their analysis of the state and the PRI differed from that of Lombardo Toledano and the PCM and provided the basis for the break with the Old Left. The Mexico of Zapata and Villa "is no longer that semi-enslaved and feudal nation of the past century but has been transformed into a rapidly developing capitalist country."[44]

The authors conceded that state capitalism had its benefits, not only for the bourgeoisie but for the proletariat as well, but they insisted on its exploitative nature. They quoted Lombardo Toledano—"every time the state takes a source of production or a public service into its hands, it automatically creates a monopoly that *receives no profits* but *public benefits*"—then countered Lombardo with a quotation from Engels—"The appropriation by the state of the productive forces *does not resolve the conflict*, but contains the elements of the solution." At the end of this paragraph was one of a very few citations: "(F.E.)" to Friedrich Engels.[45]

The Resolutions challenged orthodox communism on the leading role of industrial workers, whom they viewed as corrupted and demoralized: "now and for the near future the working class will not be able to take on an armed insurrection and maybe not even to support those initiated by other sectors." Instead, they posited the campesinos, in motion throughout northwestern Mexico, along with students as the leading force. "But unlike the working class movement, the campesinos maintain and are increasing their offensive while radicalizing and drawing into their orbit more and more social forces and sectors. The government has not been able to stop the campesino movement. . . . Although historically the campesinos are a class in the process of disappearing, we consider that, at this time, they and the progressive petty bourgeoisie in the cities are the only sectors able to undertake an armed movement in our country."[46] It is interesting that they ignored, in their analysis and literature, the wave of factory strikes in Chihuahua in 1964 organized by radical Christians.[47] The emphasis on campesinos was shared by countless revolutionaries since Mao led the Long March to victory in China in 1949 and the center of global revolution shifted from the industrialized countries to the periphery. "In underdeveloped America, the terrain of armed struggle must fundamentally be the countryside."[48]

After World War II, new social forces emerged as industrialization required administrative bureaucrats and professionals. Many students came from campesino backgrounds and had benefitted from explosive growth in higher education. In Chihuahua, these trends were pronounced: during the 1950s, half the state's population moved from the countryside to the cities, and the land they vacated was swallowed into vast empresarial holdings. The Resolutions broke with the orthodox Marxist assessment of students as members of a petty bourgeoisie. "Today the students are the vanguard in the whole world, Mexico as well."[49] They pointed to students throughout the republic mobilized not only for their own issues but in support of campesinos, railroad workers, and political prisoners; their solidarity with anti-imperialist struggles in Cuba, Panama, and Vietnam; and the militance of their protests. In Mexico City, they commandeered buses when the fares were raised and occupied schools and government offices, as they did in Chihuahua. They also noted the violence of the government's response: beatings, jail, torture, kidnapping, school closures, military occupation and martial law in the universities, and gun fire against demonstrators. They named Michoacán, Guerrero, Monterrey, Chihuahua, and Puebla as centers of student activism where "[the lack] of leadership has not been an obstacle because in the movement the masses find the leaders who substitute for their committees."[50] Here again they emphasized a mass movement producing its own leadership in the course of action.

"Participation," signed by Arturo Gámiz, was addressed specifically to students and used a question and answer format to debate whether students should take up broader issues and the extent to which formal education led to revolutionary consciousness. Gámiz maintained that action was the only school for revolutionaries. "Education is very important, but not the bourgeois education given in school but that acquired dealing with the masses, in revolutionary action, in social and political struggle. . . . But knowledge is dynamic and is constantly recreated. . . . Theory and practice . . . are absolutely inseparable."[51] This emphasis on praxis reflected a long-standing argument with the normalistas at Salaices.

The Resolutions described the student movement as "dispersed, divided, pacifist, and inoperable" and the left as "una cena de negros" (a supper of blacks—a derogatory term signifying disorder) with a proliferation of "parties, subparty groups, subgroups, little groups, and little subgroups" where "every theoretician capable of speaking of dialectics for six hours" created his own organization. On the other hand, they described "independent groups that, although they are not correct, is a good symptom, a sign of the multiplication of progressive forces that will come together in the revolutionary moment."[52] These latter groups were presumably the people Gámiz sought to make contact with during the sojourn in Mexico City and were a primary audience for the Resolutions themselves. The theme of left sectarianism was addressed more directly in "Participation," where Gámiz described a situation in which a student exhorted his or her colleagues to participate in a demonstration and they refused because of the presence of a political party; the Salaicinos were said to be against working with political parties.[53] Gámiz argued that every action has leaders who are usually members of a political party. He mentioned both the PPS and the PCM and that to refuse to take part showed "anti-communism" and promoted the "class interests of the bourgeoisie."[54]

The Resolutions insisted that the crisis of leadership could only be resolved through armed activity.

> The political parties are a great school for revolutionaries and, considered as the general staff of the proletariat, are absolutely necessary. . . . The masses create history. . . . The masses do not stop to wait for those lagging behind, be they persons or parties; what they do is to fill the posts left vacant. . . . They may lack organization, or leadership, or have a low level of revolutionary consciousness, of course, but despite all this it is possible to begin the armed struggle. During its development the conditions will develop for the workers, the campesinos, and the students to organize; beforehand, no.[55]

Once again the authors insisted on the importance of a vanguard, but a vanguard forged in the course of praxis, of everyday struggle, a concept in line with the doctrine of *foquismo*, a term not yet in use. "The duty of Latin American revolucionaries is not to wait until the change in the correlation of forces produces the miracle of social revolutions in Latin America, but to take precise advantage of everything in that change in the correlation of forces to favor the revolutionary movement—and to make revolutions!"[56]

The Resolutions promised a world to conquer:

> All opinions can, however, be reduced to two currents: those who think that *through peaceful means*, the Mexican people can break the chains that bind them, topple the capitalist regime, and install another form of government in the hands of the campesinos and workers. And those who consider that *only through armed struggle* can the Mexican people be liberated.[57]

The formulations insisted on immediate insurrection:

> It doesn't matter that the members are not masters of politicking, which is a thing of the past, but that instead they be capable of carrying through the revolution. They may lack organization, they may lack leadership, and they have a low level

of revolutionary consciousness, that is true, but despite all this it is still possible to begin the armed struggle. During its development, the basis on which the workers, campesinos, and students will organize will emerge and mature, not before. In the course of the armed struggle, the workers will join in, merge with the campesinos, and unify the students and, possibly, even the parties of the left, but not before the armed struggle. In the heat of revolution, the conditions that are lacking will mature; without it [armed struggle], nothing can be achieved, not even fraternal treatment and the end of hostilities between different forces of the left. Without it, the working class movement cannot be rebuilt; without it, the campesino movement cannot be moved from the state it is in, nor can other social sectors be attracted to an alliance with the proletariat.[58]

The authors proposed uniting the left in the course of armed struggle, and yet armed struggle requires clandestinity, secrecy, and discretion, and it creates difficult conditions where preservation of the armed nucleus becomes paramount. It removes leading actors from public activities, weakening their relationship with the popular movement. The secrecy necessary to armed struggle is the enemy of reflection, engenders paranoia and suspicion, and prevents the discussions that would allow the movement to experiment, evaluate its actions, debate future tactics, and develop, since security concerns demand that actions cannot be spoken of. The unity the authors extolled had come from open, public practice, both legal and illegal. This formulation posited a mechanical progression in which successful armed actions become a magnet attracting all progressive forces to unite in battle. Unsuccessful actions were not considered.

Armando Bartra discussed the "maximalism" that overcame the Party of the Poor in Guerrero when they took up arms. "When war becomes the center of the struggle, the question of economic, social, and political democracy is postponed until the triumph of the revolution; the attempt to realize it gradually in civic and workplace struggles is renounced, and so it stops being the object of everyday activity."[59] Without a grounding in everyday activity, the movement fails to prefigure the world it intends to make. The new world has to be built in the process of destroying the old one. If the new world is not embodied, at least partially, then the fight is wholly negative, then it is no better than what is portrayed in the *dicho*, *Quítate tú para ponerme yo* (You get down and I take your place). The new world can only be born from the movement and its everyday practices of solidarity, humanity, and justice.

> The dismantling of democratic, civic, and social organizations . . . not only leaves the majority with no defense of their civic and workplace rights but also has a disastrous effect on popular political culture because it confirms contempt for elections and workplace actions and immobilizes the ideal of liberty in an apocalyptic discourse and militarist practice. More than the cost in bloodshed, the way of the sierra always carries an enormous political cost.[60]

In Chihuahua the public movement of students and campesinos was not dismantled but continued while the vanguard moved away to organize the assault. The armed movement was crushed before the full political cost of its separation could be exacted, but the danger was clear: the militarization of the vanguard weakened the popular organizations.

> In the long run, this maximalism of the means of political action, which is the way of the guerrilla, and above all the mythology constructed around it, generate a sort of social schizophrenia. To propose politics as the vocation of wise men, reserved for the apostles of a transcendent creed, lends itself to the degrading of secular social practice.[61]

The GPG grew out of the "secular social practice" of hundreds of activists. While the Fifth Resolution may have been approved by acclamation, only a handful arrived at the assault, and even fewer understood the implications of taking that path.

The Resolutions included only one citation of Marxist authority. Rogelio Luna Jurado considered this evidence of the movement's rupture with the existing canon as an indication of the group's break with *normalismo* and an implicit criticism of the contradiction at the heart of the Cardenist project of socialist education, which is its attempt at socialism within a capitalist system.[62] He described the Resolutions as the first autonomous political program of the left and called the GPG the

> Magonistas of our times. . . . It is the result of a discovery that the generation of Madera made in practice, that becomes the essential reforming nucleus of *normalismo*. They intuit that the moment has arrived . . . to transit . . . the role mechanically imposed as a transmission belt of capitalist reform by the postrevolutionary state and of acritical proponents of textbook Marxism, to the character

of an autonomous but not anarchist movement, of a political force capable of assuming the leadership of the country's movement for reform.[63]

I have seen two versions of the Resolutions. The Primeros Vientos website reproduces all five, along with "Participation," with a brief introduction explaining that they were typed on stencils and printed on the cheap paper used in schools, each with an illustrated cover printed on cheap bond.[64] According to the website, they were intended for the Second Encounter of the Sierra in February, 1965, the date printed at the end of the Fifth Resolution, but that Encounter took place in May. The documents contain numerous spelling and typographical errors and missing diacritical marks. The introduction noted a difference in style between the Second Resolution and the others, the second being more in the style of a "political report" and less didactic. Authorship was commonly attributed to Arturo Gámiz and Pablo Gómez, although since the Resolutions were meant to be produced by the Encounter itself, they were published anonymously. There was no indication that either Gámiz or Gómez attended the Second Encounter. The introduction is signed "(-RLJ). Chihuahua, Chih. Septiembre de 2000," presumably Rogelio Luna Jurado, whose essay, "La razón maderiana" (Reasons for Madera) was included on the Primeros Vientos website and also dated September 2000.[65] The introduction included the cryptic remark, "All these characteristics have been respected in the texts [typography, errors, etc.] with the intention of approximating this presentation to a facsimile edition" which implied that the documents online are not scans of the actual documents produced in 1965 but retyped copies.

Another version consists of a thirty-eight-page PDF titled, "Segundo Encuentro en la sierra "Heraclio Bernal" / Ediciones Linea Revolucionaria. Chihuahua, México. 1965 / Torreón de Cañas, Dgo."[66] Here the text is typed in a sans serif font, in two columns, with fewer errors, and the margins are justified. Most of the illustrations appear to be woodcuts. In this version, "Participation" is not signed, but the Fifth Resolution is signed "Arturo Gámiz García, Estado de Chihuahua, February 1965." I assume this version was created later.

The Resolutions contained scathing descriptions of immorality and decadence in the United States, and mentioned the 1956 horror film *The Bad Seed*, about a murderous eight-year-old. They excoriated schools run by gangs and the 49 percent of Chicago high school students addicted to drugs, along with the Bowery, Marilyn Monroe, rock and roll's "effeminate contortions," the novels of

Françoise Sagan, *Peyton Place*, abstract painting, existentialism, and pragmatism, all "anti-scientific, sadistic, and morbid" indications of the imminent fall of capitalism.[67] This diatribe may have been intended to persuade migrant workers to stay in Mexico and fight for revolution, but it also spoke to the battle against individualism and the desire for personal transformation, described by Victor Orozco as "high ideals of solidarity, of mutual support, of general emancipation. This anticlerical and even antireligious idealism resembles a certain vocation to martyrdom and sacrifice, as assumed in the life of the saints."[68] In Spanish that devotion is often described as *mística*.

The warnings about family disintegration, homosexuality, and divorce point to a missed opportunity for gender analysis. They were consistent with the illustrations that accompanied the Resolutions and exalted the muscular male hero whose virility powered the revolution. They also underlined the group's espousal of a prudish revolutionary morality. There is no indication that the GPG or its predecessor formations indulged in the "marijuana and Marxism"[69] prevalent elsewhere in the movement or in any other ritual of the counterculture. They were straitlaced, despite Gámiz's reputation for licentiousness.[70] Their analysis echoed the rhetoric of the Catholic conservatives, who campaigned against the UNAM film club and its presentation of Luis Buñuel's *Viridiana*, along with films by "Federico Fellini, Ingmar Bergman, Max Ophüls, Tomás Gutiérrez Alea, Alejandro Jodorowsky," and others.[71] The Resolutions did not mention any literature beyond Cuban and Soviet imports, although José Revueltas had published his novels criticizing the communist party, *Los días terrenales* (Days on Earth) in 1949, and *Los errores* (The Errors) in 1964.[72] In the midsixties, the boom in Latin American literature was in full swing, featuring works such as Carlos Fuentes's *The Death of Artemio Cruz*, focused on the corruption of the revolution of 1910. Was the GPG's refusal to entertain existential ennui, self-doubt, or the writings of José Revueltas a sign of their provincialism?

While students in Mexico City were debating the value of indigenous folk music versus rock and roll imported from the United States, in Chihuahua the only music was Judith Reyes's energetic and didactic corridos. Recordings of rock and roll were still expensive imports. In the Resolutions, their defiant and sensuous rhythms were reduced to "effeminate contortions" and their spirit of rebellion unrecognized. Globalized urban culture had reached Mexico City, but its influence on Chihuahua was still faint.[73] None of the protagonists had long hair. Chihuahua had its circles of poets and painters, many of them students, with their own mimeographed journals, art galleries, performance venues, and book presentations. There would have been abundant contact between these independent left intellectuals and the GPG cadre, and there must have been defections from each side, but none of this has yet been recorded.

In the GPG iconography there were no signs of stereotypical Mexican folklore: no mariachis, no *baile folclórico*, no candy skulls, no Virgins of Guadalupe, no mention of Day of the Dead beyond the homage at the gravesite after the assault. There was no mention of food beyond the coffee, beans, and tortillas served during occupations. While Frida Kahlo may have been unknown in the North in the early 1960s, the muralists Diego Rivera and David Alfaro Siqueiros, born in Chihuahua, were widely recognized, but none of their *indigenista* and popular imagery was evident. Nor did they make use of the photographs of the revolutionary communist, Tina Modotti, active in the 1920s, such as her series of a hammer, sickle, and broad sombrero or an ear of corn, a machete, and a bandolier.

"Aesthetically, the Old Left directly referenced the imagery of a heroic caudillo figure capable of leading the masses toward liberation: male, mestizo, strict yet generous."[74] They had no use for art that was not immediately useful to their cause. They held innumerable meetings, they invaded land, they paraded downtown, they protested before the statehouse and other agencies. Chihuahua is a big state. They traveled between their base in the backlands beyond Madera City to the capital, to the Río Conchos and the southern valley, sometimes walking or sharing horses, in the backs of trucks, and in *polleros* (third-class buses or trains). They had few vehicles of their own. Their pace was frenetic and their culture was one of constant movement and austere practicality.

According to Jean Franco, the PCM forbid its militants from reading fiction "and even Marx's early writings."[75] She spoke of the way the internal life of the party was consumed in petty quarrels and changes of direction dictated from above and how militants, forbidden to question and fixed in subordinate positions, saw their determination and devotion become rigidity and intolerance.[76] "The paradox of the communist parties was always the incompatibility between egalitarian goals and party hierarchy, between the desire to eliminate social injustice and the perpetuation of patriarchal structures."[77] Militants whose only education was through the party, such as most of the normalistas and campesinos, who had never been encouraged to think independently and critically, were ill equipped to challenge their leaders. "It was there [in the rural normal schools] that there emerged a dreadful mixture of the history of Mexico with a totally coherent and gratifying political prescription that debilitated their capacity for logic with its self-sufficient citations and allegations."[78] "And the militants' extreme generosity, their desire to eliminate injustice, their intimate and public commitment, were lost in the succession of dogmas and sentences and inquisitorial requirements: one cannot greet the enemy of today who was the compañero of yesterday, we are inflexible, without pity, harsh like the hammer and the rock, tenacious, like granite."[79] Monsiváis went on to describe the lost world of communist certainty before the revelations of the Twentieth Congress: "The blindness before the crimes of Stalinism was, in some ways, perfect. It was the price paid for personal coherence, one was or was not, one contributed or not to socialism."[80] The same dogmatism was present in the Chihuahua movement in equal measure alongside the generosity and *mística* already described.

The GPG, while breaking with the old left on questions of strategy, retained its aesthetics. The illustrations in the online version of the Resolutions appear to be pencil drawings. The First Resolution ("Imperialism") shows a gathering under the trees with speakers at a podium addressing an audience. In the background of the Second ("The Colonial and Semicolonial World") are gushing oil wells, corn on the stalk, a Statue of Liberty holding a dollar sign, and in the foreground a bound and naked but struggling figure. The Third ("Brief Historical Review") shows Villa and Zapata as immobilized busts while a bedraggled creature crawls below them in chains. The Fourth ("Half-century of Bourgeois Dictatorship") shows a man in a suit with a club crushing a crawling supplicant beneath his boot. The Fifth ("The Only Path to Follow") shows a naked man with bulging thighs, bandoliers slung across his chest, flourishing a gun. "Participation" shows a young man emerging from the roof of a schoolhouse like the genie from a bottle, wearing a sweater vest with the letter *N* (*normalista*), reaching for a gun being handed to him from on high. Behind him are jagged lines signifying mountains.

In the second version of the Resolutions noted above, most of the illustrations appear to be woodcuts. The first ("Imperialism") is a globe surrounded by a crown of thorns. Others include peasants surging forward with clubs, a heroic figure rising from a barren plain, a peasant sowing his fields while a gigantic fist rises in the sky behind him, a bat with talons guarding sacks of grains while the poor line up below, a monumental fist rising from the sea to challenge a boatload of capitalists, one in a top hat, and a young man whose mouth is bound by a locked chain. There are two photographs in "Participation," one of a young man painting a mural of demonstrators surging forward with a placard, "No a las cuotas," and the other of horsemen advancing with Cuban flags.[81]

FIGURE 11 Cover of "Participación de los estudiantes en el movimiento revolucionario." Comité Primeros Vientos.

A Movement Transformed

How did a movement to enforce the constitution turn into an insurrection that sought to overthrow the regime? Was not the cause contained in the constitution itself, in the impossibility of applying the provisions of Article 27—land to the landless, to be taken from the rich and given to the poor—within a regime that respected private property? The constitution embodied the most radical demands of the subaltern fighting forces, but those forces did not come to power. Instead the entrepreneurial middle classes took power, toppled some of the former landholding elites while absorbing others, and became the new "hacendados of the revolution."[82] Surely the leaders of the agrarian movement knew their demands could be met only partially and inadequately—land, perhaps, of whatever quality, after decades of sacrifice, but land that would compensate for that sacrifice and the means to cultivate it to ensure a dignified living? And would the regime satisfy the needs of landless peasants over those of wealthy landowners? Article 27 was a provision not meant to be enforced any more than the provision of free, obligatory, and secular education for the poor or the guarantee of universal workplace rights and democracy. These were ideals meant to motivate the poor to remain within a legal framework, but in practice they were circumvented by the elites who controlled the legal terrain itself.

The movement had been fed by disparate social and ideological currents. Some of its leaders, such as the Gaytán-Escóbel clan, were unlettered rancheros from the outback. For them, armed actions against enemies with names and surnames continued a long-standing tradition, and the adoption of the strategy of armed struggle was a foregone conclusion. Many others, including Gámiz and Gómez and some of the students, were members of Marxist parties who needed ideological justification for their change of direction. By 1965, they had spent years working together in an effervescent social movement united in its implacable resistance to state authorities who refused to negotiate, a miscalculation that made the movement more determined. A series of small victories in armed actions spaced weeks or months apart made them bold. They drew on family networks for support: women and children brought food, carried messages, and hid them. An urban network provided cash and supplies. Connections between the sierra and the cities were close, and activists traveled continually throughout the state. Sporadic acts of armed insurrection created a momentum that seemed unstoppable. The political parties had contributed nothing to that momentum; they had only tried to contain it. The authorities responded to every action, whether a peaceful occupation or a violent protest, with the same repressive force and had unleashed a campaign approaching genocide in the sierra. The move from legal petitions to illegal occupations had been made long before. The movement had long ago noted that the elite, who controlled the legal terrain, were not themselves bound by it but used all kinds of "legal" maneuvers to subvert others' constitutional rights, including the rights to land and education. The armed forces that abused campesinos in the sierra daily showed themselves to be illegitimate. From illegal occupations to an attack on the army was not a big step. The leaders had already broken with their own party lines through their actions, and now they followed up with new formulations, with *Guerra de Guerrillas* as a blueprint.

It is probable that Pablo Gómez participated in the assault through solidarity with his comrades without being wholly convinced by the turn to armed struggle. He had been denied a teaching position in Chihuahua, and his plan to move to Cuba had failed as well. Gómez joined the group in Mexico City at the last minute; he may have hoped to dissuade them and consistently argued against the attack. Without questioning his commitment or sacrifice, it is possible that he followed his companions in an action that he might not have chosen.

On May 17, 1965, the guerrillas captured Roberto Jiménez, another cacique, at his ranch in El Durazno, with some of his gunmen. Days before Jiménez had murdered a young girl by slicing her throat. Jiménez forced Pima Indians to work in a clandestine still; the guerrillas destroyed the still, opened the company store to the workers, and burned the accounts of the workers' debts.[83]

On May 25, the guerrillas confronted a platoon of soldiers from the First Infantry Battalion at Las Moras. According to Salvador Gaytán, twenty-four "soldiers and civilians" captured an indigenous Pima and tortured him to make him inform. The guerrillas attacked, the Pima escaped, and the soldiers fled, abandoning six 7 mm and .22 rifles, and ammunition for the .30–06, the .30-.30, and the 7 mm super, along with radio equipment. Three soldiers were wounded. According to Salvador del Toro Rosales, other participants in the raid were Carlos and Refugio Yáñez, Manuel Ríos Torres, Mauricio Torres Coronado, and Ramón Mendoza. The DFS reported that the attack was carried out by Arturo Gámiz with eighteen men. The sergeant in charge of the platoon was court-martialed for carelessness, and the army brought in two more sections.[84]

Toro reported that the guerrillas discovered another still near the Arroyo Las Moras, belonging Ramón Molina, and that they took Molina and three workers prisoner. In a brief assembly, the *guerrilla* proclaimed sotol the poison of the poor and said the caciques got the campesinos drunk to make them stupid. They broke up the still, poured out the alcohol, and ran off the workers.[85] The animosity toward Molina had deeper causes. Salvador Gaytán told Montemayor that the campesinos of El Naranjo had asked him to denounce Ramón Molina for rape and other aggressions. Gaytán complained as sectional president, but the authorities did nothing.[86] Molina was assassinated by the successor guerrilla group in 1967.

On May 25, a UGOCM meeting at Ejido Las Parritas in Saucillo was broken up by a gang of thugs sent by the mayor, Luis Carlos Terrazas.[87]

Giner, after agreeing to a 6 percent raise in state teachers' salaries over four years to achieve parity with federal teachers, reduced that raise to 5.626 percent and deprived them of the percentage they should have earned for seniority along with the bonus for living close to the border.[88]

Indice published another report of atrocities committed by troops in search of the *guerrilla* in Madera. Soldiers killed a Pima named Arcadio on June 24 "for failing to respond to orders." On the same day, a patrol searched the home of the widow and mother of twelve-year-old Florentino Torres Corona and tortured the child, hanging him up three times by the neck, then destroyed the family's crops and stole their supplies of beans, corn, sugar, coffee, and salt. They destroyed the crops of a family living next to Los Otates. They kidnapped three campesinos—Juan Almeida, Juan Víctor Jácquez, and Señor Durán—to act as guides. Francisco Márquez and Eduardo Rodríguez Ford were kidnapped from the offices of the PPS on July 2, along with mayoral candidate Luis Estrada and Luis Homero, and taken to the barracks in Ciudad Juárez and held for three days. The army also committed unspecified abuses against women. The authorities captured thirty indigenous and killed Leonardo and Cornelio Rivera of El Durazno.[89]

On June 23, two platoons of soldiers arrived in Cebadilla de Dolores and arrested twenty people and forced them to walk to Puente de los Angeles, where they were tortured and seven of them were hanged. An indigenous man named Cornelio González tried to run away and was shot three times and buried where he lay. The state committee of the PPS protested irregularities in the Madera elections to Lombardo Toledano, who wrote to Luis Echeverría, secretary of government, and to Juan García Barragán, secretary of national defense, with a list of complaints from the serranos of Madera and a photo of the child who had been hanged.[90]

Indice published a letter protesting the arrest of Eduardo Rodríguez Ford in Madera, along with other members of the PPS, signed by Judith Reyes for the Revolutionary Bloc. The regime also arrested the editor of *Indice*, Guillermo Gallardo Astorga, and offered to free him if he refrained from attacking the governor. On September 20, 1965, Gallardo wrote an open letter to President Díaz Ordaz, a masterpiece of invective, denouncing the governor as inept, dishonest, arbitrary, idiotic, and slow-witted and warning that Gallardo did not intend to flee, commit suicide, or take part in quarrels among the prisoners.[91] He was released after fifteen days in jail.[92]

"Confident of Victory," Plans Were Made

GPG members, including Arturo Gámiz, formulated the plan to assault the army barracks in Madera while they were in Mexico City. It was a curious target for a group that had repeatedly announced that their battle was with the state and not the federal government. This insistence did not take into account the revolutionary aspirations outlined in the Resolutions of the Sierra, which aimed at broader targets than the governor, the local caciques, and the DAAC. The barracks were on the edge of town, on the highway leading south to Guerrero and Chihuahua City, next to the railway used to haul lumber. The buildings were made of wood and belonged to Bosques de Chihuahua and had been intended as workers' housing. They had been recently converted to house the army detachments sent to Madera in pursuit of the GPG.

The GPG's original plan was to assault the barracks, occupy downtown Madera, take over the bank and the radio station, and broadcast an appeal to the countryside to rise up. They had been encouraged by previous successful actions and judged that so spectacular an attack could lead the campesinos to join them in a popular guerrilla war. The group counted on acting with some thirty to forty combatants armed with the automatic weapons expropriated earlier.[93] Not everyone in the group was comfortable with the plan.

Ramón Mendoza described the September 14 departure of Arturo Gámiz, his brother, Emilio, Pablo Gómez, Antonio Scobell, and himself from the Colonia Pantitlán in Mexico City. They attempted to steal a car in Chapultepec Park without success and then boarded a bus to Aguascalientes. There they tried again to steal a car, then sent Emilio to Zacatecas to pick up Salomón Gaytán while the others continued to Torreón on the bus. There they hired a taxi to take them to Durango. In Durango Gómez injected the driver with a sedative, putting him to sleep, and took over the wheel. On their arrival in Chihuahua City, Mendoza told Lupe Jacott to call a meeting that evening in the home of Pedro Uranga and to invite Oscar González Eguiarte, Hildebrando Gaytán, and Oscar Sandoval.[94]

According to Matías Fernández, the group left Mexico City in early September having agreed to assault the base on September 16, Independence Day. Participants would be organized in three groups of ten persons each: one, led by Salvador Gaytán, to come through Sonora with the high-powered weapons stashed in Arroyo Amplio; one from Guadalupe y Calvo in the south; and one led by Gámiz to go directly to Madera. In Saucillo, they stopped so that Gómez could visit his family and pick up two pistols. There Guadalupe Jacott, Trinidad Uribes, and Carlos Armendáriz tried to join them but were told they were more valuable in the city.[95] Gómez's wife and daughter reported his appearance at their home on the evening of September 15, during the patriotic celebration. Gómez talked with his children and gave them money for school supplies. His wife was in the kitchen preparing supper, and they barely spoke.[96]

The urban brigade took charge of the kidnapped Torreón taxi driver, holding him overnight then collecting a considerable sum in donations to pay him and setting him free. Later he said that "They were good kids."[97]

At the meeting at Uranga's house, Gámiz told the participants to change into work clothes for an immediate departure for Madera. They divided the arms. The first group consisted of Gámiz, Gómez, Oscar Sandoval, Salomón Gaytán, and Lupe and Antonio Scobell. Gámiz named Mendoza commander of the second group, consisting of Rafael Martínez, "Hugo" (Florencio Lugo), "Luis" (Paco Ornelas), "Rogelio," "Camilo" (probably Matías Fernández), and "Daniel" (Emilio Gámiz), and told them to wait for an urban supporter to show up with a car. If not, they should steal one from a gas station "using the best tactic to not be discovered." They were to meet the first group in Guerrero, by the road to Ariseáchic, at 1:00 a.m. on September 16. The car arrived, and they left for Guerrero at dawn and got lost, no one knowing the town, and finally found the road to Ariseáchic. They spent the day in hiding, and when they went to meet Gámiz, no one was there.[98]

In another version, on September 16 or 17, the group met in Chihuahua City to make final plans. Gámiz warned that this was the last chance to withdraw, that afterward they would not be safe in the sierra or the city. The urban supporters fabricated a number of homemade grenades from dynamite stolen from the mines at Naica.[99] According to Lupe Jacott, she, Uranga, Juan Fernández, Paquita and Margarita Urías, Oscar Sandoval, Oscar González, and Lolita (Dolores) and Emilio Gámiz were present at that meeting.[100]

A group including Pedro Uranga, Juan Fernández, Juan and Jesús Aguila, Jesús Terres, and two or three others traveled to Madera to reconnoiter and ascertain the number of troops in the barracks. They attracted police attention, did not find the guerrilla they were supposed to meet, and after two nights sleeping in a cornfield, went back to the capital.[101]

According to *Las armas del alba*, the decision to attack the base at Madera was made on September 2 at Azcapotzalco in Mexico City. Pablo Gómez and Salomón Gaytán argued against it, since they had no information on the army's recent activities in the sierra. Gámiz responded that the political and social conditions were more important than information. Florencio Lugo pointed out that training without an enemy was not the same as actual combat, and someone countered that the taking of the base would revitalize the student and campesino movements. Salvador Gaytán and Mendoza said it was absurd for the group to be debating when they, the campesinos, were already engaged. The group finally agreed to meet again before the attack and to send Salvador Gaytán to retrieve the arms hidden near Cebadilla (other accounts said in the Arroyo Amplio near the Mineral de Dolores), gathering information along the way. The final meeting would be in Santa Rosa Ariseáchic, where Miguel Quiñónez had his school, on September 19. They calculated thirty or thirty-two combatants. Mendoza would stay with Gámiz's group since he knew the sierra, and Antonio Gaytán would accompany his brother Salvador. They would enter from Sinaloa because they were known to the authorities in Chihuahua, and they would walk because they had no money.[102] The distances traveled in this plan would be punishing, especially if the materiel were stashed at either Cebadilla or Arroyo Amplio, both relatively close to Madera City; entering the state from Sonora would have been more feasible.

The two brothers traveled north, retrieved the materiel and continued on foot, carrying thirty kilos each, under occasional rainfall. They ate corn from the fields. Then, after fasting for three days, Salvador shot a deer with his M1. They crossed the Río Tutuaca on horseback with the help of a couple of Pima and arrived at the ranch of the Durán family, who gave them two burros.[103] They arrived at Ariseáchic on September 21, where they found a note from Gámiz sending them on to Cebadilla de Dolores to wait for the others, who had left early the day before. They left the weapons in a cave, unable to carry them any farther.[104] By now the others were on their way to Matachic and Madera.

On September 17, the group including Gámiz decided to send "Camilo" (Matías Fernández or Saúl Ornelas) to Madera to meet with the compañeros who had gone there to reconnoiter while Lugo and Mendoza went to Ariseáchic to meet Miguel Quiñónez, director of the school. They must have walked from Guerrero, because they left at 10:00 a.m. and arrived at 8:00 p.m. The others were there waiting for them. They slept. The next day they took a mule and a guide and walked all night and camped near Cocomórachic. Gámiz sent the guide away, and they went to the highway by Matachic to find a truck. They pretended to be inspectors and stopped the trucks, looking for one without passengers. When they found one, they told the driver who they were and why they were fighting; he agreed to help them and took them to the Presón de Golondrinas near Madera City. There they did not find the compañeros sent to gather information because they had already returned to the capital. Two of them went to survey the base, where they saw a platoon making its rounds and other soldiers inside. Oscar Sandoval went into Madera and came back reporting that there were between one and two hundred soldiers, that some had gone into the sierra, and that he had overheard someone saying there would be war. Pablo Gómez wanted to wait, but Gámiz said they needed money and had to attack. Mendoza thought they should wait, since there were soldiers outside the base. Quiñónez said, "We're not going to fail," and so "for the love of the struggle" they made plans to go ahead.[105]

Fernández argued that they should wait for Gaytán with the arms and that he was not willing to die "*a lo pendejo*" (like a fool). Gámiz and Salomón Gaytán accused him of cowardice and pessimism; Gámiz also called him a Trotskyite. Ornelas quoted Fernández as saying, "Afraid! No! My mother told me, son, you should die before running away. And you well know that Doña Herculana doesn't give an inch." Lugo, Mendoza, Gómez, and Antonio Escóbel also argued against the attack.[106]

The group was exhausted and had hardly eaten for several days. On the morning of the attack they each ate half a tortilla and some pinole mixed with water. Among the arms they carried were three or four .22s and a single-shot shotgun, while Salvador Gaytán was bringing a .30–06, an M1, an M2, and "some short ones with forty-five shots each" in addition to sufficient ammunition. Each of the thirteen carried a pistol and a rifle; the pistols were of better quality than the long guns. It was agreed that if the attack did not succeed in the first fifteen minutes, they would retreat.[107]

In his memoir, Paco Ornelas failed to explain the photograph of his appearance at a rally for unemployed teachers in downtown Chihuahua on September 22, 1965. He said only that "all of us came from Mexico City where we had been training."[108]

The first group, firing on the north side of the base, would be Salomón Gaytán, Gámiz, Sandoval, and Mendoza. To the east, by the school and church, would be Gómez, Emilio Gámiz, and Antonio Scobell. The third group would consist of Francisco Ornelas at the Casa de Pacheco, to the south. The fourth would be made up of Guadalupe Scobell, Martínez Valdivia, Lugo, and Quiñónez to the west, near the Casa Redonda. Paco Ornelas placed Oscar Sandoval at the Casa Redonda and Miguel Quiñónez by the school.[109]

Matías Fernández would wait with the truck and the group's belongings. They agreed that if the attack went badly, Gámiz, Gómez, or Salomón Gaytán would give the signal to retreat. The first group would fire the first shots and follow up with hand grenades. The second group was to burn the building. Ornelas was to go into the Casa de Pacheco and execute the person inside. The fourth group would fire on the base from the Casa Redonda and guard the retreat. Fernández was to watch over the driver, parked near the antenna on the road to Cebadilla de Dolores. The antenna would be the first meeting place in case they failed, along with the orchard belonging to Ernesto Castellanos, the mayor, and then the watch tower in the sierra.[110]

The assault was frontal and not a guerrilla attack. They tried to cut the telephone wires but did not have the proper tools. They said goodbye to one another and took their places, waiting for 5:45 a.m. Then Salomón fired the first shot and a soldier fell. Many versions, including Montemayor's but not Mendoza's, begin with Mendoza shooting out the bulb over the door, which would have been to the attackers' disadvantage since it was still before dawn.[111] Bullets flew. The bolt fell off Mendoza's M1 after three shots; he went on firing with a pistol. A locomotive, parked by the base, lit its headlights, illuminating Gámiz and the others by the tracks. (Others reported that the lights had illuminated the soldiers and made them a target.) Either Gámiz or Salomón Gaytán called to retreat, then ran by, calling off the retreat. Then Sandoval shouted, "It's heavy, we're fucked!"[112]

A photo of soldiers running from a burning building with drawn weapons has been frequently used to illustrate articles about the assault. One recent example was Victor Orozco's series, "Guerrillas chihuahuenses de los 60," published in 2015 on the fiftieth anniversary, where the photo was captioned, "Military base at the time of the attack."[113]

Ramón Mendoza saw troops approaching around the shores of the lake behind his position, preventing their retreat. Salomón Gaytán and Gámiz were dead. The locomotive began to move away, and the conductor beckoned Mendoza; he hid behind it for some 150 to 200 meters and escaped toward Castellanos's orchard, then ran toward the hospital, where he met Guadalupe Escóbel, also running. They shot at several groups of soldiers in pursuit and took off into the sierra toward a peak called Las Lajas.[114] It began to rain. They arrived at the watch tower, where the group was to meet, and found no one there. They went to Tres Ojitos, where Mendoza was from, looking for Martín and Polo Durán, but they were told it was too dangerous; a brother-in-law of

FIGURE 12 This photo is widely reproduced alongside stories about the assault.

Mendoza's gave them a place to hide for two nights. On September 27, they arrived in Santa Rita.[115]

Pablo Gómez died with a banner in his pocket that read "Viva la libertad." Miguel Quiñónez ran into a nearby cornfield pursued by half a dozen soldiers; his corpse was dragged back to the base. Arturo Gámiz was shot as he prepared to throw a stick of dynamite, and the resulting explosion destroyed his skull; another version had Salomón Gaytán shot as he prepared to throw a grenade, which exploded in his hands, burning Gámiz as well.[116]

Ornelas crossed the alley and hid underneath a tree in someone's yard. A pair of soldiers patrolled the street, he ran behind them into a cornfield, they pursued him half-heartedly, and a bullet perforated his backpack. He found food and shelter with a campesino family. One week after the attack, he took the train from Temósachic to Chihuahua. Both the station and car were full of soldiers.[117]

Lugo was wounded in the thigh when Martínez Valdivia drew fire trying to light a grenade. He escaped, wounded, and walked for two days. Finally he hid his rifle in some bushes and approached a rancheria, where he was welcomed as a survivor of the assault. He was fed, given first aid, and hidden in a cabin behind the house. Lugo stayed for two days. When he left the family gave him money and food. He walked two or three more days and arrived in Ignacio Zaragoza at the home of his uncle, who took him to the home of Dr. Raúl Peña Garibay, who tended to his wound. Two days later he went to Los Pinos, where he met briefly with Salvador Gaytán, then went to Nuevo Casas Grandes, where he stayed with his sister. From Chihuahua City he went to Salaices, hoping to meet with Alvaro Ríos; there his identity was revealed to enthusiastic students. From Chihuahua he traveled to Mexico City, where he eventually made contact with supporters of Genaro Vásquez of Guerrero, where he was shot again in the thigh during his first action and arrested.[118]

Matías Fernández stayed with the truck, some one hundred meters from the base, while the battle raged until 8:30 a.m. The truck driver declared his intention to join in the fighting and asked for a gun. When they saw the battle lost, they took off toward Cebadilla, pursued by military jeeps. Some fifteen or twenty kilometers from Madera, Fernández got out with the baggage, which he hid under some branches, and then returned to Madera, with his arms, to the orchard chosen as the meeting place. There the foreman discovered him and brought him food and clothes. Later the foreman came back with the news that eight had died, among them Gámiz, a Gaytán, and an Escóbel. That night Fernández fled in the direction of Los Leones, leaving his rifle behind.[119]

The attack was over. The serranos did not rise up to avenge the defeat. It was left to the survivors to regroup, which they did in a surprisingly short time. The repression that followed in the sierra was harsh, while the urban networks stayed relatively untouched. The movement eventually recovered and took on new forms.

6

Aftermath

Summary

In the days after the assault, the survivors were hidden and protected, then they filtered back to Mexico City and formed a successor *guerrilla*. The press lauded the martyrs and condemned their actions. Land distributions moved forward, including some that had been stalled for many years. For decades, memory of these events was suppressed until Chihuahuan author Carlos Montemayor released a fictionalized accounting on September 23, 2003. Since then, a number of memoirs, chronicles, and academic studies have emerged. A feature film was released in 2013, and the fiftieth anniversary was celebrated throughout the country.

On the morning of September 25, Matías Fernández took the train from Temósachic to Chihuahua. Before boarding, he bought a box of apples and hid his pistol under them. There were more soldiers than civilians on the train. He went to the home of Lupe Jacott, but it was surrounded by police, as was the home of Rubén Aguilar Talamantes, so Fernández took the bus to San Pablo Meoki, went on to Delicias on foot, then traveled to Jiménez with his mother and Francisco Martínez. There were police on the highway, so his mother took his .45 pistol and hid it under her skirts. (In her interview with Montemayor, she described this incident as occurring on another occasion.) From Jiménez, Fernández took the bus to Torreón and went on to Mexico City.[1]

Eight were killed during the assault, including Gámiz, Gómez, and Salomón Gaytán. The other dead were Miguel Quiñónez Pedroza, director of the rural school at Ariseáchic; Rafael Martínez Valdivia, a teacher in Basúchil and law student at the Autonomous University of Chihuahua; Oscar Sandoval Salinas, a student at the State Normal School; Antonio Escóbel Gaytán, campesino and nephew of Salomón Gaytán; and Emilio Gámiz García, State Normal School student and brother of Arturo Gámiz. Of the thirteen attackers, only Pablo Gómez, thirty-nine and the father of five children, was older than twenty-five.

Five soldiers—Sergeants Nicolás Estrada Gómez and Moisés Bustillo Orozco, Corporal Felipe Reyna López, and Jorge Velázquez and Virgilio (or Virginio) Yáñez Gómez—were killed, and a sixth, Lieutenant Rigoberto Aguilar Marín, later died of wounds. Ten others were injured.[2] According to some accounts, twenty to forty soldiers were killed and deposited in a railway car.[3] An anonymous witness described the bodies of dead soldiers stacked like firewood.

There were several conflicting reports of civilian deaths. In one, a milkman, Rodolfo Domínguez Galaviz (or Gálvez), was thought to be a guerrilla and was shot down by troops. In another, he disobeyed an army order to halt because he was deaf and was killed; José Santos Valdés included a photo of his family watching over his corpse.[4] In Salvador del Toro Rosales's version, the day after the attack, Domínguez Galaviz rode his horse past the base where a group of women were crying and said to them, "Be quiet, noisy old women," and a soldier shot him down as he fled.[5] *El Heraldo* reported the death of another civilian, twenty-year-old Armando Aguilar Bencomo, a janitor for the railway who was hit by stray gunfire in his home during the attack.[6] According to Toro, several other civilians were wounded, either in their homes or walking near the scene, along with the driver of a taxi parked nearby, which was perforated by ninety bullets.[7]

The contradictory reports of these minor incidents are emblematic of inventions throughout by individuals who filled in gaps of memory or knowledge with whatever they found at hand. Some wanted to enhance their own participation. Others, years after the events, invented details to produce a narrative without gaps. Some with no firsthand knowledge recycled the inventions of others or guessed at what seemed most likely. "The discrepancy between fact and memory is not faulty recollection but generated by memory and imagination to make sense of events and history. Real historical fact is memory itself."[8] The social memory of these events is a vast topic that awaits further investigation.

In the novel *Las mujeres del alba*, Montemayor described the anguish of the Gaytán family, awakened by shooting and knowing their menfolk were involved.[9] They had been harassed by authorities seeking Salvador and Salomón Gaytán for months. Salvador's wife, Monserrat, took her five children, the oldest a ten-year-old girl, to the home of Albertina Gaytán, the sister of Salomón and Salvador and mother of Antonio Escóbel, who hid them. They heard the erroneous announcement on the radio that Salvador had been killed; he had been confused with Salomón. Ten-year-old Luz María went to the cemetery with her mother and cousins to see the bodies; they tried to take that of Antonio Escóbel but were prevented. They went back to Albertina's and the wake for Salomón's body, which the family had managed to rescue.[10]

On the morning of the attack, a representative of the national committee of the teachers' union telephoned Rubén Beltrán, a leader of Section Fifteen (the federal, or rural, teachers), informing him of the attack and ordering him to go to Madera immediately for information and photographs. Beltrán went to the airport, met the photographer Jolly Bustos arriving from Madera, and requested three sets of his photos. Together they went to the basement of the Hotel Hilton where Bustos had his darkroom. The photos were later confiscated by the department of government. Beltrán sent Pablo's brother, Simón Gómez; Alfonso Guaderrama, Martínez Valdivia's brother-in-law; and the journalist Pedro Muñoz Grado by plane to Madera.[11]

The corpses of Gómez and Martínez Valdivia had been placed in body bags when the order came from Giner Durán that all the bodies were to go into a common grave. The corpses were thrown on the back of a flatbed truck and paraded around town in the rain. All were mutilated, sown with machine gun fire, and Gámiz's head had been shattered. The truck parked on the central plaza overnight.

Family members arrived to claim the bodies. Emilia García, mother of Arturo and Emilio, initially identified only Emilio. Salomón's family had taken his body to the home of his sister for a wake; he was the only one buried separately. His name appears with the others on the tombstone that now covers the common grave. Families of the dead guerrillas were forced to witness the funerals with full military honors of the fallen soldiers. The bodies were lifted into a common grave on September 24 and covered with lime. *Indice* claimed that "two drunken Indians" had been hired for the occasion.[12] Jolly Bustos for *El Norte* and Juan

FIGURE 13 Tombstone over common grave. Photo by the author.

de la Torre for *El Heraldo de Chihuahua* took a number of photos of the corpses and these events; they have been widely reproduced and are available on the Primeros Vientos website.[13] Confusion continued as to the identity of several of the dead even after the hasty burial. The report published by the *Fiscalía* decades later counted fifteen attackers, listing seven who escaped.[14]

The town priest, Roberto Rodríguez Piña, refused to bless the bodies of the guerrillas. Mayor Ernesto Castellanos announced his intention to "go off in pursuit of *agraristas*." Townsfolk remarked on the satisfaction shown by "the three happy compadres," the priest, the mayor, and Rito Caldera.[15]

Supporters have speculated on various causes for the defeat as if the plan itself were not suicidal. The only hope for success would have been shooting into the base and immediately scattering to the sierra; even then they would have run considerable risks, since several kilometers of flat plains lay between the base and the foothills. Florencio Lugo offered the following points as proof they had been betrayed by Cárdenas Barojas: the absence of a watchman; the existence of soldiers outside the base; large caliber machine guns facing south;

and the seemingly reckless action of soldiers falling on them, showing that the weak number of attackers was known, since "soldiers of the enemy oppressor" are not known for bravery.[16] Other reasons offered for failure included the train engineer who turned on his headlights, illuminating Gámiz and Salomón Gaytán.[17] Paco Ornelas argued they had not been betrayed by Cárdenas Barojas; instead, the traitor had come from within, from those who "feign solidarity yet undermine those they claim to be supporting."[18]

According to Pedro Uranga, Gámiz died because he was cornered. He had been pushed to the wall by his own rhetoric and forced to act. Uranga described an era of "simple interpretations of eternity," when the Cuban victory inspired thousands throughout Latin America to take up the gun, and even people as lucid as Che embarked on adventures with little hope of victory.[19] Uranga recognized the contingent nature of the assault along with the importance of a Latin American context.

General Tiburcio Garza Zamora, chief of the Fifth Military Zone, and Giner Durán arrived in Madera that day. Giner had been in Torreón, Coahuila, with Díaz Ordaz at a ceremony celebrating the distribution of 487,000 hectares to forty-six ejidos.[20] Garza Zamora took charge of the investigation, preventing access to both state and federal authorities. Meanwhile, the army unleashed a ferocious wave of repression in pursuit of the five survivors, announcing penalties against anyone who gave them assistance.

At 6:00 p.m. on September 23, Garza Zamora assured National Defense Secretary General Marcelino García Barragán that "Everything is perfectly under control." General Bazán Guzmán, commander of the Juárez post, had taken over. Four helicopters were scouring the area.[21] Sonora sent the Twentieth Cavalry Regiment to aid the search.[22] Four T-33 jets arrived from Torreón, where they had been performing for Díaz Ordaz, along with one C-54, and one D-54 carrying sixty-eight parachuters. On September 24, fifty-three parachuters descended into the sierra while jets observed from the air.[23]

On September 24, *El Heraldo* reported that ten wounded soldiers and three civilians had been taken to the military hospital in Chihuahua City. The paper reported that fourteen persons had attacked the base with high-powered rifles, grenades, Molotov cocktails, and dynamite; six had escaped in the direction of Cebadilla de Dolores, pursued by several platoons. The weapons recovered at the scene included two 7 mm rifles, three .30–06s, two Mausers, one shotgun, and two .22 rifles. Bottles of gasoline were found hidden in nearby shrubs. Officers searched the dead guerrillas and found a plan of attack on the body of Pablo Gómez: "Task: get gasoline. Go by way of Ariseachi. Get the things down and hide them well. Two to Ariseachi. One to Madera, leaving from Guerrero. Those who stay to wait for those who go and be ready for the rest of the compañeros." On Gámiz's body, they found a sketch of the base, numbers, and corresponding noms de guerre and weapons. The only attackers who carried identification were Pablo Gómez, along with a photo of himself with his wife and five children, and Rafael Martínez Valdivia, who carried an ID from the law school of the Autonomous University of Chihuahua.[24]

The family of Pablo Gómez—his wife, his twelve-year-old daughter Alma, his brother Raúl and his wife, Rosa Cruz Ornelas Gómez, and some younger children—appeared at the offices of *El Norte*, where they were photographed. The women wore veils. They spent the initial hours of mourning restraining their grief while they waited in one office after another trying to retrieve Pablo's body.[25]

Once again, the federal attorney general sent Salvador del Toro Rosales, accompanied by Javier García Travestí, to Chihuahua to conduct investigations. They arrived to find the Chihuahua airport occupied by the military and themselves the only civilians. The next day, García Travesí went to Madera while Toro interviewed the wounded soldiers in the hospital. García Travesí returned to the capital and reported Madera in a state of siege, that the officer in charge of the investigation, Jorge Díaz Arrellano, was reluctant to give out information, and that the bodies of the attackers were destroyed by bullets and some were unrecognizable. García Travesí had suggested that the military conduct autopsies of the soldiers in order to prove homicide; they had refused. Giner had stood before the common grave of the guerrillas and had thrown in a handful of dirt, saying, "*Cabrones*, they wanted land, now they have it." García Travesí had seen "eighty to one hundred individuals with their hands tied, on the ground, guarded by soldiers" at the Madera air field. The Associated Press had arrived in Madera and sent a cable that read, "Military post in Madera City, Chihuahua, Mexico, three hundred kilometers from the border with the United States, assaulted by a communist group." Chihuahua City filled up with landowners and their families seeking safety.[26]

García Travesí gathered the townsfolk for a brief interrogation; they said that four of the attackers fled to the sierra on horseback, two of them seriously wounded and barely able to stay in the saddle. They fled in the direction of Cebadilla, which had been their refuge for the last two years. The neighbors had heard shooting and thought it was soldiers practicing, as they did every day, or explosions made by the company repairing the train tracks.[27]

Doctor Francisco Uranga Vallarta arrived in Madera looking for the bodies of his son Pedro and of the son of his friend, former state deputy Juan Fernández. He told Giner, "If my son dies, he will find himself a heroic death, but for me it will be stupid." He paid for radio announcements and leaflets tossed from an airplane over the sierra advising the two that they had been pardoned by the governor and should surrender.[28]

Raúl Gómez was arrested when he arrived on the train from Ojinaga, where he had been transferred to teach. He was interrogated and released, along with a brother or brother-in-law of Rafael Martínez Valdivia. Miguel Quiñónez had still not been identified, and Modesto Sierra Holguín was believed to be among the dead. *El Heraldo* reported that they had all been buried "in individual graves." There were rumors of armed mestizos impeding the work of the agrarian commission in Guachochi along with rumors of violence in Ojinaga and Coyame.[29]

Two railroad workers were interrogated and released. A number of homes near the base were searched. The truck driver José Dolores Lozano García was interrogated. Anyone walking within five hundred yards of the base was stopped and searched. There were rallies at the normal school of Saucillo. Antonio Becerra Gaytán and Alberto Ramírez Gutiérrez went to the office of the newspaper *Editorial*, edited by Pedro Muñoz Grado, to organize a memorial for the guerrillas. There were a number of complaints about the way they were buried.[30]

Governor Giner Durán, returning from Madera, announced, "It is not important. . . . Everything can be reduced to an adventure of crazies at the orders of Pablo Gómez; I always said he was a poisoner of inexperienced youth."[31]

On September 25, the state congress called on the federal government for aid, invoking Article 22 of the constitution and enumerating the guerrilla actions carried out by a group led by Arturo Gámiz, Pablo Gómez, Alvaro Ríos, and Salvador, Salomón, and Antonio Gaytán. (Ríos had nothing to do with any of the armed actions.) "On February 29, 1964, they destroyed a bridge. On March 5 of the same year, they killed Mr. Florentino Ibarra. On the following April 12, they burned a house and the radio station in it. On July 15, they ambushed a group of state police in Dolores, Chihuahua, taking their arms, sequestering them for several days, and wounding two of them. This year, they attacked a platoon of soldiers of the 52nd Infantry Battalion in the Sierra of Madera, wounding three, and on the 23rd, in a daring surprise attack, they attacked the army base at Madera City."[32] Given that the governor had insisted on the trivial nature of the assault and that a considerable number of troops, including air support, had been dispatched the day before, this petition was meant either to embarrass the governor or to alarm the public or both.

Six relatives of Modesto Sierra Holguín, believed to be one of the attackers, were reported arrested, along with Margarita Gámiz de Salas, age thirty-eight, believed to be a sister of Arturo Gámiz.[33] There was no other indication that Arturo Gámiz had an older sister.

A headline in *El Heraldo* announced that more than one hundred thousand hectares would be distributed to campesinos. The paper also announced the distribution of 5,339 hectares in Belisario Domínguez, to take place that day, and an unspecified distribution of the former hacienda of Palomas.[34] Meanwhile, colonists from Nicolas Bravo had invaded the former Hacienda Babícora.[35]

Pedro Uranga and Juan Fernández appeared in Mexico City. Alma Caballero persisted in demanding the return of the body of her husband, Pablo Gómez. One of the bodies buried was reported to be that of Manuel Peña González. Oscar Sandoval Salinas had been identified by his father, who said he disappeared from Chihuahua in November 1964, when the normal schools were closed.[36] In Florencio Lugo's account, he and Sandoval had left Chihuahua together in September of that year.[37]

The taxi driver from Torreón was arrested. He declared that in Torreón, on September 15, at 4:45 a.m., he picked up four individuals who had gotten off the bus from Guadalajara and said they were going to El Zarco, Durango. They carried a long bundle as their only luggage and stopped at a drugstore before leaving town. Several kilometers before El Zarco, one of them threatened him with a pistol, and the one now known to be Pablo Gómez gave him an injection to make him sleep and took over the wheel. The taxi arrived in Chihuahua at 2:00 or 3:00 a.m. the next day. (The distance between the two cities is 475 kilometers.) The driver was held overnight and then set free with 2,200 pesos (a generous amount) and told he could find the car in Cuauhtémoc. The car was found abandoned near Guerrero; its brakes had failed.[38]

José Dolores Lozano García, the twenty-six-year-old truck driver, was arrested for not reporting immediately to authorities and was accused of being an accomplice. He was interrogated by Toro Rosales. He claimed to have been assaulted on the night of September 21, to have driven all night with the guerrillas, and to have camped the next day at dawn by the Presón de las Golondrinas, where they stayed all day.[39] The guerrillas sent someone to Madera, who returned hours later, saying, "There were very few [soldiers]," and then they filled the bottles they had brought with gas from the truck. At dawn, Gámiz promised to pay the driver and left two young men with the truck and the rest took off. The three listened to gunfire for several hours until it died out. The young men kept saying to one another, "Remember we have to wait," and finally burst into tears. Lozano García took them to Matachic and later identified them as Pedro Uranga and Juan Fernández, perhaps seeking to protect Matías Fernández.[40]

On September 29, *El Heraldo* reported that the guerrillas had intended to raise flags over the army base, one with a hammer and sickle and one with the word *Libertad*. Several sources had reported a banner found on Pablo Gómez with the words, *Viva la Libertad*.[41]

Política, a national magazine close to the PPS, published long articles on October 1 and 15 blaming the attack on conditions in the state and particularly the sierra and the "repeated failures and brutal repression" that met the legal efforts of Doctor Pablo Gómez and Professor Arturo Gámiz. They quoted from the earlier article by Daniel de los Reyes concerning atrocities and from the September 11 letter of Gámiz and Salomón Gaytán.[42]

The PPS blamed the governor and "those who took the wrong path to demand compliance with the rights of the rural masses," which had been "systematically disregarded." Lombardo Toledano spoke of the "delirious left." Jesús Orta, of the national UGOCM, denied that his organization had any connection with the events of September 23, admitting that some of the attackers had once been members but saying they had resigned at the beginning of the year. The PCM blamed the attackers for their mistaken "tactic, conception, and false idea of revolution not by the masses but by small groups of revolutionaries who launch themselves alone on the attack" and called on the workers, campesinos, and students of Chihuahua to join the party.[43]

José Santos Valdés published an article titled, "Martyrs, Not Bandits," in which he corrected widespread misconceptions about the group. He noted that to Giner Durán, they were bandits, and to many others, they were agents of Castro-inspired communism and a sign that the PCM, MLN, CCI, and FEP should take power, although Gámiz was not affiliated with those groups but with the PPS and UGOCM, "whose disagreements with the PCM are well known." He pointed to the UGOCM caravan in Durango that spring as evidence that the UGOCM was still pursuing legal means, although Pablo Gómez "could not wait." Santos Valdés had known Pablo Gómez since 1948 and knew him to be consumed by "the fever for truth and justice." Santos Valdés described Miguel Quiñónez as someone beloved by both children and adults who "longed for human perfection." He ended by declaring, "Mistaken or not, they were noble."[44] Three years later, Santos Valdés wrote what would be the only sympathetic account of these events for many years.[45]

On September 30, journalist Víctor Rico Galán and photographer Rodrigo Moya traveled to Madera and Cebadilla de Dolores. Their account was published in the national news magazine *Sucesos para todos* two weeks later, receiving widespread attention. The young campesino Manuel Márquez served as their guide. His father Francisco was in jail in Juárez accused of complicity with the *guerrilla*, and Manuel was arrested after the journalists left. Driving into the sierra, Rico Galán and his escort were stopped by General Gonzalo Bazán Guzmán and his soldiers. The general greeted Rico Galán cordially, allowed Moya to photograph, and acted the politician, admitting that the campesinos faced difficulties but insisting they should protest through peaceful means. The journalists passed several trucks carrying prisoners and arrived at Cebadilla de Dolores, where the campesinos described their battle with Francisco Portillo to enlarge the ejido and told of being tortured by hanging to reveal the whereabouts of the *guerrilla*.[46]

Rico Galán noted the existence of a number of confusing and contradictory reports about the attack. He counted eight attackers dead and seven or ten escaped to the sierra. He quoted Federico García Lorca, "Señores guardias civiles / aquí pasó lo de siempre" (Gentlemen of the guard / Here happened what always happens): counterrevolution, systematic injustice, the plundering of the campesinos, barbarism. He described the "desperate slowness" of the agrarian process and concluded that Gámiz was the product and not the leader of popular desperation.[47]

One week after the assault, the military attorney general turned over his files to the federal office along with the truck driver, the arms, and other material. On October 21, Toro announced that he had interviewed eighty people to date and had accumulated a file of some three thousand pages.[48]

On October 6, the rural normal schools published a manifesto demanding justice in the name of those who died in Madera and signed by María de Jesús Moreno and José Luis Aguayo. Three students from Salaices were arrested for pasting it on walls. The director of the school next to the base in Madera and a representative of the students' parents visited the education department to ask that the school be moved, since they felt endangered by proximity to the base.[49]

Salvador Gaytán's wife Monserrat was persecuted in Madera City; her home was searched again and again, and she was taken repeatedly to the base with her five young children and interrogated. The townspeople were forbidden to help them; the children were refused their customary breakfast at the DIF (Desarrollo Integral de la Familia; Integral Family Development, a federal agency concerned with children's welfare). The family was denied credit in the shops. On November 15, they left for Mexico City.[50]

A DFS report on the first Day of the Dead following the attack appears to be largely invented. Beginning at 10:00 a.m. on November 2, five hundred people arrived at the Madera cemetery, including the parents of Arturo Gámiz, Salomón Gaytán, and Antonio Escóbel. Someone distributed mimeographed copies of verses dedicated to the martyrs. At 4:30, five horsemen jumped the fence and with lassos tried to remove the crosses from the tombs of the soldiers killed in the assault; they were chased out by municipal police, who managed to grab one of the horses. No one made any speeches.[51]

Describing the same Day of the Dead to Montemayor, Estela Quiñónez, Miguel's sister, reported traveling to Madera with Alma Caballero, her daughter Alma, her niece Rosa Ornelas, and Rosa's fiancé, José Antonio Olvera, a teacher. The townspeople were initially suspicious of them, but a taxi driver took them to the graveyard and told them that people had tried but had been prevented from providing the dead with coffins and shrouds. The graveyard was full of people, although Estela could not identify the Gámiz, Gaytán, or Escóbel families. The soldiers had followed the group from the bus; they detained Olvera briefly.[52] Alma Gómez described cleaning the grave while surrounded by soldiers who pointed machine guns at them and mocked.[53]

Despite the decimation of its leadership, the rural land invasions continued at a lower intensity throughout the state until 1988, while the student movement went on unchecked despite sporadic and ineffective repression.[54] One day before the attack on the base, a group of recent graduates of the state's normal schools marched in downtown Chihuahua demanding jobs and then encircled the statehouse. Two hundred and two June graduates had still not been assigned to schools. On September 24, *El Heraldo* announced that forty federal jobs (in rural normal schools) had been found for graduates of the State Normal School. Ten days later, five new jobs were offered, while a sizable number of demonstrators remained before the state house.[55]

On October 22, students threw Molotov cocktails at the door of the state house. Some bakers, unhappy at not being able to call a strike, had joined them; it was the bakers who had made the devices. The police dissolved the protest with tear gas and clubs. Among the arrested were the eighteen-year-old student Víctor Manuel Güereca Güereca and the baker Ernesto Amparán Orozco on the federal charge of fabrication of explosives. Two students were arrested for putting up fliers and were turned over to federal authorities, who refused responsibility.[56] On October 24, *Indice* published full-page photos of demonstrators, the women dressed in black, carrying coffins and banners that read, "Education, dead, Individual Guarantees, dead." They were surrounded by troops. The article claimed that six thousand students had demonstrated the previous Saturday.[57]

In October, Giner Durán invited Salvador del Toro and state attorney general José Melgar de la Peña to a series of breakfasts. Giner had one theme: the communists who caused all the problems, the teachers who brainwash the students, and the irresponsible, lost youth who let themselves be led. Giner gave Toro a list of enemies he expected him to arrest, starting with Guillermo Gallardo, publisher of *Indice*.[58]

According to Toro, sometime in October he was informed that President Lázaro Cárdenas had arrived in Chihuahua with his son Cuauhtémoc and the diplomat and politician Gonzalo Martínez Corbalá. They borrowed a jeep from the Agricultural Bank and headed for Madera. The management of Bosques de Chihuahua and other businessmen prepared a banquet at the tourist destination Mesa de Huracán, but Cárdenas turned them down, "preferring to eat burritos with the campesinos." Four or five days later, Toro was summoned to the Hotel Victoria to meet with Cárdenas, who said he had been sent to Madera by President Díaz Ordaz. They discussed the abuses that caused the assault, Toro insisting on his own neutrality. Cárdenas said he had just been in the sierra with one of the survivors of the attack and his family and that he himself would have done the same. He went on to speak at length about guerrilla movements in Central and South America.[59] Unless Cárdenas visited the state twice that year, Toro invented the interview or returned to Chihuahua in June 1966 and spoke with Cárdenas then.

Both Lázaro and Cuauhtémoc Cárdenas visited Chihuahua in late June 1966 as evidenced by a letter sent by Cuauhtémoc to his mother.[60] Cárdenas may have had additional motives for suggesting this trip to Díaz Ordaz: along with his perennial interest in agrarian matters, Cárdenas was negotiating for the construction of a steel-manufacturing complex on the coast of his native Michoacán at the time. Cárdenas may also have wished to intimidate Giner Durán. In his memoirs, he described the injustices committed by logging interests, who failed to fulfill their contractual obligations to the communities whose resources they exploited, leaving it to the state to provide the benefits they owed. Michoacán was an important timber-producing state. Cárdenas did not, however, discuss the *guerrilla* and their goal of socialist revolution nor did he mention the assault on the base when it occurred.[61]

Carlos Madrazo, the PRI reformer now fallen from favor, visited Chihuahua in October and paid homage to Pablo Gómez.[62] Four years later he died in a suspicious plane crash. *Indice* reprinted an article by Benjamín Laurea Lunda, president of the International Front for Human Rights, first published in *La Revista* in Mexico City, where he outlined outrages committed by troops and state police under Martínez Noriego's command in Dolores in May 1964 and quoted the letter written by Arturo Gámiz and Salomón Gaytán in September 1965. In the next issue, *Indice* reprinted José Santos Valdés's article, "Martyrs, Not Bandits," from *Política*. At the end of November, *Indice* reported Chihuahua was still "under a police regime" and that federal authorities wanted to exhume the bodies from the common grave.[63]

In December, the secretary of Hacienda and Public Credit announced that the "provincial bank" would give sixty million pesos for the development of rural Chihuahua, specifically ejidal livestock, in the milk-producing region of the Ejidos San Lorenzo and Benito Juárez, near Chihuahua City, through Melitón González, previously repudiated by the ejidatarios of San Lorenzo.[64]

On September 23, 1966, students of the rural normal schools organized memorial protests in Parral and Chihuahua City. The day before, Alma Caballero and three other women had taken the bus to Madera carrying floral wreaths. The schoolteacher Miguel Angel Parra Orozco attached a handwritten note to the doors of the former Chamizal School in Madera: "Here will be the tomb of the defenders of capitalism."[65]

On the first anniversary of the assault, Guillermo Gallardo, publisher of *Indice*, wrote an open letter warning that the state was about to explode and pointing out that every time the army declared the state at peace, there was another act of terrorism or encounter with soldiers.[66]

In 1970, 34,840 hectares of the former Hacienda Sírupa were finally distributed to the community of Cebadilla de Dolores with the expiration of the certificate of exemption.[67] In 1971, President Luis Echeverría added 252,000 hectares from Bosques de Chihuahua to the largest ejido in the republic, that of El Largo, whose ejidatarios continue to sell timber.[68] At the ceremony, Echeverría exclaimed, "I came to end the myth of Madera!"[69]

Return to Mexico City

Survivors and other members of the group gathered in Mexico City before the end of 1965, including Matías Fernández, Paco Ornelas, Ramón Mendoza, Florencio Lugo, Guadalupe Escóbel Gaytán, Guadalupe Jacott, Oscar González Eguiarte, Rubén Aguilar Talamantes, and Jesús Martínez. They lived together for some six months in Jicayán de las Flores, Guerrero, where they connected with Genaro Vásquez, who soon founded a guerrilla group in Guerrero. In 1966, they returned to Mexico City to form a new group, led by González Eguiarte, "of all the survivors and new recruits."[70]

Ramón Mendoza reported on conflicts within the group. His document began, "more than one hundred days ago, eight great compañeros . . . wrote a page of heroism in History," and went on to describe the lack of unity among the survivors, accusing the newly created Preparatory Committee for Restructuring of being a "false and fictitious authority" and rejecting any authority not attained through revolutionary action. The following page was a list of tasks involving the movement's archive, their finances, a national newspaper, and relationships with allies and supporters.[71]

Mendoza described the Mexico City school for guerrillas, where he met Oscar González Eguiarte, and they trained to return to Chihuahua and form another rural *guerrilla*. They lived together in Atzcapozalco, where they were fed but forbidden to go out, and they felt like prisoners. All of them used pseudonyms and were forbidden to speak of their families. Among their instructors was Víctor Rico Galán, who taught political theory. They also studied firearms and explosives and means of sabotage, including the use of dynamite. They traveled with disassembled arms on city buses to Ajusco, where they practiced target shooting.[72]

A letter addressed to "Compañero Carlos" and signed "Rafael Chávez Robles" detailed some of the conflicts. Undated, it began, "One year ago, we had one of the clearest guides," referring to Arturo Gámiz. "Carlos" had been the nom de guerre of Oscar Sandoval, now in the Madera cemetery; the letter's author was probably Oscar González Eguiarte. He praised Gámiz, who had formed a "small group of revolutionaries, and who confronted the deviations of both right and left; the caudillismo of [Alvaro] Ríos and his supporters, and the pragmatism and Romanticism in our own ranks." He praised the fallen comrades and then, "in lesser scale," three of the survivors: Matías, Juan Antonio (Gaytán), and "Armando" (perhaps Ramón Mendoza).[73]

Gámiz had accused Juana (Guadalupe Jacott) of pragmatism and of seeing Gómez as her father, of attending to everyday tasks without attending to her own "complete formation, to improve her morale, her way of being, her habits, her knowledge." She and Lucas (Pedro Uranga) had created a faction within the group, thwarting internal democracy, and had named themselves national leaders. In January 1966, the rest of the group formed the Committee for Restructuring (criticized in another document by Ramón Mendoza). In a meeting between the author and "Armando," Jacott, and Uranga, Uranga accused the author of being a "traitor" and creating the basis for the split. Finally, the author referred to an archive, which on September 14 Gámiz had ordered him to take immediately to Mexico City, making copies of documents held by "Carlos," an archive entrusted to the two of them, one in Mexico City and the other in Chihuahua. He urged "Carlos" to accept, temporarily, the existence of two groups and work together to prepare the "central document" for publication and to seek the alliance of both groups with regard to propaganda and mass work.[74]

According to Salvador Gaytán, when he and Mendoza arrived in Mexico City, the group was debating whether Cárdenas Barojas had been a spy and they had constituted a "bureau" to which everyone but Oscar González belonged. They, Gaytán and Mendoza, soon returned to Chihuahua.[75]

The group in Mexico City decided on Operation Pinitos in March 1966; four persons would derail and blow up a logging train in the sierra. Ramón Mendoza and Oscar González Eguiarte were sent ahead to Chihuahua City and would meet the others in the sierra at a later date. Rafael Villa Estrada got them bus passes, and they arrived late on March 9. In an aluminum suitcase they carried the plan of attack, propaganda, and the M1 Mendoza had confiscated from Emilio Rascón and used in the assault; Mendoza wore a .22 pistol in his belt.[76]

Being short of cash, they decided to walk from the station to González's parents' home and were stopped by a patrol car, and, when they refused to identify themselves, they were taken to the station. González gave his name and his parents' address while Mendoza remained silent. When an agent began to open the suitcase, Mendoza shot him in the head and they fled to González's house, the very address they had just given the police. There they were arrested after Mendoza, again, tried to shoot his way out.[77] The police found in González's possession the *Manual of the Guerrillero* and *Fifty Questions for a Guerrillero* by Commander Bay (i.e., *One Hundred Fifty Questions to a Guerrilla*, by Alberto Bayo Giroud, published in Havana in 1961), along with a letter from someone in Querétaro, promising to help him acquire explosives.[78]

Toro Rosales returned to Chihuahua and interviewed the two. Mendoza admitted to assaulting the base and to previous actions but said he had met González for the first time on the bus. González demanded his family be paid for damages to their home. In jail, Mendoza gained weight and made friends while González read every book in the library. González was released after fifteen months.[79] Mendoza was sentenced to the penal colony at Islas Marías, an island one hundred kilometers off the coast of Nayarit. Several years later, he escaped through shark-infested waters, as described in Montemayor's novel *La fuga* (The Escape).[80]

On April 3, 1966, a cargo train was derailed between Nuevo Casas Grandes and Madera. No one was hurt and no damage was incurred beyond the time and equipment needed to return the car to the track. Track had been removed and was found nearby, along with a banner that read, "People of Mexico, defend your rights. Don't support any more injustice, like the murders committed on orders of the caciques and landowners and exploitation by big business that serves imperialism. Down with cacicazgo. Long live Freedom. The 23rd of September Movement." Operation Pinitos was probably carried out by Salvador Gaytán, who left behind in a hotel room instructions for blowing up a bridge in a nearby location.[81]

On August 7, 1967, the group that would become the Grupo Popular Guerrillero–Arturo Gámiz (GPG–AG) executed the cattleman Ramón Molina, who had a long history of rape and other abuses against the serrano community.[82]

In 1968, Oscar González, Juan Antonio Gaytán, Guadalupe Escóbel Gaytán, the Tarahumara Arturo Balboa Estrada, José Luis Villa Guzmán, Carlos Armendáriz Ponce, and a few others formed the GPG–AG, whose first action was the burning of a sawmill belonging to Maderas de Tutuaca near Tomóchic on July 19. They left a message declaring themselves the heirs of the rebels of Tomóchic, precursor to the revolution of 1910, and of the guerrillas who attacked the base at Madera, now initiating the "definitive liberation" of Mexico.[83]

Carlos Armendáriz, a seventeen-year-old student, was among those who fled on foot into the inhospitable sierra, heading for the Sonora border. After a few weeks of hunger and thirst and betrayal by local campesinos, they were ambushed by troops; Armendáriz engaged the attackers in a suicidal gun battle, covering the others' escape. The rest were captured a few days later in Tezopaco, Sonora, where they were tortured and executed on September 11.[84]

Salvador Gaytán participated in several guerrilla movements in Chihuahua and Sonora during the 1970s; he claimed to have later been given refuge on the Michoacán ranch of Lázaro Cárdenas.[85] Although a presidential pardon was offered to survivors of the Dirty War in 1978, Gaytán did not return to Chihuahua until 1992. In 2004, he was elected president of the association of ex-guerrilleros at their meeting in Guadalajara.[86] In 2007, he was reelected sectional president of Dolores, forty-five years after winning the same office, which he had renounced when he took up arms. Salvador was killed in a hit-and-run accident in Sonora, in April 2011, while on a speaking tour.

Las Armas del Alba

In 1966, Chihuahua artist Alberto Carlos exhibited a charcoal drawing, commonly referred to as a painting, forty by eighty centimeters in size, titled *Ellos sabían por que* (They Knew Why), in which three young men, eyes open in death, lie in twisted poses on the ground. While not portraits of any specific individuals, the reference to the attack in Madera was clear, and the opening of the exhibition attracted crowds who did not usually attend such events. Having been warned the governor would buy the work in order to destroy it, organizers hastened to mark it "Sold." The work became an icon. While the original has disappeared, it has been reproduced countless times on posters, on the cover of Santos Valdés's book, and at the portal to the website of Primeros Vientos.[87]

The thirtieth anniversary of the attack, in 1995, may have been the first public commemoration of the events, and it introduced the term *primeros vientos*, first winds, to describe the first socialist *guerrilla* in Mexico. A committee led by Pablo Gómez's children, Alma and Eduardo Gómez Caballero, organized the event, which included roundtable discussions, speeches, and the participation of survivors.[88] The two daily papers of the capital, *El Heraldo* and *El Diario*, published a number of articles sympathetic to the guerrillas, including the story of the painting referred to above, an article by Chihuahuan social scientist Víctor Orozco in which he sketched an outline of the left in Chihuahua, and a chronology beginning with Luján's death in 1959.[89]

The initial presentation of Carlos Montemayor's novel *Las armas del alba* on September 23, 2003, at Chihuahua's Municipal Theatre marked the widening of public discussion. The audience numbered well over one thousand and spilled out into the lobby. All four of the five surviving guerrilleros who

FIGURE 14 *Ellos sabían por qué* by Alberto Carlos. Comité Primeros Vientos.

had attacked the base were speakers; Guadalupe Scobell had been killed in 1968. The event was moderated by a member of the Partido Revolucionario Democrático (PRD), and the first speaker was General Francisco Gallardo Rodríguez, who had been imprisoned for eight years for his advocacy of human rights within the armed forces. Each of the participants spoke, several at great length. The longest applause greeted the shortest speech, that of Ramón Mendoza, with his big belly and straw Stetson, who began by saying, "I am an uneducated campesino, because our education was inadequate, so I am clumsy with words." Mendoza had been arrested in 1966 with an M1 and escaped from the Islas Marías, the penal colony off the coast of Nayarit. Montemayor's speech emphasized his consistent theme, that of restoring the revolutionary battles of the recent past to popular memory, rescuing them from the web of official lies.

Montemayor was challenged to write *Las mujeres del alba* by Alma Gómez Caballero, the daughter of Pablo Gómez and an activist and former guerrilla herself, who questioned the absence of women in *Las armas del alba*.[90] Montemayor's initial response was that no woman had taken part in the assault, but he agreed to write about women involved through their relationships with male guerrillas. The book recounts the experiences of sixteen women in their own words during the days following the attack on the base, more or less in chronological order. Thirteen are the mothers, daughters, sisters, and wives of guerrillas; one is the wife of the photographer who captured some of the grisly images of the dead guerrillas; and one is from a family who protected an injured escaping guerrilla. Only one, Lupe (Guadalupe Jacott, a normalista and militant), appears in her own right. In several of his interviews, women spoke of their own political convictions, among them Laura Gaytán and Clara Elena Gutiérrez, a friend of Lupe Jacott; their interviews were not used in the book. Alma Gómez has been a lifelong activist, but the book focused on her sorrow and rage at her father's death. While many of the women were introduced to the struggle by their menfolk, the same was true of the men; many protagonists belonged to family networks, such as the Gaytán/Escóbel, Gómez/Ornelas, and Gámiz families. In an interview conducted in 2004, Hermila (Hermila Quiñónez), whose brother was a rural schoolteacher killed in the attack, recounted her mother's grief on hearing the news, to which Montemayor responded, "That's what brought me here, to hear that."[91] While he does provide a lively portrait of the indomitable Doña Herculana, mother of Matías Fernández, a poor countrywoman who brought food to prisoners, the overall tone of *Las mujeres del alba* is elegiac. Montemayor reproduced an ancient stereotype: women are emotional and only act in the shadow of their menfolk; their role is to mourn the dead warrior.

The opening of the archives of the national security services in 2002 and the appointment of a special prosecutor during the administration of former president Vicente Fox played a crucial role in the movement for recovering the memory of past social movements. Fox, a member of the National Action Party, broke the PRI's governing monopoly and opened the archives to discredit the PRI by revealing its history of coercion, surveillance, and repression. Instead, the documents demonstrated a depth of corruption and brutality from which the PAN itself was not immune. Many documents initially made public were later withdrawn from circulation. While the archive is incomplete and reflects the incapacity for analysis that characterized the intelligence services, it has been invaluable for those who know how to read it.[92]

In 2007, the tourist brochure of the town of Madera included the item "1965: 23 of September, Arturo Gámiz and Pablo Gómez, leading a group of guerrilleros, attack the military barracks of Madera" in its "Chronology of Historical Events" between "1958: The National Institute of Anthropology and History begins its investigations in Madera" and "1970: The road between Madera City and Guerrero is paved." In 2009, a monument was erected in downtown Madera that read, "The taking of the base of the city, September 23, 1965: This important event resulted in the well-being of its inhabitants, agrarian distribution, and the creation of ejidos. Madera will remember forever the heroes of the revolutionary

FIGURE 15 Monument in Ciudad Madera. Comité Primeros Vientos.

cause," followed by the names of the dead. That monument has since disappeared. Streets in Madera and the capital have been named for Gámiz, Gómez, and the others.

A movie based on *Las armas del alba*, with the same name, was released in 2013, directed and written by José Luis Urguieta and produced by Galáctica Films.[93] The production was filmed in Durango after officials in Chihuahua refused permission, and it was plagued by lack of financial support and by Montemayor's death. In 2007, another film had been in the early stages of production; the earlier film was directed by Jorge Fons with a screenplay by Xavier Robles, the team who made *Rojo Amanecer* about the massacre at Tlatelolco, and would have been produced by Jaime Casillas.[94] Casillas died in April 2008; the relation between these two films is unclear.[95] A documentary, titled *Madera 1965*, was released in 2011.[96]

The Fiftieth Anniversary in 2015 was celebrated with events throughout the country, including a three-day forum at the Escuela Nacional de Antropología e Historia in Mexico City, a special issue of *La Jornada del Campo*, and a special section in *Proceso*, both prestigious national news sources. In Chihuahua, the festivities included the presentation of Jesús Vargas's *Madera Rebelde*, film showings, and the annual commemoration at the gravesite. Local deputies voted to write the names of Gámiz and his companions in letters of gold on the wall of the state congress with the words "In memory of the martyrs of Madera 1965."

The memory of these events is vast and evolving. Tracking the scholarship and the activism undertaken in the name of Arturo Gámiz and the GPG is now a full-time job, one I hope to contribute to in the future.

CONCLUSION

But what makes these times revolutionary is not that all struggles are victorious but that the attempt at power is constantly being made.

—MARTY GLABERMAN

THE GRUPO POPULAR GUERRILLERO emerged from a broad, heterogeneous complex of agrarian and student movements that engaged in both legal and illegal protests throughout the state beginning in late 1959. They attracted national attention with articles published in Mexico City in the autumn of 1964. Recent graduates of the normal schools were massed in Chihuahua City demanding jobs at the time of the attack. The possibilities for public action had not been exhausted.

The initial actions of the GPG in the sierra in 1964 were a continuation of long-standing sporadic armed conflicts between campesinos and local strongmen. The battles escalated when the GPG emerged and the army arrived. Early victories in the field encouraged the GPG to pursue more ambitious targets. The emergence of guerrilla struggle as a conscious strategy, one dictated by their own praxis, produced fractures in the movement as a whole, and many of the leaders who supported armed struggle moved to Mexico City, returning days before the attack on the base. Meanwhile, the students organized a strike throughout the state, and the agrarian campaign expanded into neighboring Durango. These actions continued even after the assault on the base.

The GPG was the first socialist *guerrilla* in Mexico and inaugurated an unequal contest known as the Dirty War. Between 1965 and 1982, more than thirty armed insurgent groups emerged with some two thousand members, many of them urban university students.[1] In March 1973, groups throughout the country, including the Procesos (Processes), who emerged from the youth group of the PCM, formed La Liga Comunista 23 de Septiembre (LC23S; 23 of September Communist League), an urban Marxist-Leninist guerrilla organization. With the consolidation of the LC23S, all possibilities of negotiation with the government shut down. The state offered only extermination to those who took up arms no matter what their social background. It fell to Echeverría's successor, José López Portillo, to deescalate the Dirty War through a limited political reform that opened the electoral arena to certain opposition parties and awarded amnesty to some 1,500 political prisoners in 1978.[2] In their brief, sacrificial war against the state, thousands, both militants and bystanders, were killed, tortured, imprisoned, and disappeared by authorities. The damage they did in return was minimal. The suppression of those young insurgents, which was actively facilitated by U.S. training, served the armed forces as a rehearsal for the war on drugs that now devastates vast regions.

Proponents of the armed *guerrilla* have argued that it opened the way to democracy. "The physical elimination of the armed left (and in some countries, the entire left) had as its principal result the decomposition of the military dictatorships in Latin America and, in Mexico, of the dictatorship of the party of the state along with the beginning of more democratic regimes."[3] I disagree. The PRI lost its monopoly hold when global economic forces curtailed its former methods of rule, including incorporation, subsidies, and preemptive reform, all measures that required cash. By 1982, an economic crisis had fractured the Revolutionary Family, the regime could no longer buy votes the way it had, the PAN began winning elections, and civil society was organizing outside the corporate structures. In 1985, the Group of 100, artists and intellectuals, formed to combat pollution as part of an emerging environmental movement. The Mexico City earthquake of 1985 revealed the incompetence, impunity, and corruption of the government and cleared the way for the radically new: people risked their lives to pull strangers from the rubble and set up kitchens and tent cities in the streets. They refused to be helpless and expendable, performing their capacity for self-government.[4]

Five years after the earthquake, Joe Foweraker and Ann Craig published a collection of essays examining the new popular movements as the organized expression of moral outrage struggling to constitute the "people" as social actors and political subjects engaged with the institutions of the state.[5] These grassroots groupings, many led by anonymous women, did more to undermine the PRI than the armed insurgencies of the 1970s. During the 1970s and '80s a number of movements for workers' autonomy emerged, including the Democratic Tendency of the electricians' union and formations in the chronically militant teachers' union. Christian base communities proliferated, and the Colonia Rubén Jaramillo was formed in Morelos by *paracaidistas* (land invaders) and soon swelled to include thousands of people.[6]

The Dirty War was devastating to those involved, but most Mexicans knew nothing about it. In the United States, solidarity movements decried human rights violations in Brazil and the Southern Cone but knew nothing of repression in Mexico.[7] There has never been a mass public repudiation of the regime's decimation of its opponents during the Dirty War. It is only in recent years that activists and scholars have begun to reveal the dimensions of the tragedy and campaign for revindication.

Sergio Aguayo, an expert on the repressive forces of the state, made the following argument: "The guerrilla in Mexico took up arms to overthrow a regime and was defeated through extralegal means that provoked a humanitarian tragedy that unleashed a human rights movement that revolutionized political culture in Mexico and made violence, torture, and disappearances illegitimate in Mexico."[8] He is correct that the human rights movement emerged from protesters who demanded liberty for political prisoners and an accounting of the disappeared. The indomitable Rosario Ibarra de Piedra met thirty-six times with former president Echeverría demanding to know the whereabouts of her son Jesús, arrested as a *guerrilla*.[9] She and a group of mothers raised the slogan, *Ni perdón ni olvido* (Neither forgiveness nor forgetting) and occupied the national cathedral, pressuring López Portillo to offer amnesty to guerrilla members in 1978, but the violations continued unchecked, and the missing have never been accounted for. The regime punishes the legal opposition with the same barbaric methods it used on armed guerrillas, and the vast majority of violations occur against activists engaged in environmental and other peaceful protests. The massacre at Tlatelolco in 1968 was unarmed, as was the March of Corpus Cristi in 1971, and as were the normalistas of Ayotzinapa in 2014.[10] Mexico is one of the most dangerous countries in the world for journalists, targeted by both criminal cartels and security forces.[11] Despite the growth of civil society—the "revolutionized" alternate political culture Aguayo evoked— "violence, torture, and disappearances" continue.

Many of the armed revolutionaries of mid-twentieth-century Mexico were vanguards who detached themselves from broader movements and were justly accused of "dogmatism, sectarianism, militarism, and volunteerism."[12] Others, such as Lucio Cabañas's Poor People's Party in Guerrero or the Jaramillistas in Morelos, were a people in arms. I would argue that the GPG began as an embryonic people in arms and transformed itself into a vanguard. The vanguards, most notably the LC23S (who took the GPG as their inspiration), substituted their own actions for those of the people they claimed to represent. The creative agency set in motion when protesters moved beyond legality, the associations they formed working together, the attempt at embodying the world they wanted to make: these were set aside with the emergence of the armed *guerrilla*. Nothing the armed vanguard did prefigured a new world. Their taking up arms disarmed the broad movements that gave rise to them. The compelling need for secrecy, for hiding places, and for new identities kept them focused on their own survival and on the narrow military goals that became their only strategy. Most fatally, the requirements of clandestinity prevented the open discussion and evaluation of praxis necessary to their own political growth. I am not arguing that the violence of the left should be condemned because it evoked the violence of the regime—the structural violence inherent in class society was the primary cause and the state responded to every viable opposition with force—but that the violence of the left was ineffective because it failed to develop political subjects, turning its supporters into spectators and revolution into spectacle. But I would still agree with John Beverley that "with all its flaws and sometimes lethal illusions, the armed struggle revealed Latin America in its most generous, creative, courageous, and diverse aspects."[13]

The democratic *apertura* (opening) of 2000, when the PAN won the presidency away from the PRI, was not democratic and not much of a change. As John Womack remarked, the PRI did not open up but collapsed.[14] People soon referred to the PRI *emPANizado* (breaded) and the *PRIAN*. Since that year's moment of hope, neoliberal restructuring has continued, inequality has multiplied, and the drug cartels have expanded into extortion and now control the migrant routes across the U.S. border. The impunity of the powerful and the corrosive rancor of the poor threaten a war of all against all.

The roots of today's crisis can be traced to the United States. The United States encouraged the cultivation of opium poppies in Sinaloa during World War II to provide morphine to Allied troops. By the mid-1970s, an estimated fifty thousand campesinos had taken up opium and marijuana cultivation as being among the few economically viable cash crops for small producers. In 1976, at the height of the Dirty War, the LC23S attempted to kidnap the writer Margarita López Portillo, whose brother José had just been elected president.

José López Portillo instructed the DFS to exterminate the *guerrilla* and authorized a series of aggressive raids that became known as Operation Condor. This offensive brought the DFS into contact with narcotics dealers, and they soon came to terms. Thousands of troops invaded the Golden Triangle where Sinaloa, Chihuahua, and Durango meet in the sierra, ransacking villages, raping women, and hauling away young men. The crackdown on drugs served to camouflage a crackdown on rural insurgents. The DFS coordinated with the traffickers and exchanged official protection, including bodyguards and safe passage over the U.S. border, for a share of the profits. Trafficking networks formed throughout the country, protected by the authorities.[15] Alexander Aviña traced the correlation between counterinsurgency and counternarcotics efforts in Guerrero, where they developed side by side into what he called "a broader praxis of militarized rural governance" focused on "violently repressing the symptomatic manifestations of deeper structural inequalities and political factors that influence peasant participation in armed struggle or within the political economy of narcotics."[16] The military became a permanent presence in the countryside, where the only alternatives are migration or drugs.

The United States has played an insidious role. The United States furnishes an insatiable market for every kind of illegal drug, and its partial legalization of marijuana came long after the cartels had diversified. In the 1980s, Reagan declared war on drugs and challenged the Colombia-to-Florida pipeline for cocaine, which forced the Colombian cartels to switch to overland routes through Mexico, where they formed partnerships with domestic syndicates. The United States has played a double game, requiring Mexico to cooperate with antidrug measures and allow the Drug Enforcement Administration to operate on its soil in exchange for foreign aid and bank credit. On the other hand, the CIA cooperated closely with the DFS in what became known as the Iran–Contra Affair, where the two agencies organized Mexican drug dealers to sell arms to the Nicaraguan Contras, a paramilitary force that sought the overthrown of the Sandinista government. According to Boullosa and Wallace, in this instance "the CIA's anti-communist card trumped the DEA's anti-drug hand." In 1985, the DFS was disbanded, and its agents were scattered among government agencies, police forces, and criminal organizations.[17]

During the 1980s, a recession in the United States triggered a depression in Mexico's closely linked economy, which suffered currency devaluations, accelerating unemployment, and a new austerity plan. The 1980s became known as the lost decade. The NAFTA accords of 1994 further ravaged the Mexican countryside, flooding it with imported corn. International lenders imposed structural adjustments, cutting social services and devastating both the poor and middle classes. Farmers turned to drug cultivation, while the poor furnished foot soldiers to the cartels, the army, and the police. Collusion between criminal actors and police and soldiers, who are not paid a living wage, is routine and has deep historic roots.[18] NAFTA increased cross-border traffic and offered more opportunities for smugglers. Drug traffickers had once been regulated as an informal sector under the PRI's control, analogous to the blocs of workers and peasants incorporated in the CTM and CNC. Now the PRI was weakening and abandoning its former methods of rule.

> The weakening of the state and the glorification of "free enterprise" conferred authority and legitimacy on the private sector in which drug traffickers were now key players. . . . Neoliberals prioritized accumulation of profit over social welfare, ruthless competition over cooperation, and the sanctification of private property and wealth over community and civic responsibility. These propositions—the cornerstones and guiding principles of free-market ideology—also formed the dominant ideology of crime syndicates.[19]

The triumph of "free-market ideology" can also be traced to the United States. The situation has only worsened in recent years.

The GPG can only be understood as part of the wave of armed resistance that swept through Latin America and most of the world during the mid-twentieth century. By the 1980s, most of this revolutionary effervescence had dissipated. The fall of the Berlin Wall in 1989 marked a new stage in which "actually existing socialism" no longer served as either a beacon or an obstacle. New revolutionary movements face a vastly different world. They are already visible in outline in the sporadic events of mass resistance and occupation that embody, however partially, a radically new political imaginary.

Appendix

The Corrido of Arturo Gámiz (El Corrido de Arturo Gámiz)

JUDITH REYES

Ciento veinticinco sardos, de esos que defienden hoy
El latifundio del rico, llamándolo institución
Ametrallaron rabiosos, la guerrilla popular
Y desgarraron con balas, una esperanza rural.

El 23 de septiembre, muy presente tengo yo
Año de 65, en Madera sucedió
Casi por la madrugada, el cuartel se estremeció
Arturo Gámiz llegaba con los hombres que escogió.

Portaba rifle muy bueno, carabina militar
Una granada en la mano y la confianza de ganar
Ira revolucionaria, estremecía su corazón
Por que la reforma agraria era burla de la nación.

Arturo Gámiz le dijo al campesino de lugar
Por los caminos legales tierras no te van a dar
Se acapararon la tierra los Borunda y Alemán
Toma tu rifle y pelea como hacen los Gaytán.

Los persiguieron soldados y Arturo los desarmó
Y por dos de ellos supe que encuerados los dejo
Ya se traía bien cansado al gobiernito de Giner
Por que su causa era justa y por ser más hombre que él.

La concesión que el gobierno Alemanista dió a Trouyet
Para que explote los bosques de Chihuacha y de usted
Como ha dejado sin tierra al campesino del lugar
Y al Tarahumara y al Pima no se cansan de explotar.

Por eso es que Pablo Gómez no se pudo contener
Pronto se fue para la sierra para nunca más volver
Pablo murió con Arturo asaltando ese cuartel
Su rifle fue poca cosa para un corazón como de él.

Adiós Dr. Pablo Gómez adiós Salomón Gaytán
Adiós Valdivia y Quiñones ¡Ya no los perseguirán!
Adios a Emilio y Antonio y él que no supe quien fue
Arturo Gámiz no ha muerto ¡Y ustedes saben por que!

(One hundred twenty-five soldiers, of those who defend
the estates of the wealthy, believing them just,
machine gunned the popular guerrilla
and shot down the hope of the countryside.

On the 23rd of September, I remember very well,
this happened in Madera in 1965
it was almost dawn when the army base shook:
Arturo Gámiz arrived with his men.

He carried a good rifle, a military carbine,
a grenade in his hand, and faith in victory,
revolutionary wrath stirred in his heart
because the agrarian reform was a joke.

Arturo Gámiz said to the campesinos of Madera
you'll never get your land through legal channels

since the Borundas and Alemáns have stolen the land,
take up your rifle and fight, like the Gaytán family do.

Soldiers pursued them and Arturo disarmed them
And I've heard that he left them undressed.
They had worn out Giner's little government
Because their cause was just and because he was more of a man.

The concession the government had given to Trouyet
to exploit the forests of Chihuahua, that belong to you,
have left the campesinos without land
and they never stop exploiting the Tarahumara and Pima.

This is why Pablo Gómez rose up
and took off for the sierra and never returned
Pablo died with Arturo assaulting the barracks,
his rifle was nothing compared to his heart.

Goodbye Doctor Pablo Gómez, goodbye Salomón Gaytan,
goodbye Valdivia and Quiñonez, now no one will chase you any more,
Goodbye Emilio and Antonio and the one no one knew who he was,
Arturo Gámiz never died and they know why.)

NOTE ON METHODOLOGY AND SOURCES

I COMPOSED THE NARRATIVE from three streams of evidence. First, the two movement newspapers, *Acción* (1962–1964) and *Indice* (1958–1965), along with other newspapers and magazines, especially the series of articles by Mexico City reporter Daniel de los Reyes and Víctor Rico Galán's article weeks after the assault. The Chihuahua paper *El Norte* was not available in the Hemeroteca in 2011. Second, memoirs (Florencio Lugo, Judith Reyes, Paco Ornelas, Salvador del Toro Rosales, and Ramón Mendoza on the weeks before the assault), published interviews, mostly by Carlos Montemayor, and Montemayor's novels, based on his interviews. Third, the archives of the Dirección Federal de Seguridad (DFS; Federal Security Directorate) and the Dirección General de Investigaciones Políticas y Sociales (IPS; General Directorate for Political and Social Investigations) in the Archivo General de la Nación (AGN; National General Archive). While some of the reports in the archives are ludicrous, much of the information accords with the versions in the newspapers and firsthand accounts. The archives include documents produced by the movement itself, such as those of the First Encounter of the Sierra, previously unknown. I also consulted the archives in Gallery Three of the AGN (Presidents) and the Secretaria de Relaciones Exteriores (Department of Foreign Relations).

Additional primary sources included the Chihuahua state archives, being reorganized in 2011–2012, where I found Gámiz's arrest record and municipal reports from Madera City. I frequently consulted the list of Chihuahua ejidos published by the state delegation of the *Registro Agrario Nacional* in 1994, although it did not always agree with other sources; I regret I did not visit the Chihuahua office before it was boxed for shipment to Mexico City and unavailable for several years. I consulted the records of the State Normal School where several protagonists studied. Finally, there are a number of secondary sources, such as José Santos Valdés's *Madera*, the Fiscalía reports, and Jesús Vargas's chronicles. The two Fiscalía documents (one a draft) were not as well documented as they might appear, and the others were barely footnoted at all. For this reason I used them reluctantly when no other source was available.

I began by constructing a time line from the two newspapers, then I fit the other sources in chronologically. This evidence made a skeleton, which I constantly interrogated as to reliability, noting the contradictions that emerged from sifting through vast amounts of information. For example, many authors confuse two distinct places, the Mineral de Dolores and Cebadilla de Dolores, but one place is a sectional municipal head and the other is not. If a protagonist claimed to have been traveling from Mexico City with other combatants on the day his photo appeared in a Chihuahua paper giving a speech at a protest, I believed the photo. If someone described Independence Day celebrations, that gave me a more reliable date than secondary (and tertiary) accounts without dates. In *Sueños de libertad*, Ornelas reprinted undated newspaper articles published immediately after the attack with headlines referring to a distribution to Ejido Belisario Domínguez alongside another article noting the creation of the Ejido Huizopa, with 39,000 hectares, in the Madera region. Next to the article concerning Huizopa, he wrote this note: "Various hours would not pass . . . the cadavers were still warm, of soldiers and guerrillas; when the press publishes the distribution of land . . . thousands of hectares in different regions."[1] From the caption, one might conclude that the creation of the Ejido Huizopa occurred days after the attack. But according to RAN Chihuahua, the ejido was created on July 14, 1968.[2]

I was not able to conduct my own formal interviews because of the strictures of the Human Subjects protocol, which I finally declined to follow.[3] While obeying their protocol, I interviewed several individuals including some suggested by the anthropologist Augusto Urteaga, none of whom could be quoted although they furnished valuable background material.[4] Fortunately, Carlos Montemayor had made available the transcriptions of the extensive interviews that informed his trilogy of novels. I also drew on other interviews and published memoirs. Since many of the protagonists were already on record, my inability to conduct my own interviews was less significant than it might have been. I did speak with hundreds of people over the years. The memory of these events had been buried for decades and recently uncovered; many families had connections to the *guerrilla* and were anxious to talk.

I have lived in Mexico for extended periods of time, only recently as an academic. I lived in Zacatecas City and a nearby town in 1987 and 1989–1990, where I attended art school and taught briefly at Colegio Bachilleres. I then began visiting Chihuahua in 1989, often for months at a time. My adoptive family is from Guerrero City, near Madera. I visit there frequently. I have been a contributing editor to *Solar*, the journal of the Chihuahuan Institute of Culture, published poetry in Chihuahua and Zacatecas, attended a poetry workshop in Zacatecas, and published literary translations from Spanish in the United States.[5] I was a poll watcher for the presidential elections of 1994 in the sierra of Chihuahua. In 2002–2003 I worked for the Sierra Madre Alliance in Chihuahua doing sustainable development and human rights work among the Tarahumara. I conceived of this project when I attended the first presentation of Carlos Montemayor's novel, *Las armas del alba* on September 23, 2003.[6] I went back to school in 2004 to complete a bachelor's degree and continued to visit Chihuahua. I wrote my master's thesis on Madera based on secondary sources.[7] I spent a year in Mexico City and Chihuahua on a Fulbright-Hayes Doctoral Dissertation Fellowship in 2011–2012.

What was the "truth" about these events? Does it really matter who trained where in the central mountains or how two or maybe three young women were kept from joining the *guerrilla*? Isn't there a larger picture of sacrifice, solidarity, and effort? But to tell that story, one needs specific actors on specific days performing specific acts. I struggled with the discrepancies among the sources and chose what seemed most probable, guided in part by my skepticism toward the myth-making hagiography of many accounts. Every version, including my own, is partial. Many of the sources are oral histories, contributing memories created in the present from material suppressed for decades. Oral history by its nature is fluid, flowing between the interviewer and the narrator, between the past and the present, supplemented by imagination.[8] There were many ways to tell this story. The longer I worked with the raw materials, the more the argument took shape that in constituting themselves a vanguard, Gámiz and the people around him overreached. The protagonist of this book is the movement itself.

ANNOTATED BIBLIOGRAPHY

Works About Madera

Complete references for the following items are given in the general bibliography.

Víctor Rico Galán, "Chihuahua: De la desesperación a la muerte," with photographs by Rodrigo Moya (October, 1965). While this article has been frequently quoted, the conclusion he drew—that the attackers were driven by and not driving events—has been ignored. In August 1966, Rico Galán was arrested along with twenty-eight others, including his sister Ana María, and sentenced to seven years in Lecumberri. Under surveillance and infiltrated by the Group C-047 of the DFS, he had organized a group dedicated to armed struggle, the Movimiento Revolucionario del Pueblo.

José Santos Valdés, *Madera: Razón de un Martiriologio* (1968). The first book-length account, by a Communist Party member and Inspector of Schools for Northern Mexico. While his account of the group's formation and actions was incomplete, he included an impassioned report on the poverty and desperation of the landless campesinos of Chihuahua. He attributed the attack itself to the work of a provocateur who trained them.

Prudencio Godines Jr., *¡Qué poco mad . . . era la de José Santos Valdés!* (1968). A curious sequel to Santos Valdés, consisting of disinformation in the form of a recovery-from-communism memoir, at least half of which was a diatribe against Fidel's Cuba. The cover of the Godines's book bore a striking resemblance to that of Santos Valdés and was intended to deceive unwary purchasers. Godines claimed to have been present at the assault on the base as a representative of the Partido Comunista Mexicano and the Movimiento de Liberación Nacional. He awarded starring roles to both Víctor Rico Galán and Santos Valdés himself and said not a word about the years of agrarian protest and attacks on education by the governor. Today, the fraudulent nature of the volume is evident. Prudencio Godines was a pseudonym.

Jaime López, *Diez años de la guerrilla en Mexico, 1964–1974* (1974). López concluded that the *guerrilla* is an experiment—"The politician is a man who is constantly experimenting"—and "an expression of lack of confidence in the old forms of political action."[1] His account of the events that culminated at Madera followed and acknowledged the account of Santos Valdés, occupying thirteen pages; the rest of the book discussed the groups of Genaro Vásquez and Lucio Cabañas in Guerrero.

Judith Reyes, *La otra cara de la patria* (1974). A memoir with a chapter about her life in Chihuahua, where she published a newspaper dedicated to the campesino movement, by the singer-songwriter who wrote "El Corrido de Arturo Gámiz," along with a number of other protest songs.

Sergio Alberto Campos Chacón, *Barrancas rojas* (1991). A sympathetic and romantic—he added a love interest to the story—recreation of the assault on the base. The book received a national prize for testimonial literature awarded by the National Institute for Fine Arts, the National Council for Culture and the Arts, the Government of the State of Chihuahua, and the Associated Mexican Publishers.

Salvador del Toro Rosales, *Testimonios* (1996). Toro Rosales was an investigator sent by the federal attorney general's office to report on activities in Chihuahua, which he covered in several chapters. His account is sympathetic to the movement.

Minerva Armendáriz Ponce, *Morir de sed junto a la fuente: Sierra de Chihuahua 1968* (To Die of Thirst Next to the Fountain) (2001). A memoir, whose title is taken from a sonnet by the Cuban poet Nicolas Guillén, written by a former member of the Movimiento Armado Revolucionario of the 1970s. The book focused on her brother, Carlos David Armendáriz, who joined the successor organization in 1968 and was killed covering his comrades' retreat. A retired schoolteacher, Armendáriz Ponce died in 2013.

Raúl Florencio Lugo Hernández, *23 de septiembre de 1965: El asalto al cuartel de Madera; Testimonio de un sobreviviente* (2002). Written while the author, one of the five survivors of the attack, was imprisoned in Lecumberri during the 1970s, it was originally published anonymously in 2002 and then reissued under his name in two editions.[2] He followed with a second memoir, with additional information about his time in Chihuahua, and the unpublished "El reencuentro (Remembranzas)," an account of his experiences since he joined the other participants at the presentation of *Las armas del alba*.[3]

Marco Bellingeri, *Del agrarismo armado a la guerra de los pobres* (2003). The first critical analysis of these events, Bellingeri's book also focused on Jaramillo's movement in Morelos and on the two guerrilla groups in Guerrero. Bellingeri studied at the Autonomous University of Puebla and researched what became this book in the early 1980s, although it was not published until two decades later.

Carlos Montemayor, the novels *Las armas del alba* (2003), *La fuga* (2007), and *Las mujeres del alba* (2010), discussed in the introduction.

Víctor Orozco Orozco, *Diez ensayos sobre Chihuahua* (2003). A political scientist and historian at the Universidad Autónoma de Ciudad Juárez, Orozco has written extensively about northwestern Chihuahua and its serrano communities. This volume includes a critical essay about the guerrilla movement led by Arturo Gámiz, reproduced in Oikión.[4] Unlike many critics who focused on the failure of the *foco* as a model for taking power, he emphasized the importance of the GPG's break with the PPS, which opened the way for autonomous revolutionary groups such as the later Comité de Defensa Popular. It also demonstrated the possibility of breaking with the myth of the Mexican Revolution, undermining its ability to co-opt and incorporate dissident movements that allowed the creation of independent vanguards whose appropriation of Marxism departed from earlier models and took more creative forms.[5]

Francisco (Paco) Ornelas Gómez, *Sueños de libertad* (2005). A memoir by the nephew of Pablo Gómez and another survivor of the attack.

Laura Castellanos, *México armado: 1943–1981* (2007). A summary with chapters on Rubén Jaramillo, the GPG of Chihuahua, Lucio Cabañas and Genaro Vázquez in Guerrero, a number of armed groups during the 1970s, the struggle for human rights and the disappeared, and an epilogue regarding Fox's creation of the *Fiscalía*. Castellanos is a journalist and researcher who refused to use the archives of the DFS and the IPS in the AGN because "we did not wish to reconstruct the story of the repressive apparatus of the 1970s"; instead, she used interviews, newspapers, and other documents, which she cited only occasionally.[6]

Fritz Glockner, *Memoria roja: Historia de la guerrilla en México (1943–1968)* (2007). An imaginative recreation by an author and historian whose work has focused on the Dirty War and includes several novels. His father, Napoleon Glockner Carreto, was a member of the Fuerzas de Liberación Nacional, the antecedent of the Ejército Zapatista de Liberación Nacional. Despite his history degree from the Autonomous University of Puebla, Glockner refused to "cram the text with unnecessary cites."[7]

Javier H. Contreras Orozco, *Los informantes: Documentos confidenciales de la guerrilla en Chihuahua* (2007). By a journalist and university professor, this is a well-researched and well-documented but not particularly sympathetic account including a number of documents taken from the archives of the Chihuahua Office of Internal Security as well as interviews with former military personnel.

Aleida García Aguirre, "Normalistas y maestros en el movimiento campesino y guerrillero de Chihuahua, 1960–1968: Experiencias de solidaridad y relaciones reticulares en la formación de un sujeto político" (2012). A master's thesis arguing the theoretical basis of the solidarity between students and campesinos in 1960s Chihuahua. Later published as *La revolución que llegaría: Experiencias de solidaridad y redes de maestros y normalistas en el movimiento campesino y la guerrilla moderna en Chihuahua, 1960–1968* (2015).

Nithia Castorena Sáenz, "Estaban ahí: Las mujeres en los grupos armados de Chihuahua (1965–1973)" (2013). An unpublished master's thesis for the Universidad Autónoma de Ciudad Juárez analyzing gender relations among the Chihuahua armed groups. I found her analysis invaluable in understanding the impact of the movement on both the women who chose to participate and those who did not. Winner of the Chihuahua state prize for social sciences and soon to be published by the Secretaría de Cultura de Chihuahua.

Jesús Vargas Valdéz, *Madera Rebelde: Movimiento agrario y guerrilla (1959–1965)* (2015). This book is a summary of events by an important chronicler of Chihuahua.

NOTES

Preface

1. See Laura Briggs, *Reproducing Empire: Race, Sex, Science, and U.S. Imperialism in Puerto Rico* (Berkeley: University of California Press, 2002). Briggs dealt harshly with the Nationalist Party.
2. Robert F. Kennedy Jr. named his son Aidan Caohman Vieques Kennedy; he was in jail for trespassing on Navy property when the baby was born.
3. For an overview, see César J. Ayala and Rafael Bernabé, *Puerto Rico in the American Century: A History Since 1898* (Durham, N.C.: University of North Carolina Press, 2009).
4. Las cosas no se dicen, se hacen; para aquellos que luchan, su recompensa es la victoria.
5. See Michael Staudenmeier, *Truth and Revolution: A History of the Sojourner Truth Organization, 1969–1986* (Oakland: AK, 2012) and the STO electronic archive at http://www.sojournertruth.net.
6. These events have a curious sequel connecting the FALN with Chihuahua. In July 1978, William Morales, an FALN militant in New York City, lost his hands when a bomb exploded in his apartment. He was arrested and later escaped. He and his compañera, Dylcia Pagan, also an FALN member, decided to send their newborn child outside the United States for safekeeping. The child was raised in Chihuahua by lifelong activists Alma and Gabino Gómez. Alma's father, Pablo Gómez, had been a leader in the group that attacked the base at Madera in 1965. See *The Double Life of Ernesto Gómez Gómez* (San Francisco: Luna Productions, 1999), VHS.
7. Massoud Ahmadzadeh, Iranian Peoples' Fedayee Guerrillas, *Armed Struggle: Both a Strategy and a Tactic* (New York: Support Committee for the Iranian Peoples' Struggle, 1977) and online at http://www.siahkal.com/english/Massoud.htm; Beth Henson, "Armed Struggle Theories," *Urgent Tasks* 5 (Summer 1979): 25–28.

8. Henson, "Armed Struggle Theories," 26.
9. Henson, 28.
10. See Theodore W. Allen, *The Invention of the White Race* (New York: Verso, 1994) and Noel Ignatin, *White Worker, Black Worker*, http://www.sojournertruth.net/bwww.html. The journal *Race Traitor* (1993–2005) was a direct descendent of STO and can be found online at http://www.racetraitor.org. I became an editor of *RT* in 1996.
11. John Beverley, "Rethinking the Armed Struggle in Latin America," *boundary 2* 36, no. 1 (2009): 59.

Introduction

1. Various connections to that date have been suggested, but given the improvised planning of the event, I believe it was chance.
2. Carlos Montemayor, *Las armas del alba: Novela* (Mexico City: Joaquín Mortiz, 2003), 72, and Víctor Rico Galán, "Chihuahua: De la desesperación a la muerte," *Sucesos para todos*, October 15, 1965, 13. All translations from Spanish are mine unless otherwise noted.
3. Archivo General de la Nación (AGN), Dirección General de Investigaciones Políticas y Sociales (IPS), vol. 450. This evidence is difficult to reconcile with that of the official agrarian registry for Chihuahua, which showed the first presidential resolution for Huizopa dated July 15, 1966. Registro Agrario Nacional (RAN), Delegación Chihuahua, Dirección de Catastro Rural, Estructura Ejidal, April 15, 1994 (hereafter RAN Chihuahua), 27.
4. *El Heraldo*, October 1, 1965, 1. RAN Chihuahua (3) listed the amount of land distributed as 210,000 hectares to 105 beneficiaries.
5. Luis Aboites, *Breve historia de Chihuahua* (Mexico City: El Colegio de México, 1994), 166, and RAN Chihuahua, 27.
6. Aboites, *Breve historia*, 161.
7. Ana M. Alonso, *Thread of Blood: Colonialism, Revolution, and Gender on Mexico's Northern Frontier* (Tucson: University of Arizona Press, 1995); Friedrich Katz, *The Life and Times of Pancho Villa* (Stanford, Calif.: Stanford University Press, 1998); Alan Knight, *The Mexican Revolution* (Cambridge: Cambridge University Press, 1986); Daniel Nugent, *Spent Cartridges of Revolution: An Anthropological History of Namiquipa, Chihuahua* (Chicago: University of Chicago Press, 1993); Víctor Orozco Orozco, *Diez ensayos sobre Chihuahua* (Chihuahua: Doble Hélice, 2003).
8. A maquiladora is a foreign-owned factory that imports parts and exports assembled goods free of tariffs. The bracero program was an agreement signed in 1942 between the governments of Mexico and the United States providing temporary Mexican labor to the United States.
9. *Foquismo* is the belief that a small group, organized in a *foco* or magnetic center, could through guerrilla attacks demonstrate the weakness of its enemy and the possibility of victory.

10. Gladys I. McCormick, *The Logic of Compromise in Mexico: How the Countryside Was Key to the Emergence of Authoritarianism* (Chapel Hill: University of North Carolina Press, 2016), 5.
11. AGN, IPS, vol. 1025.
12. Slavoj Žižek, *Violence: Six Sideways Reflections* (New York: Picador, 2008), 1–2.
13. Carlos Montemayor collected dozens of interviews of participants and family members; they form the basis of his trilogy: *Las armas del alba* (The Weapons of Dawn), about the attack; *La fuga* (The Escape, initially translated on the Barnes and Noble website as The Leak), about Ramón Mendoza's escape from prison; and *Las mujeres del alba* (The Women of Dawn), about women's participation in these events, published after his death in 2010. Montemayor made his reputation writing poetry and fiction and as a translator of Mayan poetry; he joined the Mexican Academy of the Spanish Language in 1985. He had a personal interest in these events: he was from Parral, Chihuahua, and had met Gámiz and some of the others while working on *Acción* when he attended preparatory school. He was studying in Mexico City when the attack took place.
14. Carlos Montemayor, *La guerrilla recurrente* (Juárez: Universidad Autónoma de Ciudad Juárez, 1999), 13–14.
15. *Fundamentos de filosofía* by V. K. Afanasiev and *Cursos de filosofía* by Georges Politzer, along with Marx, Engels, and Lenin. Aleida García Aguirre, *La revolución que llegaría: Experiencias de solidaridad y redes de maestros y normalistas en el movimiento campesino y la guerrilla moderna en Chihuahua, 1960–1968* (Mexico City: n.p., 2015), 124.
16. Montemayor, *La guerrilla recurrente*, 25, describing the struggles in Morelos with Jaramillo, in Chihuahua, and in Guerrero.
17. Anonymous, "Resoluciones del Segundo encuentro en la sierra 'Heraclio Bernal,'" (Resolutions of the Second Encounter of the Sierra "Heraclio Bernal"), typescript, 1965, "Quinta Resolución: El único camino a seguir" (Fifth Resolution: The only path to follow).
18. María Teresa Guerrero Olivares, *Una generación desconocida: Movimiento social demócrata cristiano 1962–1970* (Chihuahua: n.p., 2014).
19. Barry Carr, *Marxism and Communism in Twentieth-Century Mexico* (Lincoln: University of Nebraska Press, 1992), 247.
20. See Armando Bartra, *Los herederos de Zapata: Movimientos campesinos posrevolucionarios en México, 1920–1980* (Mexico City: Ediciones Era, 1985), chap. 8.
21. See Carr, *Marxism and Communism*.
22. Carr.
23. Barry Carr, "The Fate of a Vanguard Under a Revolutionary State: Marxism's Contribution to the Construction of a Great Arch," in G. M. Joseph and Daniel Nugent, *Everyday Forms of State Formation: Revolution and the Negotiation of Rule in Modern Mexico* (Durham, N.C.: Duke University Press, 1994), 333.
24. Carr, "Fate of a Vanguard," 332.
25. The poet Efraín Huerta had this to say: "A mis viejos maestros de marxismo no les puedo entender. / Algunos están en la cárcel—otros están en el poder" (I cannot

understand my old Marxist teachers. Some are in jail and others are in power). Efraín Huerta, "Desconcierto," in *Los eróticos y otros poemas* (México: Joaquín Mortiz, 1974).

26. Carr, "Fate of the Vanguard," 339.
27. Nithia Castorena Sáenz, "Estaban ahí: Las mujeres en los grupos armados de Chihuahua. (1965–1973)" (Master's thesis, Universidad Autónoma de Ciudad Juárez, Instituto de Ciencias Sociales y Administración, Departamento de Humanidades, 2013).
28. José Santos Valdés, *Madera: Razón de un Martiriologio* (Mexico City: n.p., 1968), 84.
29. Marco Bellingeri, "La imposibilidad del odio: La guerrilla y el movimiento estudiantil en México, 1960–1974," in *La transición interrumpida: México 1968–1988*, ed. Ilán Semo (Mexico City: Universidad Iberoamericana y Nueva Imagen, 1993), 56.
30. Tanalís Padilla, "Los inquietos," *La Jornada*, October 18, 2014, http://www.jornada.unam.mx/2014/10/18/politica/006a1pol.
31. Tanalís Padilla, "Rural Education, Political Radicalism, and *Normalista* Identity in Mexico after 1940," in Paul Gillingham and Benjamin T. Smith, eds., *Dictablanda: Politics, Work, and Culture in Mexico, 1938–1968* (Durham, N.C.: Duke University Press, 2014), 342.
32. Mary Kay Vaughan, *Cultural Politics in Revolution: Teachers, Peasants, and Schools in Mexico, 1930–1940* (Tucson: University of Arizona Press, 1997), 6.
33. Bartra, *Los herederos de Zapata*, 27.
34. Bartra, chap. 5.
35. Bartra, 17–18.
36. Bartra, 18–19.
37. Bartra, 20.
38. Thanks to Christopher R. Boyer for this formulation; he added ecological preservation to the list.
39. María Guadalupe del Socorro López Álvarez, "Poder, desarrollo y medio ambiente en el ejido forestal 'El Largo' y sus anexos: Chihuahua (1971–1994)" (Master's thesis, Universidad Autónoma Metropolitana, Unidad Xochimilco), 21–36.
40. John M. Hart, *The Silver of the Sierra Madre: John Robinson, Boss Shepherd, and the People of the Canyon* (Tucson: University of Arizona Press, 2008), discussed working conditions in the Batopilas mine, just south of the Guerrero district.
41. Jorge G. Castañeda, *Utopia Unarmed: The Latin American Left After the Cold War* (New York: Knopf, 1993), 69.
42. Refugia Carrasco and Herminia Gómez, interview by Carlos Montemayor, p. 6, Fondo Carlos Montemayor, Serie Analista Político, Asalto al Cuartel de Madera. Special Collections, Library of the Universidad Autónoma de Ciudad Juárez.
43. Ernesto Guevara, *Guerrilla Warfare* (Lincoln: University of Nebraska Press, 1998), 7.
44. Andrés Becerril, quoting Jesús Zamora García, in "Madera, el asalto que detonó la insurgencia," *Excelsior*, September 23, 2015, http://www.excelsior.com.mx/nacional/2015/09/23/1047266.

45. The 23rd of September Communist League was a confederation of armed groups who took their inspiration from the attack on the base at Madera.
46. Elena Poniatowska, *Fuerte es el silencio* (Mexico City: Ediciones Era, 1980), 79.
47. In 2014, forty-three normalistas from the Rural Normal School at Ayotzinapa were attacked and disappeared. In 1997, paramilitaries massacred forty-five people at Acteal, Chiapas, who were members of the pacifist group Las Abejas (the bees). In 2006, in San Salvador Atenco, State of Mexico, demonstrations against the expansion of the Mexico City airport were violently suppressed by police, who sexually assaulted a number of women protesters.
48. See Carlos Monsiváis, *Entrada libre: Crónicas de la sociedad que se organiza* (Mexico City: Ediciones Era, 1987).

Chapter 1

1. Alexander Aviña, *Specters of Revolution: Peasant Guerrillas in the Cold War Mexican Countryside* (New York: Oxford, 2014); Armando Bartra, *Guerrero bronco: Campesinos, cuidadanos y guerrilleros en la Costa Grande* (Mexico City: Ediciones sin filtro, 1996); Marco Bellingeri, *Del agrarismo armado a la guerra de los pobres: Ensayos de guerrilla rural en el México contemporaneo, 1940–1974* (Mexico City: Editorial Casa Juan Pablos, 2003); Fernando Calderón and Adela Cedillo, *Challenging Authoritarianism in Mexico: Revolutionary Struggles and the Dirty War, 1964–1982* (New York: Routledge, 2011); Renata Keller, *Mexico's Cold War: Cuba, the United States, and the Legacy of the Mexican Revolution* (Cambridge: Cambridge University Press, 2015); Gladys I. McCormick, *The Logic of Compromise in Mexico: How the Countryside Was Key to the Emergence of Authoritarianism* (Chapel Hill: University of North Carolina Press, 2016); Verónica Oikión and Marta Eugenia García Ugarte, eds., *Movimientos armados en Mexico, Siglo XX*, 3 vols. (Mexico City: Colegio de Michoacán/CIESAS, 2006); Tanalís Padilla, *Rural Resistance in the Land of Zapata: The Jaramillista Movement and the Myth of the Pax Priísta, 1940–1962* (Durham, N.C.: Duke University Press, 2008); Jaime Pensado, *Rebel Mexico: Student Unrest and Authoritarian Political Culture During the Long Sixties* (Palo Alto, Calif.: Stanford University Press, 2013); Jeffrey W. Rubin, *Decentering the Regime: Ethnicity, Radicalism, and Democracy in Juchitán, Mexico* (Durham, N.C.: Duke University Press, 1997); Paul Gillingham and Benjamin T. Smith, eds. *Dictablanda: Politics, Work, and Culture in Mexico, 1938–1968* (Durham, N.C.: Duke University Press, 2014).
2. Barry Carr, *Marxism and Communism in Twentieth-Century Mexico* (Lincoln: University of Nebraska Press, 1992), 144–45.
3. *Acción*, June 1963, 3.
4. Sergio Aguayo Quezada, *La charola: Una historia de los servicios de inteligencia en México* (Mexico City: Grijalbo, 2001), 92–93, 124.
5. Aguayo Quezada, *La charola*, 124; AGN, DFS, 100-5-3/4, L1, H191, Versión Pública Gámiz.
6. AGN, IPS, vol. 1025.

7. Aguayo Quezada, *La charola*, 125.
8. Carr, *Marxism and Communism*, 191.
9. *Charro* means cowboy and is used disrespectfully for swaggering and corrupt union officials.
10. Carr, *Marxism and Communism*, 190–91.
11. Greg Grandin, *The Last Colonial Massacre: Latin America in the Cold War* (Chicago: University of Chicago Press, 2011), 17.
12. The IPN had been founded by Cárdenas as an alternative to the then conservative Universidad Nacional Autónoma de México (UNAM; National Autonomous University of Mexico).
13. Evelyn P. Stevens, *Protest and Response in Mexico* (Cambridge, Mass.: MIT Press, 1974), 108–26.
14. Leticia Reina, *Indio, campesino y nación en el siglo XX mexicano* (Mexico City: Siglo XXI, 2011), 70–71.
15. Carlos Fuentes, *Nuevo tiempo mexicano* (Mexico City: Joaquín Mortiz, 1971), 113. See Padilla, *Rural Resistance*.
16. José Augustín, *Tragicomedia mexicana 1* (Mexico City: Planeta, 1990), 193.
17. Aguayo Quezada, *La charola*, chap. 4.
18. Aguayo Quezada, 102.
19. Aguayo Quezada, 93–94.
20. Jorge G. Castañeda, *Utopia Unarmed: The Latin American Left After the Cold War* (New York: Knopf, 1993), 88.
21. Aguayo Quezada, *La charola*, 177; see also Hector Guillermo Robles Garnica, *La guerrilla olvidada* (Guadalajara: La Casa del Mago, 2013), Part Five: Exiles.
22. Castañeda, *Utopia Unarmed*, 88.
23. Aguayo Quezada, *La charola*, 107.
24. Julia Sweig, *Inside the Cuban Revolution* (Cambridge, Mass.: Harvard University Press, 2002), 2.
25. Castañeda, *Utopia Unarmed*, 68–69.
26. Régis Debray, *Revolution in the Revolution? Armed Struggle and Political Struggle in Latin America* (New York: Grove Press, 1967). It is interesting to note the influence Debray had on the Organization of Iranian People's Fedayee Guerrillas, a secular revolutionary group that in 1971 assaulted a military outpost in Siahkal, northern Iran. This failed assault, led by schoolteachers, was widely regarded as the first act of the revolution that defeated the Shah eight years later. See Massoud Ahmadzadeh, *Armed Struggle: Both a Strategy and a Tactic* (pamphlet circulated by the Organization of Iranian People's Fedayeen Guerrillas, n.p., n.d.) for a detailed analysis of Debray's *Revolution in the Revolution?*.
27. Ernesto Guevara, *Guerrilla Warfare* (Lincoln: University of Nebraska Press, 1998).
28. Franz Fanon, *Les damnés de la terre* (Paris: Maspero, 1961), translated as *The Wretched of the Earth* (New York: Grove, 1963).
29. Neither Richard Gott nor William J. Pomeroy includes information about Mexico in their collections. Richard Gott, *Rural Guerrillas in Latin America* (Harmonds-

worth, Middlesex: Penguin Books, 1973); William J. Pomeroy, *Guerrilla Warfare and Marxism* (New York: International, 1968).
30. Kate Doyle, "Double Dealing: Mexico's Foreign Policy Toward Cuba," http://www2.gwu.edu/nsarchiv/NSAEBB/NSAEBB83/ (accessed December 6, 2014; no longer posted).
31. Pensado, *Rebel Mexico*, 51.
32. Pensado, 8.
33. Elena Poniatowska, *Fuerte es el silencio* (Mexico City: Ediciones Era, 1980), "La colonia Rubén Jaramillo."
34. Rubin, *Decentering the Regime*.
35. Carr, *Marxism and Communism*, 236.
36. Carr, *Marxism and Communism*, 229–30.
37. When I taught briefly at Colegio Bachilleres, an elite high school in Zacatecas in 1990, dialectical materialism was on the curriculum and was taught by someone who had studied in Moscow.
38. Carlos Monsiváis, *Amor Perdido* (Mexico City: Biblioteca Era, 1977); *Días de guardar* (Mexico City: Biblioteca Era, 1970); *Escenas de pudor y liviandad* (Mexico City: Grijalbo, 1988); *Entrada libre: Crónicas de la sociedad que se organiza* (Mexico City: Biblioteca Era, 1987); and others.
39. Carr, *Marxism and Communism*, 238–44.
40. Adolfo Gilly, *The Mexican Revolution* (London: Verso, 1983).

Chapter 2

1. Mark Wasserman, *Capitalists, Caciques, and Revolution: The Native Elite and Foreign Enterprise in Chihuahua, Mexico, 1854–1911* (Chapel Hill: University of North Carolina Press, 1984), 48.
2. While most historians only speak of Apaches in this connection, with occasional references to Comanches, Brian Delay has revealed that raids on northern Mexico included extensive participation by Comanche, Navajo, and Kiowa people. See Brian Delay, *War of a Thousand Deserts: Indian Raids and the U.S.-Mexican War* (New Haven, Conn.: Yale University Press, 2008).
3. Friedrich Katz, *The Life and Times of Pancho Villa* (Stanford, Calif.: Stanford University Press, 1998), 12.
4. Fernando Jordán, *Crónicas de un país bárbaro*, 7th ed. (Chihuahua: Centro Librero La Prensa, 1989).
5. Víctor Orozco Orozco, *Diez ensayos sobre Chihuahua* (Chihuahua: Doble Hélice, 2003), 74–75.
6. Orozco, 78–79.
7. Orozco, 82.
8. Ana M. Alonso, *Thread of Blood: Colonialism, Revolution, and Gender on Mexico's Northern Frontier* (Tucson: University of Arizona Press, 1995), 162. These same Namiquipans turned against Pancho Villa and aided Pershing's punitive expe-

dition in 1916, exhausted with Villa's exacting depredations and again putting their own interests above those of the abstract nation state. The state provided additional inducements by awarding land to serranos who joined the anti-Villista local militias. During the War of Independence, many had fought on the side of Spain, which had granted them land, citizenship, and support against raiders.

9. Katz, *Life and Times of Pancho Villa*, 14.
10. Alonso, *Thread of Blood*, 35.
11. Alonso, 54.
12. Wasserman, *Capitalists*, 104.
13. See John H. Coatsworth, *Growth Against Development: The Economic Impact of Railroads in Porfirian Mexico* (DeKalb: Northern Illinois University Press, 1981).
14. Wasserman, *Capitalists*, 76.
15. Wasserman, 78–88.
16. Noé G. Palomares Peña, *Propietarios norteamericanos y reforma agraria en Chihuahua, 1917–1942* (Juárez: Universidad Autónoma de Ciudad Juárez, 1991), 22.
17. Palomares Peña, 22–23, 111.
18. Katz, *Life and Times of Pancho Villa*, 19.
19. William H. Beezley, *Insurgent Governor: Abraham Gonzalez and the Mexican Revolution in Chihuahua* (Lincoln: University of Nebraska Press, 1973), 9.
20. Katz, *Life and Times of Pancho Villa*, 19–20, and Wasserman, *Capitalists*, 40. Paul Vanderwood wrote about the Tomóchic Rebellion in *The Power of God Against the Guns of Government: Religious Upheaval in Mexico at the Turn of the Nineteenth Century* (Stanford, Calif.: Stanford University Press, 1998).
21. Heriberto Frías, *Tomóchic* (Chihuahua: Instituto Chihuahuense de la Cultura, 2006).
22. Alonso, *Thread of Blood*, 46.
23. Katz, *Life and Times of Pancho Villa*, 20.
24. Katz, 15.
25. Jane-Dale Lloyd, "Rancheros and Rebellion: The Case of Northwestern Chihuahua, 1905–1909," in Daniel Nugent, ed., *Rural Revolt in Mexico: U.S. Intervention and the Domain of Subaltern Politics* (San Diego: Center for U.S.-Mexican Studies, University of California, San Diego, 1988), 108.
26. Katz, *Life and Times of Pancho Villa*, 60.
27. Orozco, *Diez ensayos*, 154.
28. Alan Knight, *The Mexican Revolution* (Cambridge: Cambridge University Press, 1986), 120.
29. Eric R. Wolf, *Peasant Wars of the Twentieth Century* (New York: Harper and Row, 1969), 35, quoting Friedrich Katz, *Deutschland, Díaz, und die mexikanische Revolution* (Berlin: VED Deutscher Verlag der Wissenschaften, 1964), 243.
30. Wasserman, *Capitalists*, 156.
31. Knight, *Mexican Revolution*, 122.
32. Luis Aboites, *Breve historia de Chihuahua* (Mexico City: El Colegio de México, 1994), 137.

33. Mark Wasserman, *Persistant Oligarchs: Elites and Politics in Chihuahua, Mexico, 1910–1940* (Durham, N.C.: Duke University Press, 1993), 21–22.
34. Wasserman, *Oligarchs*, 35–36.
35. Aboites, *Breve historia*, 146.
36. Aboites, 143.
37. Luis Aboites Aguilar, "Agricultura chihuahuense: Trayectoria productiva, 1920–1990," in Juan Luis Sariego, coordinator, *Trabajo, territorio y sociedad en Chihuahua durante el siglo XX*, Historia general de Chihuahua 5 (Chihuahua: Gobierno del Estado de Chihuahua, 1998), 36–37.
38. Wasserman, *Persistant Oligarchs*, 43.
39. Aboites, *Breve historia*, 145.
40. Aboites, "Agricultura chihuahuense," 44.
41. Aboites, 43, 50.
42. Aboites, 40, 47.
43. Aboites, 48.
44. Aboites, *Breve historia*, 147.
45. Aboites, 159.
46. Palomares Peña, *Propietarios norteamericanos*, 112–14.
47. Palomares Peña, 128.
48. Palomares Peña, 131.
49. Aboites, *Breve historia*, 157.
50. Aboites, "Agricultura chihuahuense," 58.
51. Aboites, 52.
52. Aboites, 65, 66.
53. Aboites, *Breve historia*, 162.
54. François Lartigue, *Indios y bosques: Políticas forestales y comunales en la Sierra Tarahumara* (Mexico City: CIESAS, 1983), 15–16.
55. Lartigue, 20.
56. Samuel Truett, *Fugitive Landscapes: The Forgotten History of the U.S.-Mexico Borderlands* (New Haven, Conn.: Yale University Press, 2006).
57. Lartigue, *Indios y bosques*, 21–22.
58. Lartigue, 23–24.
59. Christopher R. Boyer, *Political Landscapes: Forests, Conservation, and Community in Mexico* (Durham, N.C.: Duke University Press, 2015), 12.
60. María Teresa Guerrero, *The Forest Industry in the Sierra Madre of Chihuahua: Social, Economic, and Ecological Impacts* (Chihuahua and Austin: Comisión de Solidaridad y Defensa de los Derechos Humanos, and Texas Center for Policy Studies, 2000), 25, http://www.texascenter.org/publications/forestry.pdf.
61. Miguel Angel Parra Orozco, *Oro Verde: Madera, vida de una región chihuahuense* (Chihuahua: n.p., 1998), 53.
62. *Mexico North-Western Railway Company* (Chicago: Corbiss Railway Printing Company, before 1911).
63. Alejandra Salas-Porras, *Grupos empresariales en Chihuahua de 1920 al presente* (Mexico City: Centro de Investigación y Docencia Económica, 1992), 17–20.

64. AGN, IPS, vol. 1027.
65. Lartigue, *Indios y bosques*, 42.
66. Aboites, *Breve historia*, 160.
67. Aleida García Aguirre, "Normalistas y maestros en el movimiento campesino y guerrillero de Chihuahua, 1960–1968: Experiencias de solidaridad y relaciones reticulares en la formación de un sujecto político" (Master's thesis, Centro de Investigación y de Estudios Avanzados, Departamento de Investigaciones Educativas, 2012), 56.
68. AGN, DFS, 100-5-1-64, L9, H109.
69. AGN, IPS, vol. 1027.
70. Tejolócachic is in the municipality of Matachic, just south of Madera; this seems unlikely, being so close to the Mineral de Dolores.
71. He was also accused of having killed Anselmo Enríquez in Tejolócachic (erroneously reported as being in Madera) on June 12, 1959; *Indice*, October 22, 1960, 2.
72. A *tienda de raya* is a company store with a monopoly on employee trade.
73. Daniel de los Reyes, "Guerrillas en la sierra chihuahuaense," *Sucesos para Todos*, September 11, 1964, 62.
74. AGN, DFS, 100-5-1-64, L9, H107–21.
75. AGN, DFS, 100-5-1-64, L9, H107–21.
76. AGN, DFS, 100-5-1-64, L9, H113.
77. Here it may be useful to look at Alan Knight's discussion of Pierre Bourdieu's concept of "habitus," a system of internalized conceptions and practices that determine what we consider normal, and apply it to the milieu of political violence in the sierra. Knight suggested that political violence is endemic at the local level, a key element of the habitus, and he sees this as a legacy of the revolution of 1910. See Knight, "Habitus and Homicide," in *Citizens of the Pyramid: Essays on Mexican Political Culture*, ed. Wil G. Pansters (West Lafayette, Ind.: Purdue University Press, 1997).
78. Alan Knight, "Caciquismo in Twentieth-Century Mexico," in *Caciquismo in Twentieth-Century Mexico*, ed Alan Knight and Wil Pansters (London: Institute for the Study of the Americas, 2005), 10–14.
79. Alan Knight and Wil Pansters, *Caciquismo in Twentieth-Century Mexico* (London: Institute for the Study of the Americas, 2005), 41–42.
80. Marco Bellingeri described the armed movements as revealing the fundamental lawlessness of the state and the lack of a clear boundary between violent and nonviolent forms of action. Marco Bellingeri, *Del agrarismo armado a la guerra de los pobres: Ensayos de guerrilla rural en el México contemporaneo, 1940–1974* (Mexico City: Editorial Casa Juan Pablos, 2003), 11. Paul Vanderwood described how nineteenth-century bandits were taken into Benito Juárez's Rural Police Force in 1861 and how outlaws and lawmen complement one another. Paul J. Vanderwood, *Disorder and Progress: Bandits, Police, and Mexican Development* (Wilmington, Del.: Scholarly Resources, 1992), 54.
81. *El Norte*, December 13, 1954, to August 12, 1955. Extensive documentation of the struggle can also be found in President Adolfo Ruíz Cortines's files in the AGN. Thanks to Benjamin Smith for these documents.

82. Founded in 1939 by the Chihuahuan Manuel Gómez Morín and strongly Catholic, the PAN was for decades the only genuine opposition to the PRI.
83. See María Teresa Guerrero Olivares, comp., *Una generacíon desconocida: Movimiento social demócrata cristiano 1962–1970* (Chihuahua: n.p., 2014).
84. See Carlos Gallegos Pérez, *Luto en Delicias: Vida y muerte de Emiliano J. Laing* (Chihuahua: Gobierno del Estado, 2003).
85. Armando Bartra, "Seis años de lucha campesina," *Investigación Económica* 36, no. 141 (1977), 157–209.
86. Rocío Martínez Carrera, *Así se fundó la colonia Villa* (Chihuahua: Doble Hélice, 1998), 17–21.
87. Martínez Carrera, 38–43.
88. Orozco, *Diez ensayos*, 14–23.
89. Julia Preston and Sam Dillon, *Opening Mexico: The Making of a Democracy* (New York: Farrar, Straus and Giroux, 2004), 117–47 ("Chihuahua, 1986").

Chapter 3

1. RAN, Chihuahua City, exp. 1160/23.
2. AGN, DFS, 100-5-1-64, L-9, H-112.
3. Alvaro Ríos, interview by Carlos Montemayor, pp. 16–17, Fondo Carlos Montemayor, Serie Analista Político, Asalto al Cuartel de Madera, Special Collections, Library of the Universidad Autónoma de Ciudad Juárez.
4. Alvaro Ríos, interview by Carlos Montemayor, 18–24.
5. Alvaro Ríos, interview by Carlos Montemayor, 24–26, 29–31.
6. Alvaro Ríos, interview by Carlos Montemayor, 3.
7. Javier Contreras Orozco, quoting Jesús Vargas with no source citation given, listed the first campesino activists to work with Ríos as Jesús Estrada (David's brother), Manuel Ríos, Carlos Ríos, Salvador Gaytán, Alberto Bustillos, and the indigenous Alberto Vargas, and the first schoolteachers as Ernesto Lugo and Alberto Ramírez. Contreras, again quoting Vargas, placed Guillermo and Eduardo Rodríguez Ford and Arturo Gámiz, all students at the State Normal School, alongside Pablo Gómez at the first protest meeting in Madera in January 1960. Javier H. Contreras Orozco, *Los informantes: Documentos confidenciales de la guerrilla en Chihuahua* (Chihuahua: Universidad Autónoma de Chihuahua, 2007), 77–78.
8. *Indice*, February 27, 1960, 1.
9. *Indice*, May 6, 1960, 3.
10. AGN, IPS, vol. 2023A, exp. 20.
11. AGN, IPS, vol. 2023A, exp. 20, 3–9.
12. José Santos Valdés, *Madera: Razón de un Martiriologio* (Mexico City: n.p., 1968), 83.
13. *Indice*, August 22, 1960, 5.
14. AGN, IPS, vol. 2023A, exp. 20, 3.
15. Santos Valdés, *Madera*, 160.

16. Jesús Vargas Valdés, *La fragua de los tiempos*, no. 925, p. 3 (no longer posted), ChihuahuaMexico.com, http://www.chihuahuamexico.com/index.php?option=com_content&task=blogcategory&id=104&Itemid=314.
17. Escuela Normal del Estado de Chihuahua, Administración Académica, Alumnos, Libros Mayores, 1958–1966, caja 27, exp. 12.
18. AGN, DFS, 100-17-1-959, L1, H172.
19. Unnumbered document included in AGN, DFS, Versión Pública Arturo Gámiz, dated June 10, 1957, signed by Leandro Castillo Venegas for the DFS.
20. AGN, DFS, 11–72, H10, L10. Jesús Vargas said Gámiz arrived in Mexico City, but the trip to Germany was cancelled "when difficulties were presented." Vargas, *Fragua*, 925, 4.
21. Andrés Becerril, "Madera, el asalto que detonó la insurgencia," *Excelsior*, September 23, 2015, http://www.excelsior.com.mx/nacional/2015/09/23/1047266. Becerril referenced *El Libro Blanco de la Liga Comunista 23 de Septiembre (The White Book of the 23rd of September Communist League)*, written by Luis de la Barreda Moreno, former director of the DFS.
22. José Antonio Reyes Matamoros, José Luis Moreno Borbolla, and Jaime Laguna Beber, "Entrevista a Alma Caballero y Alma Gómez," October 1990, Chihuahua, Chihuahua, pp. 1–5; Santos Valdés, *Madera*, 164–66; and Tanalís Padilla, "Los inquietos," *La Jornada*, October 18, 2014, http://www.jornada.unam.mx/2014/10/18/politica/006a1pol.
23. *Indice*, November 26, 1960, 1, and December 12, 1960, 1; Arturo Gámiz, "Participación de los estudiantes en el movimiento revolucionario," typescript, sec. 24, http://www.madera1965.com.mx/res6.html.
24. Aleida García Aguirre, "Normalistas y maestros en el movimiento campesino y guerrillero de Chihuahua, 1960–1968: Experiencias de solidaridad y relaciones reticulares en la formación de un sujeto político" (Master's thesis, Centro de Investigación y de Estudios Avanzados, Departamento de Investigaciones Educativas, 2012), 88.
25. *Indice*, December 12, 1960, 1.
26. *Indice*, December 21, 1960, 1; July 5, 1961, 1; February 9, 1961, 1; and June 3, 1961, 1.
27. Alicia de los Ríos Merino, "José de Jesús, Luis Miguel y Salvador Corral García: Good Bye American Way of Life, Nos vamos a la guerrilla; Procesos de radicalidad en jóvenes de la década de los setentas" (Master's thesis, Escuela Nacional de Antropologia e Historia, 2010), 99.
28. García Aguirre, "Normalistas y maestros en el movimiento campesino y guerrillero de Chihuahua," 65.
29. García Aguirre, 50, and Rogelio Luna Jurado, "Los maestros y la democracia sindical," *Cuadernos Políticos* 14 (October–December 1977): 90, http://www.cuadernospoliticos.unam.mx/cuadernos/contenido/CP.14/CP.14.7rogelioluna.pdf.
30. *Indice*, August 11, 1961, 6.
31. *Indice*, October 28, 1961, 2.

32. *Indice*, September 9, 1961, 7, and Registro Agrario Nacional (RAN), Delegación Chihuahua, Dirección de Catastro Rural, Estructura Ejidal, April 15, 1994 (hereafter RAN Chihuahua), 37.
33. *Indice*, October 25, 1961, 3.
34. *Indice*, December 2, 1961, 7, and RAN Chihuahua, 27.
35. Judith Reyes, *La otra cara de la patria* (Mexico City: Talleres Gráficos de México, 1974).
36. Reyes, 76–77.
37. Reyes, 96–98.
38. Reyes, 108–10.
39. Reyes, 103–4.
40. Reyes, 108–10.
41. García Aguirre, "Normalistas y maestros en el movimiento campesino y guerrillero de Chihuahua," 77–78.
42. García Aguirre, 75.
43. Alvaro Ríos, interview by Carlos Montemayor, 9–11.
44. Eric J. Hobsbawm, "The Machine Breakers," *Past and Present* 1 (1952): 57–70.
45. García Aguirre, "Normalistas y maestros en el movimiento campesino y guerrillero de Chihuahua," 71–73.
46. García Aguirre, 74.
47. In her memoir, Reyes told of going to the national newspaper archive and asking for the paper only to be told confidentially by an employee that "two North Americans had come to take photos of the paper" and that it was now entirely missing (Reyes, *La otra cara*, 117–18). The last copy I found at the Hemeroteca of the UNAM in 2011 was dated October 28, 1964, and various pages throughout the collection were missing.
48. *Indice*, February 2, 1963, 2, and *Acción*, February 1963, 12.
49. *Acción*, September 28, 1964, 6.
50. *Acción*, June 1963, 3 and 1.
51. *Acción*, October 4, 1962.
52. *Acción*, October 4, 1962, 9.
53. *Acción*, December 1962, 8.
54. *Indice*, April 3, 1960, 7; Vargas Valdés, *La fragua de los tiempos*, 931 (not available online); García Aguirre, "Normalistas y maestros en el movimiento campesino y guerrillero de Chihuahua," 81.
55. Yelly Alarcón and Félix Pérez, "Judith Reyes ¿Quién Cantará Tu História?" http://666ismocritico.wordpress.com/2011/11/18/judith-reyes-quien-cantara-tu-historia/, accessed December 21, 2014.
56. Vargas Valdés, *La fragua de los tiempos*, 931.
57. García Aguirre, "Normalistas y maestros en el movimiento campesino y guerrillero de Chihuahua," 80n.
58. AGN, DFS, 322–961, H274, L1.

59. *Indice*, February 19, 1961, 3.
60. AGN, DFS, 322-961, H303, L1.
61. *Indice*, February 19, 1961, 1.
62. AGN, DFS, 322-961, H330, L1.
63. *Indice*, October 22, 1960, 2.
64. *Indice*, October 22, 1960, 2.
65. *Indice*, February 27, 1960, 1, and January 30, 1960.
66. *Indice*, July 8, 1960.
67. García Aguirre, "Normalistas y maestros en el movimiento campesino y guerrillero de Chihuahua," 39–40.
68. *Indice*, July 22, 1961, 5, and August 11, 1961, 1.
69. *Indice*, February 24, 1963, 1, and March 24, 1963, 1.
70. *Indice*, January 7, 1964, 1.
71. *Indice*, October 28, 1961, 1.
72. Víctor Quintana, "Madera 65: Los ejes del contexto," *La Jornada del Campo*, September 19, 2015, 14.
73. *Proceso*, September 20, 2015, 45–46.
74. AGN, IPS, vol. 1027.
75. See Rogelio Hernández Rodríguez, *El centro dividido: La nueva autonomía de los gobernadores* (Mexico City: El Colegio de México, 2008), for a discussion of the relationships between governors and the central authority.
76. General Antonio Nava Castillo was removed from office on October 30 after he passed a law requiring the pasteurization of milk. The dairymen protested, police attacked their demonstrations, and they requested the aid of university students. More protests and repression followed. The pasteurization decree followed a long series of abuses, both by the governor and his functionaries, who were military officers from other states.
77. Santos Valdés, *Madera*, 83, 87.
78. Franklin Lee Cleavenger arrived in Chihuahua in 1900 to work as the new superintendent for the phone company, the Compañía Telefónica de Chihuahua (http://www.emersonkent.com/history_notes/franklin_lee_cleavenger.htm). This is the only reference I have found to a Lee Company. Salvador Gaytán, interview by Carlos Montemayor no. 4, 14.
79. http://www.panoramio.com/photo/75696107, downloaded January 27, 2014 (no longer posted).
80. The investigation into fraudulent or expired *certificados de inafectabilidad ganadera* (CIGs; certificates of livestock exemption) was a central demand of the UGOCM. Cárdenas had promulgated the exemption from agrarian partition in 1937, later codified in the Agrarian Code of 1942, to replenish the meat supply devastated by the revolution. The CIG exempted a landowner from partition for twenty-five years, granting him the right to anywhere from three hundred to fifty thousand hectares depending on the number of cattle, soil fertility, and climate.

CIGs required a minimum of two hundred head of cattle, excluding most smallholders. The Agrarian Code 1942 stipulated that they not be granted to landholders subject to agrarian solicitations dating back at least six months or in regions where agrarian need had not been satisfied, a stipulation that was commonly violated. One hundred five concessions had been granted in Chihuahua between 1939 and 1958, mostly in the north and northwest. García Aguirre, "Normalistas y maestros en el movimiento campesino y guerrillero de Chihuahua," 54–55, citing DAAC 1965, *Vencimiento de las primeras concesiones de inafectabilidad ganadera*, a report issued following the first round of expirations. Those granted in 1939 would expire in 1964.

In a 1964 IPS report, the author cited "official figures of the DAAC" for a total of 201 concessions in Chihuahua covering the same dates and a surface area of close to four million hectares, or one-sixth of the state. Whatever the correct figures, many holdings exceeded the required surface area; other landholders held their excess in the names of family members and associates. AGN, IPS, vol. 1025.

81. RAN, 1160/23, the actual file consulted in 2007. These figures do not agree with the figures in RAN Chihuahua, the report issued in 1994, which gives a figure of three thousand hectares for the initial dotation in 1963 and 17,282.50 hectares in 1970. The actual file is more convincing.
82. Santos Valdés, *Madera*, 71.
83. Tesorería, Asuntos Varios, oficio 84, exp. AV-17–964, State Archives, Presidencia Municipal Madera (hereafter Madera Treasurer).
84. Madera Treasurer, 7.
85. Madera Treasurer, 11–12.
86. Madera Treasurer, 2.
87. *Acción*, February, 1963, 1.
88. "Squatters Nab Chihuahua Land," *El Paso Herald-Post*, January 4, 1963.
89. *Acción*, January 1963, extra, 1.
90. García Aguirre, "Normalistas y maestros en el movimiento campesino y guerrillero de Chihuahua," 85.
91. AGN, DFS, 100-5-20-963, H94–95, L1.
92. AGN, DFS, 100-5-20-963, H100, L1.
93. *Indice*, January 19, 1963, 1.
94. *Indice*, January 26, 1963, 1.
95. *Indice*, January 26, 1963, 7, and *Acción*, January 1963, extra, 1.
96. Contreras Orozco, *Los informantes*, 81–82.
97. *Indice*, February 2, 1963, 1.
98. Various figures have been given, both for the number of latifundistas and for the hectares they held.
99. Article 27 of the constitution forbade private ownership of land within one hundred kilometers of the international border.
100. *Indice*, February 16, 1963, 2.

101. This is one of the few references to ecological damage.
102. *Indice*, February 2, 1963, 2; *Acción*, February 1963, 12; and Pablo Gómez Ramírez, "El Paracaidismo en Chihuahua," February 1963, http://www.madera1965.com.mx/parachi.html.
103. *Acción*, April 1963, 4.
104. I found no other reference to *La Voz de Chihuahua*.
105. *Indice*, July 25, 1964, 3, reprinted from *La Voz de Chihuahua*, May 12, 1963.
106. *Indice*, July 25, 1964, 3, reprinted from *La Voz de Chihuahua*, May 12, 1963.
107. AGN, DFS, 100-5-3-963, H35, L1.
108. AGN, DFS, 100-5-3-63, H84, L1.
109. AGN, DFS, 100-5-3-63, H89–90, L1.
110. AGN, DFS, 32-2-63, H112, 116, 117, L2.
111. *Indice*, June 1, 1963, 1.
112. *Acción*, July 1963, 5.
113. *Acción*, June 1963, 1.
114. This is one of very few mentions of the Terrazas family, once the largest landholders in the republic.
115. *Acción*, June 1963, 9.
116. *Indice*, June 22, 1963, 2.
117. *Acción*, June 1963, 1.
118. *Acción*, June 1963, 1.
119. *Acción*, July 1963, 1 and *Acción*, July 1963, 1. Apparently two editions were printed with the same date.
120. *Acción*, August 18, 1963, 1.
121. AGN, DFS, 32-2-63, H197, L2.
122. *Indice*, September 15, 1963, 3B, and AGN, DFS, 100-5-3-63, H102, L1.
123. *Acción*, July 1963, and *Indice*, July 5, 1963.
124. *Acción*, July 1963, 1, and *Indice*, July 5, 1963.
125. *Acción*, August 3, 1963, 1, and *Indice*, August 8, 1963, 2.
126. Roberto Blanco Moheno, *La noticia detrás de la noticia* (Mexico City.: Editorial V Siglos, 1975), 204–6.
127. AGN, DFS, 32-2-63, H125 and 132, L2.
128. AGN, DFS, 100-5-1-963, H368, L6.
129. Joe Foweraker, *Popular Mobilization in Mexico* (Cambridge: Cambridge University Press, 1993), 19.
130. Mary Kay Vaughan, *Cultural Politics in Revolution: Teachers, Peasants, and Schools in Mexico, 1930–1940* (Tucson: University of Arizona Press, 1997), 4–6.
131. Tanalís Padillo, "Rural Education, Political Radicalism, and *Normalista* Identity in Mexico after 1940," in *Dictablanda: Politics, Work, and Culture in Mexico, 1938–1968*, ed. Paul Gillingham and Benjamin T. Smith (Durham, N.C.: Duke University Press, 2014), 348.
132. García Aguirre, "Normalistas y maestros en el movimiento campesino y guerrillero de Chihuahua," 37.

133. García Aguirre, 44.
134. Padilla, "Rural Education," 350.
135. García Aguirre, "Normalistas y maestros en el movimiento campesino y guerrillero de Chihuahua," 45–46, 49–50.
136. García Aguirre, 86–87, citing Saúl Chacón López Interview.
137. García Aguirre, 70.
138. AGN, DFS, 100-5-3-963, H92–94.
139. *Indice*, June 8, 1963, 1, 4, 5.
140. *Acción*, June 1, 1963, 3.
141. *Acción*, June 1, 1963, 3.
142. AGN, IPS, vol. 1025.
143. *Acción*, June 1, 1963, 5.
144. *Acción*, June 1963.
145. *Acción*, July 1963, 8.
146. *Acción*, July 1963, 1, and August 3, 1963, 1.
147. *Indice*, August 23, 1963, 1, 3.
148. *Acción*, August 3, 1963, 1.
149. AGN, DFS, 100-5-3-963, H104–07.
150. *Acción*, September 3, 1963, 1.
151. *Indice*, September 15, 1963, 1, and *Acción*, September 3, 1963, 3.
152. Photo in "Madera, 1965," http://www.madera1965.com.mx/foto15.html.
153. This was the first mention of Gámiz in the DFS files on the UGOCM; he was not, in fact, a student at this time but had gone to Dolores some nine months earlier. His name was misspelled.
154. *Acción*, September 3, 1963, 1, and AGN, DFS, 100-5-3-63, H110–121.
155. *Acción*, September 3, 1963, 6.
156. According to RAN Chihuahua, 27, that case was executed on May 7, 1963.
157. *Acción*, September 18, 1963, 1.
158. *Acción*, September 18, 1963, 2.
159. Contreras Orozco, *Los informantes*, 82.
160. *Acción*, October 3, 1963, 1, and Contreras Orozco, 87.
161. AGN, IPS, vol. 1305.
162. AGN, IPS, vol. 2955A, exp. 5.
163. See François Lartige, *Indios y bosques: Políticas forestales y comunales en la Sierra Tarahumara* (Mexico City: CIESAS, 1983), and María Guadalupe del Socorro López Álvarez, "Poder, desarrollo y medio ambiente en el ejido forestal 'El Largo' y sus anexos: Chihuahua (1971–1994)" (Master's thesis, Universidad Autónoma Metropolitana, Unidad Xochimilco, 1996).
164. Víctor M. Quintana S., "Oro, yerba y hambre," *La Jornada*, August 6, 2011, http://www.jornada.com.mx/2011/08/05/opinion/022a1pol.
165. AGN, IPS, vol. 2955 A, exp. 5.
166. Fiscalía Especial para Movimientos Sociales y Políticos del Pasado, "Orígenes de la guerrilla moderna en México," *Informe Histórico a la Sociedad Mexicana*, National

Security Archives, https://nsarchive2.gwu.edu/NSAEBB/NSAEBB209/informe/tema05.pdf, 250.
167. Gámiz, "Participación de los estudiantes," sec. 24.
168. AGN, IPS, vol. 1305.
169. *Acción*, November 1963, 1.
170. Santos Valdés, *Madera*, 83–84.
171. Inspector General of the Police, State Police, oficio 3230, exp. 11, Chihuahua State Archives.
172. *Indice*, December 7, 1963, 4.
173. *Acción*, December 24, 1963, 1.
174. Reyes, *La otra cara*, 118–19.
175. Reyes, 120.
176. Reyes, 119–21.
177. *Acción*, February 7, 1964, 1.
178. Santos Valdés, *Madera*, photos 6 and 8, between 176 and 177.
179. Carlos Montemayor, *Las armas del alba: Novela* (Mexico City: Joaquín Mortiz, 2003), 165.
180. Santos Valdés, *Madera*, 107.

Chapter 4

1. Juan Reyes del Campillo, "El Frente Electoral del Pueblo y el Partido Comunista Mexicano (1963–1964)," *Revista Mexicana de Sociología* 50, no. 3 (July–September 1988): 219–25.
2. *Indice*, January 7, 1964, 8.
3. *Acción*, January 25, 1964, 3, 8; Registro Agrario Nacional (RAN), Delegación Chihuahua, Dirección de Catastro Rural, Estructura Ejidal, April 15, 1994 (hereafter RAN Chihuahua), 24.
4. *Indice*, January 25, 1964, 1.
5. *Acción*, January 25, 1964, 1.
6. *Acción*, January 25, 1964, 1.
7. *Indice*, February 8, 1964, 1, and AGN, DFS, 100-5-1-64, L7, H305.
8. AGN, DFS, 100-5-3-64, H36–37, L2. According to Florencio Lugo, another member of the GPG, the initial action was taken by Guadalupe Scobell Gaytán on his own. Raúl Florencio Lugo Hernández, *23 de septiembre de 1965: El asalto al cuartel de Madera; Testimonio de un sobreviviente*, 3rd ed. (Mexico City: Universidad Autónoma de Chapingo, 2006; first edition published anonymously in 2002), 56.
9. José Santos Valdés, *Madera: Razón de un Martiriologio* (Mexico City: n.p., 1968), 87.
10. Daniel del los Reyes, "Guerrillas en la sierra chihuahuense," *Sucesos para Todos*, September 25, 1964, 42.
11. AGN, IPS, vol. 1976.
12. Juzgado Primero de lo Penal, Distrito Morales, legajo no. 49, causa no. 28, 1964, Gámiz.

13. Salvador del Toro Rosales, *Testimonios* (Monterrey: Sindicato de Trabajadores de la Universidad Autónoma de Nuevo Leon, 1996), 43–44.
14. Juzgado Primero, Gámiz.
15. Juzgado Primero, Gámiz.
16. *Indice*, March 7, 1964, 2.
17. Aleida García Aguirre, "Normalistas y maestros en el movimiento campesino y guerrillero de Chihuahua, 1960–1968: Experiencias de solidaridad y relaciones reticulares en la formación de un sujeto político" (Master's thesis, Centro de Investigación y de Estudios Avanzados, Departamento de Investigaciones Educativas, 2012), 93.
18. AGN, DFS, 100-5-3-64, L1, H413–416.
19. *Acción*, February 25, 1964, 1.
20. *Indice*, March 7, 1964, 1 and AGN, IPS, vol. 1305.
21. *Acción*, February 25, 1964, 1 and October 28, 1964, 3 and Toro Rosales, *Testimonios*, 32.
22. García Aguirre, "Normalistas y maestros en el movimiento campesino y guerrillero de Chihuahua," 92.
23. Santo Valdés, *Madera*, 148.
24. Santos Valdés, 151.
25. Toro Rosales, *Testimonios*, 14, 25.
26. Toro Rosales, 26.
27. Toro Rosales, 29–30.
28. Toro Rosales, 33.
29. Agents of the Office of National Security were able to infiltrate the circles of students and campesinos in and around the UGOCM but were not able to penetrate the GPG itself in Chihuahua. Agents assigned to the case lacked sufficient training to analyze the politics of the group or the causes that led them to take up arms. As Sergio Aguayo explained, they were better at collecting than analyzing information, although some of their reports did describe the agrarian situation in the state and the governor's recalcitrance. Sergio Aguayo Quezada, *La charola: Una historia de los servicios de inteligencia en México* (Mexico City: Grijalbo, 2001), 50–53.
30. Toro Rosales, *Testimonios*, 34–39.
31. Toro Rosales, 43–44, 47.
32. Toro Rosales, 48–49, 52, 56.
33. García Aguirre, "Normalistas y maestros en el movimiento campesino y guerrillero de Chihuahua," 96.
34. Toro Rosales, *Testimonios*, 32.
35. Guadalupe Jacott, interview by Carlos Montemayor, 3.
36. García Aguirre, "Normalistas y maestros en el movimiento campesino y guerrillero de Chihuahua," 96–97.
37. *Acción*, early March, 1964, 3.
38. Fiscalía Especial para Movimientos Sociales y Políticos del Pasado, "Inicios de la guerrilla moderna en México," 14.
39. Reyes, *La otra cara*, 123–24.

40. *Acción*, April 30, 1964, 6.
41. Orozco, *Diez ensayos*, 263.
42. Toro Rosales, *Testimonios*, 70–71, and Oscar Viramontes, "Un incidente que hizo temblar a Chihuahua," *El Heraldo de Chihuahua*, October 12, 2009, based on contemporary accounts.
43. Reyes, *La otra cara*, 124, 129–32.
44. *Indice*, April 7, 1964, 1.
45. Toro Rosales, *Testimonios*, 69, 71.
46. AGN, DFS, 100-5-3-64, H53, L2.
47. Juzgado Primero de lo Penal, Distrito Morales, legajo 67, no. 612. 221/64, Jesús Hilario Cardona Rodríguez. This seems to combine two actions, 55/64 and 221/64, the first for the occupation of the DAAC and second for the events of April 6.
48. García Aguirre, "Normalistas y maestros en el movimiento campesino y guerrillero de Chihuahua," 67.
49. Francisco Ornelas Gómez, *Sueños de libertad* (Chihuahua: n.p., 2005), 270.
50. Juzgado Primero, Cardona.
51. Juzgado Primero, Cardona.
52. Juzgado Primero, Cardona.
53. Juzgado Primero, Cardona.
54. Juzgado Primero, Cardona.
55. "Declaración," http://movimientosarmados.colmex.mx/items/show/585.
56. Santos Valdés, *Madera*, 84.
57. Lugo Hernández, *El asalto*, 23–24.
58. Lugo Hernández, 25–33.
59. Lugo Hernández, 31–33.
60. Lugo Hernández, 39–41.
61. Lugo Hernández, 35–36.
62. Lugo Hernández, 41, 49–51; Guevara, *Guerrilla Warfare*, 5.
63. Lugo Hernández, *El asalto*, 51–54.
64. State Archives, Inspector General de la Policía, no. 1083, exp. IV, April 27, 1964.
65. AGN, IPS, vol. 1027.
66. *Indice*, May 2, 1964, 2.
67. *Indice*, May 2, 1964, 3, and *Acción*, April 30, 1964, 1.
68. Reyes, *La otra cara*, 111–13.
69. *Indice*, May 2, 1964, 3, and *Acción*, April 30, 1964, 1.
70. AGN, IPS, vol. 1027.
71. Fiscalía Especial para Movimientos Sociales y Políticos del Pasado, "Inicios de la guerrilla moderna en México," 19.
72. *Indice*, September 28, 1964, 1, and Reyes, "Guerrillas."
73. *Indice*, May 22, 1964, 1.
74. AGN, IPS, vol. 1027, and *Indice*, June 2, 1964, 5, 8.
75. AGN, IPS, vol. 1027.
76. AGN, IPS, vol. 1027.

77. *Indice*, June 16, 1964, 1.
78. I found an eight-page document titled "Circular Number One of the National General Command of the Popular Revolutionary Army of Mexico" in the files of the AGN, signed somewhere in the sierra of Mexico (not Chihuahua), April 1964. The first six pages described the structure of the group, dedicated to the guerra de guerrillas, and the group's duty to be connected to mass organizations. An incomplete addendum discussed the use of airfields, with a list including Flores Magón, Madera, and others in Chihuahua. It then reported on a meeting between the mayor of the city and the commander of the Fifth Military Zone about the advisability of suspending a demonstration against the United States for failing to remedy the salinization of the Río Colorado. AGN, IPS, vol. 1025.
79. Reyes, *La otra cara*, 135–36.
80. Reyes, 136–37.
81. Reyes, 137.
82. Reyes, 138–40.
83. Reyes, 140–42.
84. *Indice*, June 16, 1964, 1.
85. AGN, IPS, vol. 1027.
86. AGN, IPS, vol. 1027.
87. AGN, IPS, vol. 1027.
88. AGN, IPS, vol. 1027.
89. AGN, DFS, 100-5-23-64, H43–53, L1.
90. AGN, DFS, 100-5-1-964, H281, L8.
91. *Indice*, June 16, 1964, 1, and AGN, IPS, vol. 1027.
92. AGN, IPS, vol. 1027.
93. *Indice*, June 20, 1964, 1.
94. AGN, IPS, vol. 1027.
95. AGN, IPS, vol. 1027.
96. *Acción*, July 15, 1964, 4.
97. *Indice*, June 20, 1964, 1.
98. *Acción*, July 15, 1964, 4.
99. *Acción*, July 15, 1964, 1.
100. Reyes, *La otra cara*, 165–66.
101. AGN, IPS, vol. 1027.
102. AGN, IPS, vol. 1027.
103. Lugo Hernández, *El asalto*, 59–64.
104. State Archives, Inspector General of the Police, oficio 1772, exp. VII.
105. State Archives, Inspector General of the Police, oficio 1772, exp. VII.
106. AGN, IPS, vol. 1027.
107. Lugo Hernández, *El asalto*, 65–69.
108. State Archives, Inspector General of the Police, oficio 1813, exp. VII.
109. AGN, IPS, 100-5-1, L9, H70, in Versión Pública Arturo Gámiz.
110. AGN, IPS, vol. 1027.

111. Laura Castellanos, *México armado: 1943–1981* (Mexico City: Ediciones Era, 2007), 74.
112. AGN, IPS, vol. 1027.
113. *Indice*, July 18, 1964, 1, 2.
114. *Indice*, July 18, 1964, 4.
115. AGN, IPS, vol. 1027.
116. *Indice*, July 25, 1964, 1.
117. *Indice*, August 15, 1964, 1.
118. AGN, IPS, vol. 1027.
119. The CNOP was one of the corporate bodies of the PRI, predominantly government employees.
120. Programa Nacional Fronterizo, established in 1961 to provide economic stimulus to the border. AGN, IPS, vol. 1027.
121. AGN, IPS, vol. 1027.
122. AGN, IPS, vol. 1027.
123. Central Campesino Independiente (Independent Campesino Center), organized by the PCM as an alternative to the UGOCM.
124. One wonders who in the FEP managed whom in the PPS; since Gámiz, Ríos, and the Gómez brothers were all identified with the PPS, did someone control them? Becerra Gaytán, leader of the FEP, was never mentioned in connection with the UGOCM, leaving Judith Reyes and Salustio González as possible candidates.
125. AGN, IPS, vol. 1027. The Social Democratic Christian Movement was a leftist movement that had split from the PAN and organized factory workers, discussed briefly in the introduction.
126. AGN, IPS, vol. 1027.
127. *Indice*, September 12, 1964, 1.
128. *Indice*, September 12, 1964, 1.
129. AGN, DFS, 100-5-1, L10, H232.
130. Lugo Hernández, *El asalto*, 76–77.
131. *Indice*, September 28, 1964, 1.
132. AGN, IPS, vol. 2955 A, exp. 5.
133. Reyes, "Guerrillas."
134. Reyes, "Guerrillas," September 18, 1964.
135. Reyes, "Guerrillas," September 18, 25, 1964.
136. Reyes, "Guerrillas," September 25, 1964.
137. Reyes, "Guerrillas," September 25, 1964.
138. Reyes, "Guerrillas," September 25, 1964.
139. Reyes, "Guerrillas," September 25, 1964.
140. Reyes, "Guerrillas," September 25, 1964.
141. Nithia Castorena Sáenz, "Estaban ahí: Las mujeres en los grupos armados de Chihuahua (1965–1973)" (Master's thesis, Universidad Autónoma de Ciudad Juárez, Instituto de Ciencias Sociales y Administración, Departamento de Humanidades, 2013), 195.
142. Castorena Sáenz, 212.

143. Conversation with María Aurelia Gaytán Aguirre, Madera, Chihuahua, May 2007.
144. Reyes, "Guerrillas," September 18, 1964, 59.
145. Lugo Hernández, *El asalto*, 78–84.
146. Raúl Florencio Lugo Hernández, *Del cartel a Lecumberri* (Agua Prieta, Sonora: n.p., 2005), 24.
147. "Informe de Ramón," http://movimientosarmados.colmex.mx/items/show/596.
148. Lugo Hernández, *El asalto*, 85–86.
149. Ornelas, *Sueños de libertad*, 22–24.
150. Ornelas, 54–56.
151. Carlos Montemayor, *Las armas del alba: Novela* (Mexico City: Joaquín Moritz, 2003), 179.
152. José Juan (Matías) Fernández Adame, interview by Carlos Montemayor, 1, Fondo Carlos Montemayor, Serie Analista Político, Asalto al Cuartel de Madera. Special Collections, Library of the Universidad Autónoma de Ciudad Juárez.
153. Lugo Hernández, *Del cuartel*, 23–25.
154. Santos Valdés, *Madera*, 164, 167–68; Alma Gómez, interview by Reyes Matamoros, 5; and Alma Gómez, interview by Carlos Montemayor, 5.
155. Lugo Hernández, *El asalto*, 87.
156. Adela Cedillo Cedillo, El fuego y el silencio: Historia de las Fuerzas de Liberación Nacional Mexicanas (1969–1974) (Undergraduate thesis, UNAM, 2008), 112–14.
157. Lugo Hernández, *El asalto*, 74–76.
158. Lugo Hernández, 76.
159. Lugo Hernández, 84.
160. Lugo Hernández, 76.
161. Guadalupe Jacott, interview by Carlos Montemayor, 8, and Clara Elena Gutierrez, interview by Carlos Montemayor, 29.
162. Laura Gaytán, interview by Montemayor, 4.
163. Lugo Hernández, *El asalto*, 57.
164. Régis Debray, *Revolution in the Revolution? Armed Struggle and Political Struggle in Latin America* (New York: Grove, 1967), 44.
165. Leo Huberman and Paul M. Sweezy, *Regis Debray and the Latin American Revolution* (New York: Monthly Review Press, 1968).
166. Guadalupe Jacott, interview by Carlos Montemayor, 7.
167. Clara Elena Gutiérrez, interview by Carlos Montemayor, 30–31.
168. On a Facebook page dedicated to the memory of her mother, "Judith Reyes, tu memoria está grabado en la historia," she continues to mourn his loss.
169. Oscar González Eguiarte, "Diario de campaña," 35, Fondo Carlos Montemayor, Sección: Analista Político, Serie: Ataque Cuartel Madera, Special Collections, Library of the Universidad Autónoma de Ciudad Juárez.
170. AGN, IPS, vol. 1026, exp. 8.
171. AGN, DFS, 100-5-1, L10, H246–232, Versión Pública Arturo Gámiz.
172. AGN, DFS, 100-5-1, L16, H96.
173. Reyes, "Guerrillas," September 25, 1964.

174. AGN, DFS, 100-5-1, L9, H70 and 100-5-1, L10, H231.
175. AGN, IPS, 2023 A, exp. 20.
176. *Indice*, October 21, 1964, 1.
177. AGN, DFS, 100-5-1-64, H263–65, L9.
178. *Indice*, August 29, 1964, 1, 6.
179. *Indice*, September 12, 1964, 1, and Santos Valdés, *Madera*, 136.
180. *Indice*, October 21, 1964, 1.
181. AGN, DFS, 100-5-1-64, H291, L10.
182. Juzgado Primero, Cardona.
183. AGN, DFS, 100-5-1-64, H302, L10.
184. AGN, DFS, 100-5-1-64, H345, L10.
185. AGN, DFS, 100-5-1-64, H430, L10.
186. *Acción*, October 28, 1964, 3.
187. *Indice*, November 7, 1964. Arturo Gámiz, "Participación de los estudiantes en el movimiento revolucionario," typescript, http://www.madera1965.com.mx/res6.html.
188. AGN, DFS, 100-5-1-64, H12, L11.
189. *Indice*, November 21, 1964, 2.
190. *Indice*, November 21, 1964, 2, 3, 5, 7.
191. *Indice*, November 21, 1964, 7.
192. *Proceso*, September 20, 2015, 45–46.
193. *Indice*, December 3, 1964, 1; AGN, DFS, 100-5-1, L11, H157; and Toro Rosales, *Testimonios*, 80.
194. *Indice*, December 3, 1964, 8B.
195. AGN, DFS, 100-1-5-64, H342, L11.
196. *Indice*, December 22, 1964, 3.

Chapter 5

1. Marco Bellingeri, *Del agrarismo armado a la guerra de los pobres: Ensayos de guerrilla rural en el México contemporaneo, 1940–1974* (Mexico City: Editorial Casa Juan Pablos, 2003), 86–87. Bellingeri did not reveal his sources beyond "interviews realized in October, 1981 in Chihuahua City."
2. Aleida García Aguirre, "Normalistas y maestros en el movimiento campesino y guerrillero de Chihuahua, 1960–1968: Experiencias de solidaridad y relaciones reticulares en la formación de un sujeto político" (Master's thesis, Centro de Investigación y de Estudios Avanzados, Departamento de Investigaciones Educativas, 2012), 122.
3. Froilan Meza Rivera, "Hablan viejos dirigentes: Error táctico-militar el asalto al cuartel de Madera," *El Heraldo de Chihuahua*, September 22, 2002.
4. Meza Rivera.
5. RAN Chihuahua, 37, and Alvaro Ríos, interview by Carlos Montemayor, pp. 6–7, Fondo Carlos Montemayor, Serie Analista Político, Asalto al Cuartel de Madera, Special Collections, Library of the Universidad Autónoma de Ciudad Juárez.

6. Alvaro Ríos, interview by Carlos Montemayor, 8–9.
7. Pedro Uranga, interview by Carlos Montemayor, p. 14, Fondo Carlos Montemayor, Serie Analista Político, Asalto al Cuartel de Madera, Special Collections, Library of the Universidad Autónoma de Ciudad Juárez.
8. Letter to Compañero Carlos, reel 3, folder 20, Mandeville Special Collections Library, University of California, San Diego.
9. *Indice*, January 6, 1965, 8.
10. *Indice*, January 6, 1965, 1.
11. *Indice*, January 6, 1965, 4.
12. *Indice*, January 23, 1965, 1.
13. *Indice*, January 23, 1965, 2.
14. *Indice*, February 10, 1965, 1.
15. *Indice*, February 10, 1965, 5.
16. *Indice*, February 20, 1965, 8.
17. Javier H. Contreras Orozco, *Los informantes: Documentos confidentiales de la guerrilla en Chihuahua* (Chihuahua: Universidad Autónoma de Chihuahua, 2007), 110.
18. José Santos Valdés, *Madera: Razón de un Martiriologio* (Mexico City: n.p., 1968), 81–84.
19. Santos Valdés, 85.
20. Salvador del Toro Rosales, *Testimonios* (Monterrey: Sindicato de Trabajadores de la Universidad Autónoma de Nuevo Leon, 1996), 73–75.
21. Pedro Uranga, interview by Carlos Montemayor, 1–3.
22. Heraclio Bernal was a nineteenth-century bandit who operated in the sierra between Durango and Sinaloa.
23. *Indice*, May 29, 1965, 2.
24. Francisco Ornelas Gómez, *Sueños de libertad* (Chihuahua: n.p., 2005), 112, 116.
25. Anonymous, "Resolutions of the Second Encounter of the Sierra 'Heraclio Bernal,'" typescript, 1965; they are available on the Primeros Vientos website, http://madera1965.com.mx/resol.html; Arturo Gámiz, "Participación de los estudiantes en el movimiento revolucionario," typescript, http://www.madera1965.com.mx/res6.html.
26. Carlos Montemayor, *Las armas del alba: Novela* (Mexico City: Joaquín Moritz, 2003), 131.
27. Rogelio Luna Jurado, *La razon maderiana* (online).
28. Victor Orozco Orozco, *Diez ensayos sobre Chihuahua* (Chihuahua: Doble Hélice, 2003), 255.
29. Miguel Quiñonez's library contained the following books: Friedrich Engels, *Anti-Dühring*; Nikita Jruchov, *El imperialismo: Enemigo de los pueblos, Enemigo de la paz, Socialismo y comunismo*, and *Conjurar la guerra es la tarea fundamental*; Mario Gill, *Cuba sí, Yanquis no* (with extensive underlines) and *Episodios Mexicanos*; George Politzer, *Lecciones fundamentales de la filosofía*; Braulio Maldonado, *Los inconformes*; Lenin, *La alianza de la clase obrera y del campesinado*; Giovanni Papini, *Gogol* (probably the satirical novel *Gog*); Marx and Engels, *Obras escogidas* and *La cuestión*

agraria y el movimiento de liberación nacional; M. Illin and E. Segal, *Como el hombre llegó a ser gigante*; Mariano Azuela, *Los de abajo*; Karl Mannheim, *Diagnóstico de nuestro tiempo*; and the Agrarian Code.

30. Fourth Resolution.
31. This debate was carried on by the revolutionary intelligentsia of every developing country. In every national liberation struggle, the needs of workers and peasants were subordinated to the leadership of a flag-bearing national elite. This was the tragedy of the mid- to late twentieth century.
32. Fifth Resolution.
33. Fifth Resolution.
34. Third Resolution.
35. Recent scholars have made a compelling argument for capitalism having grown out of the English countryside and not from the transformation of artisanal to factory production in the cities. See T. H. Aston and C. H. E. Philpin, eds., *The Brenner Debate: Agrarian Class Structure and Economic Development in Pre-industrial Europe* (Cambridge: Cambridge University Press, 1985).
36. First Resolution.
37. Third Resolution.
38. Karl Marx, Preface to *Contribution to the Critique of Political Economy* (Moscow: Progress Publishers, 1977).
39. Third Resolution.
40. Second Declaration of Havana, 16.
41. Third Resolution.
42. The debate over the nature of the Mexican revolution among historians is complex and involves an assessment both of the class nature of the period leading up to it and, more importantly, the class nature of the resulting society. See Ramón Ruíz, *The Great Rebellion* (New York: Norton, 1980); Adolfo Gilly, *The Mexican Revolution* (London: Verso, 1983); Katz, *The Life and Times of Pancho Villa* (Stanford, Calif. Stanford University Press, 1998); Alan Knight, *The Mexican Revolution* (Cambridge: Cambridge University Press, 1986); John M. Hart, *Revolutionary Mexico* (Berkeley: University of California Press, 1997); John R. Womack Jr., *Zapata and the Mexican Revolution* (New York: Knopf, 1969); and many more.
43. Third Resolution.
44. Third Resolution.
45. Third Resolution.
46. Fifth Resolution.
47. María Teresa Guerrero Olivares, comp., *Una generacíon desconocida: Movimiento social demócrata cristiano 1962–1970* (Chihuahua: n.p., 2014), 182–83.
48. Guevara, Ernesto. *Guerrilla Warfare* (Lincoln: University of Nebraska Press, 1998).
49. Fifth Resolution.
50. Fifth Resolution.
51. Gámiz, "Participación de los estudiantes," sec. 4.

52. Fifth Resolution.
53. García Aguirre, "Normalistas y maestros en el movimiento campesino y guerrillero de Chihuahua," 46.
54. Gámiz, "Participación de los estudiantes," 2.
55. Fifth Resolution.
56. Guevara, *Guerrilla Warfare*.
57. Fifth Resolution.
58. Fifth Resolution.
59. "Cuando la guerra se coloca en el centro de la lucha, las cuestiones de la democracia económica, social y política se pospone al triunfo de la revolución; se renuncia a tratar de materializarlas paulatinamente en ámbitos cívicos y gremiales, y por tanto dejan de ser materia de la acción cotidiana." Armando Bartra, *Guerrero bronco: Campesinos, cuidadanos y guerrilleros en la Costa Grande* (Mexico City: Ediciones sin filtro, 1996), 144.
60. "El desmantelamiento de las organizaciones cívicas y sociales de carácter democrático . . . no solo deja en la indefensión cívica y gremial a las mayorías, también tiene efectos nefastos en la cultura política popular, pues ratifica el desprestigio de los comicios y de la acción gremial y encierra el ideal libertario en un discurso apocalíptico y una práctica militarista. Además del saldo de sangre, el camino de la sierra tiene siempre un enorme costo político." Bartra, *Guerrero bronco*, 144.
61. "A la larga, ese maximalismo de los medios de acción política, que es la vía guerrillera, y sobre todo la mitología que entorno a ella se construye, generan en una suerte de esquizofrenia social. Al hipostasiar la política como vocación de iluminados reservada a los apóstoles de un credo trascendente, se propicia el envilecimiento de la práctica social secular." Bartra, *Guerrero bronco*, 144.
62. The same might be explained, if Gámiz were the author, by a lack of access to the required sources or by his use of available but less authoritative sources, which he preferred not to cite.
63. "Es la consecuencia de un descubrimiento que obtiene en la práctica la generación de Madera, que deviene núcleo esencial reformador del normalismo. Intuyen que ha llegado el momento de transitar del papel mecánicamente impuesto como correa de transmisión de la reforma del capitalismo por el Estado postrevolucionario y de divulgadores acríticos del marxismo de manual, hacia el carácter de un movimiento autónomo, pero no anarquista; de una fuerza política capaz de asumir la dirección del movimiento reformador del país." Rogelio Luna Jurado, "La razón maderiana," unpublished essay, Microsoft Word file, http://www.madera1965.com.mx/prensa/2000/razon.docx.
64. "Resoluciones," Primeros Vientos, http://madera1965.com.mx/resol.html.
65. Luna Jurado, "La razón maderiana."
66. I obtained a digital copy of this document in September, 2010, but I do not know where.
67. First Resolution.

68. Victor Orozco, "Las guerrillas chihuahuenses de los 60: Parte 3," *El Diario de Chihuahua*, September 24, 2015, http://diario.mx/micrositios/Guerrillas-Chihuahuences-en-los-60s-Parte-3.
69. Eric Zolov, "Expanding Our Conceptual Horizons: The Shift from an Old to a New Left in Latin America," *A Contracorriente: Una Revista de Estudios Latinoamericanos* 5, no. 2 (2008): 47–73, http://acontracorriente.chass.ncsu.edu/index.php/acontracorriente/article/view/585.
70. Several young women were named in DFS reports as his girlfriends, and Judith Reyes's daughter Magaly (Yelly) Alarcón bore his child when she was a teenager. (One wonders whether that influenced the public rupture between Reyes and Gámiz in 1964.) A woman who wished anonymity described Gámiz as having a "libidinous" gaze. Gámiz and the group had frequently visited her home on the edge of the sierra; her husband had been a supporter.
71. Jaime Pensado, "'To Assault with the Truth': The Revitalization of Conservative Militancy in Mexico During the Global Sixties," *Americas* 70, no. 3 (January 2014): 489–521.
72. José Revueltas, *Los días terrenales* (Mexico City: Editorial Stylo, 1949) and *Los errores* (Mexico City: Ediciones Era, 1979).
73. On YouTube there is a five-minute video of downtown Chihuahua streets made in 1965 by a visiting tourist that shows mules bringing pulque into town and women wrapped in black and white rebozos alongside others in high heels and shirtwaist dresses. "Chihuahua in 1965," https://www.youtube.com/watch?v=cF9wXhQwisY.
74. Zolov, "Expanding Our Conceptual Horizons," 55.
75. Jean Franco, *The Decline and Fall of the Lettered City: Latin America in the Cold War* (Cambridge, Mass.: Harvard University Press, 2002), 61.
76. Franco, 61.
77. Franco, 85.
78. "Fue en ese ambiente en donde se dio una pésima mezcla de la historia de México con un recetario político sumamente coherente y gratificante que embotó la razón con citas y alegatos autosuficientes." Luna Jurado, "La razón maderiana."
79. "Y la generosidad altísima de los militantes, su deseo de extirpar la injusticia, su íntimo y público compromiso, se perdieron en la sucesión de dogmas y sentencias y requerimientos inquisitoriales, no hay que saludar al enemigo de hoy que fue el compañero de ayer, seamos inflexibles, impiadosos, acres como el martillo o la roca, tenaces, graníticos." Carlos Monsiváis, *Amor perdido* (Mexico City: Ediciones Era, 1977), 127.
80. Monsiváis, *Amor perdido*, 130.
81. A *cuota* is probably a fee, but I found no mention of that slogan nor of any murals in Chihuahua during the early 1960s.
82. See Mark Wasserman, *Persistant Oligarchs: Elites and Politics in Chihuahua, Mexico, 1910–1940* (Durham, N.C.: Duke University Press, 1993).
83. Santos Valdés, *Madera*, 86.
84. Santos Valdés, 86–87; Toro Rosales, *Testimonios*, 82; and AGN, DFS, 100-5-1, L13, H71, Versión Pública Arturo Gámiz.

85. Toro Rosales, *Testimonios*, 75–76.
86. Montemayor, *Las armas*, 181–82.
87. *Indice*, May 29, 1965, 3.
88. *Indice*, June 3, 1965, 8.
89. *Indice*, July 10, 1965, 1, and Montemayor, *Las armas*, 181–82.
90. *Indice*, July 17, 1965, 1, 2, 4.
91. *Indice*, September 11, 1965, 1, and September 18, 1; Santos Valdés, *Madera*, 103–9; "Una carta abierta," http://www.madera1965.com.mx/Carta.htm.
92. *Indice*, September 27, 1965, 8.
93. Montemayor, *Las armas*, 128–33.
94. "Informe de Ramón," http://movimientosarmados.colmex.mx /items/show/126.
95. José Juan (Matías) Fernández Adame, interview by Carlos Montemayor, p. 2, Fondo Carlos Montemayor, Serie Analista Político, Asalto al Cuartel de Madera. Special Collections, Library of the Universidad Autónoma de Ciudad Juárez.
96. Carlos Montemayor, *Las mujeres del alba* (Mexico City: Grijalbo, 2010), 67.
97. Orozco, *Diez ensayos*, 340.
98. "Informe de Ramón."
99. Orozco, *Diez ensayos*, 251–54, and Santos Valdés, *Madera*, 121–22.
100. Guadalupe Jacott, interview by Carlos Montemayor, p. 7, Fondo Carlos Montemayor, Serie Analista Político, Asalto al Cuartel de Madera. Special Collections, Library of the Universidad Autónoma de Ciudad Juárez.
101. Pedro Uranga, interview by Carlos Montemayor, 3–5.
102. Montemayor, *Las armas*, 179–88.
103. Salvador Gaytán, interview by Carlos Montemayor no. 2, Fondo Carlos Montemayor, Serie Analista Político, Asalto al Cuartel de Madera. Special Collections, Library of the Universidad Autónoma de Ciudad Juárez.
104. Montemayor, *Las armas*, 196–97.
105. "Informe de Ramón."
106. Fernández Adame, interview by Carlos Montemayor, 2–4.
107. Fernández Adame, interview by Carlos Montemayor, 2–4, 21, 23, and Ornelas Gómez, *Sueños de libertad*, 164.
108. *El Heraldo*, September 23, 1965, 1; AGN, IPS, vol. 450, exp. 2; and Ornelas Gómez, *Sueños de libertad*, 163.
109. "Informe de Ramón," and Ornelas Gómez, *Sueños de libertad*, 175–76.
110. "Informe de Ramón."
111. Montemayor, *Las armas*, 9.
112. "Informe de Ramón"; Raúl Florencio Lugo Hernández, *23 de septiembre de 1965: El asalto al cuartel de Madera; Testimonio de un sobreviviente*, 3rd ed. (Mexico City: Universidad Autónoma de Chapingo, 2006), 92; and Toro Rosales, *Testimonios*, 99.
113. Victor Orozco, *Guerrillas chihuahuenses de los 60*, parte 5, https://www.segundoa segundo.com/guerrillas-chihuahuenses-de-los-60-por-victor-orozco-parte-5/.
114. Salvador Gaytán [and Ramón Mendoza], interview by Carlos Montemayor no. 5, pp. 10–15, Fondo Carlos Montemayor, Serie Analista Político, Asalto al Cuartel

de Madera. Special Collections, Library of the Universidad Autónoma de Ciudad Juárez.
115. Salvador Gaytán [and Ramón Mendoza], interview by Carlos Montemayor no. 6, pp. 1–3, Fondo Carlos Montemayor, Serie Analista Político, Asalto al Cuartel de Madera. Special Collections, Library of the Universidad Autónoma de Ciudad Juárez.
116. Ornelas Gómez, *Sueños de libertad*, 179–81, 184, and Lugo Hernández, *El asalto*, 96.
117. Ornelas Gómez, *Sueños de libertad*, 7–9, 198–202, 228–31.
118. Lugo Hernández, *El asalto*, 9–13, 15–22, 93, 97–101.
119. Fernández Adame, interview by Carlos Montemayor, 5–8.

Chapter 6

1. José Juan (Matías) Fernández Adame, interview by Carlos Montemayor, 8–9, 14, Fondo Carlos Montemayor, Serie Analista Político, Asalto al Cuartel de Madera. Special Collections, Library of the Universidad Autónoma de Ciudad Juárez.
2. José Santos Valdés, *Madera: Razón de un Martiriologio* (Mexico City: n.p., 1968), 116.
3. Francisco Ornelas Gómez, *Sueños de libertad* (Chihuahua: n.p., 2005), 204.
4. *El Norte*, September 25, 1965; José Santos Valdés, *Madera*, photo 32, between 176 and 177.
5. Salvador del Toro Rosales, *Testimonios* (Monterrey: Sindicato de Trabajadores de la Universidad Autónoma de Nuevo Leon, 1996), 102–3.
6. *El Heraldo*, September 25, 1965, 7.
7. Toro Rosales, *Testimonios*, 102.
8. Alessandro Portelli, *The Death of Luigi Trastulli and Other Stories: Form and Meaning in Oral History* (Albany: State University of New York Press, 1991), 26.
9. Carlos Montemayor, *Las mujeres del alba* (Mexico City: Grijalbo, 2010), 17–21.
10. Luz María Gaytán, interview by Carlos Montemayor, 1–2, Fondo Carlos Montemayor, Serie Analista Político, Asalto al Cuartel de Madera. Special Collections, Library of the Universidad Autónoma de Ciudad Juárez.
11. Ornelas Gómez, *Sueños de libertad*, 216–19.
12. *Indice*, September 27, 1965, 9.
13. http://www.madera1965.com.mx/galeria.html.
14. Fiscalía Especial para Movimientos Sociales y Políticos del Pasado, "Inicios de la guerrilla moderna en México," 26.
15. Santos Valdés, *Madera*, 118–19, 121.
16. Raúl Florencia Lugo Hernández, *23 de septiembre de 1965: El asalto al cuartel de Madera* (Mexico City: Universidad Autónoma de Chapingo, 2006), 96.
17. Lugo Hernández, 92–93.
18. Ornelas Gómez, *Sueños de libertad*, 263.
19. Pedro Uranga, interview by Carlos Montemayor, 13–15, Fondo Carlos Montemayor, Serie Analista Político, Asalto al Cuartel de Madera. Special Collections, Library of the Universidad Autónoma de Ciudad Juárez.
20. *La voz del pueblo*, Torreón, September 26, 1965, 1.

21. *El Heraldo*, September 24, 1965, 1B.
22. *El Norte*, September 28, 1965, 1.
23. AGN, DFS, 100-5-3, L2, H341, Versión Pública Arturo Gámiz and *Política*, October 1, 1965, 5.
24. *El Heraldo*, September 24, 1965, 1B.
25. Ornelas Gómez, *Sueños de libertad*, 271–72, and *El Norte*, September 26, 1965.
26. Toro Rosales, *Testimonios*, 94–97.
27. *El Heraldo*, September 24, 1965, 1B, 4B.
28. *El Norte*, September 24, 1965, and Toro Rosales, *Testimonios*, 97.
29. *El Heraldo*, September 25, 1965, IB, and *Indice*, September 27, 1965, 9.
30. AGN, DFS, 100-5-3, L2, H366–370, Versión Pública Arturo Gámiz.
31. *Política*, October 1, 1965, 2, quoting *La Voz de Chihuahua*, September 27, 1965.
32. Santos Valdés, *Madera*, 123–24.
33. *El Norte*, September 27, 1965, 1.
34. The Ejido Belisario Domínguez had been formed in 1926, according to RAN Chihuahua, 15; the only amplification took place in 1964, which throws into further doubt the RAN Chihuahua document.
35. *El Heraldo*, September 28, 1965, 1B.
36. *El Heraldo*, September 28, 1965, 4, and September 25, 1965, 7.
37. Lugo Hernández, *El asalto*, 84.
38. *El Heraldo*, September 28, 1965, 1.
39. Matachic and Madera are only sixty-five kilometers apart, although the road was unpaved and may have been in poor repair.
40. *El Norte*, September 27, 1965, 1; *El Heraldo*, October 2, 1965, 1; and Toro Rosales, *Testimonios*, 87–92.
41. *El Heraldo*, September 29, 1965, 1B.
42. *Política*, October 1, 1965, 5–9.
43. *Política*, October 1, 1965, 5–9, 51.
44. *Política*, October 15, 1965, 32.
45. Santos Valdés, *Madera*.
46. Víctor Rico Galán, "Chihuahua: De la desesperación a la muerte." *Sucesos para todos*, October 15, 1965.
47. Rico Galán.
48. Toro Rosales, *Testimonios*, 105.
49. *Indice*, October 11, 1965, 6, and AGN, DFS, 100-5-3-65, L3, H8.
50. Luz María Gaytán, interview by Carlos Montemayor, 2–3.
51. AGN, DFS, 100-5-1-65, L15, H157, Versión Pública Arturo Gámiz.
52. Montemayor, *Las mujeres*, 193–94.
53. José Antonio Reyes Matamoros, José Luis Moreno Borbolla, and Jaime Laguna Beber, "Entrevista a Alma Caballero y Alma Gómez," October 1990, Chihuahua, Chihuahua, p. 7.
54. Luis Aboites, *Breve historia de Chihuahua* (Mexico City: El Colegio de México, 1994), 165–66.

55. *El Heraldo*, September 23, 1965, 1; September 24, 1965, 4B; and October 3, 1965, 1.
56. Toro Rosales, *Testimonios*, 105–6.
57. *Indice*, October 24, 1965, 1.
58. Toro Rosales, *Testimonios*, 106–8.
59. Toro Rosales, 108–12.
60. Cuauhtémoc Cárdenas to Amelia S. de Cárdenas, June 28, 1966, http://movimiento sarmados.colmex.mx/items/show/594.
61. Verónica Oikión Solano, "Lázaro Cárdenas en el laberinto de Madera," *La Jornada del Campo*, September 19, 2015, 18.
62. *Indice*, October 11, 1965, 1.
63. *Indice*, October 24, 1965, 2; October 30, 1965, 3; and November 28, 1965, 4.
64. *Indice*, December 4, 1965, 1.
65. AGN, IPS, vol. 450.
66. Toro Rosales, *Testimonios*, 129–32.
67. RAN 1160/23.
68. Aboites, *Breve historia*, 166. Once again the discrepancies are bewildering: according to RAN Chihuahua, the presidential resolution was signed on April 16, 1971, granting 256,611 hectares in the first amplification and not executed until 1976 when the amount was reduced to 251,960 hectares. RAN Chihuahua, 27.
69. Ornelas Gómez, *Sueños de libertad*, 224.
70. Fernández Adame, interview by Carlos Montemayor, 8–9, 14.
71. "Informe de Ramón," 6–7, http://movimientosarmados.colmex.mx/items/show/596.
72. Toro Rosales, *Testimonios*, 114–16.
73. "Carta al compañero Carlos," http://movimientosarmados.colmex.mx/items/show/598.
74. "Carta al compañero Carlos."
75. Salvador Gaytán, interview by Carlos Montemayor, no. 3, p. 4, Fondo Carlos Montemayor, Serie Analista Político, Asalto al Cuartel de Madera. Special Collections, Library of the Universidad Autónoma de Ciudad Juárez.
76. Toro Rosales, *Testimonios*, 116.
77. Toro Rosales, 117–21.
78. AGN, IPS, vol. 435.
79. Toro Rosales, *Testimonios*, 123–27, 137.
80. Carlos Montemayor, *La fuga* (Mexico City: Fondo de Cultura Económica), 2007.
81. Toro Rosales, *Testimonios*, 128–29, and AGN, IPS, vol. 435.
82. Minerva Armendáriz Ponce, *Morir de sed junto a la fuente: Sierra de Chihuahua 1968* (Chihuahua: M. Armendáriz Ponce, 2001), 109.
83. Víctor Orozco, *Diez ensayos sobre Chihuahua*, 271–73.
84. Orozco, 270–74.
85. *El Heraldo de Chihuahua*, May 4, 1998, 3B.
86. *El Heraldo de Chihuahua*, June 9, 2004.
87. *El Heraldo de Chihuahua*, September 25, 1995, http://madera1965.com.mx/hist1.html.

88. Miguel Angel Parra Orozco, *Oro Verde: Madera, vida de una región chihuahuense* (Chihuahua: n.p., 1998), 131.
89. Orozco, "Madera '65"; "Cronología: ¿Cómo se fue Fraguando el Ataque?," *El Heraldo de Chihuahua*, September 23, 1995.
90. Jesús Vargas Valdés, Epilogue to Montemayor, *Las mujeres*, 225.
91. Clara Elena Gutiérrez and Laura Gaytán, interview by Carlos Montemayor, 8, Fondo Carlos Montemayor, Serie Analista Político, Asalto al Cuartel de Madera. Special Collections, Library of the Universidad Autónoma de Ciudad Juárez.
92. Sergio Aguayo Quezada, *La charola: Una historia de los servicios de inteligencia en México* (Mexico City: Grijalbo, 2001), 91.
93. It is now available on YouTube, https://www.youtube.com/watch?v=VUtunSQbk4Q.
94. Monica Mateos-Vega, "Existe otro México clandestino más peligroso que la guerrilla: Entrevista con Carlos Montemayor," *La Jornada*, February 28, 2007.
95. "Muere el cineasta mexicano Jaime Casillas," *El Universal*, April 2, 2008, http://www.eluniversal.com.mx/notas/495024.html.
96. *Madera 1965*, produced by Carlos Mendoza and Irene and Xóchitl García, 2011.

Conclusion

1. Sergio Aguayo, "El impacto de la guerrilla en la vida mexicana: Algunas hypótesis," in *Movimientos armados en Mexico, siglo XX*, vol. 1, edited by Verónika Oikión Solano and Marta Eugenia García Ugarte (Zamora: El Colegio de Michoacán, 2008), 92.
2. Adela Cedillo and Ricardo Gamboa Ramírez, "Interpretaciones sobre los espacios de participación política después del 10 de junio de 1971 en México," in *Violencia y sociedad: Un hito en la historia de las izquierdas en América Latina*, ed. Verónica Oikión and Miguel Ángel Urrego (Morelia: Universidad Michoacana de San Nicolás de Hidalgo/Colegio de Michoacán, 2010).
3. Adela Cedillo Cedillo, "El fuego y el silencio: Historia de las Fuerzas de Liberación Nacional Mexicanas (1969–1974)" (undergraduate thesis, Universidad Nacional Autónoma de México, 2008), 39.
4. See Carlos Monsiváis, *Entrada libre: Crónicas de la sociedad que se organiza* (Mexico City: Ediciones Era, 1987).
5. Joe Foweraker and Ann Craig, eds., *Popular Movements and Political Change in Mexico* (Boulder: Lynn Rienner, 1990), 5.
6. See Elena Poniatowska, *Fuerte es el silencio* (Mexico City: Ediciones Era, 1980), "La colonia Rubén Jaramillo."
7. This may have shown the long arm of Cuban influence on certain solidarity movements, protecting its ally, the Mexican regime.
8. Aguayo, "El impacto de la guerrilla," 96.
9. Poniatowska, *Fuerte es el silencio*, 87.
10. In 1971, Mexico City students organized a march on June 10, the liturgical Feast of Corpus Christi, with ten thousand participants. Police vehicles arrived and

blocked the streets while *halcones* (hawks), armed initially with clubs and then with firearms, killed and wounded between twenty-five and one hundred marchers. The *halcones* appeared to be street thugs but were an elite paramilitary force created by Gustavo Díaz Ordaz in 1968 to control left-wing students, and the attack was orchestrated by security forces. Three months earlier, a group of *halcones* had been sent to the United States to train at the International Police Academy, returning to Mexico in July. President Echeverría denied responsibility and offered the mayor of Mexico City as a scapegoat. Several intellectuals, including Octavio Paz and Carlos Fuentes, blamed the events on reactionary forces seeking to undo Echeverría's *apertura*, his opening to "democracy."

11. See Periodistas en Riesgo, https://www.periodistasenriesgo.com.
12. Fernando Herrera Calderón and Adela Cedillo, *Challenging Authoritarianism in Mexico: Revolutionary Struggles and the Dirty War, 1964–1982* (New York: Routledge, 2011), 6.
13. John Beverley, "Rethinking the Armed Struggle in Latin America," *boundary 2* 36, no. 1 (2009): 58.
14. Private correspondence, June 12, 2011.
15. Julia Preston and Sam Dillon, *Opening Mexico: The Making of a Democracy* (New York: Farrar, Straus and Giroux, 2004), 327–28; and Carmen Boullosa and Mike Wallace, *A Narco History: How the United States and Mexico Jointly Created "The Mexican Drug War"* (New York: OR Books, 2015), 30–31.
16. Alexander Aviña, "Mexico's Long Dirty War," *NACLA Report on the Americas* 48, no. 2 (2016): 144.
17. Preston and Dillon, *Opening Mexico*, 329, and Boullosa and Wallace, *Narco History*, 39–40.
18. See Paul J. Vanderwood, *Disorder and Progress: Bandits, Police, and Mexican Development* (Wilmington, Del.: Scholarly Resources, 1992).
19. Boullosa and Wallace, *A Narco History*, 54–55.

Note on Methodology and Sources

1. Francisco Ornelas Gómez, *Sueños de libertad* (Chihuahua: n.p., 2005), 195 (ellipses in original).
2. RAN Chihuahua, 27.
3. I stopped conducting my own formal interviews because the federal funding I received forced me to comply with the requirements of the Human Subjects Protection Program, a federal agency focused on the rights of subjects of Biomedical and Behavioral Research, applied to ethnographic research at the discretion of the sponsoring institution. I found the procedures to be unduly burdensome and inexplicable to my subjects. The need to obtain signatures on a form that raised the issue of risk and supervision by the U.S. government engendered suspicion that was difficult to overcome, especially among serranos already leery of any government and unfamiliar with the academic milieu. I would have been additionally required

to develop interview questions in advance and submit them for prior approval. I withdrew from that procedure in 2010 and believe my work should not have been constrained by its requirements.
4. Augusto Urteaga taught at the Escuela Nacional de Antropología e Historia in Chihuahua and spent decades with the Rarámuri in the sierra before his death in late 2008.
5. Poetry of Efraín Huerta in Stephen Tapscott, ed., *Twentieth-Century Latin American Poetry* (Austin: University of Texas Press, 1996). My work appears in the second edition, replacing translations of Huerta in the first edition. Paco Ignacio Taibo II, *Life Itself* (New York: Mysterious Press, 1995), others.
6. See http://www.sierramadrealliance.org.
7. Elizabeth Henson, "Madera 1965: Armed Agrarian Revolt in the Sierra of Chihuahua" (Master's thesis, University of Arizona History Department, 2008).
8. Alessandro Portelli, *The Death of Luigi Trastulli and Other Stories: Form and Meaning in Oral History* (Albany: State University of New York Press, 1991).

Annotated Bibliography

1. Jaime López, *Diez años de la guerrilla en Mexico, 1964–1974* (Mexico City: Editorial Posada, 1974), 14.
2. Anonymous, *23 de septiembre de 1965: El asalto al cuartel de Madera* (Mexico, D.F.: Yaxkin, 2002); Raúl Florencia Lugo Hernández, *23 de septiembre de 1965: El asalto al cuartel de Madera* (Mexico City.: Universidad Autónoma de Chapingo, 2006).
3. Raúl Florencio Lugo Hernández, *Del cuartel a Lecumberri* (Agua Prieta, Sonora: n.p., 2005).
4. Victor Orozco, "La guerrilla chihuahuense de los sesenta," in *Movimientos armados en Mexico, Siglo XX*, edited by Verónica Oikión and Marta Eugenia García Ugarte (Mexico City: Colegio de Michoacán/CIESAS, 2006), 337.
5. Victor Orozco, *Diez ensayos sobre Chihuahua* (Chihuahua: Doble Hélice, 2003), 42.
6. Laura Castellanos, *México armado: 1943–1981* (Mexico City: Ediciones Era, 2007), 18.
7. Fritz Glockner, *Memoria roja: Historia de la guerrilla en México (1943–1968)* (Mexico City: Ediciones B, 2007), 15.

SELECTED BIBLIOGRAPHY

Archives

Archivo General de la Nación, Mexico City
Archivo de la Secretaría de Relaciones Exteriores, Mexico City
Archivo del Registro Agrario Nacional in Chihuahua City, Ejido Cebadilla de Dolores, Chihuahua City, Chihuahua, now moved to Mexico City
Archivo del Estado de Chihuahua, Chihuahua City, Chihuahua
Archivo de la Escuela Normal del Estado de Chihuahua, Chihuahua City, Chihuahua
Archivo del Juzgado Primero de lo Penal, Distrito Morales, Chihuahua, Chihuahua City, Chihuahua
Biblioteca de la Universidad Autónoma de Ciudad Juárez, Colecciones Especiales, Ciudad Juárez, Chihuahua

Journals and Newspapers

Acción: Voz Revolucionaria del Pueblo
Chihuahua Hoy
Cuadernos políticos
El Democrata
El Diario de Chihuahua
El Heraldo de Chihuahua
El Machete
El Monitor de Parral
El Norte
El Paso Herald Post
El Universal
Excelsior

Indice: Un Periódico sin Cadenas
La Fragua de los Tiempos, ChihuahuaMexico.com, http://www.chihuahuamexico.com/index.php?option=com_content&task=blogcategory&id=104&Itemid=314
La Jornada del Campo
La Voz de Chihuahua
Past and Present
Politica
Proceso
Sucesos para Todos

Theses

Castorena Sáenz, Nithia. "Estaban ahí: Las mujeres en los grupos armados de Chihuahua (1965–1973)." Master's thesis, Universidad Autónoma de Ciudad Juárez, Instituto de Ciencias Sociales y Administración, Departamento de Humanidades, 2013.

Cedillo Cedillo, Adela. "El fuego y el silencio: Historia de las Fuerzas de Liberación Nacional Mexicanas (1969–1974)." Undergraduate thesis, Universidad Nacional Autónoma de México, 2008.

García Aguirre, Aleida. "Normalistas y maestros en el movimiento campesino y guerrillero de Chihuahua, 1960–1968: Experiencias de solidaridad y relaciones reticulares en la formación de un sujeto político." Master's thesis, Centro de Investigación y de Estudios Avanzados, Departamento de Investigaciones Educativas, 2012.

Henson, Elizabeth. "Madera 1965: Armed Agrarian Revolt in the Sierra of Chihuahua." Master's thesis, University of Arizona, 2008.

Hijar, Andrés F. "The Myth of Madera." Master's thesis, University of Texas at El Paso, 2003.

López Álvarez, María Guadalupe del Socorro. "Poder, desarrollo y medio ambiente en el ejido forestal 'El Largo' y sus anexos: Chihuahua (1971–1994)." Master's thesis, Universidad Autónoma Metropolitana, Unidad Xochimilco, 1996.

López Rosas, Abel. "El pensamiento y estrategia política del profesor Arturo Gámiz García en las luchas campesinas y estudiantiles de Chihuahua (1962–65)." Undergraduate thesis, Universidad Autónoma de Mexico, Facultad de Filosofía y Letras, 2009.

Ríos Merino, Alicia de los. "José de Jesús, Luis Miguel y Salvador Corral García: Good Bye American Way of Life, Nos Vamos a la Guerrilla; Procesos de radicalidad en jóvenes de la década de los setentas." Master's thesis, Escuela Nacional de Antropologia e Historia, 2010.

Novels and Memoirs

Armendáriz Ponce, Minerva. *Morir de sed junto a la fuente: Sierra de Chihuahua 1968*. Chihuahua: M. Armendáriz Ponce, 2001.

Campos Chacón, Sergio Alberto. *Barrancas rojas*. Mexico City: Instituto Nacional de Bellas Artes, 1991.

Frías, Heriberto. *Tomóchic*. Chihuahua: Instituto Chihuahuense de la Cultura, 2006.

Gerardo, José. *Una alborada para Miguel: Epopeya de amor y libertad*. Torreón: Editorial sin Censura, 2013.
Lugo Hernández, Raúl Florencio. *Del cuartel a Lecumberri*. Agua Prieta, Sonora: n.p., 2005.
Lugo Hernández, Raúl Florencio. "El reencuentro (Remembranzas)." Unpublished manuscript.
Lugo Hernández, Raúl Florencio. *23 de septiembre de 1965: El asalto al cuartel de Madera; Testimonio de un sobreviviente*. 3rd ed. Mexico City: Universidad Autónoma de Chapingo, 2006. First edition published anonymously in 2002.
Montemayor, Carlos. *La fuga*. Mexico City: Fondo de Cultura Economica, 2007.
Montemayor, Carlos. *Las armas del alba: Novela*. Mexico City: Joaquín Mortiz, 2003.
Montemayor, Carlos. *Las mujeres del alba*. Mexico City: Grijalbo, 2010.
Montemayor, Carlos. *Los informes secretos*. Mexico City: Joaquín Mortiz, 1999.
Ornelas Gómez, Francisco. *Sueños de libertad*. Chihuahua: n.p., 2005.
Revueltas, José. *Los días terrenales*. Mexico City: Editorial Stylo, 1949.
Revueltas, José. *Los errores*. Mexico City: Ediciones Era, 1979.
Reyes, Judith. *La otra cara de la patria*. Mexico City: Talleres Gráficos de México, 1974.
Robles Garnica, Hector Guillermo. *La guerrilla olvidada*. Guadalajara: La Casa del Mago, 2013.
Toro Rosales, Salvador del. *Testimonios*. Monterrey: Sindicato de Trabajadores de la Universidad Autónoma de Nuevo Leon, 1996.

Reports

Aviña, Alexander. "Mexico's Long Dirty War." *NACLA Report on the Americas* 48, no. 2 (2016): 144–49.
Fiscalía Especial para Movimientos Sociales y Políticos del Pasado. "Inicios de la guerrilla moderna en México" [draft version]. *Informe Histórico a la Sociedad Mexicana*. National Security Archives. http://www.criterios.com/Documentos/050_El_inicio_de_la_Guerrilla_Modernia_en_Mexico.pdf (accessed March 15, 2006; no longer posted).
Fiscalía Especial para Movimientos Sociales y Políticos del Pasado. "Orígenes de la guerrilla moderna en México." *Informe Histórico a la Sociedad Mexicana*. National Security Archives. https://nsarchive2.gwu.edu/NSAEBB/NSAEBB209/informe/tema05.pdf.
Guerrero, María Teresa. *The Forest Industry in the Sierra Madre of Chihuahua: Social, Economic, and Ecological Impacts*. Chihuahua and Austin: Comisión de Solidaridad y Defensa de los Derechos Humanos and Texas Center for Policy Studies, 2000. http://www.texascenter.org/publications/forestry.pdf.
"Registro Agrario Nacional, Delegación Chihuahua, Dirección de Catastro Rural, Estructura Ejidal," typescript, April 15, 1994. Photocopy in author's possession.

Books

Aboites, Luis. *Breve historia de Chihuahua*. Mexico City: El Colegio de México, 1994.
Aguayo Quezada, Sergio. *La charola: Una historia de los servicios de inteligencia en México*. Mexico City: Grijalbo, 2001.

Aguilar Terrés, María de la Luz, comp. *Memoria del primer encuentro nacional de mujeres ex guerrilleras: Analisis y reflexión sobre la participación de las mujeres en el movimiento armado socialista.* Mexico City: n.p., 2003.

Aguilar Terrés, María de la Luz, comp. *Guerrilleras: Antología de testimonios y textos sobre la participación de las mujeres en los movimientos armados socialistas en México, segunda mitad del siglo XX.* Mexico City: n.p., 2007. 2nd ed., 2014.

Almada, Francisco R. *Resumen de historia del Estado de Chihuahua.* Chihuahua: Ediciones del Gobierno del Estado de Chihuahua, 1986.

Almada, Francisco R. *El ferrocarril de Chihuahua al Pacífico.* México: Editorial Libros de México, 1971.

Alonso, Ana M. *Thread of Blood: Colonialism, Revolution, and Gender on Mexico's Northern Frontier.* Tucson: University of Arizona Press, 1995.

Augustín, José. *Tragicomedia mexicana 1.* Mexico City: Planeta, 1990.

Aviña, Alexander. *Specters of Revolution: Peasant Guerrillas in the Cold War Mexican Countryside.* New York: Oxford, 2014.

Badiou, Alain. *Polemics.* London: Verso, 2006.

Bartra, Armando. *Guerrero bronco: Campesinos, cuidadanos y guerrilleros en la Costa Grande.* Mexico City: Ediciones sin filtro, 1996.

Bartra, Armando. *Los herederos de Zapata: Movimientos campesinos posrevolucionarios en México, 1920–1980.* Mexico City: Ediciones Era, 1985.

Beezley, William H. *Insurgent Governor: Abraham Gonzalez and the Mexican Revolution in Chihuahua.* Lincoln: University of Nebraska Press, 1973.

Bellingeri, Marco. *Del agrarismo armado a la guerra de los pobres: Ensayos de guerrilla rural en el México contemporaneo, 1940–1974.* Mexico City: Editorial Casa Juan Pablos, 2003.

Blanco Moheno, Roberto. *La noticia detrás de la noticia.* Mexico City: Editorial V Siglos, 1975.

Boullosa, Carmen, and Mike Wallace. *A Narco History: How the United States and Mexico Jointly Created "The Mexican Drug War."* New York: OR Books, 2015.

Boyer, Christopher R. *Political Landscapes: Forests, Conservation, and Community in Mexico.* Durham, N.C.: Duke University Press, 2015.

Calderón, Fernando Herrera, and Adela Cedillo. *Challenging Authoritarianism in Mexico: Revolutionary Struggles and the Dirty War, 1964–1982.* New York: Routledge, 2011.

Carr, Barry. *Marxism and Communism in Twentieth-Century Mexico.* Lincoln: University of Nebraska Press, 1992.

Castañeda, Jorge G. *Utopia Unarmed: The Latin American Left After the Cold War.* New York: Knopf, 1993.

Castellanos, Laura. *México armado: 1943–1981.* Mexico City: Ediciones Era, 2007.

Coatsworth, John H. *Growth Against Development: The Economic Impact of Railroads in Porfirian Mexico.* DeKalb: Northern Illinois University Press, 1981.

Contreras Orozco, Javier H. *Los informantes: Documents confidentiales de la guerrilla en Chihuahua.* Chihuahua: Universidad Autónoma de Chihuahua, 2007.

Debray, Régis. *Revolution in the Revolution? Armed Struggle and Political Struggle in Latin America.* New York: Grove, 1967.

Delay, Brian. *War of a Thousand Deserts: Indian Raids and the U.S.-Mexican War.* New Haven, Conn.: Yale University Press, 2008.

Domínguez Rascón, Alonso. *La política de reforma agraria en Chihuahua, 1920–1924: Sus efectos hasta 1940.* Mexico City: Instituto Nacional de Antropología e Historia, 2003.

Domínguez Rascón, Alonso. *Procesos agrarios en Chihuahua.* Juárez: Cuadernos de Investigación, Unidad de Estudios Históricos y Sociales–Chihuahua, Universidad Autónoma de Ciudad Juárez, 2004.

Fanon, Franz. *The Wretched of the Earth.* Translated by Constance Farrington. New York: Grove, 1963.

Foweraker, Joe. *Popular Mobilization in Mexico.* Cambridge: Cambridge University Press, 1993.

Foweraker, Joe, and Ann Craig, eds. *Popular Movements and Political Change in Mexico.* Boulder: Lynn Rienner, 1990.

Franco, Jean. *The Decline and Fall of the Lettered City: Latin America in the Cold War.* Cambridge, Mass.: Harvard University Press, 2002.

Franco Rosales, María Concepción. *Imágenes, voces y recuerdos: Una historia de la Escuela Normal del Estado de Chihuahua.* Chihuahua: Doble Hélice, 2006.

Fuentes, Carlos. *Nuevo tiempo mexicano.* Mexico City: Joaquín Mortiz, 1971.

Fuentes Mares, José. . . . *Y México se refugió el en desierto: Luis Terrazas, historia y destino.* Mexico City: Editorial Jus, 1954.

Gallegos Pérez, Carlos. *Luto en Delicias: Vida y muerte de Emiliano J. Laing.* Chihuahua: Gobierno del Estado, 2003.

García Aguirre, Aleida. *La revolución que llegaría: Experiencias de solidaridad y redes de maestros y normalistas en el movimiento campesino y la guerrilla moderna en Chihuahua, 1960–1968.* Mexico City: n.p., 2015.

García Sánchez, Liliana. *Judith Reyes: Una mujer de canto revolucionario (1924–1988).* Mexico City: Redez, 2007.

Gillingham, Paul, and Benjamin T. Smith, eds. *Dictablanda: Politics, Work, and Culture in Mexico, 1938–1968.* Durham, N.C.: Duke University Press, 2014.

Gilly, Adolfo. *The Mexican Revolution.* London: Verso, 1983.

Glockner, Fritz. *Memoria roja: Historia de la guerrilla en México (1943–1968).* Mexico City: Ediciones B, 2007.

Godines, Prudencio, Jr. *¡Qué poco mad . . . era la de José Santos Valdés!* Mexico City: n.p., 1968.

Gott, Richard. *Rural Guerrillas in Latin America.* Harmondsworth, Middlesex: Penguin Books, 1973.

Grandin, Greg. *The Last Colonial Massacre: Latin America in the Cold War.* Chicago: University of Chicago Press, 2011.

Guerrero Olivares, María Teresa, comp. *Una generacíon desconocida: Movimiento social demócrata cristiano 1962–1970.* Chihuahua: n.p., 2014.

Guevara, Ernesto. *Guerrilla Warfare.* Lincoln: University of Nebraska Press, 1998. First published in English 1961 by Monthly Review Press (New York). First published as *La guerra de guerrillas,* 1960.

Gutiérrez Lozano, Ramón, and Fernando Sandoval Salinas. *Así enseñaban nuestros profesores*. Chihuahua: Instituto Chihuahuense de la Cultura, 2003.

Hart, John M. *Empire and Revolution: The Americans in Mexico Since the Civil War*. Berkeley: University of California, 2002.

Hart, John M. *Revolutionary Mexico*. Berkeley: University of California Press, 1997.

Hart, John M. *The Silver of the Sierra Madre: John Robinson, Boss Shepherd, and the People of the Canyon*. Tucson: University of Arizona Press, 2008.

Hernández Rodríguez, Rogelio. *El centro dividido: La nueva autonomía de los gobernadores*. Mexico City: El Colegio de México, 2008.

Herrera Calderón, Fernando, and Adela Cedillo. *Challenging Authoritarianism in Mexico: Revolutionary Struggles and the Dirty War, 1964–1982*. New York: Routledge, 2011.

Huberman, Leo, and Paul M. Sweezy. *Regis Debray and the Latin American Revolution*. New York: Monthly Review Press, 1968.

Jordán, Fernando. *Crónica de un país bárbaro*. 7th ed. Chihuahua: Centro Librero La Prensa, 1989. First published 1956 by Asociación Mexicana de Periodistas (Mexico City).

Joseph, G. M., and Daniel Nugent. *Everyday Forms of State Formation: Revolution and the Negotiation of Rule in Modern Mexico*. Durham, N.C.: Duke University Press, 1994.

Katz, Friedrich. *The Life and Times of Pancho Villa*. Stanford, Calif.: Stanford University Press, 1998.

Katz, Friedrich, ed. *Riot, Rebellion, and Revolution: Rural Social Conflict in Mexico*. Princeton, N.J.: Princeton University Press, 1988.

Katz, Friedrich. *The Secret War in Mexico: Europe, the United States, and the Mexican Revolution*. Chicago: University of Chicago Press, 1981.

Keller, Renata. *Mexico's Cold War: Cuba, the United States, and the Legacy of the Mexican Revolution*. Cambridge: Cambridge University Press, 2015.

Knight, Alan. *The Mexican Revolution*. Cambridge: Cambridge University Press, 1986.

Knight, Alan, and Wil Pansters, eds. *Caciquismo in Twentieth-Century Mexico*. London: Institute for the Study of the Americas, 2005.

Lartigue, François. *Indios y bosques: Políticas forestales y comunales en la Sierra Tarahumara*. Mexico City: CIESAS, 1983.

López, Jamie. *Diez años de la guerrilla en Mexico, 1964–1974*. Mexico City: Editorial Posada, 1974.

Martínez Carrera, Rocío. *Así se fundó la colonia Villa*. Chihuahua: Doble Hélice, 1998.

McCormick, Gladys I. *The Logic of Compromise in Mexico: How the Countryside Was Key to the Emergence of Authoritarianism*. Chapel Hill: University of North Carolina Press, 2016.

Meyer, Michael C., and William H. Beezley. *The Oxford History of Mexico*. New York: Oxford University Press, 2000.

Meyer, Michael C., William L. Sherman, and Susan M. Deeds. *The Course of Mexican History*. New York: Oxford University Press, 2003.

Monsiváis, Carlos. *Amor perdido*. Mexico City: Ediciones Era, 1977.

Monsiváis, Carlos. *Días de guardar*. Mexico City: Ediciones Era, 1970.

Monsiváis, Carlos. *Entrada libre: Crónicas de la sociedad que se organiza*. Mexico City: Ediciones Era, 1987.

Monsiváis, Carlos. *Escenas de pudor y liviandad*. Mexico City: Grijalbo, 1988.

Montemayor, Carlos. *La guerrilla recurrente*. Juárez: Universidad Autónoma de Ciudad Juárez, 1999.

Nugent, Daniel, ed. *Rural Revolt in Mexico: U.S. Intervention and the Domain of Subaltern Politics*. San Diego: Center for U.S.-Mexican Studies, University of California, San Diego, 1988.

Nugent, Daniel. *Spent Cartridges of Revolution: An Anthropological History of Namiquipa, Chihuahua*. Chicago: University of Chicago Press, 1993.

Oikión, Veronica, and Marta Eugenia García Ugarte, eds. *Movimientos armados en Mexico, Siglo XX*. 3 vols. Mexico City: Colegio de Michoacán/CIESAS, 2006.

Orozco Orozco, Víctor. *Diez ensayos sobre Chihuahua*. Chihuahua: Doble Hélice, 2003.

Padilla, Tanalís. *Rural Resistance in the Land of Zapata: The Jaramillista Movement and the Myth of the Pax Priísta, 1940–1962*. Durham, N.C.: Duke University Press, 2008.

Palomares Peña, Noé G. *Propietarios norteamericanos y reforma agraria en Chihuahua, 1917–1942*. Juárez: Universidad Autónoma de Ciudad Juárez, 1991.

Parra Orozco, Miguel Angel. *Oro Verde: Madera, vida de una región chihuahuense*. Chihuahua: n.p., 1998.

Pensado, Jaime. *Rebel Mexico: Student Unrest and Authoritarian Political Culture During the Long Sixties*. Palo Alto, Calif.: Stanford University Press, 2013.

Pomeroy, William J. *Guerrilla Warfare and Marxism*. New York: International, 1968.

Poniatowska, Elena. *Fuerte es el silencio*. Mexico City: Ediciones Era, 1980.

Portelli, Alessandro. *The Death of Luigi Trastulli and Other Stories: Form and Meaning in Oral History*. Albany: State University of New York Press, 1991.

Preston, Julia, and Sam Dillon. *Opening Mexico: The Making of a Democracy*. New York: Farrar, Straus and Giroux, 2004.

Reina, Leticia. *Indio, campesino y nación en el siglo XX mexicano*. Mexico City: Siglo XXI, 2011.

Ruíz, Ramón. *The Great Rebellion*. New York: Norton, 1980.

Rubin, Jeffrey W. *Decentering the Regime: Ethnicity, Radicalism, and Democracy in Juchitán, Mexico*. Durham, N.C.: Duke University Press, 1997.

Salas-Porras, Alejandra. *Grupos empresariales en Chihuahua de 1920 al presente*. Mexico City: Centro de Investigación y Docencia Económicas, 1992.

Santos Valdés, José. *Madera: Razón de un martiriologio*. Mexico City: n.p., 1968.

Sariego, Juan Luis. *El Indigenismo en la tarahumara: Identidad, comunidad, relaciones interétnicas y desarrollo en la Sierra de Chihuahua*. Mexico City: Instituto Nacional Indigenista, 2002.

Sariego, Juan Luis, coordinator. *Trabajo, territorio y sociedad en Chihuahua durante el siglo XX*. Historia general de Chihuahua 5. Chihuahua: Gobierno del Estado de Chihuahua, 1998.

Staudenmeier, Michael. *Truth and Revolution: A History of the Sojourner Truth Organization, 1969–1986*. Oakland: AK, 2012.

Stevens, Evelyn P. *Protest and Response in Mexico.* Cambridge, Mass.: MIT Press, 1974.
Sweig, Julia. *Inside the Cuban Revolution.* Cambridge, Mass.: Harvard University Press, 2002.
Truett, Samuel. *Fugitive Landscapes: The Forgotten History of the U.S.-Mexico Borderlands.* New Haven, Conn.: Yale University Press, 2006.
Vanderwood, Paul J. *Disorder and Progress: Bandits, Police, and Mexican Development.* Wilmington, Del.: Scholarly Resources, 1992.
Vanderwood, Paul J. *The Power of God Against the Guns of Government: Religious Upheaval in Mexico at the Turn of the Nineteenth Century.* Stanford, Calif.: Stanford University Press, 1998.
Vargas Valdés, Jesús. *La patria de la juventud: Los estudiantes del Politécnico en 1968.* Chihuahua: Nueva Vizcaya Editores, 2008.
Vargas Valdés, Jesús. *Madera Rebelde: Movimiento agrario y guerrilla (1959–1965).* Chihuahua: Ediciones Nueva Vizcaya, 2015.
Vaughan, Mary Kay. *Cultural Politics in Revolution: Teachers, Peasants, and Schools in Mexico, 1930–1940.* Tucson: University of Arizona Press, 1997.
Wasserman, Mark. *Capitalists, Caciques, and Revolution: The Native Elite and Foreign Enterprise in Chihuahua, Mexico, 1854–1911.* Chapel Hill: University of North Carolina Press, 1984.
Wasserman, Mark. *Persistant Oligarchs: Elites and Politics in Chihuahua, Mexico, 1910–1940.* Durham, N.C.: Duke University Press, 1993.
Wolf, Eric R. *Peasant Wars of the Twentieth Century.* New York: Harper and Row, 1969.
Womack, John R., Jr. *Zapata and the Mexican Revolution.* New York: Knopf, 1969.
Žižek, Slavoj. *Violence: Six Sideways Reflections.* New York: Picador, 2008.

Articles

Aboites Aguilar, Luís. "Agricultura chihuahuense: Trayectoria productiva, 1920–1990." In Sariego, *Trabajo, territorio y sociedad*, 27–91. Chihuahua: Government of the State of Chihuahua, 1998.
Aguayo, Sergio. "El impacto de la guerrilla en la vida mexicana: Algunas hypotesis." In *Movimientos armados en Mexico, siglo XX*, vol. 1, edited by Verónika Oikión Solano and Marta Eugenia García Ugarte, 91–96. Zamora: El Colegio de Michoacán, 2008.
Alonso, Ana María. "U.S. Military Intervention, Revolutionary Mobilization, and Popular Ideology in the Chihuahuan Sierra, 1916–1917." In Nugent, *Rural Revolt*, 207–238.
Bartra, Armando. "Seis años de lucha campesina." *Investigación Económica* 36, no. 141 (1977): 157–209.
Bellingeri, Marco. "La imposibilidad del odio: La guerrilla y el movimiento estudiantil en México, 1960–1974." In *La transición interrumpida: México 1968–1988*, edited by Ilán Semo, 49–73. Mexico City: Universidad Iberoamericana y Nueva Imagen, 1993.
Beverley, John. "Rethinking the Armed Struggle in Latin America," *boundary 2* 36, no. 1 (2009): 47–59.

Carr, Barry. "The Fate of a Vanguard Under a Revolutionary State: Marxism's Contribution to the Construction of a Great Arch." In Joseph and Nugent, *Everyday Forms*, 326–52.

Castellanos, Laura. Interview by Mario Casasús. http://www.cedema.org/uploads/MEXARM.pdf.

Cedillo, Adela, and Ricardo Gamboa Ramírez. "Interpretaciones sobre los espacios de participación política después del 10 de junio de 1971 en México." In *Violencia y sociedad: Un hito en la historia de las izquierdas en América Latina*, edited by Verónica Oikión and Miguel Ángel Urrego. Morelia: Universidad Michoacana de San Nicolás de Hidalgo/Colegio de Michoacán, 2010.

Craig, Richard B. "Human Rights and Mexico's Antidrug Campaign." *Social Science Quarterly* 60, no. 4 (March 1980): 691–701.

Doyle, Kate. "The Corpus Christi Massacre: Mexico's Attack on Its Student Movement, June 10, 1971." National Security Archive, June 10, 2003. https://nsarchive2.gwu.edu/NSAEBB/NSAEBB91.

Estrada López, Juvencio. "Los primeros vientos: Entrevista con Paco Ornelas." *El Diario de Chihuahua*, September 22, 1995.

Gilly, Adolfo. "Chiapas and the Rebellion of the Enchanted World." In Nugent, *Rural Revolt*, 261–331.

Gómez, Pablo. "El paracaidismo en Chihuahua." *Indice*, February 2, 1963, 2.

Gómez Caballero, Alma. "Una breve cronología que enmarca: Madera 1965; las causas." http://www.jornada.unam.mx/2005/11/07/informacion/87_madera (accessed May 31, 2006; no longer posted).

Guevara, Ernesto Che. "Lessons of the Cuban Revolution" and "What Is a Guerrilla?" In Pomeroy, *Guerrilla Warfare and Marxism*, 287–90.

Hobsbawm, Eric J. "The Machine Breakers." *Past and Present* 1 (1952): 57–70.

Knight, Alan. "Caciquismo in Twentieth-Century Mexico." In *Caciquismo in Twentieth-Century Mexico*, edited by Alan Knight and Wil Pansters, 1–48. London: Institute for the Study of the Americas, 2005.

Knight, Alan. "Habitus and Homicide." In *Citizens of the Pyramid: Essays on Mexican Political Culture*, edited by Wil G. Pansters, 107–30. West Lafayette, Ind.: Purdue University Press, 1997.

Lloyd, Jane-Dale. "Rancheros and Rebellion: The Case of Northwestern Chihuahua, 1905–1909." In Nugent, *Rural Revolt*, 107–33.

Long, Ryan. "An Interview with Carlos Montemayor." *World Literature Today*, March–April, 2006.

Luna Jurado, Rogelio. "La razón maderiana." Unpublished essay. Microsoft Word file. http://www.madera1965.com.mx/prensa/2000/razon.docx.

Luna Jurado, Rogelio. "Los maestros y la democracia sindical." *Cuadernos Políticos* 14 (October–December 1977): 72–103. http://www.cuadernospoliticos.unam.mx/cuadernos/contenido/CP.14/CP.14.7rogelioluna.pdf.

Mateos-Vega, Monica. "Existe otro México clandestino más peligroso que la guerrilla: Entrevista con Carlos Montemayor." *La Jornada*, February 28, 2007. http://www.jornada.com.mx/2007/02/28/index.php?section=cultura&article=a04n1cul.

Montemayor, Carlos. "Romper los cercos del silencio." Prologue to *Rodrigo Moya: Foto insurecta.* Text by Alfonso Morales Carrillo and Juan Manuel Aurrecoechea. Mexico City: Ediciones El Milagro, 2004.

Oikión Solano, Verónica. "Lázaro Cárdenas en el laberinto de Madera." *La Jornada del Campo*, September 19, 2015, 18.

Orozco, Víctor. "La guerrilla chihuahuense de los sesenta." In Oikión and García Ugarte, *Movimientos armados*, 337–60.

Ortiz Pinchetti, Francisco. "El asalto al cuartel de madera, el 23 de septiembre de 1965." http://madera1965.com.mx/Asalto.htm.

Padilla, Tanalís. "Ayotzinapa: Indignación y justicia." *La Jornada del Campo*, September 27, 2015. http://www.jornada.com.mx/2015/02/14/opinion/018a1pol.

Padilla, Tanalís. "Espionage and Education: Reporting on Student Protest in Mexico's Normales Rurales, 1960–1980." *Journal of Iberian and Latin American Research* 19, no.1 (2013): 20–29.

Padilla, Tanalís. "Los inquietos." *La Jornada del Campo*, October 18, 2014, http://www.jornada.unam.mx/2014/10/18/politica/006a1pol.

Padilla, Tanalís. "Rural Education, Political Radicalism, and *Normalista* Identity in Mexico after 1940." In Gillingham and Smith, *Dictablanda*, 341–59.

Pensado, Jaime. "'To Assault with the Truth': The Revitalization of Conservative Militancy in Mexico During the Global Sixties." *Americas* 70, no. 3 (January 2014): 489–521.

Petrich, Blanche, "Ciudad Madera: Un legado con raíz viva." *La Jornada*, September 25, 2000. http://www.madera1965.com.mx/prensa/2000/jornada.pdf.

Reyes, Daniel de los. "Guerrillas en la sierra chihuahuense." *Sucesos para Todos*, September 11, 18, and 25, 1964.

Reyes del Campillo, Juan. "El Frente Electoral del Pueblo y el Partido Comunista Mexicano (1963–1964)." *Revista Mexicana de Sociología* 50, no. 3 (July–September 1988): 217–28.

Rico Galán, Víctor. "Chihuahua: De la desesperación a la muerte." *Sucesos para todos*, October 15, 1965.

Roseberry, William. "Hegemony and the Language of Contention." In Joseph and Nugent, *Everyday Forms*, 355–66.

Vargas Valdés, Jesús. "Las armas del alba: 23 septiembre 1965." *El Heraldo de Chihuahua*, September 21, 2003.

Zolov, Eric. "Expanding Our Conceptual Horizons: The Shift from an Old to a New Left in Latin America." *A Contracorriente: Una Revista de Estudios Latinoamericanos* 5, no. 2 (2008): 47–73. http://acontracorriente.chass.ncsu.edu/index.php/acontracorriente/article/view/585.

Zolov, Eric. "Latin America in the Global Sixties." *Americas* 70, no. 3 (January 2014): 349–62.

INDEX

1960s, 18–19

Acción, 6, 12–13, 67–69, 77–78, 80, 82–84, 89–90, 92, 98–99, 101–2, 105, 125, 146
agrarian reform, 25, 42–43, 58, 61, 66–67, 68, 71, 79–80, 87, 152, 205–7; 1994 reforms, 17, 203–4; Agrarian Code of 1942, 7, 13, 50, 87, 130, 155, 230n82, 241n29; Article 27, 16, 17, 43, 66, 90, 167–168, 231n101; Chihuahua Land Law of 1922, 43
agrarismo, 14–15, 16–18, 25, 44, 85
Alarcón Reyes, Magaly [Yelly], 123, 143, 244n70, 229n58
Alemán, Miguel, 6, 12, 21, 22, 27, 50, 74, 89
Almeida, Esteban, 79, 85, 101
Alvarado, Luisina, 141–42
Alvarez, Francisco Javier, xix, 82, 91, 94, 105, 145–47
Amigos de Cuba, 62, 121
anticommunism, 23–24, 61, 62, 74, 86, 108, 160
armed struggle, xv–xvi, 4–6, 9–10, 19, 30, 88, 97, 117, 149, 155, 158–62, 168–69, 199, 201–3, 213. *See* guerrilla warfare.
Armendáriz, Carlos, 54, 172, 193, 214
Arroyo Amplio, 118, 126, 127, 135, 171, 173
Asociación Revolucionaria de Mujeres, 101, 154

assault on base September 23, 1965, xix, xx, xxi, 3–4, 7–8, 13, 19, 54, 57, 139, 140, 149, 150, 171–77, 178, 182, 186, 190, 193, 199; consequences, 3–4, 177–90; execution, 3–4; planning, 151, 171–72
Avila Camacho, Manuel, 22, 86

Balboa, Arturo, 16
Barrios, Roberto, 71–72, 94, 106
Bay of Pigs Invasion, 26, 62
Becerra Gaytán, Antonio, 56, 62, 94, 101, 112, 119, 184, 101, 113, 124
Becerra Gaytán, Ema, 112, 124
Beltrán, Rubén, 180
Borunda, Teófilo, xix, 50, 72, 74, 81, 85, 89–90, 113, 130
Bosques de Chihuahua, 3, 4, 6, 9, 34, 46, 50, 51, 52, 57, 59, 61, 62–63, 68, 69, 72–73, 75–76, 80–81, 83–84, 89–90, 93, 104–5, 128, 131, 152, 171, 189, 190
Bracero Program, 7, 17, 45, 92, 134, 141, 148, 218n8

Caballero, Alma, xix, 185, 188, 190, 61
caciquismo, 3, 4, 6, 7, 14, 20, 29, 31, 36, 39, 52–53, 80, 81, 82, 96, 108, 118, 128, 129, 134, 137, 147, 152–153, 169, 171, 193, 199

Caldera, Rito, xi, 127–128, 129, 134, 144, 181
Calles, Plutarco Elías, 43, 44, 104
campesinos, 3–6, 7, 9–10, 14, 15, 16–18, 22, 23, 25, 29, 31, 32, 42, 48, 50, 52, 54, 57–58, 59, 61, 62, 63, 65, 66, 67, 68, 69, 70, 71–72, 73, 77–99 *passim*, 101, 102, 103, 104–111, 113, 116–121 *passim*, 123, 124, 125, 126, 128, 129, 131, 132, 138, 140, 144, 147, 148, 150, 152, 154, 162, 169–70, 171, 173, 185, 186, 187, 189, 193, 199, 202, 213, 216, 235n29; in Five Resolutions, 155, 157–61, 165, 168
capitalism, 9, 15, 18, 22, 24, 133, 155, 164, 190, 242n35, 243n63; as discussed in Five Resolutions, 156–58
Cárdenas Barojas, Lorenzo, xix, 140
Cárdenas, Lázaro, xix, 6, 7, 15, 17, 22, 25, 26, 27, 61, 86, 88, 189, 194
Cardona Rodríguez, Jesús Hilario, xix, 106, 111–16, 119–21, 123–25, 129–30, 132, 146
Castellanos, Ernesto, 102, 134, 144, 175, 181
Castorena, Nithia, xviii, 13, 136, 216
Castro, Fidel, 27–29, 30, 67, 90, 95, 117, 140, 154, 213
cattle industry, 9, 38–39, 43, 44–45, 46, 50, 66
Cattlemen's Association, 9, 74, 81, 83, 89, 90, 107–8, 111
Cebadilla de Dolores, 58, 59, 63, 75, 80, 83, 95, 121, 142, 152, 170, 173, 175, 182, 187, 190, 210
Celulosa de Chihuahua, 49, 50, 60, 72–74
Central Campesina Independiente (CCI), xxiii, 54, 131, 132, 144, 186
Central Intelligence Agency (CIA), 27, 106, 203
Cereceres, Juan, 53
Certificado de Inafectabilidad Ganadera (CIG), xxiii, 7, 45, 70, 75–76, 78–80, 85, 93, 101, 131, 190, 230n82
Chacón, Saúl, 88, 92, 97, 109, 113, 142
Chávez, Alfredo, 82, 85, 130
Chihuahua City, 47, 58, 66, 73, 75, 78, 117, 123, 130, 133, 137, 139, 153, 154, 171, 172, 177, 182, 183, 190, 192, 199; occupations and marches in public space in, 5, 57, 58, 109, 190; urbanization and CDP in, 5, 10, 32, 55
Ciudad Juárez, xvii, 7, 38, 44, 45, 46, 47, 70–71, 90, 108, 125, 130, 132, 145, 170, 182, 187, 215, 216; organizing of unemployed in, 45, 110, 131; and PRONAF, 131, 238n120

Cold War, 11, 30, 68, 74, 78, 95; context of, 5, 21–23, 27–28; in documents of First Encounter, 26, 95–96
Colonia Francisco Villa, 5, 32, 55
Comité de Defensa Popular (CDP), xxiii, 5, 10, 32, 34–35, 54–55
Comité Pro Defensa de las Garantías Individuales y Sociales (Comité Pro), xxiii, 93, 101, 105–6, 119, 124, 125, 132
Communism, 11, 23, 30, 33, 62, 74, 118, 158, 186, 213
Conchos Valley, 5, 34, 44, 154
Confederación de Trabajadores Mexicanos (CTM), xxiii, 11, 131, 204
Confederación Nacional de Campesinos (CNC), xxiii, 11, 17, 61, 70, 71, 79–80, 83, 94, 131, 204
Cotton industry, 11, 34, 44, 45, 46, 50, 58, 78, 119–20; Anderson, Clayton and Company, 44, 78
Cuauhtémoc City, 44, 49, 54, 78, 146, 185
Cuban Revolution of 1959, 5, 18–19, 21, 25–29, 30, 31–32, 61, 67, 87, 95, 96

Danzós Palomino, Ramón, 101, 112, 113, 121, 122, 129, 144
Delicias, 35, 44, 46, 54, 59, 61, 81, 82, 85, 89–93 *passim*, 98, 104, 105, 107, 109, 110, 111, 112, 121, 130, 142, 178
Departamento de Asuntos Agrarios y Colonización (DAAC), xxiv, 4, 23, 51, 54, 57, 63, 67, 69, 70, 72, 78, 80, 81, 83, 84–85, 88, 90, 91, 99, 101, 103, 105–6, 108, 109, 111, 129, 130, 131, 132, 141, 144, 146, 151, 152, 171, 230–231n82; 1964 occupation of offices, 54, 57, 91, 92–95, 105–6, 117, 141, 146, 236n47
Dirección Federal de Seguridad (DFS), xxiv, 22–23, 27, 28, 51–52, 60, 82–83, 97, 104, 111, 124, 133, 143, 144, 145, 169, 188, 203, 209, 213, 215, 233n155, 244n70
Dirección General de Investigaciones Políticas y Sociales (IPS), xxiv, 23, 95, 97, 124–126, 128, 129, 130, 133, 209, 215
Díaz Ordaz, Gustavo, xix, 28, 74, 100–101, 110–13, 115–16, 122–23, 125, 127–28, 132, 141, 146, 149, 155, 170, 182, 189, 250n10; protest against candidate, 110–16, 122, 127–28, 141, 145–46

Index

direct action, 10, 77, 104; and creation of political subjects, 4–6, 66, 200, 202
Dirty War, 7, 8, 20, 23, 194, 199–203, 216

Echeverría, Luis, 4, 27–28, 58, 170, 190, 200, 201, 250n10
Economic Miracle, 4, 14, 17, 20, 21–22, 45
education, 26, 28, 77, 82, 86–92, 131, 133, 146, 147, 152, 157, 158, 159, 165, 168, 189, 195, 214; rural normal schools, 6, 14–15, 26, 32, 61, 86–87, 99, 106, 111, 122, 130, 147, 154, 165, 187, 188, 190; students, xiv, 4, 5, 7, 8, 9–10, 12–13, 15, 18, 21, 24, 25, 28, 29, 31, 32, 54, 57, 60, 61, 62, 68, 73, 86–97 *passim*, 99, 100, 102, 104, 105, 106, 108–113 *passim*, 119–125 *passim*, 130, 131, 132, 138, 143, 145–48 *passim*, 150, 154, 158–64, 168, 177, 186–90 *passim*, 199, 216, 227n7, 230n78, 235n29, 250n10; socialist, 5–6, 14–15, 86–88, 162
ejidos, 3, 4, 7, 9, 13, 16–18, 34, 43, 44, 45, 50, 54, 57, 58, 63, 69, 72, 75–76, 78, 79, 81, 83, 85, 90, 91, 93–94, 96–99 *passim*, 103, 130, 131, 135, 152, 157, 170, 182, 187, 190, 196, 209, 210, 220n39, 247n34; legal basis of, 16, 17. *See* agrarian reform.
El Heraldo de Chihuahua, xviii, 4, 106, 179, 181, 182, 184, 185, 186, 188, 194
El Norte, 6, 53, 180, 183, 209
elections, 20, 24; of 1964, 12, 100–102, 155
Escóbel (Scobell) Gaytán, Guadalupe, xxi, 75, 118, 174, 191, 193, 195, 234n8
Escóbel (Scobell), Juan Antonio, xxi, 75, 102–3, 118, 119, 126, 127, 139, 171, 172, 174
Estrada, Amador, 126, 135
Estrada, David, 58
Estrada, Luis, 60, 126, 135, 170

Federal Army, 9, 36, 40, 106
Federal Bureau of Investigation (FBI), xi–xiv, 22, 27, 90, 106
Federación Estudiantil de Chihuahua (FECH), xxiv, 32, 88, 89, 109, 111, 121, 123, 125, 145
Federación de Estudiantes Campesinos Socialistas de Mexico (FECSM), xxiv, 88, 138
Fernández, Juan, 139, 153, 172, 184, 185, 186

Fernández, Matias (José Juan), xix, 139, 171–75 *passim*, 177, 178–79, 186, 191, 196,
First Encounter of the Sierra, 26, 57, 75, 95–99, 209
Foquismo, xv, 7, 28–29, 32, 67, 150, 160, 218n9
foreign investment, 11, 21–22, 39, 40–41, 46, 47, 96, 155. *See* United States.
forestry industry, 3–4, 5, 6, 34, 46–50, 52, 57, 60, 62, 63, 69, 72, 76, 83–84, 96, 123, 131, 189, 192
Four Friends, xx, xxi, 6, 34, 51–53, 59, 63, 81, 102
Frente Electoral de Pueblo (FEP), xxiv, 12, 13, 23, 93, 100–101, 105, 109, 111, 112, 113, 123, 124, 125, 127, 129, 132, 144, 186, 238n124

Gallardo Astorga, Guillermo, 67, 68, 170
Gámiz García, Arturo, xix, 8, 9, 13, 14, 19, 20, 25, 27, 60–64, 67, 75, 77, 79, 80–81, 88–89, 92–97, 101, 103, 104–5, 108–10, 113, 118–19, 126–29, 131–34, 137–44, 146–50, 152, 154, 159–60, 163–64, 168–69, 171–77, 179–80, 182–88, 190–93, 196–98, 209, 211, 214, 215, 219n13, 227n7, 228n20, 233n155, 238n124, 243n62, 244n70
Gámiz García, Dolores, 147, 154, 172
Gámiz García, Emilio, xix, 171–172, 174, 179
García Aguirre, Aleida, 67, 78, 87, 104, 216
García Barragán, Marcelino, 182
García de Gámiz, Emilia, 146, 180
Garcia Travestí, Javier, 183
Garcia Valseca newspapers, 74
Garza Zamora, Tiburcio, 152, 182
Gavilondo, Hilario, 78–79, 81, 85, 93, 101
Gaytán Aguirre, Juan Antonio, xix, 75, 135, 136, 193
Gaytán Aguirre, Salomón, xix, 14, 75, 102–3, 119, 126, 127, 133, 134, 135, 137, 138, 144, 147, 148, 171, 172, 174, 175, 176, 179, 180, 182, 186, 188, 190
Gaytán Aguirre, Salvador, xx, 59, 75, 76, 77, 116, 133, 134, 139, 152–53, 169, 171, 173, 174, 177, 187, 192, 193, 194, 227n7
Gaytán Valdez, Rosendo, xix, xx, 60, 75
Gaytán, Hildebrando, 88, 154, 171
Gender, 5, 13–14, 32, 37, 118, 136–37, 145, 151, 195–96; discourse, 13–14; gendered violence, 6, 14, 37, 51–52, 81, 116, 123, 169, 193,

Gender (*continued*)
203; land invasions and, 13–14; in Resolutions, 13, 163–166; and women's participation; 13, 55, 61–62, 65, 70–71, 85, 87, 99, 104, 105, 107, 141–43, 168, 200–201

Gil Valenzuela, Fortunato, 59–60, 134, 151

Giner Durán, Práxedes, xx, 3, 9, 14, 74, 78, 83, 85, 89–90, 94, 98, 99, 105, 107–8, 111, 112, 121, 123, 124, 125, 129, 130–31, 143–48 *passim*, 151, 152, 170, 180, 182, 183, 184, 186, 189

Gómez Caballero, Alma, 61, 143, 188, 195, 196

Gómez Ramírez, Pablo, xx, 10, 13, 25, 60–64, 67, 68, 79–80, 82–83, 88–89, 93–96, 98, 101, 104–5, 108, 109, 111, 113, 138–42, 145, 149, 152, 163, 169, 171, 172, 174, 176, 179, 183–86, 190, 194, 195, 196, 215, 217n6, 227n7

Gómez Ramírez, Raúl, xx, 13, 61, 82–83, 89, 91–93, 95, 101, 110, 154, 184

Gómez Ramírez, Simón, 13, 61, 82–83, 89, 101, 180

Gómez Velazco, Antonio, xx, 82, 101, 123, 128, 132, 136, 152

González Delgado, Salustio, 121, 122, 132, 154, 238n124

González Eguiarte, Oscar, xx, 95, 98, 120, 123, 140, 143, 152, 153, 154, 171, 172, 191, 192, 193

González Herrera, Saúl, 78, 93, 112

González, Margarito, 119, 133

Greene, William C., 39, 47–48

Grupo Popular Guerrillero (GPG), xxiv, 3, 4, 8, 9, 10, 19, 23, 25, 29, 34, 54, 60, 62–63, 75, 100, 102–4, 116–19, 120–21, 127, 129, 147–48, 149, 153, 154, 162, 164, 165, 166, 171, 193, 198, 199–200, 202–4, 215, 234n8, 235n29; assault on base by, 3–4, 7–8, 150, 151, 171–77; in Mexico City, 8, 137–43, 148, 149, 151, 159, 171, 191–94; study groups of, 10, 154

Grupo Popular Guerrillero–Arturo Gámiz, 54, 143, 193

Grupo Vallina, 50, 59

Guerra de Guerrillas, 9, 19, 29, 118, 125, 151, 168, 237n78

Guerrero District, 24, 34–39 *passim*, 41, 47, 54, 83, 94, 110, 133–134, 138, 159, 161, 171–173, 177, 183, 185, 191, 196, 201–202, 203, 211, 214, 215, 219n16, 220n40

Guerrero, Antonio, 49, 50, 62, 85

guerrilla warfare, 19, 25, 28, 29, 34, 52, 75, 116–119, 131, 137–143, 149–150, 151, 153, 162, 199–200, 201–202; rural and urban, 9–10. *See foquismo*.

Guevara, Ernesto (Che), 9, 19, 28, 29, 67, 154, 182

Gutiérrez Barrios, Fernando, 27–28

Gutiérrez Zamora, Manuel, 106–7, 109

Gutiérrez, Clara Elena, xx, 89, 95, 98, 113, 142, 196

Hacienda Babícora, 6, 39, 45–48 *passim*, 66, 75–77, 152, 185

Hacienda Santo Domingo, xxi, 69–72, 85, 89, 90

Hacienda Sírupa, xxi, 59, 75–76, 83, 97, 190

Hearst, William Randolph, 39, 45–47 *passim*

Hernández Gómez, Enrique, 85, 89–90, 131

Huizopa, 3, 51, 58, 59, 60, 96, 126, 131, 133, 135, 150, 152, 210, 218n3

Ibarra, Florentino, xx, 51–52, 59, 102–3, 126, 128, 134, 135, 184

Ibarra, José, xx, 3, 14, 34, 51–53, 58–59, 62, 80–81, 82, 97, 102, 119, 126–28, 134, 136, 137, 144–45, 151

Indice, 6, 59, 62, 63, 67, 68, 71–72, 73–74, 78–84 *passim*, 89, 90, 98, 101, 105–6, 111, 121, 122, 124, 125, 129–30, 133, 134, 143–48 *passim*, 151, 154, 170, 180, 189, 190, 209

indigenous people, 7, 15–16, 32, 34, 35–38, 40–41, 43, 47, 59, 63, 68, 86, 96, 129, 152, 154, 164, 169, 170; nineteenth century incursions by, 34, 35–37, 42, 57, 84; Apache, 34, 38, 57, 75, 84, 223n2; Pima, 15–16, 52, 59, 169, 170, 173; Tarahumara (Rarámuri), 15–16, 35, 46–47, 65, 79, 83, 110, 122, 128, 129, 193, 205–7, 211, 251n4

Instituto Politécnico Nacional (IPN), xxiv, 31, 60; 1956 strike at, 24–25, 60

Irrigation Zone Five, 44, 45, 46, 54, 78, 85, 88, 93. *See* Conchos Valley.

Jacott, Guadalupe, xx, 141–42, 152–53, 171–72, 178, 191–92, 196

Juárez Santos Coy, Eduardo, xx, 69, 78, 90, 105, 108–9

Index

Juventud Comunista de México (JCM), xxiv, 32, 124
Juventud Popular (JP), xix, xxiv, 60, 87–88, 95–96, 113, 138, 153

La Liga Comunista 23 de Septiembre (LC23S), 200, 202–3
land invasions, 4, 5, 6, 13–14, 17, 18, 19, 23, 45, 54, 55, 65–66, 68, 69–72, 77–83 *passim*, 88–89, 90, 91, 100–105 *passim*, 107, 108, 109, 113, 117, 132, 141, 168; rural, 7, 75–76, 78, 188; urban, 5, 10, 31–32, 54
Las armas del alba [film], 67, 197. *See* Carlos Montemayor.
Liga de Comunidades Agrarias (LCA), xxiv, 70–71, 131–32
Lombardo Toledano, Vicente, xx, 11–12, 100–101, 132, 140, 149, 155, 157–58, 170, 186
López Mateos, Adolfo, xx, 22, 25, 26, 55, 59, 61–62, 65, 67, 69, 71–72, 74, 75–76, 78–79, 92–93, 94–95, 109
López Portillo, José, xiv, 20, 200, 201, 202–3
López, Jacinto, xx, 58, 59, 71, 108
Lugo Hernández, Raúl Florencio, xx, 116–18, 127–28, 133, 137–42, 172–74, 176–77, 181, 185, 191, 209, 214, 234n8
Luján Adame, Francisco, xx, 52, 57–60, 61, 73, 79
Luján, Leonel, 59, 61

Madera City, 3, 4, 8, 11, 16, 29, 45, 47, 51, 52, 54, 57–63 *passim*, 68, 72–77 *passim*, 80, 82, 83, 88, 90, 94, 95, 96, 99, 101, 102, 103, 104, 109, 118, 123, 126, 128, 130–36 *passim*, 141–45 *passim*, 149, 151, 152, 154, 162, 163, 165, 170–74 *passim*, 189, 190, 191, 193, 194, 196, 197, 198, 205–7, 209, 210, 211, 213, 214, 217n6, 221n45, 226n70, 226n71, 227n7, 237n78, 243n63, 247n39; origins of, 34, 39, 48–50; post-assault repression in, 54, 178–188
Mariñelarena, José (or Jesús), 110, 113–14, 145–46
Márquez, Francisco, 61, 170
Martínez Noriega, Roberto, xx, 78, 83, 126
Martínez Valdivia, Rafael, xx, 10, 113, 139, 179, 183, 184

Marxism, xv, 4, 9, 10, 11–12, 21, 26, 28, 30–33, 60, 87, 144, 154–55, 158, 162, 164, 168, 200, 215, 243n63; *guevarismo*, 7–8
Melgar de la Peña, José, 120, 146, 189
Mendoza Domínguez, Manuel, xx, 90, 98, 105, 107
Mendoza, Ramón, xx, 10, 60, 102, 133, 153, 169, 171, 175, 191, 192, 195, 209, 219n13
Mennonites, 7, 44, 78–79, 101
Mexico City, 6, 8, 10, 11, 13, 18, 20, 23–24, 25, 26, 31–32, 33, 37, 38, 40, 46, 49, 50, 55, 58, 60, 61, 63, 64, 71, 78, 83, 85, 90, 95, 99, 100, 106, 108, 110, 116, 125, 126, 130, 137, 138, 139, 140, 141, 146, 148, 149, 150, 151, 159, 164, 169, 177, 178, 179, 185, 188, 190, 191, 192, 198, 199, 200, 209, 210, 211, 219n13, 221n47, 228n20, 250n10; decision to move to, 137–143; influence on Gámiz and Gómez, 25; journey from, 171–174; training in 1964–65; 138–139, 140
Mexico, 12, 17, 20, 27, 28, 33, 35, 36, 41, 81–82, 164, 183, 193, 194, 199–204; history of, 21–25, 30, 155–59, 165–66
Mineral de Dolores, 51, 52, 59, 75–85, 96, 127, 134, 144, 173, 210, 226n70
mining industry, 10, 18, 22, 34, 36, 38, 39, 42, 45, 47, 80, 96, 126, 130
Molina, Ramon, 62, 83, 116, 152, 169, 193
Montemayor, Carlos, xxi, 9–10, 67, 178, 193, 209, 210, 219n13; *Las armas del alba*, 67, 172, 194–198, 211, 215, 218n2, 219n13; *Las mujeres del alba*, 180, 195–196, 215, 219n13
Movimiento de Liberación Nacional (MLN), xv, xxiv, 26, 74, 144, 186, 214
Movimiento Revolucionario del Magisterio (MRM), xxiv, 24, 55, 101
Muñoz Grado, Pedro, xviii, 103, 113, 122, 180, 184
Muñoz Leyva, Carlos, 61, 81, 104

New Left, 21; contrast with Old Left, 30–33, 165; Cuba and, 31
Normal Night School, 62, 73, 82, 87, 88, 112, 119, 145–48
normalistas, 4–5, 12–15 *passim*, 24, 74, 86–87, 97, 104, 105, 109, 141, 143, 159, 165, 201, 221n47

Obregón, Alvaro, 7, 44
Ornelas, Francisco (Paco), xxi, 112, 172, 174, 182, 191, 209, 215
Ornelas, Saúl, 139, 173
Orozco, Victor, xvii, 154, 164, 175, 194, 215
Orta, Jesús, 95, 186

Partido de Acción Nacional (PAN), xxiv, 10, 35, 53, 55–56, 111, 113, 132, 196, 200, 202, 227n82, 238n125
Partido Auténtico de la Revolución Mexicano (PARM), xxiv, 93, 132, 133
Partido Comunista Mexicano (PCM), xxiv, 11–13, 20, 23, 26, 32, 33, 54, 56, 62, 67, 68, 87–88, 93, 98, 100, 101, 111, 122, 133, 138, 155, 157, 160, 165, 186, 200, 238n123
Partido Popular Socialista (PPS), xxiv, 5, 11–13, 26, 58, 60, 61, 62, 68, 75, 79, 82, 87, 93, 94, 100–101, 110, 111, 112, 132, 133, 138, 149, 150, 155, 160, 170, 186, 215, 238n124
Partido Revolucionario Institucional (PRI), xxv, 9, 20, 22, 25, 27, 31, 32, 33, 55–56, 68, 70, 74, 88, 93, 98, 100, 110, 122, 124, 125, 131, 132, 157, 190, 196, 200, 202, 204, 227n82, 238n119
pax priísta, 22–23
Picazarri, Amador, 101, 109
Pinoncely, Emilio, 69, 85
Política, 33, 62, 68, 110, 186, 190
Porfiriato, 6, 38–42, 43, 47, 79, 157
porros, 31
Portillo, Francisco, xxi, 75, 83, 97, 152, 187
Prieto, Alejandro, 51
Prieto, Rosario, 81, 92–93, 101, 103
Primeros Vientos, 5, 163, 181, 194

Quiñónez, Miguel, xxi, 10, 88, 154, 173, 174, 176, 179, 184, 186, 241n29

Railroads, 22, 34, 38–39, 46, 47, 48; Chihuahua to Pacific Railway, 47, 50; Northwest Railroad of Mexico, 48, 49, 50; railway workers, 18, 22–23, 24–25, 31, 42, 49, 55, 101, 159, 184; railway workers strike, 10, 24; Río Grande, Sierra Madre, and Pacific Railroad, 47;
Rascón, Emilio, 97–98, 153, 192

Rascón, Manuel, 60
Revolution of 1910, xxi, 5, 6, 15–16, 18, 26, 33, 34, 38, 41–44, 45, 81, 86, 156–58, 164, 193, 226n77
Reyes, Daniel de los, 134, 141, 144, 186, 209
Reyes, Judith, xxi, 6, 12–13, 14, 21, 23, 25, 64–69, 70–71, 82, 90, 98–99, 101, 109–12, 113, 119–20, 121–24, 126, 127, 130, 143, 154, 164, 170, 209, 214, 229n47, 238n124, 244n70
Rico Galán, Victor, 26, 138, 187, 191, 209, 213, 214
Ríos, Alvaro, xxi, 6, 10, 11, 13, 25, 57–60, 61, 62, 65, 66, 67, 78, 81–83, 89–90, 93, 95, 97, 98, 100, 104, 111, 113, 121, 123, 124, 130, 132, 133, 134, 143, 150, 151, 152, 177, 184, 191
Ríos Torres, Carlos, xxi, 16, 52, 59, 61, 79, 102, 134, 227n7
riot police (*granaderos*), 23–24, 31, 105
Rodríguez Ford, Eduardo, 88, 170, 227n7
Rodríguez Ford, Guillermo, 88, 105, 106, 132, 133
Ruíz Cortines, Adolfo, 22, 45, 226n81
Rural Normal School of Salaices, 6, 13, 62, 88, 97, 104–6, 107, 119, 138, 139, 154, 159, 177, 187
Rural Normal School of Saucillo, xx, 6, 61, 88, 95, 104–6, 107, 109, 119, 141, 145, 184
Rural Normal Schools, *See* Education

Salazar Ramírez, Othón, 24, 101, 113
Sánchez Calderón, Hector, 98, 131
Sanchez Lozoya, Dionisio, xxi, 69, 71–72, 78
Sandoval Salinas, Oscar, xxi, 113, 137, 139, 148, 171, 172, 174, 179, 185, 191
Santa Rita, 10, 63, 79, 81, 94, 103, 150, 151, 176
Santos Valdés, José, xxi, 67, 98, 140, 143, 151, 179, 186, 190, 210, 213
Schneider, Roberto, 51, 85, 93
Second Encounter of the Sierra, 26, 97, 149, 153–166; Five Resolutions of, 13, 26, 95–96, 129, 149, 151, 153–66, 171
Secretaría de Educación Pública (SEP), xxv, 24, 86
Sierra Holguín, Modesto, 184, 185
Sierra Madre Land and Lumber Company, 39, 47–48

Social Democratic Christian Movement, 10, 53–54, 238n125
state (rural) police, 51–53, 59, 63, 98, 100, 107, 126, 127, 131, 134, 135, 137, 144, 184, 190, 226n80
State Normal School, 12–13, 60, 61, 62, 73, 87, 88, 102, 109, 111, 123, 124, 139, 145–46, 147, 148, 153, 179, 188, 210, 227n7; 1964 graduation of, 122–24

Technical School, 62, 73, 87, 88, 102, 111, 112, 123, 145, 146
Technical School for Young Ladies, 73, 87, 111, 145, 146
Temósachic, xxi, 16, 37, 40, 45, 47, 48, 51, 63, 73, 81, 82, 103, 144, 145, 150, 152, 176, 178
"The Participation of Students in the Revolutionary Movement", 97, 146, 154, 159
Toro Rosales, Salvador del, xxi, 9, 103, 106–11, 153, 169, 179, 183, 185, 187, 189, 193, 209, 214
Tres Ojitos, 94, 102, 103, 175
Trouyet, Carlos, 50, 84

Unidades Industriales de Explotación Forestal (UIEF), 48–50 *passim*
Unions, 17, 23, 24, 25, 26, 38, 49, 53–54, 55, 58, 72–73, 90, 91, 110, 132, 146, 147, 201; Teachers' Union, 82, 89, 91–92, 113, 131, 152, 180, 201; *See* Unión General de Obreros y Campesinos Mexicanos.
Unión General de Obreros y Campesinos Mexicanos (UGOCM), xix, xx, xxi, xxv, 4–6, 10, 11–13, 16, 23, 25, 26, 34, 52, 53, 58–62 *passim*, 63, 65, 66, 70, 71, 77–78, 80, 81, 88–89, 91–101 *passim*, 104–5, 108, 109, 111, 113, 117, 119, 123, 131, 132, 140, 142, 152, 154, 170, 186, 230n82, 233n155, 235n29, 238n123, 238n124; Federación de Obreros y Campesinos del Estado de Chihuahua (FOCECH), xxiv, 59; split in 1965, 100, 149–51
United States, 7, 12, 17, 18, 27, 28, 29, 42, 49, 58, 62, 64, 65, 67, 68, 79, 82, 85, 87, 123, 134, 148, 163–64, 183, 200, 201, 202–4, 217n6, 218n8, 237n78, 250n10; anti-communism of, 23–24, 26–27, 30, 74, 77–78, 155, 203; borderlands of, 36–37, 38, 40, 44, 46, 79, 125–126, 157; investment in Mexico by, 22, 38–39, 40, 43–48 *passim*, 50, 155; and security services, 21
Uranga, Pedro, xxi, 139, 150, 153, 171, 172, 182, 185, 186, 192
Urbanization, 7, 17, 21–22, 46, 81
Urías, Luis, 87, 124

Vallina, Eloy Santiago, xxi, 49, 50, 68, 73, 84, 85, 130
Vega Portillo, Tomás, 3, 51, 80–81, 126, 128, 134, 151
Vietnam War, 18, 159
Villa Estrada, Rafael, 60, 192
Villa Rentería, Francisco Hipólito, xxi, 83, 107, 120
Villarreal, Lázaro, xxi, 53, 93, 112, 113, 119, 121, 123, 124, 132–33
violence, 3, 6–10, 11, 13–14, 21, 23, 31, 40, 51–53, 57–60, 62, 63, 67, 68, 71, 77, 80–81, 84, 90, 96–103 *passim*, 105, 106, 112, 113–14, 116, 119, 120–21, 126–29, 132, 134–36, 147–48, 152–53, 155, 159, 168, 169–70, 184, 193, 199–204, 226n77, 226n80. *See* Gender.

white guards, 45, 84, 127
working class, 117, 158, 161
World War II, 17, 21, 22, 35, 45, 46, 50, 148, 157, 158, 202

Yáñez, Carlos, 62, 83, 94, 133

ABOUT THE AUTHOR

Elizabeth Henson has been a lifelong activist. She received a doctorate in history from the University of Arizona in 2015. She continues to write and research in Bisbee and Douglas, Arizona. She has both traveled extensively through and lived in Mexico.